Process and Difference

SUNY SERIES IN
CONSTRUCTIVE POSTMODERN THOUGHT
David Ray Griffin, *Editor*

Process and Difference

*Between Cosmological and Poststructuralist
Postmodernisms*

edited by

CATHERINE KELLER and ANNE DANIELL

STATE UNIVERSITY OF NEW YORK PRESS

Published by
State University of New York Press, Albany

Chapter 3, "Whitehead, Deconstruction, and Postmodernism," by Luis Pedraja was previously published in *Process Studies* (PS 28.1-2).

Chapter 4, "Whitehead and the Critique of Logocentrism," is adapted from Joseph Bracken, S.J., *The One in the Many*, © 2001 Wm. B. Eerdmans Publishing Co., Grand Rapids, MI. Used by permission; all rights reserved.

Chapter 8, "A Whiteheadian Chaosmos?" by Tim Clark was previously published in *Process Studies* (PS 28.3-4).

For information, address State University of New York Press,
90 State Street, Suite 700, Albany, NY 12207

Production by Judith Block
Marketing by Patrick Durocher
Composition by Doric Lay Publishers

Library of Congress Cataloging-in-Publication Data

Process and difference : between cosmological and poststructuralist postmodernisms / Catherine Keller and Anne Daniell, editors.
     p. cm. — (SUNY series in constructive postmodern thought)
    Includes index.
    ISBN 0-7914-5287-5 (alk. paper) — ISBN 0-7914-5288-3 (pbk. : alk. paper)
    1. Process philosophy. 2. Poststructuralism. 3. Postmodernism. I. Keller, Catherine, 1953– II. Daniell, Anne, 1965– III. Series.

    BD372 .P719 2002
    146´.7—dc21

2001032204

10 9 8 7 6 5 4 3 2 1

Contents

Introduction to SUNY Series in Constructive Postmodern Thought*

The rapid spread of the term *postmodern* in recent years witnesses to a growing dissatisfaction with modernity and to an increasing sense that the modern age not only had a beginning but can have an end as well. Whereas the word *modern* was almost always used until quite recently as a word of praise and as a synonym for *contemporary,* a growing sense is now evidenced that we can and should leave modernity behind—in fact, that we *must* if we are to avoid destroying ourselves and most of the life on our planet.

Modernity, rather than being regarded as the norm for human society toward which all history has been aiming and into which all societies should be ushered—forcibly if necessary—is instead increasingly seen as an aberration. A new respect for the wisdom of traditional societies is growing as we realize that they have endured for thousands of years and that, by contrast, the existence of modern civilization for even another century seems doubtful. Likewise, *modernism* as a worldview is less and less seen as The Final Truth, in comparison with which all divergent worldviews are automatically regarded as "superstitious." The modern worldview is increasingly relativized to the status of one among many, useful for some purposes, inadequate for others.

Although there have been antimodern movements before, beginning perhaps near the outset of the nineteenth century with the Romanticists and the Luddites, the rapidity with which the term *postmodern* has become widespread in our time suggests that the antimodern sentiment is more extensive and intense than before, and also that it includes the sense that modernity can be successfully overcome only by going beyond it, not by attempting to return

---

*The present version of this introduction is slightly different from the first version, which was contained in the volumes that appeared prior to 1999.

to a premodern form of existence. Insofar as a common element is found in the various ways in which the term is used, *postmodernism* refers to a diffuse sentiment rather than to any common set of doctrines—the sentiment that humanity can and must go beyond the modern.

Beyond connoting this sentiment, the term *postmodern* is used in a confusing variety of ways, some of them contradictory to others. In artistic and literary circles, for example, postmodernism shares in this general sentiment but also involves a specific reaction against "modernism" in the narrow sense of a movement in artistic-literary circles in the late nineteenth and early twentieth centuries. Postmodern architecture is very different from postmodern literary criticism. In some circles, the term *postmodern* is used in reference to that potpourri of ideas and systems sometimes called *new age metaphysics,* although many of these ideas and systems are more premodern than postmodern. Even in philosophical and theological circles, the term *postmodern* refers to two quite different positions, one of which is reflected in this series. Each position seeks to transcend both *modernism,* in the sense of the worldview that has developed out of the seventeenth-century Galilean-Cartesian-Baconian-Newtonian science, and *modernity,* in the sense of the world order that both conditioned and was conditioned by this worldview. But the two positions seek to transcend the modern in different ways.

Closely related to literary-artistic postmodernism is a philosophical postmodernism inspired variously by physicalism, Ludwig Wittgenstein, Martin Heidegger, a cluster of French thinkers—including Jacques Derrida, Michel Foucault, Gilles Deleuze, and Julia Kristeva—and certain features of American pragmatism.* By the use of terms that arise out of particular segments of this movement, it can be called *deconstructive, relativistic,* or *eliminative* postmodernism. It overcomes the modern worldview through an antiworldview, deconstructing or even entirely eliminating various concepts that have generally been thought necessary for a worldview, such as self, purpose, meaning, a real world, givenness, reason, truth as correspondence, universally valid norms, and divinity. While motivated by ethical and emancipatory concerns, this type of postmodern thought tends to issue in relativism. Indeed, it seems

---

*The fact that the thinkers and movements named here are said to have inspired the deconstructive type of postmodernism should not be taken, of course, to imply that they have nothing in common with constructive postmodernists. For example, Wittgenstein, Heidegger, Derrida, and Deleuze share many points and concerns with Alfred North Whitehead, the chief inspiration behind the present series. Furthermore, the actual positions of the founders of pragmatism, especially William James and Charles Peirce, are much closer to Whitehead's philosophical position—see the volume in this series entitled *The Founders of Constructive Postmodern Philosophy: Peirce, James, Bergson, Whitehead, and Hartshorne*—than they are to Richard Rorty's so-called neopragmatism, which reflects many ideas from Rorty's explicitly physicalistic period.

to many thinkers to imply nihilism.* It could, paradoxically, also be called *ultramodernism,* in that its eliminations result from carrying certain modern premises—such as the sensationist doctrine of perception, the mechanistic doctrine of nature, and the resulting denial of divine presence in the world— to their logical conclusions. Some critics see its deconstructions or eliminations as leading to self-referential inconsistencies, such as "performative self-contradictions" between what is said and what is presupposed in the saying.

The postmodernism of this series can, by contrast, be called *revisionary, constructive,* or—perhaps best—*reconstructive.* It seeks to overcome the modern worldview not by eliminating the possibility of worldviews (or "metanarratives") as such, but by constructing a postmodern worldview through a revision of modern premises and traditional concepts in the light of inescapable presuppositions of our various modes of practice. That is, it agrees with deconstructive postmodernists that a massive deconstruction of many received concepts is needed. But its deconstructive moment, carried out for the sake of the presuppositions of practice, does not result in self-referential inconsistency. It also is not so totalizing as to prevent reconstruction. The reconstruction carried out by this type of postmodernism involves a new unity of scientific, ethical, aesthetic, and religious intuitions (whereas poststructuralists tend to reject all such unitive projects as "totalizing modern metanarratives"). While critical of many ideas often associated with modern science, it rejects not science as such but only that *scientism* in which only the data of the modern natural sciences are allowed to contribute to the construction of our public worldview.

The reconstructive activity of this type of postmodern thought is not limited to a revised worldview. It is equally concerned with a postmodern world that will both support and be supported by the new worldview. A postmodern world will involve postmodern persons, with a postmodern spirituality, on the one hand, and a postmodern society, ultimately a postmodern global order, on the other. Going beyond the modern world will involve transcending its individualism, anthropocentrism, patriarchy, economism, consumerism, nationalism, and militarism. Reconstructive postmodern thought provides support for the ethnic, ecological, feminist, peace, and other emancipatory movements of

---

*As Peter Dews points out, although Derrida's early work was "driven by profound ethical impulses," its insistence that no concepts were immune to deconstruction "drove its own ethical presuppositions into a penumbra of inarticulacy" (*The Limits of Disenchantment: Essays on Contemporary European Culture* [London: New York: Verso, 1995], 5). In his more recent thought, Derrida has declared an "emancipatory promise" and an "idea of justice" to be "irreducible to any deconstruction." Although this "ethical turn" in deconstruction implies its pulling back from a completely disenchanted universe, it also, Dews points out (6–7), implies the need to renounce "the unconditionality of its own earlier dismantling of the unconditional."

our time, while stressing that the inclusive emancipation must be from the destructive features of modernity itself. However, the term *postmodern,* by contrast with *premodern,* is here meant to emphasize that the modern world has produced unparalleled advances, as Critical Theorists have emphasized, which must not be devalued in a general revulsion against modernity's negative features.

From the point of view of deconstructive postmodernists, this reconstructive postmodernism will seem hopelessly wedded to outdated concepts, because it wishes to salvage a positive meaning not only for the notions of selfhood, historical meaning, reason, and truth as correspondence, which were central to modernity, but also for notions of divinity, cosmic meaning, and an enchanted nature, which were central to premodern modes of thought. From the point of view of its advocates, however, this revisionary postmodernism is not only more adequate to our experience but also more genuinely postmodern. It does not simply carry the premises of modernity through to their logical conclusions, but criticizes and revises those premises. By virtue of its return to organicism and its acceptance of nonsensory perception, it opens itself to the recovery of truths and values from various forms of premodern thought and practice that had been dogmatically rejected, or at least restricted to "practice," by modern thought. This reconstructive postmodernism involves a creative synthesis of modern and premodern truths and values.

This series does not seek to create a movement so much as to help shape and support an already existing movement convinced that modernity can and must be transcended. But in light of the fact that those antimodern movements that arose in the past failed to deflect or even retard the onslaught of modernity, what reasons are there for expecting the current movement to be more successful? First, the previous antimodern movements were primarily calls to return to a premodern form of life and thought rather than calls to advance, and the human spirit does not rally to calls to turn back. Second, the previous antimodern movements either rejected modern science, reduced it to a description of mere appearances, or assumed its adequacy in principle. They could, therefore, base their calls only on the negative social and spiritual effects of modernity. The current movement draws on natural science itself as a witness against the adequacy of the modern worldview. In the third place, the present movement has even more evidence than did previous movements of the ways in which modernity and its worldview *are* socially and spiritually destructive. The fourth and probably most decisive difference is that the present movement is based on the awareness that *the continuation of modernity threatens the very survival of life on our planet.* This awareness, combined with the growing knowledge of the interdependence of the modern worldview with the militarism, nuclearism, patriarchy, global apartheid, and ecological devastation of the modern world, is providing an unprecedented impetus for people to see the evidence for a postmodern worldview and to envisage postmodern ways of relating to each other, the rest of nature, and the cosmos as a whole. For these reasons, the failure of the previous antimodern movements says little about the possible success of the current movement.

Advocates of this movement do not hold the naively utopian belief that the success of this movement would bring about a global society of universal and lasting peace, harmony and happiness, in which all spiritual problems, social conflicts, ecological destruction, and hard choices would vanish. There is, after all, surely a deep truth in the testimony of the world's religions to the presence of a transcultural proclivity to evil deep within the human heart, which no new paradigm, combined with a new economic order, new child-rearing practices, or any other social arrangements, will suddenly eliminate. Furthermore, it has correctly been said that "life is robbery": A strong element of competition is inherent within finite existence, which no social-political-economic-ecological order can overcome. These two truths, especially when contemplated together, should caution us against unrealistic hopes.

No such appeal to "universal constants," however, should reconcile us to the present order, as if it were thereby uniquely legitimated. The human proclivity to evil in general, and to conflictual competition and ecological destruction in particular, can be greatly exacerbated or greatly mitigated by a world order and its worldview. Modernity exacerbates it about as much as imaginable. We can therefore envision, without being naively utopian, a far better world order, with a far less dangerous trajectory, than the one we now have.

This series, making no pretense of neutrality, is dedicated to the success of this movement toward a postmodern world.

David Ray Griffin
Series Editor

Acknowledgments

Joseph A. Bracken, S.J.'s chapter, "Whitehead and the Critique of Logocentrism," was adapted from Joseph A. Bracken, S.J., *The One in the Many: A Contemporary Reconstruction of the God-World Relationship*, © 2001 Wm. B. Eerdmans Publishing Company, Grand Rapids, MI. Used by permission; all rights reserved.

The chapters by Luis G. Pedraja and Tim Clark were both published in 1999 issues of the journal, *Process Studies*. Pedraja's "Whitehead, Deconstruction, and Postmodernism" appeared in vol. 28/1–2, and Clark's "A Whiteheadian Chaosmos?" appeared in vol. 28/3–4.

This volume was conceived among the exciting lectures and conversations of the third International Whitehead Conference, which took place in the summer of 1998 in Claremont, California. We became aware that there were a number of scholars across the planet already exploring convergences between process and poststructuralist thought. Our special thanks, of course, go to the series editor, David Ray Griffin, for his monumental organizational work in this and countless other major conferences, for his immense scholarly productivity as a theorist and host of postmodern readings of Whitehead, and specifically for his support of this volume. The adept assistance of Jane Bunker, Judith Block, Marilyn Silverman, and Katy Leonard of the State University of New York Press is also greatly appreciated.

Reference Key to Frequently Cited Texts

Process Philosophy

Alfred North Whitehead:

AI   *Adventures of Ideas* [1933]. New York: Free Press, 1967.

CN   *The Concept of Nature.* Cambridge: Cambridge University Press, 1920.

ESP   *Essays in Science and Philosophy.* New York: Philosophical Library, 1947.

MG   "Mathematics and the Good" in *The Philosophy of Alfred North Whitehead.* New York: Tudor Publishing, 1951.

MT   *Modes of Thought* [1938]. New York: Free Press, 1968.

PR   *Process and Reality: An Essay in Cosmology* [1929]. Corrected Edition. David Ray Griffin and Donald W. Sherburne, eds. New York: Free Press, 1978.

RM   *Religion in the Making.* Cambridge: Cambridge University Press, 1926.

S   *Symbolism: Its Meaning and Effect.* New York: Macmillan, 1927.

SMW   *Science and the Modern World* [1925]. New York: Free Press, 1967.

Henry Nelson Wieman:

IA   "Intellectual Autobiography," in *The Empirical Theology of Henry Nelson Wieman,* Robert Bretall, ed. Carbondale and Edwardsville: Southern Illinois University Press, 1969.

ITG   *Is There a God?* Chicago: Willett, Clark and Company, 1932.

MUC *Man's Ultimate Commitment.* Carbondale and Edwardsville:
Southern Illinois University Press, 1958.

SHG *The Source of Human Good.* Carbondale and Edwardsville:
Southern Illinois University Press, 1946.

with Regina Wescott Wieman:

NPR *Normative Psychology of Religion.* New York: Thomas Y. Crowell
Company, 1935.

Poststructuralist Philosophy

Judith Butler:

BTM *Bodies that Matter: On the Discursive Limits of "Sex."* New York:
Routledge, 1993.

CF "Contingent Foundations: Feminism and the Question of 'Postmodernism'" in *Feminists Theorize the Political,* Judith Butler
and Joan W. Scott, eds. New York: Routledge, 1992.

GP "Gender as Performance" in *A Critical Sense: Interviews with
Intellectuals.* New York: Routledge, 1996; first published in
Radical Philosophy 67, summer 1994.

GT *Gender Trouble: Feminism and the Subversion of Identity.*
New York: Routledge, 1990.

IGI "Imitation and Gender Insubordination" in *inside/outside:
Lesbian Theories, Gay Theories,* Diana Fuss, ed. New York:
Routledge, 1991.

Gilles Deleuze:

B *Bergsonism.* New York: Zone Books, 1991.

DR *Difference and Repetition.* Paul Patton, trans. New York: Columbia
University Press, 1994.

EP *Expressionism in Philosophy: Spinoza.* New York: Zone Books,
1990.

LS *The Logic of Sense.* Mark Lester with Charles Stivale, trans.
New York: Columbia University Press, 1990.

TF *The Fold: Leibniz and the Baroque.* Tom Conley, trans.
Minneapolis: University of Minnesota Press, 1993.

with Felix Guattari:

AO   *Anti-Oedipus: Capitalism and Schizophrenia.* Robert Hurley,
      Mark Seem, and Helen Lane, trans. Minneapolis: University
      of Minnesota Press, 1983.

TP   *A Thousand Plateaus: Capitalism and Schizophrenia.*
      Brian Massumi, trans. Minneapolis: University of Minnesota
      Press, 1987.

WP   *What Is Philosophy?* New York: Columbia University Press, 1994.

Jacques Derrida:

D   *Dissemination.* Barbara Johnson, trans. Chicago: University of
      Chicago Press, 1981.

LI   *Limited Inc.* Gerald Graff, ed. Evanston, IL: Northwestern
      University Press, 1988.

OG   *Of Grammatology.* Gayatri Chakravorty Spivak, trans. Baltimore:
      Johns Hopkins University Press, 1976.

MP   *Margins of Philosophy.* Alan Bass, trans. Chicago: University of
      Chicago Press, 1982.

P   *Positions.* Alan Bass, trans. Chicago: University of Chicago
      Press, 1981.

SP   *Speech and Phenomena.* Evanston, IL: Northwestern University
      Press, 1973.

Donna J. Haraway:

MW   *Modest_Witness@Second_Millennium.FemaleMan©_Meets_Onco
      Mouse™: Feminism and Technoscience.* New York and London:
      Routledge, 1997.

Preface

Transmutation is the way in which the actual world is felt as a community. . . .

—Alfred North Whitehead, *Process and Reality*

Process and Difference brings into creative conversation what may at one level appear to be incommensurable theories: process thought, which espouses cosmology and ontological relationality, and poststructuralist or deconstructive theory, which embraces disruption and heterogeneity. Although both are labeled *postmodern,* their own proponents often take them to be so dissimilar as to be opposed. The editors and contributors to this book believe, however, that *processing* at a deeper level these *differences* of theory may cultivate fertile and innovative modes of reflection. Conversant with both genres of postmodernism, the various contributors partake of a prevailing mood of critical appreciation and enthusiasm for the fresh kinds of thinking to be generated by this process-poststructuralist proposition. Indeed, as theologians, philosophers, and religionists, the contributors herein could be said to share a certain "faith" in the potential for creativity to spring forth in surprising ways at the meeting grounds of these different postmodernisms.

This book is not meant to introduce to a wider public some already existing conversation between proponents of two postmodern theories, since such interchange has barely begun. And since both theories already exercise a wide interdisciplinarity, they might better be described as methods to be practiced in one's various discourses. As is explored in several of the chapters in this volume, both help to unmask the abstractions (process) or power-knowledge regimes (poststructuralism) which claim a status of absolute or unmediated "Truth." Additionally, both ways of thinking disclose the constitutive interrelations (process) or traces of the Other (poststructuralism) within identities, historical contexts, and disciplines, revealing the complexity at work to produce any such entity. Thus, while there may be important surface differences between these two postmodernisms, examining them at a deeper level may also reveal an array of kindred methods and hermeneutical aims.

Given the force of their differences, however, this book will not attempt to splice together a new "superbreed" of postmodernism. What, then, might it achieve? Perhaps it may act as a fertilizer, stimulating the growth of conversations among the disciples of these distinct but related theories, as well as among those who already conceive of their thought as springing from the intermixture of a variety of postmodern strains. Admittedly, the intent is to coax a certain conversion—not in the sense of affiliating exclusively with one postmodern denomination so as to disavow the other, but of allowing the continuous conversion of one's own thinking into creative and pertinent ways of attending to vital communal issues.

It may be said that all of the contributors compare key texts of the process and poststructuralist canons, with a common desire to counter modern, Western assumptions of a substance-based, dualistic cosmology with expressions of a more fluid, multifaceted, ever-materializing cosmology. Yet among these contributors flourishes a diversity of concerns and emphases. Indeed, the "difference" of our title alludes in part to the variety of subjects, perspectives, and indeed postmodernisms explored in this volume. The contributors variously deconstruct and reconstruct notions of divinity, realign science and religion, address identity politics and public policies, and offer unsentimental terms for peace. A bit of "difference" also describes the contributors' various social locations. Although cultural pluralism within both process and poststructuralist discourses remains still more of an ideal than an actuality (in this series and volume, as well), the editors feel heartened that there is a range of difference—especially with regard to nationality, ethnicity, gender, race, and sexuality—embodied (if not always thematized) by the contributors to this book. It is our hope that the differences brought forth through this volume may be indicative of an even greater future diversity—in both topic and social particularity—to be fostered by the process-poststructuralist proposition.

Following the introduction, the chapters are arranged thematically. The first two chapters disclose surprising historical conjunctions of process and poststructuralist theories. In "The Roots of Postmodernism" (chapter 1), Arran Gare reveals the common Schellingian roots of process and poststructuralism, thereby recontextualizing the intellectual history of their convergences and divergences. Catherine Keller, in "Process and Chaosmos" (chapter 2), makes manifest moments of admiration for, and reliance upon, Whitehead within the recent work of the radical constructivists Donna J. Haraway and Gilles Deleuze. Such "process punctures" in what may at times appear to be a "monocultural postmodern surface" portend, in Keller's words, the transformation of poststruturalist thought "beyond the anticosmological stasis of much francocentric theory."

The next two chapters compare pivotal concepts from the works of Whitehead and Jacques Derrida, the "founding figures" of process and poststructuralism, respectively. In "Whitehead, Deconstruction, and Postmodernism" (chapter 3), Luis G. Pedraja elucidates parallel lines of thought running through Whitehead's and Derrida's critiques of modernity and linguisitic hermeneutics. He contends that examining Whiteheadian hermeneutics in light of deconstructive theories will make the case for Whitehead as "a potential contributor to and predecessor of our current postmodern philosophers." Exploring kindred congruencies, Joseph A. Bracken, S.J. in "Whitehead and the Critique of Logocentrism" (chapter 4), conjoins Derrida's key concept of *différance* with Whitehead's categorical imperative of creativity to envision a divine Logos that simultaneously differentiates and unites.

Chapters 5 and 6 venture process-poststructuralist engagements with theories of subjectivity. Specifically, they address the tensions found in identity constructions, especially pertaining to gender, as well as in our very understanding of the concept "identity." In "Unconforming Becomings" (chapter 5), Christina K. Hutchins situates the Whiteheadian concept of "becoming" in a dialogue with the sex/gender or "queer" theory of Judith Butler, and from out of this convergence urges a "holy expansion" of definitions of subjectivity. Anne Daniell, in "Figuring Subjectivity for Grounded Transformations" (chapter 6), compares the identity-figuration proposed by the feminist-poststructuralist, Rosi Braidotti, with that of the process theologian, John B. Cobb Jr., and reconciles them with the ecological imperative to value the continual interplay of grounding and transition in both ecological and social constructions.

The next three chapters explore ways in which process-poststructuralist amalgamations might bear upon religious and theological thinking. Carol Wayne White's "Processing Henry Nelson Wieman" (chapter 7) interweaves "creativity," as the divine element of life (conceptualized by another influential source for process thought, Henry Nelson Wieman), with what she esteems as the always "open-ended textuality" of poststructuralist thought. Synthesizing certain process and poststructuralist themes, White imparts her own "postmodern religious valuing." Tim Clark, in "A Whiteheadian Chaosmos?" (chapter 8), on the other hand, moves in precisely the opposite direction. Conducting a discriminating comparison of the cosmological schemes of Whitehead and Deleuze, he finds them incommensurable for *theological* integration. By contrast, Roland Faber in "De-Ontologizing God" (chapter 9) constructs a cosmological vision through which the alterity privileged by Emmanuel Levinas and the immanence accentuated by Deleuze may be synthesized in a "Whiteheadian contrast," prompting a conception of the divine as "eschatological ad-vent."

The volume culminates with a chapter by Isabelle Stengers, a philosopher who construes her own scholarship as a coalescence of Whiteheadian and Deleuzean theoretical positions. "Beyond Conversation" (chapter 10) warns of strong socio-intellectual barriers on the part of "the French tradition," impeding the likelihood of conversations between process theorists and deconstructionists. Working at the interface of theory and praxis, Stengers proffers, nonetheless, a spiritually charged Whiteheadian "peace-making proposition," described as "the kind of experimental togetherness that makes peace a challenge and not the condition for a polite conversation." It is the editors'pleasure to introduce Stengers's "cosmopolitics," already influential in Europe, to a particularly compatible English-speaking audience.

The editors hope that this book will attract not only process thinkers already familiar with the innovative work of the State University of New York Press Series in Constructive Postmodern Thought, but also other postmoderns who may be intrigued by the hybridity stimulated by the process-poststructuralist proposition. We share a commitment to working toward scholarship in which diversity, creativity, and a critically attuned interrelatedness may flourish. For the germination of such a project, a yearning for community may be a prerequisite—if not in the full but contested sense of Cobb's "common good," then in the sense of encounters in which mutual respect and openness lead to self-transformation. Even as the contributors herein correlate process and poststructuralist texts, this volume already emerges from, and aims toward, actualizations of such community.

Several of the chapters in this book found their first incarnations within a context of "creating the common good," as they were prepared for the third International Whitehead Conference, "Process Thought and the Common Good," an interdisciplinary meeting held in Claremont, California, in August 1998 to celebrate the silver anniversary of the Center for Process Studies. Surprised by the occurrence of several presentations sympathetically coordinating process and poststructuralist themes, the editors conceived of the idea for this volume and then solicited other articles. This is the first collection of its kind, bringing together much of what has been written thus far on the topic.

While this book seeks to lure process and poststructuralism toward a more synthetic, less oppositional connection, the differences of subject matter and opinion within the collection demonstrate that—beyond perhaps the critique of modern subjectivity and substance—there is no single purpose or positive thesis already common to process and other postmodernist thinkers. Rather, forged in the fires of interdisciplinary and multimethodological imagination, the chapters all risk their own adventures of ideas. The editors suspect that those readers already influenced by process thought will find themselves readily drawn to this experiment, given their Whiteheadian bent for nudging contradictions into contrasts. Indeed, to incorporate into their hermeneutics such poststructuralist emphases as fluidity, difference, and disruption may recall process people to their own cosmological radicalism. Likewise, for those readers influenced primarily by deconstructive strains of postmodernism, to behold such process ideals as novelty, interrelationality, and cosmology in a poststructuralist light may permit certain promising metamorphoses, away from anthropocentric privilege and toward more contextual concrescences.

Anne Daniell
Drew University

Introduction
The Process of Difference,
the Difference of Process

CATHERINE KELLER

> We are separated by so many similar things that the flow which attracts us
> to each other is exhausted as it beats against these obstacles. It no longer
> flows, held back by boundaries that are too watertight. We are divided by
> that part of the selfsame and its theater, which cannot be traversed.
>
> —Luce Irigaray, *Elemental Passions*[1]

The present collection stages a meeting between two postmodernisms that
have never been one. Process and poststructuralist discourses pursue divergent aims, conflicting methods, and discordant styles. They emanate from disparate sources and from different cultural traditions.[2] So this volume
expresses not a nostalgia for reunion but a desire for *différance*. Is this the
rather foolish, fleeting infatuation of an otherwise rational philosophy with a
younger, fashionable, flirtatious theory—a cartoon of the dignified older man
who falls for the coquette? Or is there a more interesting eros in evidence
here? Does it display the potentiality for reciprocal transmutation, if not for
any abiding mutual commitment? By positioning these chapters in a series
dedicated to the production of a reconstructive postmodernism, by including
three European contributions, by concluding it indeed with an essay by an
important francophone philosopher, we signal the intensity that the contributors to this volume attribute to this attraction.

Of course if so-called deconstructive and reconstructive postmodernisms are never likely to become one, neither would either movement claim
to be unitary in itself. As in Irigaray's titular pun, *Ce Sexe Qui N'en Est Pas
Un*,[3] neither is singular—or singularly masculine. So we do not anticipate a
romance between a single process thought and a single poststructuralism.
Indeed as each comprises a radical pluralism, each has already generated a
nest of divergent trajectories. At their different scales, these movements both
continue to proliferate internationally, decolonizing their own centers, without
thereby obscuring the strong family resemblances that mark each as a movement. But as movements toward each other?

1

Certainly within Whiteheadian thought there is massive mistrust, if not outright antagonism, toward the French style of inquiry that is still largely identified—despite the gallant efforts of this series—with postmodern thought. This mistrust could hardly be avoided. The academic force of poststructuralism delegitimates any project that can be called "metaphysics," "ontology," "cosmology," or "worldview." It withers away any appeal to "universals," to "coherence," "consistency," "reason," "totality," or "God." Process thinkers wring their hands at the insouciant irrationality with which incommensurable, indeed opposed, meanings of all these signifiers get conflated. We have found ourselves repeatedly within intellectual spaces where Alfred North Whitehead's linguistic strategies get swept, indistinguishably from the very metaphysics he opposed, into the dustbin of philosophy. Such dismissive tactics may indeed exhaust "the flow which attracts us." For they often take place among progressive and creative thinkers, often in faculties of religion, often engaged in feminist theory. Beneath these obstacles to coalition lie serious questions as to the capacity or the desire of deconstruction to engage the problems of the world, indeed to offer a discourse with which one can even refer to a world—that which infinitely precedes and exceeds language; that which will not relieve language of the task of responsible reference within our endangered terrestrial swathe of relations.

Nonetheless, some of us within the process trajectory have outgrown the terms and tenor of our own mistrust of "deconstructive postmodernism." Within Whiteheadian thought the "lure for feeling" that poststructuralism conveys may too readily get dismissed, as though it is nothing but infatuation with modish jargon. Yet if we repress this lure as morally lightweight and philosophically incoherent, do we not caricature deconstruction—as the seductress, against whom younger scholars must be warned? Yet both schools of thought are equipped to deal affirmatively, even irenically, with difference.

Deconstruction as Elimination?

Let me first articulate the difference as falling within reconstructive postmodernism—that is, as a difference in the modes of prehension or reception of deconstruction. Permit me to pursue a more specific argument on behalf of this volume. We in these chapters would have little objection to the series' editor's criticisms of the "eliminative postmodernism" of Mark C. Taylor and Richard Rorty.[4] David Ray Griffin's general argument with deconstruction— that Other in opposition to which the *reconstructive* alternative *constructs* itself—introduces his historical account of the postmodernity he prefers. It frames his account of the founders of constructive postmodern philosophy (among whom Whitehead figures prominently, but with the important parallels of Charles Sanders Peirce, Charles Hartshorne, Henri Bergson, and

William James).[5] I will suggest that his analysis suffers from a "fallacy of misplaced opposition."

Griffin's characterization of modernity as antirational belongs in the toolkit of any serious postmodernism. It builds upon Whitehead's disruption of the hackneyed identification of the last half millennium and its science as a triumph of rationality.[6] In a tight tour de force, Griffin's historical analysis of the foundational incoherence of modernity demonstrates the constitutive role of the rejection of "panexperientialism" (or pananimism) in shaping modern reason.[7] He does not however engage Derrida, who coined the term *deconstruction*, nor Gilles Deleuze, Michel Foucault, Luce Irigaray, or Julia Kristeva, or indeed any of the French theorists whom one thinks of as originators of the "deconstructive postmodernism" to which this series offers the preferred alternative. Instead, he disputes with U.S. philosophers like Karl Popper, Wilfrid Sellars, and Keith Campbell. They are no doubt worthy opponents. Yet their questions, terms, and analytic methods simply do not represent what is known as "deconstruction." Indeed there is if anything less tolerance between North American philosophy and French deconstruction than between the latter and process thought.

Griffin makes the aggressive assertion that the antirationality of modernity, as exemplified in these anglophone philosophers, "finds its logical conclusion in deconstructive postmodernism."[8] Whether or not there is any validity in such a culminating accusation cannot, however, be ascertained within the terms of his own argument. For he has mounted the argument against a "deconstruction" of his own invention. Griffin claims, more specifically, that deconstructive postmodernists make a "tacit identification of perception with sense-perception" and thus of the latter with "the given." Yet the founder of deconstruction *propre* would, as I will show, reject precisely that identification. I am not interested however in arguing against Griffin's critique. Rather, to continue with Whitehead's criteria, it is in "applicability" and "adequacy" to the relevant body of texts that this critique has been lacking. The fallacious opposition does not invalidate Griffin's argument with U.S. philosophy.[9] The present volume decenters the opposition in order to advance the positive agenda of the series.

It is the passion of reconstructive postmodernism rather than the nits it picks that stimulates this entire debate, including of course the present volume and its "difference" within the series. Griffin's immense project does not lack applicability and adequacy to the problems of the earth. In Griffin's specific argument this passion takes the form of this "rhetorical question":

Given a world with a growing ozone hole, imminent global warming, and an enormous stockpile of nuclear weapons, any of which could bring the human race and much of the rest of the life of the planet to a grossly premature end, and given a host of other interconnected problems of gargantuan proportions, should we not say, from this type of pragmatic point of view, that a philosophy that results in a strenuous contributionism is "truer" than one that promotes ironic detachment?[10]

Unfortunately, however, this particular deployment of apocalyptic rhetoric permits the caricature of (all) deconstruction as irresponsible and of irony itself as disengaged. Griffin had claimed that "Richard Rorty's 'irony' is probably the best term for the stance toward life that follows from deconstructive postmodernism."[11] Again, I agree with Griffin's judgment of Rortian pragmatism; I also read Rorty's "liberal ironism" as inadequately pragmatic and incoherently postmodern. But I find it a mediocre and indirect substitute for the continental poststructuralism, which thereby—at least in the minds of any poststructuralist reader—gets damned by association. It is not that poststructuralism (and all other ironists, Nietzschean, Kierkegaardian, Socratic, or Joban) should be defended from such questions of accountability to the earth and to its vulnerable species. Nor have feminists and postcolonialists working from within the deconstructive heritage ever ceased to ask these questions. But then Griffin's particular question must become a real and not a rhetorical one. Otherwise the reconstructive challenge, however carefully framed, will continue to be read as a polemical dismissal of French-based theory. And *as such* it remains almost as ill-grounded in the relevant literature as are blithe dismissals of "metaphysics."

If Griffin's "strenuous contributionism" is not to be used to discipline those drawn to poststructuralism—as though they have succumbed to some irresponsible relativism, some (globally) fatal attraction—then the chapters in this volume will be permitted to make their own strenuous contribution to process postmodernism. Such a postmodernism, as Griffin insists, "should have been officially dubbed '*reconstructive*' to indicate more clearly that a deconstructive moment is presupposed."[12] By inviting the process poststructuralists out of their methodological closet, this volume seeks to prolong and not merely presuppose that "moment." Only so can deconstruction play a constructive role within process thought. The latter may then show the way out of an unsatisfactory and uncharacteristic opposition. If, that is, the Whiteheadian criterion of "contrast" be consistently entertained, then the "lure for feeling," which some process thinkers take from poststructuralism, will exceed the impulse either to separate the two movements as incommensurable or to merge them as one. Thus reconstructive postmodernism depends upon deconstruction as much as deconstruction depends upon the speculative schemes it deconstructs. What Isabelle Stengers calls a "peace-making proposition" emerges out of the nexus of disputation and divergence by which difference heightens in relation. Indeed, while Whitehead predates by half a century the eruption of the thought of difference as such—as *différance*—this pluralism radicalizes the particularity of the other, but precisely as an other-in-relation. Contrast hybridizes a new one from many. It does not appropriate the others for the selfsame identity of the one, and as "feeling" it resists reduction either to rationality or to language.[13]

Perhaps the proposition entertained by this volume augurs the coming of process poststructuralisms and deconstructive cosmologies. Or perhaps it merely opens up a third space, for now as positively unnameable as the subject of the "postmodern" itself. At any rate, the chapters in this volume, whether working more on the common history of the postmodernisms or more on the potentiality for future contrasts, do not conceal the sympathetic feeling motivating the rather abstract comparisons of these two distinct and nonparallel postmodernities.

Imbalanced Attractions

Of course the opening romantic comedy, casting poststructuralism in the feminine role, reverses gender rather quickly in the light of an analysis of cultural power. Poststructuralism, for all its postures of subversion, occupies a position of virtual ideological hegemony in the liberal arts academy, while process thought, dependent as it is upon theological studies, has faced not only the ongoing attack of various Christian orthodoxies but the loss, due to its metaphysical taint, of much potential solidarity on its progressive flank. While we in Griffin's series inherit a style and a polemic that I would be hard-pressed to fit to any feminized subject-position, we do find ourselves in some analogy to a stereotype of the woman who does not even rise into visibility as a worthy opponent. Poststructuralist scholars do not need to bother with any argument at all against constructive postmodernism. Whether or not we extend a desirously inclusive "we" to the poststructuralist, one can hardly imagine a conversation between the two movements, so unequal are their powers of influence, so imbalanced is the attraction. So this volume does not pretend to represent a dialogue. It is not as though this project emerges from any version of equal representations, but within a minority of poststructurally inclined process thinkers, embedded within the minority of which process thought represents within the academy. But we do not bemoan the impossibility of what Stengers (chapter 10), anyway, finds suspicious in the call for "civilized conversation."

Rather, like the Irigarayan "woman," this form of process thinking will seek out textual points of rupture in the "watertight" boundary, certain intersections, interactions, and interfluencies, where poststructuralist and process streams have already mingled. Thus we might read Irigaray's opening utterance as parable for the present task: "The flow which attracts us to each other," like the "lure for feeling" in the sense of a Whiteheadian proposition, can be ignored and exhausted. When elsewhere she questions the seamless privilege of language we can imagine her speaking not only *comme femme* but as reconstructive postmodernist:

Is the domination of language's rule unshakable? Allowing merely the addition of stylistic devices, of rhetorical flourishes, of still unsung melodies, of lyrics or words yet to ring out, within an empire of unchanging delineation. Will man speak to himself, still and always, through a medium that is determined by him, through an other defined in him? . . . *Forgetting of Air in Martin Heidegger*[14]

Our parable cuts both ways. "How can we still approach each other if there are only coverings which are not porous enough? . . ." Seeking to soften and transgress the boundaries of an androcentric subjectivity, Irigaray might speak either for process or poststructuralist challenges to the "separative self" and its language games.[15] So my (admittedly ironic) gender positionings of both postmodernisms must remain a bit queer; that is, ambiguously bounded, subject to hybrid identities and reciprocal permeabilities.

Porous Proposition

The particular proposition proposed by this anthology will partake, like any "complex propositional feeling," of a hybrid series of events unfolding within a nexus of affinity and difference. It partakes of the uncertainty that Whitehead relished in quantum theory as in his definition of a proposition: a tale "that perhaps might be told about particular actualities" (PR, 256). The tale, familiar in its contours, but requiring restatement from the present perspective, runs this way:

Toward the end of the second Christian millennium, Western philosophy had unleashed successive and simultaneous waves of resistance to the "selfsame": to the metaphysical premise of "substance," *ousia*, as the simple unity of self-identically subsisting subjects and objects. Among anglophone thinkers, Whitehead and his school posed the major alternative, while the Nietzschean-Heideggerian-French lineage developed a continental antiessentialism. The one fights substance with *process,* the other with *difference.* Both have exercised a wide interdisciplinary appeal largely outside of philosophy proper. And both can claim the title "postmodern" with ancestral legitimacy.[16]

The profound parallels may still startle those who have the patience to untangle both skeins of arcane vocabulary. Both jubilantly privilege becoming over being, difference over sameness, novelty over conservation, intensity over equilibrium, complexity over simplicity, plurality over unity, relation over substance, flux over stasis. Both repudiate the inherited "truth-regimes" of unifying metanarratives, which objectify reality from the vantage point of a stable, underlying subject. Both deconstruct—or, in Whitehead's language, "criticize the abstraction of"—any essentialized substance or subject. And both accomplish this critique by exposing the Western linguistic structures that fabricate the illusory common sense of what Derrida calls "self-presence" and what Whitehead calls "the subject-predicate form of proposition."

But of course poststructuralism is one long revolt against the authority of metaphysical first principles. By contrast, many process thinkers continue to presume upon the metaphysical truth and unexceptionable explanatory power of Whitehead's categoreal scheme. Poststructuralism maintains a playful cadence of ironic indirection, dispersive of any propositional claims and shunning holistic, unifying language. Process thinkers continue to construct additions to their integrative worldview, in which the many do not merely multiply but become one. If only for an instant. The latter understands its claims to correspond more-or-less, however imperfectly, with things-in-themselves: language constructs *from* something, the nature of which we can infer by a process of speculation and description. Poststructuralism has, with Kant, nothing to say about any *Ding an sich*—except about the self-deceptions of language when it claims to discover the "pure presence" of anything. So language cannot "represent"—make present again, mirror—that real presence: linguistic construction goes "all the way down," because any substratum of "common experience" can itself only be recognized *in and by language*.[17]

So far these differences of rhetorical style and self-definition, operative within the imbalance of cultural power, have obviated exploration of the massive similarities that exercise such a gravitational force on this volume. Of course it is more characteristic of the process "worldview" to seek out such divergent similitudes as grist for "contrast." I hope this characterization is not too flat or too unfair. It only recapitulates rather familiar generalizations in order to surface the width of the proposition. Put provocatively, if not apocalyptically: The current waves of process and poststructuralist thought may, for all their inequality, be quite equally in peril. They may be in danger of exhausting their own respective modes of resistance to the systems of "the selfsame." Might we suggest that precisely inasmuch as reconstructive and deconstructive postmodernisms remain poised in impermeability to each other—however oblivious each may be of the other's existence—they will both tend to an ineffectual scholasticism? If they cannot honor each other's "approach"—not as schools or fronts of thought but rather as *styles of responsible engagement*—they may lose their own creative edges. In other words, without each other, each might lose the world.

Here, when one needs to warn against the danger of world-loss, one is immediately tempted to continue the same practice of caricature that each school continually defends against. That is, as soon as we name the problems—problems that may dissipate when one studies the primary texts, but that continue to function, to "circulate" in the Foucaultian way of knowledge-regimes—we risk a form of that irresponsibility. But certain generalizations that do not apply to the primary texts remain descriptive at the level of widely dispersed discursive effects, rhetorical styles, and propositional feelings.

The ontophobia, the self-proclaimed ethical undecidability, the ecological indifference, the anti-essentialist "witch-hunt" of which so many progressive scholars accuse deconstruction in America—these problems have not decreased with widespread tenure.[18] They accompany a general cultural tendency toward political burnout and failed coalitions, with concurrent academic regression to specialized, if differently disciplined, discourse.[19] More importantly, they symptomatize a tendency, born of exhaustion with the conventions of representation rather than of political indifference, to replace the world with language. In the meantime language for "world"—cosmos, universe, totality, worldview, nature, community, and perception (sensory and extra)—has all been helpfully problematized but often irresponsibly abandoned.[20]

Similarly, reconstructive postmodernity sacrifices broader academic credibility, attractive power, and therefore its own potential for broad-based cultural alliances to the extent that it backs itself into a metaphysical corner. It might with its confident system—assuredly an open and growing one—capture "some of life in its meshes" but lose access to the cultural world in which it must test and change its language.[21] The profound pragmatism of the reconstructive project will be best served by a livelier sense of rhetorical strategy.

The former by its élan for negation and dissipation, the latter by its dogged insistence on the language of rationalist ontology, hurt their own capacities to make a difference (however you spell it). Clearly, the editors of and the contributors to this volume and its series do not think such an outcome inevitable. They propound not some romantic union of the two schools, by which love redeems the world. But more modestly, they practice a discourse of the overlap, an interstitial language in which a certain regenerative flow becomes possible.

The positive form of this complex propositional feeling would read as follows: The "multiple contrast" (Whitehead) generated in this volume exemplifies the potential of a "disjunctive conjunction" (Deleuze) of the poststructural and process trajectories. They will not merge. Certain coverings—by which the one wards off metaphysics, by which the other shields it—can however become *more porous toward that which they fear*. Key concepts can, like pores, get unclogged. A whole membrane of relevant concepts are becoming more permeable in the present anthology. In what follows, I will raise the question of two such conceptual pores, which remain pivotal to the interchange constitutive of what might be called "a process poststructuralism," or a "deconstructive cosmology."

Metaphysics: Foundation vs. Ground

While studying in Claremont, I happened to see the first *Star Wars*. For more than a decade afterward I suffered from a recurrent phantasm: whenever I would be trying to put some problem of life or theology in process terms, an image of Luke Skywalker's control panel would flash through my mind. It was as if I were flying this little ship at incredible speeds, through impossible intergalactic labyrinths, steering by the radar grid on his screen. Actual entities, prehensions, the primordial nature of God, the subjective aim . . . these categories seemed to be serving as the grid by which my Skywalker-persona zoomed in on its conceptual target. As a slow, pacific, low-tech, and earthbound feminist, I would swat the image away. But the "initial aim" often taunts like a trickster. Was it mocking my dependence on metaphysics for getting around in the universe? Was it cartooning my crypto-foundationalism?

I do not confuse process theology in the Claremont mode with the Force of *Star Wars,* its geophilic cosmology with "spacey" journeys of groundless abstraction, its embracing vision with any certain or self-enclosed system. Nonetheless, I cannot miss my own temptation to cling to these categories as though they comprised a foundation—*fond* in French, meaning "bottom"—a lowest ground of belief upon which one can build a stable edifice of thought, life, and faith. Do the categories of Whitehead comprise a foundation? Certainly Whitehead uses the language of "metaphysics" to justify an all-inclusive system of concepts, which is to encompass in its text the description, indeed the very "texture," of all possible experience. He summons the pantheon of rationality, coherence, consistency, platonic realism, and system, which seems at best passé, or worse, totalizing and reactionary. Inconveniently for lovers of both process and poststructuralism, one cannot erase this metaphysical terminology like some dirty secret. The text insists. But does Whitehead's commitment to a certain sense of "metaphysical categories" arrayed in systematic form amount to a *foundation,* even if he does not use that word?

We might define foundationalism as "the powerful thesis that our beliefs can indeed be warranted or justified by appealing to some item of knowledge that is self-evident or beyond doubt." [22] Foundationalism becomes a problem for postmodern thought inasmuch as it appeals to the certainty or self-evidence of first principles to justify belief. Revelation, reason, or any combination might be asked to deliver such first principles, which then serve as the firm foundations upon which to build the arguments of the system. It can thus stand on its own, with a certain architectural self-sufficiency. Undoubtedly Whiteheadianism serves for many of its disciples ipso facto as such a foundation. But that much may also be true of the feverishly antifoundationalist disciples of poststructuralism. Does Whitehead himself, however, provide such warrants?

If so, how can one account for his insistent, indeed systematic, assault on precisely such epistemic certainties? "Philosophy has been haunted by the unfortunate notion that its method is dogmatically to indicate premises which are severally clear, distinct, and certain; and to erect upon those premises a deductive system of thought" (PR, 8). This is not just an appeal for intellectual modesty. It is as clear a statement of antifoundationalism as one can find prior to the formulation of the problem in current terms. If some of us are tempted to deduce our own utterances from his scheme, we are clearly violating its own first principles. Those first principles, while not simply unknowable, require the "asymptotic approach" (PR, 4) of an ongoing "imaginative experiment" (PR, 5).

With his good-humored radicalism, Whitehead went about puncturing the false certainties of philosophy: "the chief error in philosophy is overstatement" (PR, 7). He did not substitute for them new and improved certainties. Rather, he launched into the very space of metaphysics his "categoreal scheme," an entire fleet of "metaphors mutely appealing for an imaginative leap." His "tentative formulations" voyaging on "an experimental adventure" inscribe within that discursive space an alternative matrix of concepts "systematic" enough—that is, organically intercohering—to prevent, one might say, the recourse to conventional habits (PR, 4-9). Contrary to the pursuit of a principle of Sameness by which the new, the other, the strange can be domesticated or excluded, Whitehead practices an empiricism, which demands revision of, rather than reduction to, the system. "We habitually observe by the method of difference" (PR, 4). This difference, as will become manifest in the course of these chapters, has much in common with the Derridean and Deleuzean strategies of difference, even while it stresses more than the former the role of perception and the positive potentialities of science and religion in the production of difference itself. Even of science he argues, as though anticipating Irigaray's fluid plea, that "the systematization of knowledge cannot be conducted in watertight compartments" (PR, 10). Whitehead thawed out the metaphysical tradition of the West, melting the unchanging, eternal Reality of its Being into the turbulent flow of an endless Becoming. "Creativity," as the first principle, cannot constitute a foundation as just defined. But then his disciples are ever tempted to cling to his tropes like life rafts amid the very flux that his philosophy has unleashed. Irony abounds.

So while some of us would prefer to de-emphasize the currently dysfunctional terminology of "metaphysic" and "ultimate generality," we might nonetheless find Griffin's key argument for the nonfoundationalism of his own Whiteheadianism compelling. He develops "Whitehead's antifoundationalist belief that epistemology cannot be discussed in isolation from metaphysics." Whitehead is in this move making a specific case against Cartesian and Lockean epistemologies of representation. Griffin's contention is intriguing: "By prehending our bodies, we thereby indirectly apprehend the actualities beyond our bodies *insofar as those actualities beyond our bodies are present within actualities comprising our bodies.*"[23] Put less technically, by learning again to think with our bodies, we discern what a complex and porous community they comprise; and how they themselves open out into the endless interrelatedness of their worlds. It is a matter of letting the body—as a densely hermeneutical embodiment of world—back into the philosophical heritage that had variously but consistently excluded it. Indeed it had most perniciously excluded it by its insistence on the foundational role of sense perception—hence the importance, which one might too readily miss, of amplifying Whitehead's broader, sometimes mysterious ("vague," "primitive," "obscure," etc.), but rather concrete understandings of perception.

Let us fill out the earlier citation of Irigaray: "How can we still approach each other if there are only coverings which are not porous enough, and *a void between those who no longer dwell in their bodies*?" (emphasis mine). Irigaray seems to be directing her plaint at theorists in her own discursive tradition, perhaps indeed at a simulacrum of Jacques Lacan. It would be a serious mistake to assume that, despite all the feminisms reading the text as body and body as text, deconstruction more successfully inhabits its bodies than any metaphysics. The difficulty in finding the conceptual pores with which to open language into the speech and the silence of the body, when concepts are constructed "all the way down," is notorious. Judith Butler's poignant "what about the body, *Judy*?" marks the trouble at the heart of feminist poststructuralism.[24] Griffin's process thought may more consistently avoid both essentialism and the linguistic idealism to which deconstruction is prone, while actually performing a "solution"—but in overtly metaphysical terms that will remain incompatible with poststructuralism.

What shall those of us do, however—those of us for whom reconstructive postmodernism does not beat, absorb, or supersede deconstruction—with the Whiteheadian language of metaphysical system? Of course we can contextualize it historically and defend it on its own terms, as Griffin does. We can also strategically deemphasize the language that is not pragmatically useful, as John B. Cobb Jr. has done in his construction of a Christian theology and of a life-centered economics. I want to make a further suggestion: we can read Whitehead's most stubbornly rationalist language as a deconstructive strategy. His antifoundationalist scheme is based on intricate readings of the key texts of substantialist metaphysics. His categories enter the cracks that fissure the thought of Plato, Aristotle, John Locke, René Descartes, Gottfried Wilhelm Leibniz, and Benedict de Spinoza; they probe with uncanny precision, and remain—precisely because they fit well enough—like a wedge, which, once inserted, prevents the closure by which the system contains and sustains itself. Or in Derrida's language, like a hinge, "brissure"—at once "fracture," "fragment," and "joint" (OG, 65).

In that case however we must understand deconstruction itself more like its originator means it, and less like his English-speaking disciples (a literary assembly, remarkably free of philosophical education) use it: that is, like an inside job. "Operating necessarily from the inside, borrowing all the strategic and economic resources of subversion from the old structure, borrowing them structurally, that is to say without being able to isolate their elements and atoms, the enterprise of deconstruction always in a certain way falls prey to its own work" (OG, 41). So of course Whitehead's system—as system—"falls prey" to its own antifoundationalist dynamism.

It is not just that Whiteheadians will commit fallacies of misplaced concreteness with the very abstractions Whitehead designed to counter such over-generalizations. We will need to continue to *risk* metaphysics. (Cf. Isabelle Stengers's chapter in this book on putting oneself at "risk" in the peace-making process.) That is, even if we experiment with postmetaphysical, postontological, or posttheological varieties of Whiteheadianism (as some of us do, to very different effect, in this volume[25]), the continuation of that which we find indispensable in the process project will entail, to distort Gayatri Spivak's famous phrase, a certain "strategic metaphysics." We need to speak about "world." We cannot always be coy. We need to think as bodies very concretely about our earth context and with our communities. We need operable language, theological and cultural, with which to confront the hegemony of a transnational economy bent on consuming world, earth, and community. For all its own formidable barrage of technical language, process thought, perhaps due to its dependence upon the progressive educational arms of religious institutions, still evinces a robust capacity to interact with social movements (e.g., trying to arise from the *fin-de-millennium* "battle of Seattle"). *Au contraire,* French-based theory may in the United States exercise a more purely academic range of effects.

We need not argue about degrees of political impact, however. Rather the question remains methodological. Whitehead now belongs to the origins of a past century. Many of us do not consider that which is precious in his philosophy indelibly yoked to impressive but dated linguistic strategies. Defense of traditional metaphysical language, like polemics against deconstruction, exhausts "the flow which attracts us." We may let certain codes fade into history (precisely not oblivion). But others—the language of prehension, event, concrescence, actual entity, and "interconnected relations of difference in contrast"—remain fresh enough to operate "from the inside"—as lures to feeling for a poststructuralist process cosmology. But what is it to which we are appealing, if not a foundation, if not necessarily a metaphysical template, with such interrelated figures of speech?

We might consider, for example, a distinction thus far usually missed, or actively denied: that between foundation and ground. Antifoundationalists tend to use the terms synonymously. This is partly a problem of the particularity of the French language: *fond,* in *fondation,* translates as both "bottom" and "ground." Therefore one can understand a tendency to con/found the two, which equates antifoundationalism with groundlessness. However in English the terms remain distinct: a foundation designates that which is sunk into the ground. The cultural artifact is not the same as the earth-ground that is given—however much we name, form, construct from, poison, erode, or ignore the earth.

Too literal, such terrestrial "ground?" *Pardon,* but I think the distinction opens up ground that cannot be ceded. It is precisely as metaphor that the conflation of ground with foundation becomes dangerous. Diane Elam performs a standard instance of the literary-critical posture of groundlessness: arguing valiantly for a coalitional feminism of "shared ethical commitments" within Derridean terms, she ends up proposing faithfully "a groundless solidarity" within a "politics of undecidability." For, as feminists, "we are all concerned for women, yet we don't know what they are." She merrily expands the claim to this axiom: "what binds us together is the fact that we don't know."[26] While one can readily unpack what is actually meant, the use of these gross but slick overstatements would benefit from some Whiteheadian deconstruction of their abstraction. Decision is confused with certainty, as ground is reduced to foundation. This is the sort of irresponsible indifference to the difference that language makes—all in the name of *différance*—that sends many back into the arms of Mama metaphysics. But then this is not Derrida, but a disciple. Unlike Sophocles' Athena, I do not in general "prefer the male." I simply cannot imagine a politically meaningful public to whom I would want to propose this "groundless feminism." It merges with deconstruction at precisely the point at which feminism offers its more fruitful resistances.[27]

Anyone serious about feminism or any other form of resistance to power will surely want to offer ground—to give reasons, to cede turf, and to remember the shared earth that provides the one common ground in which all of our contexts nest. Might the bodily and earthly ground—*adamah*—be permitted to offer itself as trope for the most embracing perspective in which *earthlings* live, breathe, and have our discourses? Or must we continue to mistake "ground" for fixity, the self-present, the changeless—for the Same? Yet the dirt shakes, shifts, creeps, and crawls. "Neither humus nor humans are humble at all."[28] Literal ground, recycled stardust like us, oozes with life-forms. Yet nothing is more sustaining of life than the densely relational, *relative* stabilities of the spinning earth-ball. I propose this apparently retrograde metaphor for the shared project precisely *not* as a shared foundation, but as a possible perspective in which to read our differences. So no set of texts will provide the ground, but they will variously inhabit and honor it. Their concepts will either attend to their own "ground," the earthly habitat that endlessly and differently gives rise to thought, or they will drift in the conventional groundlessness that has provided the very foundation of *classical* metaphysics.

Here we share the series' (counter)apocalyptic urgency: in an epoch of accelerating ecological suicide, the cultural elite of our species surely will not want to continue unwittingly the long tradition of degrading the earth, of taking *mater* for granted, of ignoring the suffering of bodies, of constructing ground once again as the inert, the lifeless, the dull, the opaque to knowledge—that which without *logos* does not exist. Theologically the classical tradition, which constitutes the very heart of what Heidegger and Derrideans call "ontotheology," grounded itself in the denial of this ground: in the release of thought into ever more transcendent abstractions, ever more unchecked generalizations, ever more transcendental subjects. So might there be a possibility for something like an intentionally *grounded* poststructuralism? Could this ground not support the wide-ranging dynamisms of the Deleuzean "nomadology," which will figure in this volume—for do nomads not inhabit the earth with all the more poignant versatility?[29]

If we cannot converse within the reverberation of the moving earth, I suspect the barrier of the Same will continue to loom too large between these schools. But there is ground for hope. For instance, Donna J. Haraway, the most influential voice within the deconstructive movement of science studies, proposes not another groundless anti-ontology but a "dirty ontology." Standing in the gulf between scientific and poststructuralist discourse, a margin not dissimilar to the present one, she—in the persona of the "modest witness"— offers one of the rare moments of the desired distinction:

> S/he is about telling the truth, giving reliable testimony, guaranteeing important things, providing good enough grounding—while eschewing the addictive narcotic of transcendental foundations—to enable compelling belief and collective action. (MW, 22)[30]

We may impute at least an intuitive convergence between the dirt and the ground of Haraway's multidimensional argument. The figure of the "modest witness" embodies a challenge to scientific overgeneralization while claiming the moral and empirical obligation to observe in the fullest and most worlded sense. Not coincidentally this challenge will turn out to be well versed in Whitehead.

The Trace of Correspondence

I hope that the antifoundationalist reading of Whitehead appears plausible and a bit surprising. Its helpfulness would lie in its capacity to help us feel our complex, continuous bodily exchange with our worlds, and thus to intensify our sense of ourselves as fellow creatures nesting within the precarious and precious ecologies of our carbon-based complexity.[31] But this feeling and this intensity will not translate into the wider coherence it politically seeks, without *minding its language*: that is, bearing its own linguistic constructivity always in mind. Yet on the whole, we of the process heritage tend to speak as though we are describing the world-as-it-is, albeit humbly and imperfectly. However practical such realistic rhetoric may be in nonacademic contexts, however insistent Whitehead was upon his "platonic realism," however well we may distinguish naive from "pluralistic realism" (PR, 78), and however many battles we can win by appeal to common sense, we forfeit the possibility of "common ground" with deconstruction if we tread heavily through the post-Kantian marshlands. On this path, the widespread impatience of process thought with issues of language, rhetoric, and textuality only makes matters worse. The alternative is not, I trust, to get mired in linguistic narcissism. But we may perhaps pick up our text and walk. The chapters in this volume perform various forms of this double attention—to language and to the world. Each of them moves closer to a deconstructive critique of linguistic representation, and moves there on *process* grounds.

Does treading more lightly on language mean, as some would surely suppose, that process thinkers should give up the idea of correspondence? Certainly the Heideggerian influence on continental philosophy has delegitimated the theory that language corresponds more or less truthfully with reality. Yet especially in his critique of Rorty, Griffin has advanced a careful argument in favor of correspondence. Rorty (with the sweeping simplification to which the American reception is prone) has reduced all sense of linguistic reference to the world beyond language to correspondence, and reduced correspondence to the fallacious "mirror of nature."[32] Whiteheadians of course also repudiate any foundationalist claim that language can with transparency or certainty mirror anything (except at best itself, in the form of analytic tautologies). But to smash the mirror is not the same as to cut the link between language and the world within which language takes place.

We may perhaps agree that our Logos creates the world-as-we-*know*-it. Indeed we may agree that our understandings and our sensations of the world are radically constructed—constructed at least as far down as our consciousness can reach. Whatever we *know together* ("con/sciousness" is, after all, always collective) we have already prefabricated together. Whitehead's theory of symbolic reference surely suggests a process of reference so elaborately indirect that it can justify no one-to-one correspondence, no mirroring or naive realism.

But we do not believe that our language has created the world-as-it-is. This would be a mere replication of the *creatio ex nihilo*—which Whiteheadians do not even grant to God![33] Moreover, we do not just *believe* that something exceeds and precedes language. With the intriguing doctrine of causal efficacy, we learn to attend to the very filaments of memory, visceral feeling, and mood that make us aware of "a circumambient world of causal operations" (PR, 176). In this causal preconsciousness—for we can never "know" the cause and therefore mirror its process in a concept—is embedded the link to the world in its immediacy. Our concepts cannot therefore directly correspond to anything beyond concepts. Yet this indirection remains critically important to Whitehead. It is the entire basis of his critique of Kantian subjectivism as well as of foundational objectivisms (and thus pivotal for Griffin's argument). Whitehead's language about this prelinguistic modality remains striking:

> In the dark there are vague presences, doubtfully feared; in the silence, the irresistible causal efficacy of nature presses itself upon us; in the vagueness of the low hum of insects in an August woodland, the inflow into ourselves of feelings from enveloping nature overwhelms us; in the dim consciousness of half-sleep, the presentations of sense fade away, and we are left with the vague feelings of influences from vague things around us. (PR, 176)

It may be that the efficacy of Whitehead's theory of causal efficacy rests on this sort of stylistic shift: he moves into a language of poetic invocation, appropriate to a subject matter, which, if reduced to its categories, presents a rather flimsy platform upon which to build the whole nondualist edifice.

It is not as though poststructuralism, especially where it joins with psychoanalysis, has been lacking in such attention to the preconscious. Indeed it benefits from the scaffold of decades more of Freudianism to lean upon. Let me just allude to Kristeva's concept of the "semiotic," which cries out for interchange with Whitehead's odd doctrine of "causal feeling." She identifies the semiotic (by contrast to the Lacanian "symbolic") with Plato's cosmological concept of the "chora": "the chora precedes and underlies figuration and thus specularization, and is analogous only to vocal or kinetic rhythm." She reads this cosmological concept into a theory of the unconscious. The notion of the subject thus proposed "will allow us to read in this rhythmic space, which has no thesis and no position, the process by which significance is constituted. Plato himself leads us to such a process when he calls this receptacle or chora nourishing and maternal, not yet unified. . . ."[34] Of course, for Kristeva the semiotic remains a "psychosomatic modality of the signifying process"[35]—the emphasis being upon the presymbolic generation of language, not upon the impact of the world. But this is a matter of differing emphases: for Whitehead the point of the description of causal feeling is also, precisely, to account for symbolization through the traces of a rhythmic presymbolic process.

This introduction can only raise and complicate these questions of the relation of Whitehead's theory of language to that of deconstruction. Griffin considers "eliminative" in Rorty, Taylor, and their followers, that which purges from theory the causal links, however dark, dim, and presymbolic, to the world; that which in short erases the traces of the world in language. If we underscore his own *proviso*—that he does not claim that his critique applies to a thinker such as Derrida[36]—we find ourselves in agreement with this criterion of postmodernism. Therefore we need not identify the eliminative with the deconstructive. Certainly the leading female poststructuralists, Kristeva and Irigaray, seek more to protect the presymbolic, the presensory (especially the previsual) from the "specular" transparency of the normative Western and certainly male gaze.[37] But Derrida, who also disavows the "phallogocentric" gaze, may provide a clear test case on the question of the reference of language to world.

Setting aside for the time being the mere term *correspondence,* what might Derrida's critique of the "transcendental Signified" entail for process thinkers? This question will be taken up more fully in Joseph A. Bracken's and Luis G. Pedraja's chapters. We may at least indicate the problem. Derrida's formative deconstruction of the binary of signifier and signified comprises an argument that all that is signified also signifies: that there is no logos, no ultimate subject, no consciousness, or Presence or Being, where the signifying chain stops; that is, no Platonic, changeless original of which all signs are mere imitations. As there is no pure Signified, there is also no pure Origin: signified also signifies; cause is also effect. This news should not surprise Whiteheadians, though the language and its tones may. Derrida used the metaphor of "text" to indicate all that signifies, all sign-systems—including especially nonphonetic ones, even nonhuman ones such as genetic codes. The argument, however, issued in the claim that "there is no world outside the text,"[38] a phrase since chanted as a mantra of literary criticism. If it means that there is literally no world outside of language, we reconstructors truly must join the chorus of critics appalled at this unrelenting linguistic idealism and its solipsistic textualism—at this festival of writers worshiping "Pure Writing."

The critique of *logocentrism,* Derrida's term for the Platonized understanding of language as something exterior to that which it signifies, has, however, been widely misconstrued as what he calls the error of "linguisticism."[39] Derrida sought liberation not from the nonlinguistic, not even from the theistic, but rather from the quasi-theological claims of the transcendental Signified. Standing in for the divine Logos in its mid-Platonic incarnation in classical theism, this unchanging, intelligible, fixed reference of speech oriented Western philosophy, according to Derrida, even structuralist linguistics. *Il n'y a pas de hors-texte* in the context of Derrida's text does not mean there is nothing outside the text, but rather that there is no significance outside of context; and that the context itself is comprised of signifiers. Derrida means to dispute *"the tranquil assurance that leaps over the text toward its presumed content, in the direction of the pure signified"* (OG, 159, his emphasis). Every element of meaning of which we can say anything is enmeshed in a "web of significations," that is, in relations rather than substantives corresponding to substances. Thus he is trying to rescue the context of the text from the violent abstraction of representation—of the illusion that language makes "present again" the thing. The critique of representation however cannot be read as repudiation of reference to the world. Derrida himself has become understandably impatient with the misunderstanding: "It is totally false to suggest that deconstruction is a suspension of reference." His own terminological preference would be however not "reference" or "correspondence," and certainly not representation with its associations with the "metaphysics of Presence" (substantialism), but rather "the other of language":

> I never cease to be surprised by critics who see my work as a declaration that there is nothing beyond language, that we are imprisoned in language; it is, in fact, saying the exact opposite. The critique of logocentrism is above all else the search for the "other" and the "other of language."[40]

Because that other of language only appears in language as language, Derrida's project—incommensurable even if after all not incompatible with Whitehead's—contents itself with the investigation of the "traces" in language itself. If we take Derrida at his word (how else?) when he proposes the concept of "trace" as "strategic nickname" for *différance*—following Bracken's clue that we read *différance,* Derrida's substitute for, and deferral of, a first principle, as "creativity"—we may find more positive analogies between deconstruction and Whitehead's much earlier critique of the Same of modernity.

"Trace" names *différance* when it conveys something ancient, a primordial process of signification, an "archiwriting," "'older' than the . . . truth of Being" (MP, 22). By trace he does not mean graphic marks of human language but rather something "which must be thought *before the opposition of nature and culture*, animality and humanity, etc., [and] belongs to the very movement of signification" (OG, 70, my emphasis). Because of its quasi-metaphysical implications, its insinuation of the primordiality of *différance,* this is a side of Derrida's thinking largely ignored by his disciples. Yet it should appear evident to us that this critique of logocentrism does not reduce signified to signifier any more than it reduces nature to culture or world to text. Rather, it exposes the self-deceptions of dualisms that pretend to derive language from a nonlinguistic and unchanging original, which language can re/present. That presence, or substance, subjects "the other of language" to the inflations of a language that authorizes itself as representation of the same. In short, Derrida has reinvented for an other and later context the fallacy of misplaced concreteness.

If we would temporarily put Derrida *en procès*—letting resonate here Kristeva's *sujet en procès,* the double entendre of the French phrase, which means both "in process" and "on trial"—we must come again to the question of the sensory. Derrida's argument with Edmund Husserl comprises another aspect of the quasi-metaphysical thought lost upon most literary-critical users of deconstruction. "Since the trace is the intimate relation of the living present to its outside, the opening to exteriority in general, to the nonproper, etc., the temporalization of sense is, from the outset, a 'spacing.'" Thus "archewriting is at work at the *origin of sense*."[41] In other words, we find in Derrida a felicitous analog to Whitehead's and Griffin's arguments against the primordiality of sense perception: sense is already inscribed, interpreted, or, in Whitehead's terms, *abstracted.* Indeed Derrida's "spacing" as exteriority puts space in time but also temporalizes space. This exteriority will become the "deferred presence" of *différance* itself: "*Différance* as temporization, *différance* as spacing.

How are they to be joined?" (MP, 9). Derrida has already suggested the answer, in the notion of "the becoming-time of space" and "the becoming-space of time" (MP, 8). We may consider vis-à-vis the problem of language and perception Whitehead's notion of "the presented locus" as a "common ground" between causal efficacy and presentational immediacy (sense perception):[42] "It must be remembered that the presented locus has its fourth dimension of temporal thickness 'spatialized' as the specious present of the percipient" (PR, 169). Despite the unappetizing technicality of both texts at this point, the convergence seems inviting. Might there not be significance in how both thinkers at once temporalize space and spatialize time in their articulations of that which always already imprints and precedes sense perception?

Derrida's delicate analysis of the present as nonpresence, as not constituted in the purity of substantial self-presence transmitted in the habits of *res cogitans,* yields instead a fractured tracery of past and future not incompatible with Whitehead's composite and interrelational "drop" of the present. Moreover, as Derrida rules out any possibility of a one-to-one correspondence between language and thing, by which one could merely mirror, so surely does Whitehead. Whitehead's analysis of the fragile emergences of consciousness as a spatiotemporal effect of contrasts between past and future surely precludes what Derrida calls "Presence," or its re/presentation in language. Indeed Whitehead anticipates the precise contours of the critique of representation: "Anyhow 'representative perception' can never, within its own metaphysical doctrine, produce the title deeds to guarantee the validity of the representation of fact by idea" (PR, 54).

If then we sense a convergence of criticisms in the repudiation of representation, what is to be said of correspondence? Must the reconstructive postmodern argument for a nonfoundational theory of correspondence remain incompatible with the radical critique of representation as logocentrism? Certainly Griffin has protected correspondence from its reduction to Rorty's mirror—to an imitation of reality by language. Whitehead's notion of proposition had inserted a wedge between language and reality, guarding against any such unmediated representation.[43]

By returning to the root sense of "correspondence" we might release another set of its resonances. The etymology of correspondence can help to free it from the onus of a one-to-one and one-way relation of signifier and signified. The word, as H. Richard Niebuhr notes in his articulation of a "responsible self," originally denotes a relational activity of co/responding, that is, of "answer[ing] to something else in terms of fitness," as the size of the nose may be "responsible" to the head.[44] First, therefore, it suggests an aesthetic sense of fit, and then an ethical sense of responsibility. So might we consider in a process-poststructural sense of correspondence an active and constitutive interrelation of language and world, in which the truth we tell is measured in the co/responsibility we produce? That is, the correspondence of our language to its world will be experienced in the beauty and the justice of the relations we answer to?

Perhaps we may consider such a hermeneutic of correspondence as a grounding referentialism suitable to a dirty ontology: it may not suit many Derrideans but it does answer to what many Whiteheadians find beautiful and just in deconstruction. At any rate, it has opened the second node, brissure, or conceptual pore, for the present state of imbalanced attraction.

The Chaosmos

> But how then can we proceed in philosophy if there are all these layers that sometimes knit together and sometimes separate? Are we not condemned to attempt to lay out our own plane, without knowing which planes it will cut across? Is this not to reconstitute a sort of chaos? That is why every plane is not only interleaved but holed, letting through the fogs that surround it, and in which the philosopher who laid it out is in danger of being the first to lose himself.
>
> —Deleuze and Felix Guattari, *What Is Philosophy?*

Thus Deleuze and Guattari on the difficulties that confront the project of this very collaboration. If we do not seek to subsume the deconstructive under the reconstructive moment, the chapters in this volume begin to constitute a third space: not in the abyss "between" two established methodologies so much as in the overlap, in the interleaf. But does such a process poststructuralism or a deconstructive cosmology then begin to lay out what Deleuze and Guattari have called "a plane of immanence" of its own? Or does it merely unfold certain implications of process thought, as already process theology has done so munificently? Perhaps such explication, as long as it does not appeal to Whitehead's scheme as a foundation, is always already its own creation. Such a creation takes place of course not from nothing but amid the chaos that fogs our lenses. In the early attempt to construct a third or planar space—neither metaphysics nor deconstruction, nor opposed to either—we may only be more acutely aware of the danger.

Thinkers of the French tradition (for whom the etiquette "constructivism" is more properly applied than "deconstruction"), whose abstruse work is only recently coming into prominence, Deleuze and Guattari are not recommending disorderly thinking but rather a constant confrontation of chaos. They understand the function of philosophy to be the production of concepts. A concept "crosscuts the chaotic variability and gives it consistency [reality]." Consistency? Reality? Whiteheadian ears will be perking up. "A concept is therefore a chaoid state *par excellence;* it refers back to a chaos rendered consistent, become Thought, mental chaosmos" (WP, 208). Might the chaosmos symbolize at once the form and the content of the third space sketched out in this volume? Perhaps then we may be together constituting a speculative chaosmology, which by its defining contrast of chaos/order amplifies rather than diminishes the uncertainty upon which the entire project is grounded.

It so happens that the chaos to which Deleuze and Guattari refer signals a profound affinity with Whiteheadian thought. It is not a coincidence that their thought plays a disproportionately prominent role in this volume. (Isabelle Stengers, Roland Faber, and Tim Clark could each in a way be characterized as Deleuzean Whiteheadians, as could my more recent theology.) Deleuze's *Difference and Repetition* situates itself within an entire cultural moment of "difference," and somewhat precedes its Derridean rendition. Thus toward the end of that major work we may read with special interest Deleuze's startling appraisal of Whitehead. Here, by way of summing up the Nietzschean countertradition he had cultivated, he argues against "categories," which "belong to the world of representation," for "descriptive notions":

> That is why philosophy has often been tempted to oppose notions of a quite different kind to categories, notions which are really open and which betray an empirical and pluralist sense of Ideas: "existential" as against essential . . . or indeed the list of empirico-ideal notions that we find in Whitehead, which makes *Process and Reality* one of the greatest books of modern philosophy. (DR, 284-285)

In other words we have here a major French thinker finding in Whitehead an ideal type of the nonessentialist, nonrepresentational, and descriptive thinking he was developing.

Deleuze's growing readership can neither be identified with deconstruction nor separated from poststructuralism. Deleuze's enchantment with Whitehead bursts into full view two decades later in his exegesis of Leibniz and the Baroque in *The Fold*. (Stengers's and my chapters will discuss the Deleuzean transmutation of monadology into nomadology, while Anne Daniell's work considers Rosi Braidotti's feminist Deleuzeanism with respect to process ecology.) This French imprimatur should at least reassure those who seek a third space that the attraction is not totally unrequited. More importantly, Deleuze performs in refreshingly unfamiliar terms a nonrepresentational reading of Whitehead. He writes with approval of Whitehead's sort of pluralist empiricist notions that they "preside over completely distinct, irreducible and incompatible distributions: the nomadic distributions carried out by the phantastical notions as opposed to the sedentary distributions of the categories" (DR, 285). The notion of the "phantastical" resonates with the illusory status of pure possibility in *Adventures of Ideas*: ideas signalling their own lightness of being, their mere abstraction.

Might the Deleuzean "distributions," which morph later into Deleuze with Guattari's "chaoid concepts," suggest the sort of thought appropriate to the world—the chaosmos—we seek to materialize? Could we hope in this fragile, promising conversation for the strengthening of a certain kind of chaosmological coalition? What difference does this conversation make—this attempt to think without foundation and representation, but toward the reality of our relations? Might such thinking—a difference *within* not *from* White-headianism and poststructuralism—matter in the constitution of a certain kind of material-social common ground?

Of course we cannot now appeal to some common denominator, as though it would provide us the "fond," the bottom line, in this project's exchange. The ground continually shifts, and the commons remains in conceptual as well as ecological peril. What Deleuze calls the *pro/fond*—"before the bottom"—churns up perpetual chaos for any confident statements of the common good. But I am convinced that, for instance, the "common good" that Cobb has advanced as an alternative to late capitalist economics and that provided the context for much of the following discussion, does not misplace its own concreteness. It does not mistake creaturely anguish and planetary threat, which can only be analyzed now with the help of global "distributions," with abstract universals. Its urgency flows from a quite concrete—but not asphalt—context: that of progressive Christianity, interpreted through a particular Anglo-American philosophical language, at the intersection with the social movements and an encompassing environmentalism.

This volume seeks to widen and enliven the philosophical discourse not just for the sake of propositional complexification but also to fine-tune the terms of the urgency. Everyone in this volume seems to think that this interchange between movements matters, that more is at stake than, for instance, justifying process studies to a new generation. The concern is rather to stimulate a kind of solidarity. If we seek some solidity in that solidarity, some shared ground irreducible to a common denominator, it will be flowing ground, dense perhaps and lavic, dependent upon continually clearing the Irigarayan channels. Its chaoid universe, its mattering world, requires neither dogmatic reconstruction nor dogged deconstruction so much as, first of all, what is called "poetic listening" by Isabelle Stengers: "The time has come," she writes, "for new alliances, which have always existed but for a long time have been ignored, between the history of humankind, its societies, its knowledges, and the exploratory adventure of nature."[45]

Oh, "God"

What about God? Does the very name undermine whatever alliance we might have imagined? This introduction can only postpone the question, hoping to have cleared a bit of a space in which the chapters can in their very different ways answer. When meditating upon process and difference, such deferring of the subject of *theo*logy may be not only forgivable but inevitable. But not endlessly. Or rather, if the *eschaton* is itself subject to an indefinite deferral, talk about that which comes, or came, or does not come, or always comes, is not. If God matters—becomes embodied—in our discourse, in this dialogue, then theology would take at least the form of penance for the repressive exclusions and imperial inclusions that the doctrine of the incarnation covers. Yet, of course, much of this conversation, like most reading of Whitehead in America, is not accidentally sponsored by living, dissenting forms of Christian theology. Process theology as postmodern theology has profoundly if not always evidently influenced all of the forms of progressive theology, especially feminist and ecological, which construe the creation to be the scene of salvation, and creation's character to be that of interdependent events rather than separate subjects and things.

At least for this author, the very symbol "chaosmos" offers a nonsynonymous translation of what theology calls "the creation." If process theology alone among constructive theologies has forthrightly disavowed the *creatio ex nihilo,* it is only fair—if I may borrow from chaos science's vocabulary—to let the self-similarity of its content iterate as its form. The theology that arises within such a chaosmos has much in common with process theology; its difference lies less in its propositions than in the styles, strategies—the arts—of their articulation. Its contours have suggested themselves already. Such a theology, in cahoots with the Whiteheadian rejection of any Creator who could *do* an absolute beginning and a final end, deconstructs the metanarrative of a linear providence. It cuts free of the logocentric antecedents of a *creatio ex nihilo.*[46] But it does so—in the name of Spirit. Love. Even "God," the cumbersome monosyllable.

God-language, *theologos,* does not name, however, the common ground or even goal of this volume. Yet the question of "God" remains vital to all. Does this postmodern mattering of God-talk extend beyond the wishful thinking of a few theologians? Or does it capture, as Griffin's entire series suggests, a vital postmodern possibility? Surely the end of the Enlightenment signals the exhaustion of thought inspired by disenchantment—that is, by its foundational critique of classical theism and its theocratic social structures, coded as superstition, authoritarianism, antiscience, and by its own continuation of the classical theist project of despiriting nature.[47] The critique of modernity, of course, has been long the province of a theological confessionalism, or neo-orthodoxy, enshrined preeminently in the Barthian opus. In a move whose resemblance to the present strategy cannot be denied, many theologians now revive neo-orthodoxy by referring its "system against systems," its critique of enlightenment subjectivity, to that of Derrida.[48] We also note the nominal proximity to the present project of another theological postmodernism, that of "radical orthodoxy."[49] This orthodox Christian postmodernism claims a confessional, communal, or revelatory starting point, as against the pseudo-universalisms of modern foundationalism. However, the assertion of theology as a "metadiscourse" (John Milbank) or as centered around "hard core beliefs" (Nancey Murphy), resembles precisely that which a process postmodernism (followed by poststructuralism) eschews as misleading certainty. Indeed, J. Wentzel Van Huyssteen exposes the "spectacular fideism" of such claims as little more than "cryptofoundationalism."[50] Moreover, the transparent agenda of conserving classical doctrinal rhetoric from feminist or deconstructive critique, of substituting liturgical practice for theoretical contestation, of purifying an impermeable "language game" for religious tradition, has nothing to do with the theologies at work in this volume. Milbank's conservative Augustinianism, for instance, eschews the progressive political impulses that energize reconstructive as well as deconstructive postmodernisms.

At any rate, a return to Niceno-Chalcedonian orthodoxy, the heart of classical Christianity, can hardly count, however credal, as a *credible* postfoundationalism. As a theologian I imagine that "soon and very soon," as the spiritual puts its eschatology, post-Enlightenment thought will outgrow the feedback loop between classical theism and classical atheism. Perhaps we all do, however, share a common hope: that postmodernity might signal the dissipation of the autonomic antitheology that from the beginning sharpened the cutting edges of modernism.

Perhaps from the other side this is happening already in Derrida's inability to let the question of (his) negative theology go, in his "Circonfessions," in his meditation on Abraham/Kierkegaard and "the Gift"; in Kristeva's preoccupation with Mary, faith, and medieval love mysticism.[51] Its most striking revelation may come in the essays of Luce Irigaray, which, unlike her sardonic flirtation with female mystics in *Speculum of the Other Woman,* can only be described as feminist theology.[52] Yet for the most part deconstruction has promoted an undifferentiating anti-Christianity, presuming stereotypes of ontotheology unrecognizable to anyone who has actually studied the so-called Logos in its multiple and mutually conflictual contexts. Deconstruction as theology has not yet produced an affirmative, activating alternative. As Griffin's earlier critique of Taylor suggests, a/theology plays the Trojan horse within the camp of Christendom, rekilling "God" from the inside. Taylor's scintillating deployment of Derrida unfortunately closes some of the most promising gaps, loopholes, and fissures, which Derrida himself keeps insistently—perhaps ever more insistently—open.[53] As Bracken's chapter demonstrates, Derrida's critique of logocentrism can be mobilized to critically strengthen Whiteheadian *theism.* Should we ignore or disparage the affinity of deconstruction to Whitehead's challenge to classical theism, just because the final theological utterances remain incommensurable? Because, that is, the one silences its metaphors just where the other reconstructs them? The echo in that silence may initiate the reconstruction. "In the beginning is the echo."[54]

Between these theological poles of the postmodern, our volume weaves its spider's web of sometimes crisscrossing, sometimes paralleling, alternatives. While Stengers and Faber study the way in which Deleuze also—at least in relation to Spinoza, Leibniz, and Whitehead—leaves "God" open for reinterpretation, Clark argues for an uncompromising Deleuzean atheism, or polytheism, as the standard by which to continue the (Sherburnean) project of reading God out of Whitehead. Faber, by contrast, makes an intriguing argument for the Deleuzean "insistence," rather than "existence," of God through an eschatological collapse of the two ultimates, God and creativity, into one. Carol Wayne White's discussion of the preliminary postmodernism of Henry Nelson Wieman, a process thinker who went his own way, similarly redefines God as the "creative event," as creativity itself. According to Clark, "creativity" in *Process and Reality* functions analogously to "difference" in Deleuze's *Difference and Repetition*. With startling congruence, Bracken shows the analogy of creativity to Derridean *différance*. This is to say that in the present encounter, "God" comes through sufficiently questioned, multiplied, suspended or released, flirted with, or reconstructed, to demonstrate that at the very least the language of "God" matters. That possibly, theological discourse helps to materialize a difference, without which postmodernity falls prey to the Same of the modern saeculum.

This virtual life of theology before, through, and beyond the modern actualizes itself, for instance, in Irigaray's feminist quasi-Christology pitched not against God but against the "sublime and unattainable distance of a God-Father": "Any detour is valuable [to His followers] if it can hide this revelation: the divine wishes to dwell in the flesh."[55] The divine does not remain in the sky, in the text, or in one man. Try as we might, theologians cannot confine it to a mono-Logos. For that dwelling, process theology in its carnal immanence always prepares a ground. The complex sacrality of the present proposition would not require that anyone swallow the name of "God." (Nor I presume would God.) These ancient *logoi* still carry the trace of something irreducible to a name, irreducible to *theos* or *a/theos*. That trace—here peacefully propositioned—always disrupts the "one foundation" of religious nostalgia. Yet we could imagine it temporarily pitching its tent in this third space.

Notes

1. New York: Routledge, 1992, 104.

2. Cf. Arran Gare's chapter in this volume for a startling disclosure of a common ancestor for process and deconstructive postmodernisms.

3. *This Sex Which Is Not One,* Catherine Porter with Carolyn Burke, trans. (Ithaca: Cornell University Press, 1985).

4. David Ray Griffin, William A. Beardslee, and Joe Holland, *Varieties of Postmodern Theology,* SUNY Series in Constructive Postmodern Thought (Albany: State University of New York Press, 1989).

5. Griffin, *Founders of Constructive Postmodern Philosophy: Peirce, James, Bergson, Whitehead, and Hartshorne,* SUNY Series in Constructive Postmodern Thought (Albany: State University of New York Press, 1993).

6. See Alfred North Whitehead, *Science and the Modern World* (New York: Free Press, 1967).

7. Griffin disputes the "sensationalist view of perception," showing how widely the identification of perception with sense perception is presupposed, and using this analysis to show (a) that the incoherence of modern thought stems from this presupposition, which leaves only a "vacuous actuality" and (b) that the truly postmodern alternative will require a return to the panexperientialism nipped in the bud for orthodox theological as well as for mechanistic scientific reasons early in modernity. Introduction to *Founders of Constructive Postmodern Philosophy,* 14ff.

8. Griffin, *Founders of Constructive Postmodern Philosophy,* 4.

9. Griffin means by "deconstructive postmodernism" an amalgam "inspired variously by" pragmatism (Dewey), physicalism (Quine), Wittgenstein, and Heidegger, as well as by Derrida and other French writers. He does not even mention "poststructuralism" prior to the revised series introduction. Given the contested nature of all these terms—especially by those to whom they are applied—Griffin's definition of deconstruction is not so much false as misleading. The present volume seeks to relieve the series of the confusion thus generated.

10. Griffin, *Founders of Constructive Postmodern Philosophy,* 30.

11. Ibid., 30.

12. See Griffin's new series introduction, in this volume.

13. "That the heightening of intensity arises from order such that the multiplicity of components in the nexus can enter explicit feeling as contrasts, and are not dismissed into negative prehensions as incompatibilities" (PR, 83).

14. Austin: University of Texas Press, 1999, 142. In the context of her argument with Heidegger, Irigaray implicitly marks her own difference within the continental scene of *différance.*

15. I had developed, with some early help from Irigaray, a "between" the "separative" and the "soluble" self-structures, to which a "connective self" signaled a third, gender-fluid location. See Catherine Keller, *From a Broken Web: Separation, Sexism and Self* (Boston: Beacon, 1986).

16. John B. Cobb Jr. first used the term *postmodern* with reference to Whitehead in 1964, in the *Centennial Review* 8 (spring, 1964), 209-220. Griffin used it already in 1972. Cf. his summation of the process usage, in *Founders,* 33 n.1.

17. Cf. Terry Eagleton, *The Illusions of Postmodernism* (Oxford and Cambridge, MA: Blackwell Publishers, 1996).

18. See Frederic Jameson, *Postmodernism, or, The Cultural Logic of Late Capitalism* (Durham, NC: Duke University Press, 1991); David Harvey, *The Condition of Postmodernity: An Enquiry into the Origins of Cultural Change* (Oxford and Cambridge, MA: Blackwell, 1989); and Terry Eagleton, *The Illusions of Postmodernism.* Feminists have raised questions of the dehistoricizing loss of world, agency, subjectivity, and identity within feminism since its first reception. For a recent summation of

the problematic cf. Susan Stanford Friedman, "Negotiating the Transatlantic Divide: Feminism After Poststructuralism," in *Mappings* (Princeton: Princeton University Press, 1998) 181ff. Cf. also the internal debate, *The Essential Difference,* Naomi Schor and Elizabeth Weed, eds. (Bloomington: Indiana University Press, 1994).

19. Cf. Cobb's critique of academic specialism as it harnesses the university to the economism of transnational capitalism in *For the Common Good: Redirecting the Economy Toward Community, the Environment, and a Sustainable Future,* coauthored with Herman Daly, (Boston: Beacon, 1994 [1989]).

20. For the best defense of Derrida's own work against such charges, cf. John D. Caputo, *The Prayers and Tears of Jacques Derrida: Religion without Religion* (Bloomington and Indianapolis: Indiana University Press, 1970), esp. 16ff.

21. Zora Neale Hurston, *Their Eyes Were Watching God* (Harper Collins, 1999), 186.

22. J. Wentzel Van Huyssteen, *The Shaping of Rationality: Toward Interdisciplinarity in Theology and Science* (Great Britain: Eerdmans, 1999), 62.

23. Griffin, *Founders of Constructive Postmodern Philosophy,* 22.

24. Judith Butler, *Bodies that Matter: On the Discursive Limits of "Sex"* (New York: Routledge, 1993), 9. Cf. Christina Hutchins's persuasive reading of Butler via Whitehead in this volume.

25. Especially the Europeans, Isabelle Stengers (chapter 10), Roland Faber (chapter 9), and Tim Clark (chapter 8).

26. Diane Elam, *Feminism and Deconstruction: Ms. en abyme* (London: Routledge, 94), 85. The titular pun, from Derrida's radicalizing "mise en abime," refers to the abysmal rift that opens in the ground, and thus "the infinite displacement brought about by feminism and deconstruction: the displacement of the subject, of identity politics, of the subject of feminism and deconstruction" (25).

27. *Derrida and Feminism: Recasting the Question of Woman,* Ellen K. Feder, Mary C. Rawlinson, and Emily Zakin, eds. (New York: Routledge, 1997).

28. "We are audacious, like nature herself. We are wet, fecund, protean, dangerous. When we start to comprehend this in widening circles of the world, we know something worth knowing. We know that we must become responsible." William Bryant Logan, *Dirt: The Ecstatic Skin of the Earth* (New York: Riverhead Books, 1995), 16.

29. Cf. esp. Gilles Deleuze and Felix Guattari, *A Thousand Plateus: Capitalism and Schizophrenia* (Minneapolis: University of Minnesota Press, 1987).

30. For more on Haraway, see my chapter in this book.

31. Griffin, *Postmodern Politics for a Planet in Crisis: Policy, Process, and Presidential Vision* (Albany: State University of New York Press, 1993).

32. Richard Rorty, *Philosophy and the Mirror of Nature* (Oxford: Blackwell, 1990).

33. Catherine Keller, *Face of the Deep* (London: Routledge, forthcoming).

34. The term *semiotic* means mark, trace, and figuration, and for her then suggests the inscription upon the subject of "various constraints imposed on this body—

always already involved in a semiotic process—by family and social structures." *The Kristeva Reader,* Toril Moi, ed. (New York: Columbia University Press, 1986), 93f.

35. Ibid., 96.

36. Griffin, *Varieties of Postmodern Theology,* 30, 53, n.5.

37. The widespread influence of Whitehead on feminism in North America reflects a disjunctive but analogous attraction to a language that honors its own poetic edges, where women find expressive options beyond emulation of the andromorphic subject or surrender to objectification.

38. *Il n'ya pas de hors-texte* (OG, 158).

39. Jacques Derrida, *Deconstruction in a Nutshell: A Conversation with Jacques Derrida.* Edited with a commentary by John D. Caputo (New York: Fordham University Press, 1997), 104.

40. Derrida, "Back from Moscow, in the USSR," in *Politics, Theory and Contemporary Culture,* Mark Poster, ed. (New York: Columbia University Press, 1993), 197–235.

41. Derrida, "Speech and Phenomena," in *A Derrida Reader: Between the Blinds,* Peggy Kamuf, ed. (New York: Columbia University Press, 1991), 26, 27. Emphasis added.

42. Whitehead sometimes equates sensory perception with "presentational immediacy" (which Griffin calls "pure sense-perception"), sometimes with "symbolic reference" (as Cobb does, and that Griffin calls "full fledged sense-perception"); cf. Introduction to *Founders.*

43. For a compact discussion of truth and language cf. also Paul Nancarrow, "Realism and Antirealism: A Whiteheadian Response to Richard Rorty," *Process Studies* 24 (1995).

44. H. Richard Niebuhr, *The Responsible Self: An Essay in Christian Moral Philosophy* (New York: Harper, 1963).

45. Isabelle Stengers, *Power and Invention: Situating Science* (Minneapolis and London: University of Minnesota Press, 1997), 59.

46. Catherine Keller, *Face of the Deep* (London: Routledge, forthcoming). A poststructuralist and reconstructive theology of creation from the chaos—*ex profundis.*

47. Cf. Griffin, *Religion and Scientific Naturalism* (Albany: State University of New York Press, 2000), chap. 5.

48. Cf. Walter Lowe, *Theology and Difference: The Wound of Reason* (Bloomington: Indiana University Press, 1993) and Graham Ward, *Barth, Derrida, and the Language of Theology* (Cambridge and New York: Cambridge University Press, 1995.)

49. In conjunction with the arguments represented by "postsecular philosophy," postcritical and narrative theology, and so forth. See *Radical Orthodoxy,* John Milbank, Catherine Pickstock, and Graham Ward, eds. (London and New York: Routledge, 1999); *Post-Secular Philosophy: Between Philosophy and Theology,* Phillip Blond, ed. (London and New York: Routledge, 1998); John Milbank, *Theology and Social Theory: Beyond Secular Reason* (Oxford: Blackwell, 1990), *The Word Made*

Strange: Theology, Language, and Culture (Oxford and Cambridge, MA: Blackwell, 1997); and *Truth in Aquinas,* John Milbank and Catherine Pickstock, eds. (London: Routledge, 2000).

50. J. Wentzel Van Huyssteen, *The Shaping of Rationality: Toward Interdisciplinarity in Theology and Science* (Great Britain: Eerdmans, 1999), 77, 81.

51. Harold Coward and Toby Foshay, eds., *Derrida and Negative Theology* (Albany: State University of New York Press, 1992); Derrida, *The Gift of Death* (Chicago: University of Chicago Press, 1995); *Religion,* Derrida and Gianni Vattimo, eds. (Stanford: Stanford University Press, 1998); Geoffrey Bennington, *Jacques Derrida* (Chicago: University of Chicago Press, 1993); Caputo and Michael J. Scanlon, eds., *God, the Gift, and Postmodernism* (Bloomington: Indiana University Press, 1999).

52. See esp. Luce Irigaray, *Speculum of the Other Woman* (Ithaca: Cornell University Press, 1985), Gillian C. Gill, trans., and "Divine Women," in *Sexes and Genealogies* (New York: Columbia University Press, 1993); also *An Ethics of Sexual Difference* (Ithaca: Cornell University Press, 1993); *Marine Lover of Friedrich Nietzsche* (New York: Columbia University Press, 1991); and *This Sex Which Is Not One* (Ithaca: Cornell University Press, 1985). Cf. also *Transfigurations: Theology and the French Feminists,* C. W. Maggie Kim, Susan M. St. Ville, and Susan M. Simonaitis, eds. (Minneapolis: Fortress Press, 1993).

53. Mark C. Taylor, *Erring: A Postmodern A/theology* (Chicago: University of Chicago Press, 1984).

54. Gilles Serres, *Genesis* (Ann Arbor: University of Michigan Press, 1995), 119.

55. Irigaray, *Marine Lover of Friedrich Nietzsche,* Gillian C. Gill, trans. (New York: Columbia University Press, 1991), 186.

1

The Roots of Postmodernism
Schelling, Process Philosophy,
and Poststructuralism

ARRAN GARE

Fundamental questioning of the assumptions of modernity has reached its apogee in process philosophy and poststructuralism. That these philosophies are both reacting against modernity is enough to warrant a closer examination of their similarities and differences. But there is a more compelling reason for undertaking such an examination. Even a superficial consideration of these movements of thought reveals them to have common central themes. There appear to be resonances between these philosophies, and the task of revealing these resonances has only just begun.

However, while such work can be illuminating, it risks losing sight of the bigger picture—the relationship between ideas, broader traditions of thought and cultural traditions, and the society we live in. My contention is that it is only when we can relate philosophers and their ideas to deeper, often submerged traditions of thought that the full benefit of contrasting particular thinkers and particular ideas can be gained. We can then evaluate each movement of thought, each philosopher, and each idea as contributions to these deeper traditions and in so doing, evaluate these deeper traditions.

Traditions and the Search for Origins

Traditions of thought provide the matrix within which ideas are developed, evaluated, and transcended. They are characterized by diverse views contending with each other and with views from opposing traditions. Such traditions are core components of the cultures of societies and civilizations, justifying and developing or opposing the principles on which they are based. It is in relation to this broader context that ideas should be understood.

Modernity, the civilization that now dominates the globe, has as its foundation a "master tradition" of thought, characterized by Alfred North Whitehead as scientific materialism. This is accompanied by a countertradition which, taking the subject as its point of departure rather than nature, is idealist rather than materialist and treats the world, including nature, as a human or social construct. Scientific materialism is, and always has been, a developing tradition of inquiry, aiming to provide not only a coherent understanding of the physical, biological, and social worlds, but also the foundations for ethics and political philosophy, and to define the ultimate goals for society, civilization, and humanity.[1] Its components include not only mainstream natural science but also mainstream psychology and economics. The market is construed as a self-steering automaton, driven by the greed of individuals, which must be allowed to progress, although this involves subjugating or destroying all life-forms, communities, and individuals revealed to be of no use to the economy.

As the dominant tradition of inquiry, these ideas have come to be embodied and have formed the basis of social organization and of people's orientation to the world.[2] It is an essential component of a self-reproducing configuration of beliefs, practices, social relations, and social institutions which, having emerged in Britain, Holland, and France, expanded to encompass first Europe and America, then the entire world, subjugating, destroying, or transforming every other culture and civilization. The market is the ultimate power in the scientific materialist world. Driven by the appetites and aversions of individuals, it must be allowed to progress, although this involves subjugating all nonhuman forms of life and destroying all traditions and communities that do not serve its expansion. The ultimate aim of this civilization is the complete technological domination of not only the physical and biological world, but also of humans who do not conform to this vision of the world and its future. The idealist countertradition, while sharing the commitment to the domination of nature, differs in treating human subjects as above nature and in celebrating human rationality. The process of realizing the technological domination of the world is called "modernization," and proponents of modernization are modernists. The latest phase of globalization indicates how powerful the modernists are. Postmodernists are, preeminently, those who reject modernism in one or more of its variants or manifestations, but also the society formed by modernity and by the path being taken by modern civilization.

Postmodernism should be understood as one of the traditions that emerged in opposition to modernity's dominant tradition of thought, which has sought to question its assumptions and to develop an alternative basis for orienting people to the world and to each other. While there were survivors of older traditions of thought who opposed modernity, and while there were individual thinkers, such as Giambattista Vico and Jean-Jacques Rousseau, who were precursors to postmodernism, postmodernism only crystallized as a tradition in Germany at the end of the eighteenth and the beginning of the nineteenth centuries, as a more radical alternative to the idealist challenge of Immanuel Kant, Johann Gottlieb Fichte, and G. W. F. Hegel to scientific materialism. Only then was there a movement of thought with a diversity of people responding to and building upon each other's achievements. It was at this stage that certain individuals could be identified who forged the basic direction of the tradition. Preeminent among these were Johann Herder, Johann Wolfgang von Goethe, and Friedrich von Schelling.

In terms of his breadth of vision and his characterization of the crucial issues, Herder can be taken as the defining figure in this tradition. Herder argued against the primacy attributed by Enlightenment philosophers to universal principles and abstractions and defended the concrete, the particular, sense experience, quality over quantity, and diversity against the pressures within modernity toward uniformity. He saw tendencies to justify suffering in the name of abstractions—the human species, civilization, and progress—as cruel and sinister. He rejected the mechanistic view of nature, instead representing nature as active and purposeful, a unity in which dynamic, purpose-seeking forces flow into each other, clash, combine, and coalesce. Correspondingly, he opposed atomistic, utilitarian thinking and promulgated an ethics of self-expression or self-realization, calling on peoples and individuals to express the potentialities unique to them. Herder argued that different cultures have incommensurable but equally defensible values and ideals. He held that all *cultures* (the plural term was coined by him), both in the past and in the present, are significant in their own right and equally valuable, although he expressed considerable hostility to Europeans for their greed and aggression. However, while Herder had the greatest breadth of vision, it was Schelling who elaborated upon these ideas most rigorously and creatively and who had the greatest influence on subsequent philosophers.

Schelling's influence has been enormous. Hegel was deeply in his debt, as were those who reacted against Hegel. Ludwig Feuerbach, Søren Aabye Kierkegaard, Friedrich Engels, and Mikhail Aleksandrovich Bakunin attended his lectures. He influenced Samuel Taylor Coleridge, Karl Marx, Arthur Schopenhauer, Friedrich Nietzsche, Fyodor Dostoyevsky, and Martin Heidegger. Charles Sanders Peirce described himself as a "Schellingian, of some stripe."[3] Indirectly, mainly through his influence on science, Schelling's earlier work was a major influence on process philosophy and his later work was a major influence on the poststructuralists. My contention is that through Schelling we can appreciate the coherence of this tradition of opposition to modernity, and that through understanding the relationship between Schelling's earlier and later work we can discern and evaluate the relationship between process philosophy and poststructuralism.

Schelling's Early Philosophy

Schelling was central to the development of post-Kantian philosophy. Kant construed the world as understood by science as the product of sensations organized by the imagination, forms of intuition, and categories of the understanding of a transcendental ego. The "thing-in-itself" was deemed to be unknowable except indirectly in relation to moral action. To overcome this division between the subject and the object, between the phenomenal world and the real world, and between science and ethics, Fichte had postulated an "Absolute I" that is the source of all intuitions and thereby of the objective world and the empirical ego. Nature was seen as the objective world posited by the Absolute I, as something against which the moral will could develop and realize itself. This is idealism. The focus on the active, controlling subject is the obverse of the reduction of nature to a mechanical world of matter in motion.

Schelling, while influenced by these thinkers, departed radically from them. Characterizing one of his first works, "System of Transcendental Idealism," he was consequently characterized as an idealist. However, while his transcendental idealism was designed to analyze and elaborate the categories through which the world is understood, it was not meant to be a self-sufficient philosophy. Taking up Friedrich Hölderlin's criticism of Fichte, that it is inconceivable that an Absolute I could become conscious of itself, Schelling argued that the self-conscious I needs to be explained as the product and highest potentiality of nature. Transcendental philosophy therefore needs to be complemented by a philosophy of nature, which he developed in *Ideas for a Philosophy of Nature*.[4] As Schelling put it, "both sciences together are [required]."[5] Schelling later pointed out that his philosophy was neither materialist nor spiritualist, neither realist nor idealist; it contained within itself these oppositions.[6] And he affirmed the priority of the philosophy of nature over transcendental idealism.

Nature must be conceived as capable, at its highest level of development, of giving rise to the self-conscious subject that could arrive at knowledge of nature. Schelling's philosophy of nature, developing the insights of antimechanistic thinkers such as Herder and Goethe, was an attempt to understand nature in this way.[7] His procedure was to subtract from self-consciousness to arrive at the lowest conceivable potential and then to construct the path upward to show how the conscious self could be conceived to emerge from this. The lowest potential arrived at was the "pure subject-object," which Schelling equated with nature; he claimed, moreover, that the "unconscious" stages through which consciousness emerges can only become conscious to an I that has developed out of them and realizes its dependence upon them. Nature was conceived as essentially activity or, simultaneously, "productivity" (or process) and "products." Without productivity, there could be no products, and without products, there could be no productivity. This productivity consists in opposed activities limiting each other. Schelling proclaimed, "give me a nature made up of opposed activities . . . and from that I will bring forth for you the intelligence, with the whole system of its presentations."[8] From opposed activities emerge force and matter, space and time, chemicals, and nonliving and living organisms. According to Schelling, the process of self-constitution or self-organization, rather than being a marginal phenomenon, must be the primal ground of all reality.[9] Whatever product or form exists is in perpetual process of forming itself. Dead matter, in which product prevails over productivity, is a result of the stable balance of forces where products have achieved a state of indifference. Organisms are self-organizing beings in which productivity cannot easily maintain products in a state of indifference. Living organisms differ from nonliving organisms in that their complexity makes it even more difficult to maintain a state of indifference. They must respond creatively to changes in their environments to form and reform themselves as products. Life is the condition for the emergence of spirit, with its social forms and their history. With spirit, we have the emergence of freedom to choose evil or good. Evil is the domination of the blind self-seeking urge. It is creative power out of control, like cancer; but, without such creative power, there would be no existence and no good.[10]

With nature conceived as a self-organizing unity, this philosophy is fundamentally anti-Cartesian. We ourselves are part of nature. There can be no Archimedean point outside of nature from which we can view nature as an object. As Schelling saw it, what we encounter in empirical nature, either immediately or through experiments, are products, and it is these that the particular sciences deal with. The particular sciences by themselves can never grasp the conditions of their possibility, nor can they grasp the world as a whole. As Schelling characterized scientific knowledge,

> Every experiment is a question addressed to nature that nature is forced to answer. But every question contains a hidden a priori judgement; every experiment which is an experiment is prophecy; experimentation is itself a production of a phenomena. . . . The fact that experiment never leads to . . . [absolute] knowledge is evident in the fact that it can never get beyond the natural forces which it itself uses as its means . . . the last causes of the phenomena of nature no longer appear themselves. . . . [If] every new discovery throws us back into a new ignorance, and as one knot is untied, another is tied, then it is conceivable that the complete discovery of all connections in nature, that therefore our science itself, is also an endless task.[11]

The original productivity, which is neither subject nor object, must be grasped in some other way. It requires intuition or imagination. Art, which "reflects to us the identity of the conscious and unconscious activities,"[12] is this intuition become objective. It is accessible to all, while philosophical intuition is a special ability limited to philosophers with exceptional imagination.

Schelling and Process Philosophy

It is not difficult to see in this brief account of Schelling's early philosophy the ideas central to process philosophy. Schelling clearly anticipates Henri Bergson's arguments for the inadequacy of thought that objectifies (by spatializing) the world, the role of intuition in grasping durational becoming, and therefore the superiority of art over science for grasping reality. Whitehead's critique of scientific materialism and his philosophy of organism can be interpreted as efforts to develop Schelling's ideas more rigorously in the light of more recent physics.[13] For Whitehead, as for Schelling, nature is "unconscious mind." To use Whitehead's terminology, the ultimate existents are proto-conscious (or feeling) "actual occasions," which constitute themselves or "concresce" by "prehending" other actual occasions along with their potentialities, or "forms of definiteness," and then become "objects," that is, potentialities to be prehended in the self-creation of other actual occasions (PR, 23). With these characteristics, the emergence of both inert objects and the higher levels of consciousness in "societies" of such actual occasions can be explained (AI, 207; PR, 88f.). While there is no evidence that Whitehead studied Schelling's work, he was acquainted with Schelling's basic ideas through the writings of N. O. Lossky. He reproduced a quotation from Schelling in *The Concept of Nature*, in which Schelling characterized the essence of his philosophy of nature (CN, 47).[14] This book was written shortly before Whitehead elaborated on his own metaphysics. However, virtually every idea in science that inspired Whitehead was influenced in some way by Schelling's philosophy of nature. It was the influence of Schelling that led scientists to postulate the conservation of energy and to promote energy as a core concept of science.[15] Whitehead made energy, reconceived as "creativity," a core category (a category of the ultimate) of his metaphysics.[16] H. C. Oersted's discovery of electromagnetism, central to the development of J. C. Maxwell's ideas, was inspired by Schelling.[17] Maxwell's work was a major point of departure for Whitehead. More fundamentally, Schelling's evolutionary cosmology, in which nature was conceived as self-organizing, together with his argument that explanation should ultimately be genetic, was incorporated into biology by those Schelling inspired. Karl von Baer's ideas on embryology, informed by Schelling, formed the core of Herbert Spencer's evolutionary theory of nature, which then had a major influence on both Bergson and Whitehead. Finally, both Bergson and Whitehead were strongly influenced by the "Schellingian" Peirce, mainly through the latter's influence on William James. When the influence of Schelling on subsequent science and philosophy is traced out, it is clear that both Bergson and Whitehead were, like Peirce, Schellingians of some stripe.

But this is also true of the poststructuralists. The poststructuralists were, to begin with, philosophers attempting to critique and go beyond phenomenology and structuralism. But their deeper opposition was to Hegelian philosophy, and their major source of inspiration was the anti-Hegelian work of Nietzsche and Heidegger.[18] Both Nietzsche and Heidegger were (directly or indirectly) strongly influenced by Schelling's critique of Hegel's philosophy,[19] and poststructuralism is essentially a continuation of Nietzsche's and Heidegger's attempts to further Schelling's attack on Hegelian philosophy. To fully understand and properly evaluate poststructuralism, it is necessary to see it in relation to the opposition between Hegel and Schelling.

Schelling's Confrontation with Hegel

The crucial point of opposition between Schelling and Hegel pertained to the concept of the Absolute. Schelling had construed nature as everything that is and is not and as that from which conscious subjects and their experience of objects emerge. This involved rejecting Fichte's notion of the Absolute as the "Absolute I." Schelling, reluctantly, proposed to use the term *Absolute* to characterize that which is the "absolute identity" underlying all differences and the totality of these differences.[20] Elaborating on this, Schelling wrote, "It is that which never was, which, as soon as it is thought, disappears and Is only ever in what is to come, but is only in a certain manner there as well, thus Is only really in the end. There then, it also first assumes the name being as well as that of the Absolute."[21] It cannot be made an object of thought, but is presupposed by the thought of subjects and in the experience of objects. It is not thought in thinking but by self-disclosure or revelation.[22] This involves an "intellectual intuition." Hegel attacked this notion and the place given to intuition in such disclosure:

> Dealing with something from the perspective of the Absolute consists merely in declaring that . . . all is one. To pit this single insight . . . to palm off its Absolute as the night in which, as the saying goes, all cows are black—this is cognition naively reduced to vacuity. . . . The True is the whole. But the whole is nothing other than the essence consummating itself through its development. Of the Absolute it must be said that it is essentially a *result,* that only in the *end* is it what truly is; and that precisely in this consists its nature, viz. to be actual, subject, the spontaneous becoming of itself.[23]

The system developed by Hegel was strongly influenced by Schelling's genetic form of explanation, his dialectical method of developing categories, and his philosophy of nature and philosophy of history. But Hegel followed Fichte in taking the Absolute as "Absolute I" or Spirit. Hegel's system begins with the Logic, conceived to be the ground plan of the whole of reality, which "shows forth God as he is in his eternal essence before the creation of Nature and finite Spirit."[24] Being, the first category of the Logic, was presented as the most abstract and most empty category, the starting point from which all the categories required to understand the world and our consciousness of it could be dialectically generated. This Logic requires the positing of Nature. Nature is posited by Spirit and Spirit emerges as the truth of Nature, the negation of Nature's negativity. The Philosophy of Spirit describes the moral as opposed to the physical aspect of reality. It displays humanity in its development from Subjective Spirit in which it struggles to overcome the vestiges of its natural heritage with its bonds of individualism, to Objective Spirit in which humanity battles to construct objective institutions: the family, civil society, and the State. The sequence of social forms has provided increasingly better vantage points for Spirit to attain a view of itself as Absolute Spirit through Art, Revealed Religion, and Philosophy. The Absolute emerges here, as a result.

Hegel's attack on Schelling provoked a sustained response from Schelling, who defended and elaborated his philosophy to expose the defects in Hegel's philosophy. He charged Hegel with having produced a self-enclosed dance of abstractions dealing with essences without any place for existence. The crucial move made by Schelling was to show that a system of reason cannot explain the fact of its own existence. Criticizing Hegel's starting point in Being, treated as the most abstract category, Schelling argued,

> This being had to transform itself for no reason into existence *(Dasein)* and the external world and then into the inner world of the concept. The consequence was that the living substance, as a result of the most abstract concepts, was only left in thought.[25]

Schelling argued that there is an "unprethinkable Being"—*unvordenkliches Sein,* which precedes all thought and that is presupposed by it.[26] While such a notion is closely associated with Schelling's earlier notion of the Absolute, its development led to a greater preoccupation with the nature of human existence, which he saw not as a transparent consciousness, but as itself problematic. "Far . . . from man and his activity making the world comprehensible," Schelling wrote, "he is himself what is most incomprehensible."[27] Consequently, along with negative philosophy concerned with articulating concepts needed to comprehend the world, Schelling argued for a positive philosophy that would be measured by life, taking its force from reality itself and producing something actual. Although Schelling never repudiated his philosophy of nature, at this stage he disavowed the quest for system.[28] Positive philosophy is empirical. It must follow the real development of our world. Rationality is not presupposed, as in idealism, but shown to emerge from an original chaos. Schelling then embarked on a study of mythology and revelation as they had developed historically as the means by which people had confronted the human condition and become aware (or been made aware) of the possibility of redemption.

Schelling's arguments against Hegel and his call for a positive philosophy brought about a philosophical revolution. Nietzsche and Heidegger were products of this revolution. The poststructuralists, Jacques Lacan, Jacques Derrida, Michel Foucault, Jean-François Lyotard, Gilles Deleuze, and Felix Guattari, have continued to develop the arguments of these philosophers and sought to free civilization of the (defective?) forms of thinking that have engendered an oppressive and domineering social order. Hegel is the thinker whose ideas have to be overcome.

Nietzsche and Heidegger

Friedrich Nietzsche is the first point of departure for these "Schellingian" thinkers. Nietzsche characterized nature as consisting of "dynamic quanta, in a relation of tension to all other dynamic quanta," centers of force characterized by "will to power." Each center of force was seen to have its own perspective on the world. On this assumption Nietzsche launched a ferocious attack on the tendency in philosophy to take abstract concepts for reality.[29] He affirmed the reality of becoming and criticized philosophy's traditional fixation on being and abstract thought, and the ethics based on such thought, as an attack on life itself, as the will to power turned against itself.

On the assumption that we are part of a dynamic world, Nietzsche argued that knowledge is a process of accommodating ourselves to the world and the world to us. Truths are humanly constructed instruments designed for human purposes. Any knowledge that is of use to people "involves the *identification of things which are not the same,* of things which are only similar"[30] through metaphor. That is, it is based on operations that are usually dismissed as rhetorical tropes: on transferring things from one sphere to an entirely different sphere (metaphor), on confusing a thing with its attributes (metonymy), on taking a part for the whole or the whole for a part (synecdoche), and on illicit generalizations. Concepts are formed by equating unequal things, and then overlooking what is individual and actual. Words become concepts when they no longer refer to any one particular but fit countless more or less similar instances. Language denies difference, freezes the process of becoming, and creates the illusion that we are enduring subjects in a world of enduring substances:

> In order to think and infer it is necessary to assume beings: logic handles only formulas for what remains the same. That is why this assumption would not be a proof of reality: "beings" are part of our perspec-

tive. . . . The fictitious world of subject, substance, "reason," etc., is needed: there is in us a power to order, simplify, falsify, artificially distinguish.[31]

Truth, then, is nothing but confusions and simplifications that have become conventional:

> What then is truth? A movable host of metaphors, metonymies, and anthropomorphisms: in short, a sum of human relations which have been poetically and rhetorically intensified, transferred, and embellished, and which, after long usage, seem to a people to be fixed, canonical, and binding. Truths are illusions which we have forgotten are illusions; they are metaphors that have become worn out and have been drained of sensuous force, coins which have lost their embossing and are now considered as metal and no longer as coins.[32]

The repository of dead metaphors is language. Science is the extension of the labor of language in the construction of a great, rigidly regular edifice of concepts. "[S]cience works unceasingly on this great columbarium of concepts, the graveyard of perceptions."[33] It is thereby incapable of grasping what is most important in life. "How much of a piece of music has been understood when that in it which is calculable and can be reduced to formulas has been reckoned up?"[34] Nietzsche rejected the quest for a transcendent perspective beyond the world of becoming, from which a total view of the world could be gained, as a delusion. With this, he also rejected the effort to create a coherent system of thought. For Nietzsche, the will to system is the will to self-deception. There is no reason to believe that all valid insights will cohere. And, Nietzsche argued, "linguistic means of expression are useless for expressing 'becoming'."[35] Accordingly, he adopted an aphoristic style of writing and experimented with different genres.

Although strongly influenced by Nietzsche, Heidegger argued that Nietzsche's starting point in forces and the will to power is still a form of metaphysics. Following Schelling's later philosophy, Heidegger took Being as the central focus of his philosophy.[36] In his seminal work, *Being and Time,* Heidegger defined his project as treating the "question of Being," and mapped out two distinct tasks requiring two parts: first, "the Interpretation of *Dasein* in terms of temporality, and the explication of time as the transcendental horizon for the question of Being," and second, to map out the "basic features of a phenomenological destruction of the history of ontology, with the problematic of Temporality as our clue."[37]

Heidegger argued that since Plato, Being has come to be forgotten, so we no longer dwell in the world in a way that the meaning of Being is revealed to us. The Greeks began the process of conceiving of Being as an underlying and constantly present "ground" of the presencing of things; however, the Romans conceived this ground as that which produces things. "Being" itself was reduced to the status of a superior kind of entity that produces the world, and the world came to be seen as the totality of all created beings, as composites of form and matter bearing various traits that are ready at hand for use. Western civilization came to be dominated by metaphysics, by "onto-theo-logy" (identifying being, God, and reason) through which all particular beings are conceived as merely products of some ultimate ground. The debasement of the world to objects to be used is accompanied by a fantasy of the self-empowerment of the subject. Descartes's philosophy is a crucial turning point in this regard. For Descartes, it is reason that is the ground for reality and truth, and in Descartes we have the beginning of subjectivism where the subject is conceived of as the self-determining, as certain of itself, and as that which knows and places value on an objective world. Subsequently, the subject becomes the focus of philosophy, a development that culminates in the philosophy of Fichte and Hegel. The subject, representing the world as a picture, discloses Being only as a collection of calculable, controllable things. This development has been accompanied by the degeneration of language. Language, as Heidegger construed it, "the house of the truth of Being," has surrendered itself "to our mere willing and trafficking as an instrument of domination over beings."[38]

Science, and most importantly, modern science as inaugurated by Descartes, manifests this orientation. As Heidegger noted, echoing and developing Schelling's characterization of science,

> Modern science's way of representing pursues and entraps nature as a calculable coherence of forces. . . . Because physics, indeed already as pure theory, sets nature up to exhibit itself as a coherence of forces calculable in advance, it orders its experiments precisely for the purpose of asking whether and how nature reports itself when set up in this way.[39]

While initially this technological character was confined to the natural world, it is now coming to dominate the human world. The almighty subject, liberated from all constraints in Descartes's philosophy, has become itself an object of control:

> In the planetary imperialism of technologically organized man, the subjectivism of man attains its acme, from which point it will descend to the level of organized uniformity and there firmly establish itself. This uniformity becomes the surest instrument of total, i.e., technological, rule over the earth. The modern freedom of subjectivity vanishes totally in the objectivity commensurate with it.[40]

The Poststructuralists: The Case of Derrida

Heidegger, along with Nietzsche, was the major source of inspiration for the poststructuralists. Some poststructuralists, such as Foucault and Deleuze, were more influenced by Nietzsche; others, notably Derrida, were more influenced by Heidegger. However, poststructuralism is characterized by an increasing focus on discourse and its relation to power within societies, and by a further distancing from and rejection of the concerns of Schelling's earlier philosophy (although this is less true of Deleuze). The preoccupation with the relation between language, metaphysics, the human sciences, and the workings of power, has been associated with increasing skepticism about the capacity of language to facilitate an understanding of the world and a growing hostility to totalizing discourses, including metaphysics. Lacan, for instance, argued that the symbolic order (which includes language) separates people from reality. Foucault portrayed claims to knowledge as expressions of power. And Derrida attempted to expose the way in which language sustains existing power relations. How the poststructuralists developed Nietzsche's and Heidegger's insights, and how they further turned their backs on the concerns of Schelling's earlier work, is best illustrated by the work of Derrida.

Using Nietzsche to develop Heidegger's ideas,[41] Derrida criticized metaphysics, specifically what he refers to as "logocentric metaphysics," the quest for an origin or foundation in truth, reason, or the Logos, and the "metaphysics of presence," taking what is claimed to be present or immediately given—the subject, objects of thought, what is perceived, concepts, or propositional assertions—as such an origin or foundation.[42] For Derrida, even Heidegger is guilty of striving for a foundation in what is immediately and self-evidently present. Derrida has striven to show that what appears to be given and self-evident is actually generated by, and dependent upon, language and other systems of signs.

To develop this notion, Derrida accepted Ferdinand de Saussure's argument that signs have significance only as parts of systems, but attacked Saussure for subordinating the signifier to what it signifies and rejected Saussure's abstraction of sign systems from the temporal process of signifying. Following Nietzsche, Heidegger, and Peirce, Derrida argued that the play of difference must be temporal as well as spatial, and introduced the term *différance,* implying both "differ" and "defer," to deal with this. *Différance* is *"sameness* which is not identical . . . referring to differing, *both* as spacing/temporalizing and as the movement that structures every dissociation" (SP, 129–160, 129f.). This term is almost identical to Schelling's characterization of the Absolute, and it plays essentially the same role in his philosophy.[43] On this basis Derrida argued "[t]hat the play of differences supposes, in effect, syntheses and referrals which forbid at any moment, or in any sense, that a simple element be *present* in and of itself, referring only to itself. . . . [N]o element can function as a sign without referring to another element which itself is not simply present. This interweaving results in each "element" . . . being constituted on the basis of a trace within it of the other elements of the chain or system. . . . There are only, everywhere, differences and traces of traces" (P, 26). Reality itself is, to use Peirce's terminology, endless semiosis, and the subject is an effect of this. As Derrida put it (again in terms similar to those used by Schelling), "The subject, and first of all the conscious and speaking subject, depends upon the system of differences and the movement of *différance,* that the subject is not present, nor above all present to itself before *différance,* that the subject is constituted only in being divided from itself, in becoming space, in temporalizing, in deferral. . . ." (P, 29).

According to Derrida, the deepest desire of the Western philosophical tradition, that is, the tradition of metaphysics, has been to deny all this, to find some fixed, permanent center, a transcendental signifier that will give meaning to all other signs. It has tried to freeze the play of *différance* in Platonic Forms, in God, in clear and distinct ideas, in material substance, in the transcendental ego, in Absolute knowledge, in "Man," or in the logical essence of language. To reveal what is being denied and to expose the arbitrary nature of all such efforts is what Derrida calls, following Heidegger's call for a "destruction" of the history of ontology (ontotheology), "deconstruction."[44] Derrida argued that in each attempt to fix the play of *différance,* a binary opposition is assumed, one term of which is taken to be prior to and superior to the other (LI, 93). The second term is made out to be derivative, accidental, and unimportant in relation to the first, which is taken either as an ideal limit or the central concept of a metaphysical system. The second term is then either effaced or repressed. This repression takes place because the second term—abnormal, parasitical, void, nonliteral, nonideal, absence, difference, falsity, and undecidability—suggests the breakup of the values assured by the first term—normal, standard, fulfilled, literal, ideal, presence, identity, truth, and knowability conceived of as conscious mastery. In this way metaphysics establishes ethical-ontological hierarchies based on subordination. These hierarchies are embedded in everyday language, which, according to Derrida, "is the language of Western metaphysics, and it carries with it not only a considerable number of presuppositions of all types, but also presuppositions inseparable from metaphysics, which, although little attended to, are knotted into a system" (P, 19). Derrida deconstructs ideal limits and the central concepts of metaphysical systems by showing how what is excluded as secondary and derivative is in fact at least as primordial and general as the metaphysical original. Deconstruction reveals a root system beneath metaphysics that never touches ground, exposing the arbitrary nature of what have been taken as absolutes. It reveals that "transcendental essences," which have been taken as absolute points of reference, are arbitrary signifiers arrested from the chain of signifiers and privileged, or made to seem "natural," thereby freezing the play of differences and imposing a fixed structure and hierarchy on society. By subverting the fixation of meaning that legitimizes exclusive groups, deconstruction enables those who have been suppressed and marginalized by Western civilization—the colonized, women, those outside the academies—to be heard.

Evaluating the Postmodernists

We are now in a position to understand what are the commonalities and what are the differences between process philosophy and poststructuralism, and to evaluate them accordingly. Clearly, they do have much in common, and this is what we would expect as different branches of the tradition of which Schelling was the first major philosopher. They are both highly critical of the civilization of modernity. Both give a central place to the notion of becoming and see one of the greatest problems of modern civilization as the denial of the reality of becoming. Both are critical of mainstream science for construing the world as a realm of predictable entities to be controlled. They are both concerned with freeing society from such forms of thinking and with opening a space for spontaneity and creativity. They differ in what they focus upon. Process philosophers are primarily concerned with elaborating a cosmology that can replace scientific materialism. For poststructuralists, the notion of the "all-controlling rational subject" rather than nature as "matter in motion" is regarded as the major flaw in the culture of modernity. Their attack on modernist culture has taken the form of a critique of metaphysics and rationality, with the major focus being on the illusions and power structures created or sustained by discourse. They have promoted the proliferation of new perspectives and celebrated diversity in order to relativize metaphysics and science and to free discourse and people from coercive constraints. This, it is believed, will allow the suppressed Others—those excluded by the dominant discourse—to speak and assert themselves.

What is the basis of this divergence? And what is its significance? The divergence reflects the failure to reconcile Schelling's philosophy of nature, developed in opposition to the mechanical view of the world and concerned with what is accessible to reason and amenable to formulation in concepts, with positive philosophy, developed in opposition to Hegel's notion of the rational, controlling consciousness and concerned with existence.

Nietzsche, Heidegger, and the poststructuralists are most at fault here. Belonging to the subtradition inspired by Schelling's later work, they generally have presupposed Schelling's dynamic view of nature and critique of science but otherwise have ignored the earlier work. In particular, they have ignored Schelling's efforts to show how nature might be conceived such that it could produce conscious subjects, and they have ignored Schelling's commitment to a reformulated notion of rationality on this basis. While the natural and human sciences are debunked, little effort is made to show what could replace them.

Nietzsche offers a relatively crude version of a dynamic conception of nature as consisting of nothing but forces. This underlies his whole critique of modern culture. But Nietzsche's position is clearly self-contradictory as, in contrast to Schelling, he outlines a theory of knowledge based on this characterization of nature that precludes the possibility of arriving at or defending such a conception of nature. This tension in Nietzsche is evident in his analyses of language and science. By assuming the truth of a particular conception of nature as the basis of his analysis, he not only debunks claims to absolute truth deriving from the use of dead metaphors, but suggests that metaphors necessarily prevent us from grasping any truth. Schelling had already appreciated the inconsistency in this move and avoided it. Furthermore, Schelling had already exposed the flaws in the philosophy of nature embraced by Nietzsche. As Andrew Bowie points out in his critique of Nietzsche, "The notion of such a 'force in general' is, as the *Naturphilosophie* showed, problematic, because it is impossible to suggest that all is force: 'For we can only think of a force as something finite. But no force is finite in terms of its *nature* unless it is limited by an opposed force. Hence, when we think of a force (as we do in matter), we must also think of an *opposed* force.'"[45] Failing to appreciate this prevents Nietzsche from recognizing that limits are productive of higher levels of existence. Nietzsche's diagnosis of the problems of civilization as the will to power turned against itself, and the solution suggested by this diagnosis, are therefore fundamentally flawed. The solution suggested (and largely embraced by Foucault and Deleuze), although not always upheld, is that the will to power should be freed from all constraints, including the constraints of rationality. But if Schelling is right, then the very existence of any organism derives from limits, and the rationality that emerges from an original chaos is a limit that makes human existence possible.

Heidegger criticized Nietzsche, to some extent rightly, for still being in the thrall of ontotheology; but by characterizing this as metaphysics and dismissing metaphysics as such, Heidegger precludes any consideration of Schelling's real metaphysics (as opposed to his misrepresentation of it as a form of idealism).[46] Schelling's metaphysics upheld the primacy of Being over consciousness, rejected the possibility of grasping Being as an object of thought, while still upholding the quest for a philosophy of nature through which the emergence of humans would be intelligible and rationality could be appreciated as an emergent within nature. While Heidegger defended the first two propositions, he had no place for the third. As Karl Löwith, a former student of Heidegger, noted, "In Schelling, the problem of being in the anti-Hegelian movement arrived at the point where Heidegger once more took it up. . . . The difference with Schelling lies in the fact that Heidegger erects on Kierkegaard's basis a 'system of existence' *(Dasein)* which lacks Schelling's tension between the negative and the positive philosophy, of 'reason' and 'existence'."[47] As a consequence, Heidegger could contrast how the ancient Greeks revealed reality as a self-bringing-forth into full presencing with how technological modernity reveals nature as standing reserve to be exploited, but had no basis for claiming that one form of revealing was better than the other. And having rejected the effort to get technology spiritually in hand, the only response to our present predicament Heidegger offered was that by questioning technology we can allow the saving power to shine.[48]

In upholding this attenuated challenge to modernity, Heidegger misrepresented the history of European thought by characterizing it as the triumph of metaphysics construed as the forgetting of Being. This involved identifying metaphysics with ontotheology and then with idealist philosophy, philosophy in which the subject is taken as the starting point. But Schelling had already argued against this approach and developed a metaphysics that took the self-conscious subject to be derivative. More importantly, the most influential metaphysics, particularly in Anglo-Saxon countries, is still that of Thomas Hobbes, which reduces the subject to little more than the effect of the mechanical motion of matter. This was the ultimate target of Schelling's philosophy. Heidegger's overly schematic cultural history focuses on idealism and leaves no place to appreciate the dominant metaphysics, nor Schelling's challenge to it.

Heidegger's characterization of history has informed the work of most of the poststructuralists.[49] Derrida, for instance, takes it for granted that *metaphysics* is a term of censure, and this allows him, despite the echoes of Schelling in his work, to more completely forget his origins than did Nietzsche or Heidegger. For Derrida, what is central to metaphysics is a self-reflexive presence that recognizes the Other as ultimately the same. It is this that must be opposed if the Other is to be heard. Heidegger's preoccupation with Being was abandoned by Derrida as still too metaphysical. But his characterization of metaphysics not only does not fit Schelling's philosophy; Schelling's notion of the Absolute was designed to avoid self-reflexive presence and to give a place to difference. This was central to his opposition to Hegel. As Deleuze wrote of Schelling in this regard, "The most important aspect of Schelling's philosophy is his consideration of powers. How unjust, in this respect, is Hegel's critical remark about the black cows! Of these two philosophers, it is Schelling who brings difference out of the night of the Identical, and with finer, more varied and more terrifying flashes of lightning than those of contradiction: with *progressivity*" (DR, 190f.).

Having rejected both metaphysics and Heidegger's preoccupation with Being, Derrida embraced Nietzsche's perspectivism. The result is a view of the world as an endless play of language. For Derrida "there is no extratext. . . . There is nothing before the text; there is no pretext that is not already text" (D, 328). This does not mean that there is no world beyond the text; rather, his argument is that there is nothing beyond the text that can anchor the play of *différance*.[50] The world itself is, as Nietzsche suggested in "On Truth and Lies in a Non-Moral Sense," an unstable foundation of "running water."[51] As with Nietzsche, although in a more disguised form, a particular conception of the world underlies arguments that deny the possibility of truth claims for such a conception of the world. The effect of this is to trivialize language, to undermine the struggle to understand the world, and thereby to undermine any basis for effective political action. Derrida's philosophy leaves no place to attack the dominant conception of the world as false, nor any basis to strive for a social order based on a more adequate understanding of the world.

What these analyses suggest is that philosophers inspired by the tradition begun by Schelling's later work, without acknowledging the point of his earlier work, have undermined the force of their own arguments against modernity and undermined the basis for political action to oppose it. Generally, they have presupposed a nonmechanistic, dynamic view of nature while at the same time dismissing efforts to develop and justify such a view. This has been associated with a preoccupation with language as an autonomous realm unconnected to the real world, while at the same time deluding people about its real nature. But by denying any possibility of understanding the world through language, these philosophers have trivialized their own critiques of modernity while obscuring more fundamental challenges to it. Poststructuralists require Schelling's earlier philosophy or developments of it to sustain their arguments.

In Defense of Process Metaphysics

Starting where Schelling began, process philosophers are in a better position than the poststructuralists to comprehend and develop Schelling's whole philosophy. As we have seen, Schelling did not repudiate the earlier philosophy of nature. In fact, it was working out the implications of his earlier work that led Schelling to his later views. Whitehead moved in the same direction. Taking as his starting point that we as conscious subjects are products of, and part of, the world, he appreciated that being precedes consciousness and that the world as a whole cannot be grasped as an object. Consequently, he was faced with issues raised in the later work of Schelling and those influenced by it. The crucial question is, How did he deal with these issues? Or, what amounts to the same thing, Does positive philosophy, even if it presupposes and requires the negative philosophy of the philosophy of nature, undermine negative philosophy as the poststructuralists concluded?

Whitehead's defense of metaphysics and speculative philosophy provides an answer to this question. He defended the quest for coherence. By coherence, Whitehead meant that the fundamental ideas, in terms of which the [philosophical] scheme is developed, presuppose each other so that in isolation they are meaningless. . . . In other words, it is presupposed that no entity can be conceived in complete abstraction from the system of the universe, and that it is the business of speculative philosophy to exhibit this truth. (PR, 3)

This quest for coherence Whitehead regarded as "the great preservative of rationalistic sanity" (PR, 6). Why should this be so? Coherence in this sense enables us to think about the relations between aspects of the world and between different discourses about it, to understand their domains of validity in relation to each other, and to expose one-sided thinking that abstracts from the totality of relations. It does not deny difference in the world; it is the condition for understanding what difference is. In this regard Whitehead's notion of coherence entirely accords with Schelling's notion of the Absolute.

But how can such coherence be achieved? Have not Nietzsche, Heidegger, and Derrida shown the impossibility of such a quest? And even if we could gain coherence in thought, have not these philosophers shown that this coherence would bear no relation to reality? What Nietzsche's critique of substance-thinking, Heidegger's critique of ontotheology, and Derrida's critique of logocentric metaphysics have shown is the incoherence of efforts to grasp the world as a totality from some privileged vantage point outside the flow of becoming. But Schelling had already argued this point, and Whitehead's notion of coherence does not entail such a vantage point.

In fact, Whitehead accepted the fact that there is more to the world than will ever be grasped by language, criticized the tendency to take abstractions for reality (the "fallacy of misplaced concreteness"), and accorded a primary role to metaphors in thought, language, philosophy, and science. What Whitehead condemned as "The Dogmatic Fallacy" is the result of a superficial appreciation of the nature of language:

The error consists in the persuasion that we are capable of producing notions which are adequately defined in respect to the complexity of relationship required for their illustration in the real world. . . . Except perhaps for the simpler notions of arithmetic, even our more familiar ideas, seemingly obvious, are infected with this incurable vagueness. (AI, 144f.)

This suggests that Whitehead fully appreciated the linguistic issues that Nietzsche, Heidegger, and poststructuralists have addressed, without drawing the conclusion that metaphysics is impossible.

Whitehead defined metaphysics as "the science which seeks to discover the general ideas which are indispensably relevant to the analysis of everything that happens" (RM, 72n). The elaboration of such general ideas is speculative philosophy. Whitehead redefined categories as schemes of ideas arrived at by articulating metaphors, and defended speculative philosophy and the elaboration of categoreal schemes as a fallibist undertaking:

> Philosophers can never hope finally to formulate these metaphysical first principles. Weakness of insight and deficiencies of language stand in the way inexorably. Words and phrases must be stretched towards a generality foreign to their ordinary usage; and however such elements of language be stabilized as technicalities, they remain metaphors mutely appealing for an imaginative leap. (PR, 4)

What is achieved by such imaginative leaps is understanding of the world, not just of language. Describing what is involved in the quest for understanding, Whitehead wrote,

> [U]nderstanding is never a completed static state of mind. It always bears the character of a process of penetration, incomplete and partial. . . . Of course in a sense, there is a completion. But it is a completion presupposing relation to some given undefined environment, imposing a perspective and awaiting exploration. (MT, 43)

To this end, Whitehead called for the production of a diversity of metaphysical schemes. While "we cannot produce that final adjustment of well-defined generalities which constitute a complete metaphysics . . . we can produce a variety of partial systems of limited generality" (AI, 145). The resulting rival schemes, inconsistent with each other, but each with its own merits and its own failures, will then warn us of the limitations within which our intuitions are hedged. This simultaneously opposes the quest for absolute truth while allowing that understanding can be advanced.

Opening the possibility of gaining a better understanding of the world and of the rational justification of process metaphysics as an alternative cosmology to scientific materialism provides a way beyond the Nietzschean affirmation of the will to power (or the Deleuzean affirmation of desire) on the one hand, and the quietism of Heidegger and Derrida's odd notion of play on the other. Construing nature as "something autonomous, something self-positing and self-activating,"[52] as Schelling put it, and people and societies in the same way, allows us to appreciate the diversity, irreducible difference, and intrinsic significance of Others, and to appreciate that ways of thinking, practices, and institutions which fail to appreciate such differences are fundamentally flawed. We are then provided with a goal: not only to advance understanding but to create a society based on a better understanding of the world and ourselves than has been possible with either scientific materialism or idealism.

Postmodernism against Modernity

Whitehead's defense of metaphysics bridges the gap between Schelling's earlier and later philosophy. Once this gap is bridged, the two traditions deriving from Schelling can be combined. The work of Nietzsche, Heidegger, and the poststructuralists can be reinterpreted to augment the critique of modernity by process philosophers, while the philosophy of nature and a reformulated notion of knowledge and rationality deriving from process philosophy can be used to defend the most important ideas and critiques deriving from Nietzsche, Heidegger, and the poststructuralists. Upholding metaphysics as construed by Whitehead is not to privilege a particular discourse. It is to uphold a discourse that enables people to question and attempt to replace the abstractions that presently dominate civilization. What we now need is the development of new abstractions that will allow us to understand the immanent dynamics, intrinsic significance, and the diversity of processes participating in the creative becoming of the world, including ourselves. This is the condition not only for an effective opposition to the destructive imperatives of modernity. It is the condition for overcoming it.

Notes

1. This is most clearly shown by Stephen Toumlin in *Cosmopolis: The Hidden Agenda of Modernity* (Chicago: University of Chicago Press, 1990).

2. I have shown how this has taken place in *Nihilism Inc.: European Civilization and Environmental Destruction* (Sydney: Eco-Logical Press, 1996).

3. See Joseph L. Esposito, *Schelling's Idealism and the Philosophy of Nature* (Lewisburg, PA: Bucknell Univeristy Press, 1977), 202f.

4. See F. W. J. Schelling, *Ideas for a Philosophy of Nature* [1804], E. E. Harris and Peter Heath, trans. (Cambridge: Cambridge University Press, 1988).

5. Schelling, *System of Transcendental Idealism* [1800], Peter Heath, trans. (Charlottesville: University Press of Virginia, 1978), 2.

6. See Schelling, *On the History of Modern Philosophy*, Andrew Bowie, trans. (Cambridge: Cambridge University Press, 1994), 120.

7. Schelling's clearest exposition of this was in "The Philosophy of Nature," in ibid., 114–133.

8. Schelling, *System of Transcendental Idealism*, 72.

9. On this, see Marie-Luise Heuser-Kessler, *Die Producktivität der Natur: Schellings Naturphilosophie und das neue Paradigma der Selbstorganisation in den Naturwissenshcaften* (Berlin: Duncker & Humblot, 1986).

10. Schelling develops his ideas about freedom in *Of Human Freedom*, James Gutmann, trans. (La Salle, IL: Open Court, 1954).

11. *Schelling's Werke*, vol. 1, 276, 277, 279, translated and cited by Bowie, *Schelling and Modern European Philosophy* (London: Routledge, 1993), 39f.

12. Schelling, *System of Transcendental Idealism*, 225.

13. The influence of Schelling on Whitehead has been traced by Antoon Braeckman, "Whitehead and German Idealism," *Process Studies* 14 (1985), 310–326.

14. Whitehead cites N. O. Lossky, *The Intuitive Basis of Knowledge*, Mrs. Duddington, trans. (Macmillan, 1919) as the source of his quote from Schelling.

15. See Thomas Kuhn, "Energy Conservation as an Example of Simultaneous Discovery," in *The Essential Tension* (Chicago: University of Chicago Press, 1977).

16. See Dorothy Emmett, "Creativity and the Passage of Nature," in *Whitehead's Metaphysics of Creativity*, Friedrich Rapp and Reiner Wiehl, eds. (New York: State University of New York Press, 1990).

17. On this see Esposito, *Schelling's Idealism*, 137.

18. This is shown most clearly by Jürgen Habermas in *The Philosophical Discourse of Modernity*, Frederick G. Lawrence, trans. (Cambridge: Polity Press, 1987).

19. As Julian Roberts noted, "Schelling, or at least Schellingian thought (however transmitted) had a decisive impact on . . . Kierkegaard, Nietzsche and Heidegger." In *German Philosophy* (Oxford: Blackwell, 1988). The influence of Schelling on Nietzsche was largely mediated by Schopenhauer.

20. In developing his notion of the Absolute, Schelling drew upon both Fichte and Bruno, and has been interpreted accordingly. My contention is that Schelling was working toward a new notion of the Absolute. For a careful and illuminating analysis of Schelling's notion of the Absolute, see Bowie (1993), chapter 4, esp., 60–67.

21. Schelling, *On the History of Modern Philosophy*, Bowie, trans., 152. Schelling here clarifies his differences with Hegel.

22. Schelling, *System of Transcendental Idealism*, 209.

23. *Hegel's Phenomenology of Spirit*, A. V. Miller, trans. (Oxford: Clarendon Press, 1977), 9, 11.

24. *Hegel's Science of Logic*, W. H. Johnston and L. G. Struthers, trans., 2 vols. (London: Allen & Unwin, 1929), vol. 1, 60.

25. Schelling, *System der Weltalte* (1827–1828), S. Peetz, ed. (Frankfurt: Klosterman, 1990), 58, Bowie, trans., in *Schelling and Modern European Philosophy*, 143.

26. Schelling, *Philosophie der Offenbarung* (The philosophy of revelation), Manfred Frank, ed. (Frankfurt: Suhrkramp, 1977), 160.

27. Schelling, *Sämmtliche Werke*, K. F. A. Schelling, ed., 14 vols. (Stuttgart and Augsburg: Cotta, 1856–1861), II, 3, 7.

28. Schelling, *Philosophie der Offenbarung*, 127.

29. Friedrich Nietzsche, *The Will to Power*, Walter Kaufmann and R. J. Hollingdale, trans. (New York: Vintage, 1968), §635, §636, §619.

30. Nietzsche, "The Philosopher," in *Philosophy and Truth*, Daniel Breazeale, ed. (Atlantic Highlands, New Jersey: Humanities Press, 1979), 51.

31. Nietzsche, *Will to Power,* §517, 289.

32. Nietzsche, "On Truth and Lies in a Non-Moral Sense," *Philosophy and Truth,* 84.

33. Ibid., 88.

34. Nietzsche, *Will to Power,* §624.

35. Ibid., §715, 380.

36. Sonya Sikka shows that Heidegger was far more indebted to Schelling than he acknowledged. See "Heidegger's Appropriation of Schelling," *Southern Journal of Philosophy* 32 (4) (1994), 421–428.

37. Martin Heidegger, *Being and Time,* John Macquarie and Edward Robinson, trans. (Oxford: Blackwell, 1962), 63.

38. Heidegger, "Letter on Humanism," in *Basic Writings,* David Farrell Krell, ed. (London: Routledge & Kegan Paul, 1978), 199.

39. Heidegger, "The Question Concerning Technology," in *Question Concerning Technology and Other Essays,* William Lovitt, trans. (New York: Harper, 1977), 21.

40. Heidegger, "The Age of the World Picture," in ibid., 152f.

41. Derrida's relation to Heidegger is analyzed by Herman Rapaport in *Heidegger and Derrida* (Lincoln: University of Nebraska Press, 1989). The complex relation between Derrida, Nietzsche, and Heidegger is analyzed in Ernst Behler's *Confrontations: Derrida, Heidegger, Nietzsche,* Steven Taubeneck, trans. (Stanford: Stanford University Press, 1991). Derrida's relation to Kant, Schelling, Fichte, Hegel, and Heidegger is analyzed in Rudophe Gasché, *The Tain of the Mirror: Derrida and the Philosophy of Reflection* (Cambridge: Harvard University Press, 1986).

42. See Derrida, "*Ousia* and *Grammé*" in *Margins of Philosophy* [1972], Alan Bass, trans. (Sussex, England: Harvester Press, 1982).

43. As Bowie noted in *Schelling and Modern European Philosophy,* 69.

44. "Deconstruction" is a very complex notion. For its full explication see Rudophe Gasché, *The Tain of the Mirror: Derrida and the Philosophy of Reflection* (Cambridge: Harvard University Press, 1986), part 2.

45. Bowie, *Schelling and Modern Philosophy,* 68f., citing Schelling, *Werke,* vol. 2, 49–50.

46. Heidegger wrote in the appendix to *Schelling's Treatise on the Essence of Human Freedom,* Joan Stambaugh, trans. (Athens: Ohio University Press, 1985), 193, that "Schelling's idea of identity and of the groundless as in-difference is more primordial within the absolute metaphysics of subjectivity, but only within it." This fails to do justice to the place accorded to the philosophy of nature in Schelling's metaphysics.

47. Karl Löwith, *From Hegel to Nietzsche* (London: Constable, 1964), 118.

48. Heidegger, "The Question Concerning Technology," 35.

49. I have examined other poststructuralists in these terms in chapter 2 of *Postmodernism and the Environmental Crisis* (London and New York: Routledge, 1995).

50. In an interview with Richard Kearney, Derrida denied that he meant that there is no world beyond the text. See Kearney, *Dialogues with Contemporary Continental Thinkers* (Manchester: Manchester University Press, 1984), 123.

51. Nietzsche, *Philosophy and Truth,* 85.

52. Schelling, *On the History of Modern Philosophy,* 130f.

2

Process and Chaosmos
The Whiteheadian Fold in
the Discourse of Difference

CATHERINE KELLER

Every person, place and thing in the chaosmos of Alle anyway connected
. . . was moving and changing every part of the time: the traveling inkhorn
(possibly pot), the hare and turtle pen and paper, the continually more and
less intermisunderstanding minds of the anticollaborators. . . .

——James Joyce, *Finnegan's Wake*

i

Process thought writes the connections. Poststructuralism traces the differences. And these movements, themselves "moving and changing," have remained anticollaborators indeed.

Let me back up to the occasion for this reflection, John B. Cobb Jr.'s
sense of "the common good."[1] His transtheological challenge has in part
directed itself toward the university. He has rightly assessed the damages to
the earth produced by the socialization of the intellectual power of the West
to an epistemological grid of territorial borders. The patrol of these borderlines by the guardians of cultural privilege assures that intellectuals do not
learn to address the powerful intersections of technoscience, political economy, and religious fantasy. Thus for all its tradition of radical spin-offs, the
university has organized knowledge/power according to standards of universality and objectivity that mask the special interests of race, class/economics,
sex/gender, and species.

There have been promising tendencies toward the breakdown of such
borderlines, as the academic institutionalization of movement politics in

women's, African-American and Hispanic, environmental studies, and so forth by their nature cut across and beyond the disciplines. As the twentieth century concluded, these socially transformative reconstructions of knowledge have coalesced in the university with a pervasive shift in discursive formations, based on a heightened attention to the politics of discourse itself. Variously called "discourse theory," "critical theory," "deconstruction," "constructivism," "poststructuralism," "postcolonialism" and, rather nakedly, "theory," we have here a vast postmodern movement, pretty much tenured in the United States for the next several decades. Its cross-disciplinary attention to the politics of discourse, to the power of knowledge, has taken root in the universities. It has absorbed into itself and changed the original movement of feminist and ethnic identity politics in the North American academy.[2] Really it comprises a movement only in a loose, paradigmatic sense, and no unified school—unity after all being one of its impermissibles. It, if "it" exists, is more a shifting matrix of attractive assumptions, emanating from privileged texts and tropes. In its understanding of itself as performative discourse, and thus as political practice, it churns up new articulations of ethnicity as plurality and hybridity, of sexuality as "a many-gendered thing."

However subversively or effectively these deconstructive academic trends transgress the boundaries of traditional scholarship, for Whiteheadians they pose serious problems. Yet process thought and other postmodernisms claim in common a startling width of conceptual commitments (far exceeding their inter- and transdisciplinary methods). Chiefly they overlap in their critique of any fixed, self-identical essence of being or corollary habit of substantialism. Positively they share the assertion of a fluid nexus of mutually constitutive events, always already perspectival. Therefore they both exercise a relentless attention to the sociocultural production of the Real, or what claims to be such.

Yet these striking similarities hardly come to speech, let alone to the table. For the discursive *différance* of poststructuralism so far functions to disqualify anything like a Whiteheadian methodology. We come up against a quite nonfluid rejection of any kind of cosmology, ontology, or ground for referring to a world before or beyond language. But the familiar process strategy—of demanding metaphysics as common ground—will provoke a snicker that can be heard all the way to Paris.

Poststructuralism has deconstructed the concepts whereby one might posit the existence of an original nature distinct from human culture, or a prelinguistic depth that churns up the textual surface. The postmodern "surface espousal" (as the early Edward W. Said receives Gilles Deleuze and Jacques Derrida[3]) may seem in its U.S. reception to resemble the total facade exposed in the powerful satiric film, *The Truman Show,* which the sea itself lay captive to the media construction, its horizon a mere painted scrim for the performance.

We can, of course, as Whiteheadians, claim to be the original postmoderns; or we can erect our own wall between the abominable and the acceptable postmodernism, the noxious and the nice. We can show how they, the Other of postmodernism, really need Whitehead, whom we are generously prepared to deliver. These tactics of combat, conversion, or condescension may not conduce to creative contrast however—let alone to the common good. I am not claiming that this conversation is more important than others; that process thinkers should stop what they are doing and read Derrida, Michel Foucault, Luce Irigaray, Donna J. Haraway, Deleuze, Rosi Braidotti, Said, Homi K. Bhabha, and Judith Butler. They may not even wish to tarry with *this* cross-dressing process-poststructuralist.

If, however, they feel some attraction to poststructuralist styles of writing or tactics of thought, there may be available another point of entry. It is not one we could have devised. It is shockingly straightforward: Find points where poststructuralism confesses its own love of Alfred North Whitehead. Then we could consider the difference as mutual attraction. But such points seem inherently impossible, since, to repeat, one can hardly miss Whitehead's metaphysics, ontology, cosmology, rationalism, naturalism, and theology— more or less that which deconstruction exists to deconstruct. So if indeed an eros for Whitehead were to manifest itself within any major texts of poststructuralist theory, it would constitute not just an interesting twist, but a rupture in the basin of assumptions, a leak in the dam of pure cultural-linguistic constructivism. But, of course, poststructuralism takes its own greatest pleasure in rupture, gap, fissure, break, and lag. In difference. Such fissures open up the text to its own hidden intertext:

> Intertextuality is, in a sense, the way that history, understood as cultural and ideological change and conflict, records itself within textuality. . . . These fragments of the previous system and the fissures they create on the surface of the text reveal conflictual dynamics which led to the present textual system. (Daniel Boyarin, *Intertextuality and the Reading of Midrash*[4])

So it gives me great pleasure to discover, against all expectations, a Whiteheadian intertext within the texts of poststructuralism. If this chapter provides any specific service, it will be to introduce you to the two texts in which I have found embedded major fragments of Whiteheadian intertext. Each of these texts is concentrated, pointed, erudite, and very different, indeed independent, of the other. Each would call itself "constructivist," operating within the influence of the French philosophical eruption of "difference," and each sits at a current cutting edge of influence. So we will wonder—why do they resort to Whitehead? What meaning for process thinkers, what meaning for poststructuralists, can be ascribed to such a "resort to Whitehead"—a resort that may only temporarily serve as a holiday scene of refreshment, of the relaxation of tiresome oppositions, but from which some new resource may "issue forth," *resortir.*

ii

The first such intertext cracks through a little work of Deleuze called *The Fold.*[5] Simultaneously with Derrida and Foucault, but only now coming into a wider appreciation, Deleuze was a great mouthpiece for the idea of difference.[6] As coauthor with Felix Guattari, Deleuze is known for a "nomadology"—his earlier concept of the nomadic subject-event, a mobile, machine-like force of multiple power shifts and surface subversions.[7] If Foucault declared that "perhaps one day this century will be known as Deleuzean," certainly Deleuze's Foucault gently shifts the Nietzschean/Parisian lineage in a surprising direction.[8] "Things, living creatures and words need only fold back on this depth as a new dimension, or fall back on these forces of finitude. . . . The fold, as Foucault constantly says, is what constitutes a 'thickness' as well as a 'hollow'." And yet this language of "fold" can only be spotted in Foucault by way of Deleuze, as he himself seems to have undergone certain shifts by which he enfolded his thought in early modern metaphysics. *The Fold* is an interpretation of Leibniz's monad in terms of folds of space, time, and movement. The Leibnizian fold is reread in terms of an historic aesthetic of drapes, pleats, and labyrinths: "the Baroque fold unfurls all the way to infinity" (TF, 3). The world itself is read as an infinite body twisting endlessly into the "pleats of matter" and the "folds in the soul" (TF, 4). Deleuze traces affinities between current developments in science, mathematics, and art to this complex Baroque folding motion. At the end of *The Fold,* he suggests that the present aesthetic—by contrast to the Baroque—does "not allow the differences of inside and outside, of public and private, to survive. They identify variation and trajectory, and overtake monadology with a 'nomadology'" (TF, 137). Yet the nomad, which supercedes the monad, does not after all return us to the abrupt discontinuities of a more Foucaultian Deleuze, of machine-nomads making raids on all settled centers. He concludes with a quite cosmological postulate: "We are discovering new ways of folding, akin to new envelopments, but we all remain Leibnizian because what always matters is folding, unfolding, refolding" (TF, 137).

How against the Parisian backdrop of difference itself does one account for this trajectory of thought—this journey that culminates in a *nomad* revised through a revised *monad,* that is, a nondualistic, nondeterministic monad understood as event of enfolding and outfolding differentiations? Certainly the kinship to quantum theory, indeed to the physicist David Bohm's ontological interpretation of the quantum wave as the "implicate order," has been recognized.[9] But the ontologizing gesture roots in more familiar territory for

Whiteheadians. I refer especially to the opening of *The Fold*'s sixth chapter, "What Is an Event?"

"Whitehead," writes Deleuze, "is the successor, or *diadoche,* as the Platonic philosophers used to say, of [Leibniz]. The school is somewhat like a secret society" (TF, 76). Whitehead, he continues, "stands provisionally as the last great Anglo-American philosopher before Wittgenstein's disciples spread their misty confusion, sufficiency, and terror" (TF, 76). Invoking the microcosmic extension shared by Leibniz's and Whitehead's notion of event, he writes, "[t]he event is a vibration with an infinity of harmonics or submultiples, such as an audible wave, a luminous wave, or even an increasingly smaller part of space over the course of an increasingly shorter duration" (TF, 77). Continuing with his close reading of *Process and Reality,* he pounces appreciatively upon the notion of "prehension" and of "satisfaction" as "self-enjoyment" (TF, 78), noting here also depth resonances with Leibniz:

> this becoming is not completed without the sum of perceptions tending to be integrated in a great pleasure, a Satisfaction with which the monad fills itself when it expresses the world, a musical Joy of contracting its vibrations, of calculating them without knowing their harmonies or of drawing force enough to go further and further ahead in order to produce something new. (TF, 79)

Having established this Baroque counterpoint, he claims that with Leibniz "the question surges forth" that will haunt Whitehead: "not how to attain eternity, but in what conditions does the objective world allow for a subjective production of novelty, that is, of creation" (TF, 79). The vibratory event in which prehensions produce the subject functions here as the folding motion. Perhaps one can say quite straightforwardly that the Whiteheadian prehension becomes the Deleuzean fold. But it is precisely through the concept of prehension that Deleuze designates the "great difference" from "Leibniz's Baroque condition" (TF, 80):

> For Whitehead [the difference] involves prehensions being directly connected to each other, either because they draw on others for data and form a world with them, or because they exclude others (negative prehensions), but always in the same universe in process. . . . [F]or Leibniz, it is because the monads' being-for the world is submitted to a condition of closure. . . . (TF, 80-81)

For Whitehead, "to the contrary, a condition of opening causes all prehension to be *already* the prehension of another prehension. . . ." (TF, 81).

Thus the folding motion is retained or regained through the theory of prehension, but now unfolded, beyond its Leibnizian gesture, into an open universe of mutually constitutive relations. This radical relationality is lacking not only in Leibniz, but, I would claim, in the vocabulary of the poststructuralist French theories (except perhaps with reference to the text as textile of endless interdependent signifiers, à la Derrida). Might the constructivism for which Deleuze counts as a growing eminence be read in its difference from the sheer linguistic play of difference—as enabling poststructuralism to consider now a modulation to an energetic physico-animate field of differential relations?

Such openness to the world, this radical connectedness in other words, might account for another difference—that marked by the dissolution of the Leibnizian borders between incompossible worlds:

> For Whitehead . . . on the contrary, bifurcations, divergences, incompossibilities, and discord belong to the same motley world *that can no longer be included in expressive units*, but only made or undone according to prehensive units and variable configurations or changing captures . . . captures instead of closures. (TF, 81)

Thus, self-contained monads seem to have become bands of nomads, no longer as mere bursts of divergence, but now understood as a complex connectivity in which beings are "kept open through divergent series and incompossible totalities that pull them outside" (TF, 81). He finds the breakdown of the static privacy of the monad in Whitehead's rhythm of privacy and publicity.

Especially intriguing is his use of Whitehead's cosmos to conceptualize chaos: "In a same chaotic world [the Whiteheadian cosmos] divergent series are endlessly tracing bifurcating paths" (TF, 81). Bifurcations, we note, belong to the language of chaos theory and iteration, the nonlinear mathematics with which Deleuze, a polymath as well, seems to have been well acquainted as it made its Parisian rise in the late 1960s.[10] Events, he writes, paraphrasing Whitehead, "are produced in a chaos, in a chaotic multiplicity, but only under the condition that a sort of screen intervenes" (TF, 76). With Leibniz, the screen sifted incompossibles; with Whitehead, I presume, it is the categoreal grid of process itself that he likens to the contemporary composer Pierre Boulez's "polyphony of polyphonies" (TF, 82). It is this bottomless plurality, in conjunction with such unresolved polytonality, that constitute what Deleuze—citing James Joyce—calls a "chaosmos" (TF, 81).[11]

Deleuze returns to the idea of the chaosmos in his final constructive passage. I submit that it is precisely the resort to Whitehead that allows him to move, without polemic, beyond the anticosmological stasis of much francophone theory. His own semiotic move, twisting from Leibniz to Whitehead, does not reduce meaning to language, but rather reads multifaceted signs in motion in all the space-time folds. The Whiteheadian visitation in his text cannot be described, as my opening questions may have suggested, as mere rup-

ture or break; rather, Whitehead enables the articulation of a plural, conflictual, yet radically relational nomadology. This is a postmodernism no longer
content with its earlier—and yet also Deleuzean—"surface espousal."[12] It
lays out a postmodern surface in the alternative form of his "plane of immanence,"[13] which now enfolds, by means of a distinctively Whiteheadian pattern of pleats, a cosmological depth without classical closure. Yet even as the
secondary literature on Deleuze and Guattari proliferates, and as the prima
facie purely negative relation of Deleuze to theology becomes itself a subject
of inquiry, I have found—outside of the work of Isabelle Stengers, Tim Clark,
and Roland Faber, contributors to this volume—a stunning paucity of reference to the Whiteheadian fold within the Deleuzean plane.[14]

iii

If left to the idiosyncracy of a single philosopher, the Whiteheadian crack in
the facade of postmodern anticosmology would be nothing but a puncture.
Only the discovery of another intertextual fissure, one independent of Deleuze, enabled me to imagine a crack—it takes two points to make a line, even
a jagged one. This one appears in Haraway's recent book with a title in the
form of an E-mail address: *Modest_Witness@Second_Millennium.Female
Man©_Meets_OncoMouse*™.[15] Haraway works within the new interdisciplinary field known as "science studies." She has emerged as one of the most
influential feminist theorists in the United States, first bursting onto the scene
with her distinctly antinaturalist "Cyborg Manifesto."[16] Critical of the naive
romanticism of much ecofeminism, she calls feminism to educate itself scientifically well enough that it can engage technoscience critically. Only so can
feminism challenge the net of power/knowledge it has so profitably and per-
ilously cast round the globe. Yet her cyborg is not a figure of techno-terror like
"Hal" of *2001: A Space Odyssey,* but a poignant, ambiguously gendered,
ambiguously specied creature, powerful in its complex hybridity, confusing
our identities, deserving our respect.[17]

The cyborg marks for Haraway the site of the nonhuman. But it marks
it as a cultural product. It shares with biological organisms a claim to be
acknowledged as "sign interpreters." Of course, technically Whiteheadians
consider any machine an aggregate rather than an individual and thus incapable of subjectivity. We may sidestep the matter of Artificial Intelligence and
cybernetic prehensions here, and note instead the specific function of the figure of the cyborg in her argument. Like Deleuze, Haraway stretches the semiotic field well beyond its modern or postmodern anthropocentrisms.

"In the 1990s," she writes, "across the former divide between subjects
and objects and between the living and nonliving, meaning-in-the-making—
the physiology of semiotics—is a more cyborg, coyote, trickster, local, open-

ended, heterogeneous, and provisional affair" (MW, 127). The playful unpre-
dictability of the trickster, the traditional mythogram of the boundary-trans-
gressive chaos in which culture and nature cannot be separated, figures, as
Braidotti has demonstrated, something very like the flight of the Deleuzean
nomad.[18] The indeterminate, nonlinear character of postmodern science
seems as with Deleuze to be facilitating a new sense of cosmological interconnectedness. But she makes a leap of her own, in moving from semiotics to
ontology:

> Sign interpreters are ontologically dirty; they are made up of provision-
> ally articulated, temporally dispersed, and spatially networked actors
> and actants. In the most literal and materialist sense, connections and
> enrollments are what matter. (MW, 127)

What *matters*—what at once materializes and demands a nonreductionist val-
orization—is for Haraway, as for Deleuze, connections, enrollments, and
enfoldments. Here the unlimited width of nonhuman subject-agents belies the
modern dualisms as well as the postmodern culture-monism. This relationality appears not as a harmonious grid of categories, not as a neat solution to all
dualisms, but in the epistemological struggle for her "dirty ontology." Not
unlike Deleuze, Haraway wants to maintain an open semiotic constructivism,
without forfeiting the right to reference the more-than-human worlds, and
therefore to address the mineral, vegetable, animal, and technological cosmoi
heretofore colonized by the natural sciences.

Without nostalgia for a classically foundational Nature or Culture, she
manages also to repudiate the slickly synthetic culture of nature characteristic
of modern technoscientific production (à la *The Truman Show*). She seeks
instead—and this move I also find radical within its poststructuralist milieu—
"an always contingent practice of *grounding or worlding*" (MW, 113, my emphasis). Her scientific care for matter seems to rescue her from the facile disdain of any grounding moves, pervasive among those theorists who do not
distinguish "ground" from "foundation."[19]

Haraway locates her own voice as a "modest witness" within "the net of
the virtual community of feminist science studies," especially close to Sandra
Harding's "strong objectivity" and the physicist Karen Barad's "agential realism" (MW, 116). She is, in other words, unwilling to sacrifice a sense of
agency, realism, social location, or even objectivity to an irresponsible deconstruction of all subjectivity and positionality—all worldhood. In league with
Harding, she eschews any mere deconstruction of false, interested appeals to
scientific "objectivity" (MW, 36f., 95).[20] Thus she calls for a nondualistic,
pluriform language of the object. "Strong objectivity" was Harding's way
within feminist science studies to challenge the self-universalizing absolutes
of traditional science, which sought objectivity by ignoring its own gender,

race, class and species, and privilege and perspective.[21] But their point is that the opposite is true: By ignoring our own situated specificity, our knowledge loses so-called objectivity. With her understanding of context as "dynamic material webs of human and nonhuman actors" (MW, 116), Haraway performs not an anti-ontology but an alternative ontology.

If it seems by now irresistible to enroll Haraway in a Whiteheadian project, we do not have to do it for her. Hear how Haraway characterizes her own project: "[I]t is a commitment to avoiding what Whitehead called 'the fallacy of misplaced concreteness,' where simple location and a metaphysics of substantives with primary and secondary qualities . . . get mistaken as reality" (MW, 269). Haraway, whose original discipline was biology, uses this famous fallacy in her critique of the biopower of current genetic research. Given her analysis of the corporate economic might carrying the biology, her deployment of Whitehead's concept resembles Cobb's monumental critique of global economism's supreme version of the same fallacy.[22]

Specifically she diagnoses a "gene fetishism," which mistakes the gene for some literal mechanism *simply located* within "naturally bounded bodies" mapped upon a fixed space-time territory:

> [Whitehead's] notion of objectifications is very close to that held by my mutated witness: "A nexus is a set of actual entities in the unity of the relatedness constituted by their prehensions of each other, or—what is the same thing conversely expressed—constituted by their objectifications in each other." Objectifications had to do with the way "the potentiality of one actual entity is realized in another actual entity." Prehensions could be physical or conceptual, but such articulations, such reachings into each other in the tissues of the world, constituted the most basic processes for Whitehead. (MW, 147)

Haraway takes Whitehead so seriously as to grant him the standpoint of her titular "modest witness." This is no fleeting reference: "Without at present going further into his special terminology, I ally myself with Whitehead's analysis to highlight the ways that gene fetishists mistake the abstraction of the gene for the concrete entities and nexuses that *Modest_Witness@Second_Millennium* monomaniacally affirms" (MW, 147). In an extended footnote Haraway discusses reading Whitehead as a graduate student with her teacher, the ecologist G. Evelyn Hutchinson, but notes the wider trajectory: "I also read Whitehead as an undergraduate, and I believe this philosopher-mathematician lurks in the tissues of many a resister to gene fetishism in feminist science studies and elsewhere" (MW, 297, n.21).

Haraway interweaves bell hooks's "yearning"[23]—for an "affective and political sensibility" (MW, 128)—with Whiteheadian "prehension." Both require a sense of our own embodied, situated difference that enters into active relationship with other worlds of difference—and so takes responsibility for actualizing some differences and not others. Together they allow her to translate an irreducible but unstable eros for collective historical change "into a worldwide tissue of coalitions for a more livable technoscience" (MW, 129). Such a coalitional field of interactions would be constituted by a hope for what Cobb means—for all its discursive perils—by the "common good." In Haraway's language:

> How do the differently situated human and nonhuman actors and actants encounter each other in interactions that materialize worlds in some forms rather than others? My purpose is to argue for a practice of situated knowledges in the worlds of technoscience, worlds whose fibers infiltrate deep and wide throughout the tissues of the planet, including the flesh of our personal bodies. (MW, 130)

To express this differential connectivity, Haraway has crafted the beautiful trope of "totipotent stem cells"—"those cells in an organism that retain the capacity to differentiate into any kind of cell." "Stem cells," she continues, "are the nodes in which the potential of entire worlds is concentrated. . . . Out of each of these nodes or stem cells, sticky threads lead to every nook and cranny of the world" (MW, 129).

iv

What common motives appear to account for the poststructuralist resort to Whitehead? In the wake of this examination of Deleuze and Haraway as two possible, if also of course contestable cases, we may venture the following four points: First, both authors engage natural science with much greater seriousness than most of their peers in theory, yet always with the intent to disarm its objectivisms, determinisms, fetishisms, and closures. They seem, moreover, to find themselves in need of a world, even perhaps a cosmology— if one that remains provisional, unsettled, and ontological only in the most slippery and nonfoundational way. So while resisting scientific objectivism, they also, without marking their difference polemically, find themselves in a different rhetorical situation than those poststructuralists who have been known to mark cosmology as the enemy. Thirdly, therefore, Deleuze and Haraway quietly disrupt the Foucaultian privilege of rupture and discontinuity over connection. And finally, they take from Whitehead a vocabulary with which to embrace the chaotic complexity of difference. The play of difference as such does not take account of the objectifications of the other in us and of us in the other. It may find itself in a new kind of closure, enmeshed in network, however fluidly enunciated, of mutually exclusive impermeabilities, of opaque incommensurabilities strictly bounded by human language. This is where relativism and relationalism part company—there where relativism freezes into a deconstructive undecidability.

Deleuze and Haraway seek, instead, the fold of the infinitely interconnected in the one case and the fibrous worlds of connection and enrollment in the other. Differences, then, do not remain neatly incommensurable, but rather seek mutual enrollment. Prehensions of difference shift social location into complicating hybridities, which mess up not only the centers of identity but also the boundaries of alterity—thus not anti-ontology but dirty ontology; not anticosmology but the chaosmos.

Let me suggest that the Whiteheadian intertext has appeared at a delicate moment in the evolution of postmodern theory: a moment of yearning for a world that resists and redirects our cultural constructions of it; a cosmos open to our construction precisely because it constructs us with the capacity to imagine it back to itself new. Only as worlded in such a cosmos can we imagine our differences as grounded in a common matrix of preconditions, and so as yearning for a future common good. But the only common good that can actually exist, if only for an instant, is that which we create in our mutual prehensivity. In our technoscience as well as in our aesthetics, in our politics as well as in our theology, a radical relationism begins where mere celebration of difference breaks down—that is, where the exuberant affirmation of pluralism seeks more than the rupture of old boundaries and the proliferation of new ones.[24] The resort to Whitehead is not a return to metaphysics; yet it does entail a provisional admission of cosmology and of the need for the cross-disciplinary movement between a humane philosophy of mutual relations and a mathematicizing science, between the infinity of objects and the immediate urgency of ecology. It commits itself, I would think, to a transdisciplinary practice that theorizes the inequality of differences and the limits of relativism.

Those limits, I would suggest, encounter us where social orders encounter their own self-contradictions within us. In other words, the limits of relativism encounter us at the border of chaos. "[I]f there is to be progress beyond limited ideals," writes Whitehead, "the course of history by way of escape must venture along the borders of chaos in its substitution of higher for lower types of order" (PR, 111). Chaos, as such, as a pure disorder, does not exist: thus Deleuze, on Whitehead. What appears there under the no/thingness of the name of chaos is neither nonbeing nor the opposite of order but a boiling ocean of incessant relatedness. Its crash and clash of difference not yet organized into contrast, threatening incommensurability, is what must be faced at the point of evolutionary rupture, at the point of insight, at the point of economic and political negotiation for justice, at the point of systemic shift. Here we may learn much from the contributions of chaos theory, and particularly of the complexity biologist Stuart Kauffman's "edge of chaos"—the critical phase transition at which a complex, self-organizing system may emerge from far-from-equilibrium states that had seemed too unstable to sustain any ordered complexity.[25] At that edge or that border, of chaos, traced in the filigreed self-similarities of fractal geometry, we may perceive—if we can adjust our conceptual eyes to the darkness over its roiling deep—the fluttering of life itself.

"The complexity of nature is inexhaustible," writes Whitehead (PR, 106). Indeed his radical pluralism inscribes itself in the first principle of creativity, whereby the many become one and are increased by one—the oceanic drive of the universe toward complexity. The drive, the voraciousness, the yearning can get, as it does in process theology, personified as the lure of God. While Whitehead has a more restricted use of the term *chaos,* I cannot think chaos as anything, or no/thing, distinct from this infinite creativity, felt as the originality and the catastrophe of all finitudes. Perhaps this reading of Whitehead only becomes possible by letting his "category of the ultimate"— the creativity of which God is the first creature—try on the names of the mythical and repressed chaos of the Bible: *tohuvabohu* and *tehom,* first materialized as *leviathan* and *mayim.*[26] *Process and Reality* suggests the threat of this originative creativity in numerous ways. For instance, "Apart from canalization, depth of originality would spell disaster for the animal body" (PR, 107). This anticipates the science of the edge of chaos, as well as an even later theology of *tehom.* The channeling or self-organizing of this "depth of originality" allows organic life to stabilize, evolve, and socialize. The social order thus derived depends upon "hybrid prehensions" that have as "immediate environment" a "living, non-social nexus" (PR, 107).

That nonsocial nexus of life is so charged with multiplicity, so catalytic of intense immediacy, that evolution depends upon channeling it without subduing it—that is, on attentive balancing acts on the edge of chaos. Might we say—on negotiating with the trickster? Does that nonsocial life-nexus not answer to Whitehead's use of chaos, as the border along which creativity takes place, that is, takes body? Thus it corresponds to the hypothesis of life evolving to "the edge of chaos." Whatever the scientific metaphors, however, I find in this matrix of concepts a hospitable sanctuary for meditation on the good, common and uncommon, in the postmodern period. The borderline is a rich zone, not a linear separation, within the emerging "interstitial perspective" (Bhabha) of postcolonial theory—but here Whitehead had already found that "[l]ife lurks in the interstices" (PR, 105).

The Whiteheadian intertext in Deleuze and Haraway may seem to their usual readers like an embarrassing rupture upon a smoothly postmetaphysical surface. A methodological chaos of ontological depth wells up, threatening some return to romanticism, to speculative metaphysics, indeed to a primitive, prelinguistic monstrosity.[27] Up closer, the crack may appear—as do the algorithms of fractal chaos—rather less threatening. Perhaps then the Whiteheadian intertext emerges as a semiotic pleat, or as a totipotent stem cell. This particular postmodern recourse to Whitehead, more deconstructive and constructivist than in itself reconstructive, is good news for reconstructive postmodernism—if we seek not to control the terms of discourse but allow our thought to be prehended, folded into a wave of discursive originality that had seemed for all its interdisciplinarity to exclude us. We may then trust that cosmology, cast on the *mayim* of a wilder postmodernity, will return to us—differently.

What matters is not that process thinkers gain prestige in the elite discourses of academic postmodernism, but that through such mutual enfoldments process thinkers may help to hold postmodernity accountable to the transdisciplinary yearning, indeed to that "common good." Explicating (unfolding) this fresh Whiteheadian fold within the postmodern, implicating ourselves in its contextual actualizations, may help us to conceptualize the wider solidarity. At any rate, the Whitehead-of-poststructuralism may function as a kind of precreased intertext, which should permit deeper and clearer articulation of our shareable yearnings.

v

As would be obvious to any Whiteheadian, every relationship constitutes a reciprocal enfoldment. If that inevitable mutual implication is to reach the level, at least among some process thinkers, of an enrollment and not a mere capture (of, e.g., some poststructuralist knowledge/power by Whiteheadian operatives) then of course process thought itself must change accordingly. To elaborate the specific changes exceeds the capacities of this chapter but is pursued throughout this book.[28] But let me sketch somewhat expressively, in closing, certain so-far implied criteria. These are criteria not for some total conversion of process thought, but for the conversation among those who wish to transform its incompatibilities with deconstruction into contrast. One can argue in each case that the needed adjustment unfolds a potentiality of Whitehead's text more faithfully than have certain traditions and habits of its interpretation.

We would need, first of all, to overcome the habit of metaphysical deduction if not the metaphysics, that is, the starting point in the categoreal scheme if not the scheme itself. I think, as I argue in the introduction, that this means a postfoundational process thought.[29] Such a style of thinking emphasizes Whitehead's own attention to uncertainty, plurality, and the metaphoric language that protects them, while de-emphasizing his own appeal to rationalism, coherence, objectivism, and totality. It is not that those appeals, read within his historical context, can be ignored by any who engage his discourse seriously, or indeed any who pursue some interchange between philosophy and science. They encode the indelibly modern terms of the postmodern radicalism of his still open text. The needed shift of emphasis does not entail more sacrifice of received vocabulary; it does historicize aspects of Whitehead's rhetoric, which may ill serve the present context of conversation.

To enjoy the occasional deconstructive resort to Whitehead, then, is not to gloat but to sniff out our own inevitable fallacies of misplaced concreteness. It is to "criticize the abstraction" in our own tendencies to morph Whitehead's experimental categories into eternal first principles, and his "principle of the ultimate" into something that is, that is some *thing,* which takes the place of Platonic Being and so hardens the "intuitive appeal" into an intellectual certainty. To cease to *found* our thinking upon Whitehead is to read his thought as itself a porous construction still "in the making." His historical contribution remains for many—including the many who do not acknowledge it—part of the historical *ground* upon which we construct our present conceptual habitation.

To *ground* is not to *found.* Our constructions do not need to turn the dense ecology of that which precedes and supports us into a substructure, substratum, and substance. For those of us attracted to process thought, as a living "community of interpreters" (Josiah Royce) rather than a founding authority, it is the support process thinkers provide for our projects of social justice, ecological sustainability, and spiritual solidarity that keep us also returning to this arcane, increasingly past, discursive practice. There is even among process thinkers a "resort to Whitehead." Erstwhile Whiteheadians may drift away like nomads, but like nomads also return. But such habitations as we construct will remain of necessity makeshift, improvised of local elements and strange imports—and ready to *fold.*

This would mean of course that always our formulation of that "common good" would itself remain suspect. For if we absorb on our journeys some Foucaultian sense for "regimes of knowledge," then the terms of "the common" and "the good" register subtle relations of subjugation. If in our nomadology we can no longer avoid the Deleuzean sense that "the basic series are divergent" (DR, 123), then we cannot hope for any simple convergence of our own series of process and poststructuralist thoughts. They diverge "not relatively, in the sense that one could retrace one's path and find a point of convergence, but absolutely" (DR, 123). That is, they remain divergent "in the sense that the point or horizon of convergence lies in a chaos or is constantly displaced within that chaos" (DR, 123). Yet that chaos "is itself the most positive, just as the divergence is the object of affirmation" (DR, 123). The French and cutting edge of difference may slice painfully against our process sense of cosmic harmony and relationship. It may also reinscribe the complexity of the commons—socially, ecologically, and indeed intertextually—upon the ever-shifting, self-recycling ground of our Whiteheadian antecedence.

The common cracks always into the different. Standing at the edge, the common appears not as utopian stability and not as empty abyss, but as the positive chaos within which our interconnections take place. For Whiteheadians "the common" has never suggested the ground of a settled order—however neat our scheme—but something not accidentally resembling the Joycean chaosmos. We do not hope for final justice or total community. We cannot even finally solve the conflicts marked by the intertext. But we may hold out for some collaborative limit to our intermisunderstanding.

The surface espousal of postmodernism, its linguistic self-reference, its relativism of undecidability, begins to break open; its surface vibrates with extrahuman rhythms; its very "face" discloses its depth as the chaos of creation itself.[30] At that border of chaos, that fold of soulful matter, we become conscious that the great social injustices, the ecological terrors, have enfolded us as well. These transcontextual, structural deformations of the web of relations are always already our own wound: we do not heal anything from the outside. In the dirt, the disease, and the denial, we remain "anyway connected." If we are less common than Cobb might hope, we are less uncommon than other postmoderns might imagine. What is suffering, what matters, has already metastasized within our insubstantial but totipotent organisms. But the inside that enfolds the world, folds it out again. Differently.

Notes

1. John B. Cobb Jr.'s *For the Common Good: Redirecting the Economy toward Community, the Environment, and a Sustainable Future* (Boston: Beacon, 1989/1994), coauthored with Herman E. Daly, is only one major text in the living, cross-disciplinary, multileveled library of his writings, and the practices they inspire. But his critique of free trade first developed therein—well before most other academics offered any resistance to the "GNP orthodoxy," except perhaps in terms of Marxist critiques, which did not specifically direct themselves against the global, homogenizing destruction of ecology and community entailed by neoliberal economics unleashed. The critique of the socialization of university economists to avoid interdisciplinary exchange already played a key role in this text.

2. This absorption and friction was early addressed in the anthology *Feminism/Postmodernism,* Linda J. Nicholson, ed. (New York and London: Routledge, 1990). A flood of works around and since then have entered into the fray, investigating from either side the possible depoliticizing effects of the deconstruction of identity politics and the corrolary anti-essentialism. Cf. Naomi Schor and Elizabeth Weed, eds., *The Essential Difference* (Bloomington and Indianapolis: Indiana University Press, 1994); Diana Fuss, ed., *Essentially Speaking: Feminism, Nature and Difference* (New York and London: Routledge, 1989); Nancy Fraser, *Justice Interruptus: Critical Reflections on the 'Postsocialist' Condition* (New York and London: Routledge, 1998); and Susan Stanford Friedman, *Mappings: Feminism and the Cultural Geographies of Encounter* (Princeton: Princeton University Press, 1998).

3. Edward W. Said, *Beginnings: Intention and Method* (New York: Basic, 1975), 376.

4. Daniel Boyarin, *Intertextuality and the Reading of Midrash* (Bloomington: Indiana University Press,1990), 94.

5. Gilles Deleuze, *The Fold: Leibniz and the Baroque,* Tom Conley, trans. (Minneapolis: University of Minnesota Press, 1993 [1988]).

6. Cf. Deleuze, *Difference and Repetition,* Paul Patton, trans. (New York: Columbia University Press, 1994 [1964]).

7. See esp. Deleuze and Felix Guattari, *A Thousand Plateaus: Capitalism and Schizophrenia,* Brian Massumi, trans. (Minneapolis: University of Minnesota Press, 1987 [1980]); also with Guattari, *Anti-Oedipus: Capitalism and Schizophrenia,* Robert Hurely, trans. (New York: Viking Press, 1977 [1972]). For a good secondary source, cf. Eleanor Kaufman and Kevin Jon Heller, eds., *Deleuze and Guattari: New Mappings in Politics, Philosophy, and Culture* (Minneapolis: University of Minnesota Press, 1998).

8. The Foucault citation, printed on the cover of Deleuze, *Negotiations* (New York: Columbia University Press, 1995) is from *Theatrum Philosophicum.* Cf. Deleuze, *Foucault* (Minneapolis: University of Minnesota Press, 1986/1988), 128.

9. Timothy S. Murphy, "Quantum Ontology," in *Deleuze and Guattari: New Mappings in Politics, Philosophy, and Culture,* Eleanor Kaufman and Kevin Jon Heller, eds. (Minneapolis: University of Minnesota Press, 1998), 211–229.

10. He regularly cites the chaos mathematician who invented the "fractal," Benoit Mandelbrot, as well as Rene Thom, whose metaphor of "catastrophe folds" quietly intersects the Deleuzean oeuvre. He frequently cites the progenitor of contemporary chaos theory, Ilya Prigogine, who also was an avid reader of Whitehead, and whose collaborator, Isabelle Stengers, has contributed to the present volume. His frequent coauthor has developed the metaphor independently, arguing in language relevant to the present case that "chaos is not pure indifferentiation; it possesses a specific ontological texture." See Guattari, *Chaosmosis* (Bloomington and Indianapolis: Indiana University Press, 1995), 81. Brian Massumi has further exfoliated their use of the metaphoricity of chaos theory, in "vortexes," "creative turbulence," and "double bifurcations" in *A User's Guide to Capitalism and Schizophrenia: Deviations from Deleuze and Guattari* (Cambridge: Massachusetts Institute of Technology Press, 1996), 62ff.

11. Cf. also Deleuze and Guattari, *What Is Philosophy?* (New York: Columbia University Press, 1994 [1991]) and Guattari, *Chaosmosis* (Bloomington and Indianapolis: Indiana University Press, 1995 [1992]).

12. Cf. Said's disucssion of Deleuze and Derrida within the context of his own espousal of surface versus depth in his *Beginnings: Intention and Method* (New York: Basic, 1975), 377.

13. "From chaos the plane of immanence takes the determinations with which it makes its infintie movements or its diagrammatic features. Consequently, we can and must presuppose a multiplicity of planes, since no one plane could encompass all of chaos without collapsing back into it; and each retains only movements which can be folded together" (WP, 50).

14. The link does get a footnote in Daniel Smith, "The Doctrine of Univocity," in *Deleuze and Religion,* Mary Bryden, ed. (London and New York: Routledge, 2001),

182 n.32. Also cf. a hopeful allusion to the secular theological promise of the Whitehead-Deleuze intersection in Clayton Crockett's preface to Charles Winquist, *Epiphanies of Darkness* (Albany: State University of New York Press, 2000).

15. Donna J. Haraway, *Modest_Witness@Second_Millennium.FemaleMan©_Meets_OncoMouse™: Feminism and Technoscience* (New York and London: Routledge, 1997).

16. "A Cyborg Manifesto: Science, Technology, and Socialist-Feminism in the Late Twentieth Century," in Haraway, *Simians, Cyborgs, and Women: The Reinvention of Nature* (New York and London: Routledge, 1991), 149–181. A version of this essay was first printed under the title, "A Manifesto for Cyborgs: Science, Technology, and Socialist Feminism in the 1980s," in the *Socialist Review* 80 (1985): 65–108.

17. Haraway, *Simians, Cyborgs, and Women: The Reinvention of Nature* (New York and London: Routledge), 1991.

18. Cf. Rosi Braidotti, *Nomadic Subjects: Embodiment and Sexual Difference in Contemporary Feminist Theory* (New York: Columbia University Press, 1994).

19. Cf. my introduction in this book.

20. That Haraway, as a constructivist, colludes with Sandra Harding, the feminist science theorist whose "standpoint feminism" had been the subject of debate between them, indicates the intertextual direction of Haraway's own thinking.

21. Harding, *Whose Knowledge? Whose Science? Thinking From Women's Lives* (Ithaca: Cornell University Press, 1992).

22. Cobb and Daly, *For the Common Good.*

23. bell hooks, *Yearning* (Boston: Southend Press, 1990).

24. Cf. also Friedmann, "Beyond Difference," in *Mappings: Feminism and the Cultural Geographies of Encounter* (Princeton: Princeton University Press, 1998).

25. Stuart Kauffman, *At Home in the Universe: The Search for Laws of Self-Organization and Complexity* (New York: Oxford University Press, 1995).

26. "The unformed and empty" and "the deep"; "the sea monster" and "the sea." In Christian theology these figures have been necessarily repressed or demonized by the doctrine of *creatio ex nihilo,* which in *The Face of the Deep* I am at pains to deconstruct. Yet while Whitehead disdained the doctrine, and outlined the best alternative so far, he also contributes to the repression of the biblical alternative. Mistakenly designating that doctrine as "the Semitic theory of a wholly transcendent God creating out of nothing an accidental universe," he persists in a footnote with this displacement of his battle with other Christian theories upon the racially marked, intellectually superceded Other: "The book of Genesis is too primitive to bear upon this point" (PR, 95 n.8).

27. Cf. Thomas Cousineau's critique of Deleuze's insistence upon a quasi-theological "originality" in his article, "The Future of an Illusion: Melville's Deconstruction of Deleuze's A/theology" in Bryden, *Deleuze and Religion.*

28. Indeed, the elaboration of the criteria for such a shift, especially pertaining to the troubled defense of metaphysics, foundationalism, and the correspondence theory of truth, is discussed in more depth in my introduction, a later text than the present chapter.

29. As I argue in the introduction, this is already kin to David Ray Griffin's project. While he would be more careful to distinguish between good and bad versions of foundationalisms, I find J. Wentzel Van Huyssteen's espousal of "postfoundationalism," argued at a distance from the Whiteheadian debate, especially helpful (see Van Huyssteen's *Shaping of Rationality: Toward Interdisciplinarity in Theology and Science* [Great Britain: Eerdmans, 1999]). But the point to stress again here is the distinction, germinal in Haraway and Deleuze, of founding versus grounding.

30. My book, *The Face of the Deep* (London: Routledge, forthcoming), examines potential readings of the metaphor of *panim*, "face," by way of Emmanuel Levinas's "face of the other" and the problematic of depth/surface in Derrida, Deleuze, and Said.

3

Whitehead, Deconstruction, and Postmodernism

LUIS G. PEDRAJA

Alfred North Whitehead's critique of modernism is similar to what are now considered "postmodern" critiques. In particular, Whitehead's philosophy and critique of modernism parallel many of Jacques Derrida's epistemological and contextual concerns. Although Whitehead's and Derrida's philosophies are similar in some respects, there is nothing to link them beyond a few references to common sources such as Charles S. Peirce, Henri Bergson, and to a lesser extent for Whitehead, Friedrich Nietzsche (OG, 48).[1] Nevertheless, with the exception of a few process philosophers, most postmodern thinkers ignore Whitehead as a potential source for postmodern thought.

To propose that Whitehead shared concerns similar to those of postmodern philosophers is not a novel idea in itself. David Ray Griffin and John B. Cobb Jr. have written about Whitehead's postmodern agenda. For instance, Griffin, along with other writers in the series on *Constructive Postmodern Thought,* has argued convincingly that Whitehead was indeed aware of both the dangers and the demise of modernism. In addition, these writers correctly claim that people like Peirce, William James, Bergson, Whitehead, and Charles Hartshorne go beyond the deconstruction of modernity by providing the context for a constructive postmodernism. According to them, these constructive postmodern thinkers recognized both the fallacies of modernism and the need for reconstructing its worldview.[2] According to Cobb, the development of the new physics and James's philosophy led Whitehead to an awareness of the onset of a radical shift in world views. Cobb goes on to argue that although Whitehead never used the term *postmodern,* he spoke of the modern world in "postmodern tones," recognizing both the accomplishments and the limitations of modernity.[3] This leads Cobb to examine how Whitehead moves from the substance-oriented language of modernity to a "postmodern" understanding of events-in-relation that overcomes the subject-object dichotomy of modernity.[4]

However, regardless of these arguments by Cobb and Griffin, White-head's metaphysical concerns continue to obscure his postmodern views in the minds of most of his readers. As a result, the "presence" of postmodern views in Whitehead's writings still remains largely ignored in most of the works that trace the development of postmodernism and deconstruction.[5] This failure is partially due to a simplistic understanding of Whitehead's project. Whitehead attempts to tread a fine line between what he considers the two primary fallacies of philosophy: the dogmatism that presupposes its ideas are irrefutably absolute and the antirationalism that discards all philosophical methods (AI, 223). The first concern leads him toward a critique of modernism; the second leads him toward a constructive reconception of his philosophical worldview. Because of the latter concern, Whitehead is characterized unfairly as a passé metaphysician by most students of postmodernism and is readily dismissed as a potential source of postmodern thought.

Although Whitehead maintains a certain degree of the "rationalism" disavowed by proponents of deconstruction, he does not merely continue the Enlightenment project. The premature burial of Whitehead's thought in the grave of modernism and metaphysics by some postmodern writers obscures the rich diversity of Whitehead's works. In a sense, we need to "deconstruct" the primacy given to his metaphysics to recover his original hermeneutical and "postmodern" stance. To accomplish this task, I will examine several areas in Whitehead's writing to demonstrate how they are both postmodern and similar to Derrida's concerns.

In doing this, I am also breaking ranks with those who, like Griffin, place Whitehead in direct contrast to postmodern deconstructionists. Griffin interprets Whitehead's philosophy as a constructive revision of modernism. According to him, the weakness of modernism is its attempt to eliminate a transcendent view of God while retaining the ideologies that presupposed this view of God. Because modernism retained these ideological presuppositions, the "modern self" also retained the notions of detachment, isolation, and individualism ascribed to the transcendent God. Griffin believes constructive postmodern theologies can overcome these modern views without eliminating notions of a centered universe, self, and history.[6] Although Griffin is correct in this preliminary assessment of modernity, he goes on to contrast White-head's constructive approach to deconstruction or, as he calls it, "eliminative postmodernism."[7] Griffin's intent is to combat the dangers of a radical relativism and nihilism, which he correctly believes are inherent in some postmodern approaches. However, in creating this oppositional contrast between Whitehead and deconstruction, he alienates an important aspect of postmodern philosophy and risks missing the similarities that exist between White-head's and Derrida's projects.

Countering deconstruction with Whitehead's philosophy in this way places these two important philosophies at odds with one another. In addition, it limits the potential for a deeper dialogue and exchange between these philosophies. One exception to this polemic against deconstruction is an essay by William Dean that presents a valid possibility for comparing Whitehead's empirical concerns to Derrida's historical deconstruction through a naturalistic and pragmatic view of history.[8] This opens a possibility for further dialogues and exchange between process and postmodern philosophies. Although Dean begins to address this possibility in a specific area, I intend to further extend this comparison in a broader scope with the hope of engendering further research.

While Griffin's interpretation of Whitehead merits serious consideration, it still attempts to salvage a "centeredness" that is difficult to maintain in Whitehead's philosophy. It is true that Whitehead wants to recover certain metaphysical categories and to develop a constructive project. This is part of his attempt to develop a comprehensive interpretive system (PR, 3-4) and his desire to combat the antirationalistic fallacy. However, we also must recognize that Whitehead's critique of modernism radically deconstructs the possibility of an unbiased, axiomatic center that can be abstracted from the whole. This does not mean that Whitehead advocates a radical relativism or a denial of freedom as do some advocates of deconstruction. But neither does Derrida's philosophy in its basic presuppositions advocate a radical relativism and a denial of freedom as some of his interpreters propose. What they both advocate is a suspicion of abstractions that pose as absolute universal truths and the need to acknowledge philosophy's failure to recognize the limitations of its particular contextual perspectives and standpoints. Underlying this suspicion of abstract absolute truths is a shift in their respective philosophies from Western views that give primacy to *being, permanence, presence, space, detachment,* and *individual substances,* to views that incorporate *becoming, change, time, interrelations,* and *fluidity.*

Although it may not seem evident, Whitehead does not want to establish an absolute metaphysical system. What he wants is to develop a comprehensive hermeneutical scheme to serve as an interpretive context in which individual experiences can acquire meaning (PR, 10). According to Whitehead, the task of the speculative philosopher is "the endeavor to frame a coherent, logical, necessary system of general ideas in terms of which every element of our experience can be interpreted" (PR, 3; AI, 222). The comprehensive nature of Whitehead's project leads him to create a neometaphysical system as a hermeneutical tool. However, his metaphysics do not replace his hermeneutical concerns. Rather, his metaphysics are a result of his basic assumption that all propositions, and hence, all interpretations, always and inescapably assume a metaphysical context within which they acquire meaning (PR, 11-12). Whitehead uses the term *metaphysics* to refer to a broad metacontext or matrix of experience, not to an overarching, transcendent logocentric ontology. Whitehead's hermeneutical concerns lead him toward an examination of language as the mediator of experience and philosophy. As a result, his philosophy struggles with questions regarding meaning and its simple location in "objective" linguistic assertions.[9] The neglect of Whitehead's hermeneutical concerns in favor of his metaphysics prevents a true appreciation of his postmodern views and limits comparisons to Derrida's agenda.

Language and the Task of Philosophy

Language plays a crucial role in mediating, interpreting, and constituting human experience. It is the tool of the philosopher, the medium that both crafts and conveys the philosophical world. Thus, we encounter some of the most striking parallels between Whitehead and Derrida as they examine language's role and effect upon the work of the philosopher. This eventually leads them both to recognize that language itself carries limitations and interpretative presuppositions that influence philosophy (PR, 11-13; OG, 157-158). Whitehead's writings demonstrate a strong concern with language both as the tool of philosophy and as the means for conveying human experience (PR, 11). It is the latter that emerges as central to Whitehead's empirical philosophy, leading him to explore the role of language in both the construction and expression of experience. As a result, he turns his attention toward both hermeneutics and the deconstruction of philosophical presuppositions. Whitehead's and Derrida's shared suspicion of how philosophy and metaphysics use language is evident. Derrida's project questions the order of both language and rationality by denying the philosophical presumption that language reflects and conforms to the rational order of some external reality apart from human interpretive activity. According to Derrida, Jean-Jacques Rousseau's condemnation of writing as the destruction of presence reveals language's inability to seize presence (OG, 141). Rousseau, says Derrida, understands writing as a mediate form of speech that becomes a dangerous supplement that usurps the place of speech by forgetting its vicarious nature and by making itself "pass for the plenitude of a speech whose deficiency and infirmity it nevertheless only *supplements*" (OG, 144). Thus, Rousseau's desire is to eliminate the mediative role that language plays between presence and absence (OG, 157). However, for Derrida, the mediative role of language, and most significantly, writing, is inescapable. Thus, it is the graphic differentiation of the "silent play" of *différance* that serves as the condition for both the possibility and the function of signs and phonemes (MP, 5). Without it, speech and language would be impossible. Writing differs from speech in that writing neither presupposes the presence of Being, nor its transparency to it. As a result, writing is primarily an interpretive exercise enmeshed in the "play" of interpretation that takes primacy over speech. This has several implications for Derrida's philosophical insights (OG, 6–26).

First, since the differentiation of the sign precedes even speech, Derrida gives writing primacy over speech. Second, he notes the elusive nature of presence in language and argues that every representation is a continual play between absence and presence. In other words, every representation both discloses and hides something; it is always an abstraction. Therefore, Derrida concludes that it is impossible to efface the linguistic venue of philosophy in hopes of presenting its supposed signified content (OG, 160). This leads Derrida to challenge both the philosophical presumption that linguistic signifiers can convey an accurate picture of an extratextual reality and the tendency of metaphysicians to privilege these philosophical assertions as higher expressions of truth. Derrida rejects the philosopher's assumption that there is something outside the text to which signifiers point, since "there is nothing outside the text" (OG, 158).

The force of Derrida's argument comes from his understanding that the play of difference (spatialization) and defer-*ence* (temporalization) in the linguistic context of the sign is the prime source of meaning. As a result, there is no external referent to language that language can approach for verification. Language is primarily interpretive. Derrida rejects the presumption that philosophy presents being, presence, and reality more accurately than literature and other forms of linguistic expression.[10] Therefore, Derrida's arguments break down the sharp distinctions that separate and privilege philosophy over other forms of linguistic expression. This forcefully presents the philosopher with the inescapability of prejudices, intentions, presuppositions, and biases. There is no external "truth" or "essence" that can serve as an objective test for the accuracy of philosophical presuppositions beyond the linguistic structure of the text.

This recognition of the limits of both philosophy and language is also evident in Whitehead's philosophy. Whitehead notes that "[a]n old established metaphysical system gains a false air of adequate precision from the fact that its words and phrases have passed into current literature" (PR, 13), leading to a false presumption of descriptive precision that assumes the obvious simplicity of the philosophical statements offered. Like Derrida, he recognizes the privileged position accorded to certain types of philosophical assertions by virtue of the language system they presuppose. Although Whitehead is reacting primarily to the popularity of logical positivism during the early part of the 20th century, he also takes to task the presupposition that the method of philosophy should lead to "premises which are severally clear, distinct, and certain; and to erect upon those premises a deductive system of thought" (PR, 8).

Instead of a verifiable system of presuppositions that conforms to an external reality, Whitehead favors an ongoing, progressive, interpretive "scheme" that measures success by its pragmatic ability to interpret experience within a given context (PR, 8-9). Whitehead is indebted to Peirce and James for his conclusion. However, unlike Peirce who believed that an absolute and final interpretation was finally attainable, Whitehead's interpretive system maintains an ultimate nonfinality to it (PR, 9). Whitehead's interpretive system is dynamic in its rationalism and does not limit valid interpretation to philosophers and scientists. On the contrary, Whitehead acknowledges the role of artistic insight and poetic imagination in the advancement of productive thought. In addition, he sees it as necessary for transcending attempts to create a direct representation of what appears to be obvious (PR, 9).

Whitehead explodes the boundaries of philosophy and denies it a privileged position over artistic and imaginative enterprises. According to him, the parameters imposed by philosophy's formal and structural presuppositions constrain attempts to "stray" beyond their established limits (AI, 228-229). These limits prevent innovations in philosophy and criticize new expressions as unnecessary neologisms. Naturally, these presuppositions do not prevent Whitehead from manipulating language to create new metaphors that could open new philosophical perspectives, nor does it prevent Derrida from coining the term *différance*.

Both writers share a tacit recognition of the inherent limitations that language imposes on the philosopher. Thus, Whitehead turns his attention to language as the tool of philosophy. Like Derrida, Whitehead notes that even simple subject-predicate propositional forms such as "The whale is big," can "conceal complex, diverse meanings" (PR, 13). The dependence of a statement's meaning upon its context prevents a singular monolithic expression of truth in Whitehead's philosophy. Truth is always and necessarily contextual. Even when Whitehead moves beyond language, he still locates meaning and "truth" within the complex play of interrelatedness (MG, 675-681). Ultimately, the interconnectedness of reality and form takes primacy over the Cartesian preference for substance and quality in Whitehead's philosophy (PR, xiii).

Admittedly, Whitehead does not go as far as Derrida in noting the dependence of thought on language. According to Whitehead, language cannot be "the essence of thought." If language were the basis for thought, any attempt at translation would be impossible.[11] Instead, Whitehead states that thought originates from the way a particular fragmentary sense experience impresses us in relation to other experiences. In the constitution of our bodies and the way they relate to the environment there are certain common elements with which we can identify. However, Whitehead also contends that the retention, recollection, communication, and integration of thought into higher complex ideas is impossible without language. Like Derrida's play of *différance*, Whitehead concludes that it is in the relating and contrasting of experiences that thought emerges. As a result, he recognizes that without language, thought would be impossible (MT, 32-36).

Whitehead maintains that language functions as a mediator of present experiences to both the past and to other experiences (MT, 33). According to Whitehead, both language and thought emerge together, but, logically, thought must have primacy over language. The importance of language to Whitehead's philosophy is stated most clearly in the final sentence of lecture 2 of *Modes of Thought,* entitled "Expression": "The account of the sixth day should be written, He gave them speech, and they became souls" (MT, 41). Nevertheless, Whitehead does not go as far as deconstruction in placing language at the forefront of all thought and experience.

On the other hand, as this quote reveals, Whitehead maintains a connection between speech and presence and a representational understanding of language—concepts repudiated by Derrida. For Whitehead, writing is an artificial and modern development while speech is the embodiment of human nature (MT, 37). Even further, Whitehead gives primacy to speech due to its representative character. He writes that in the breath of speech there is the intimation of the core of organic existence, hence, life (MT, 32). However, in fairness to Whitehead, he also makes a distinction between writing and speech, indicating that the former is a beneficial innovation that, in discussions about language, often gets intermingled with the latter (MT, 37). As a result of this recognition, Whitehead calls for a more precise distinction between writing and speaking, but not for a dichotomy that places one over the other. According to Whitehead, symbols predate the onset of writing and play a crucial role in the formation of linguistic practices (MT, 37). Even if symbols do not precede speech, Whitehead's use of "symbols" in this manner indicates an awareness of a strong relationship between thought, writing, and speech, which he felt other scholars had neglected.

Whitehead also makes a remark regarding linguistics that merits further attention. He notes in passing how the accessibility of writing and reading to the masses is a fairly recent innovation (MT, 37). According to him, through countless eras, at least in Europe, writing had been primarily the domain of the aristocrat, the politician, and the academician. In this respect, we can add that writing can be both a source of power and a source of oppression. Scholars often ignore the socioeconomic power of writing to disseminate, control, and shape ideas. The control of the written word by aristocrats, clergy, academicians, and politicians skews our understanding of culture and history in the West—a history portrayed by those in control of society. Our interpretive venture must continually recognize the inherently oppressive nature of written documents that were and often still are controlled by the educated and the powerful. Although Whitehead does not elaborate upon the theme, he opens the door to some of the socioeconomic implications of writing that now play an important role in the hermeneutical concerns of deconstructionism.

Whitehead understands language as connecting different aspects of sense experience in a unity that reflects the connectedness of the world or a common activity (MT, 33-34). This suggests an external referent to language. However, this suggestion should not be taken as too strongly logocentric. Language, according to Whitehead, still abstracts and reproduces elements of experience that can be "most easily reproduced" in human consciousness (MT, 34). Thus, the abstract quality of language in itself is already an interpretive enterprise. Humans continually use abstracted elements of experience, associate them with a contextual framework of meaning, and even suggest a particular world that they represent (MT, 34).

On the other hand, his assertion regarding the dynamic interconnectedness of language as reflecting the interconnected activity of the world creates a new possibility for preserving a connection between language and the world without falling into logocentrism. In an article in the *American Journal of Theology and Philosophy,* Marjorie Hewitt Suchocki posits a viable thesis of the connection between language and reality in response to the American deconstructionists Carl Raschke and Charles Winquist.[12] We can also apply this response to Derrida. Although language interprets reality, preventing a referential logocentrism, its interconnected play represents the interconnected creative activity of the world, ultimately providing a possible link between Whitehead and Derrida.

Language can never capture the fullness of reality, nor can any linguistic function ever predict the total possibility of its meaning. On the contrary, language presents a distorted picture of reality in which single words, "bounded by full stops, suggest the possibility of complete abstraction from any environment" (MT, 66). This tendency gives the false appearance that philosophy can conceive of the interconnection of things, discretely understandable, without making reference to other things (MT, 66). Whitehead's rejection of this presupposition denies the philosopher the possibility of absolute unbiased descriptions of reality devoid of any interpretive system. In recognizing the limitations created by our finite perspectives, he acknowledges the need to move beyond a "narrow" epistemology based merely upon sense-data and introspection, and appeals to literature, ordinary language, and practice as other sources (AI, 228).

Whitehead understands language as originating from the characteristic functions of "emotional expression, signaling, and [the] interfusion of the two" (MT, 37). In both instances, these characteristics are reactions to particular situations within a particular environmental context (MT, 38). The origins of language are predominantly functional rather than representational. In addition, Whitehead notes that this characteristic function of language fades into the background as language advances, leaving a suggestion (trace?) of something that has lost its dominating position (MT, 37-38). Since the specific context in which language originates is no longer present, language can never be identically reproduced in its original function. Only certain elements, abstracted from their original context by the linguistic function, can be repeated, thus leaving the appearance that something has disappeared from the language. Eventually, linguistic functions move toward higher levels of abstractions, which both facilitate civilization and obscure the abstract, and hence, interpretive nature of language. Therefore, Whitehead recognizes the dilemma of philosophers who must use language to express their philosophies, but who cannot escape the biases and interests inherent in their languages.

Like Derrida, Whitehead rejects the possibility that language might express "propositional truths" outside of its linguistic context. Thus, Whitehead writes in *Process and Reality,*

> every proposition refers to a universe exhibiting some general systematic metaphysical character. Apart from this background, the separate entities which go to form the proposition as a whole, are without determinate character. Nothing has been defined, because every definite entity requires a systematic universe to supply its requisite status. Thus every proposition proposing a fact must, in its complete analysis, propose the general character of the universe required for that fact. There are no self-sustained facts, floating in nonentity. (PR, 11)

Although the last sentence points toward Whitehead's "ontological principle," which grounds every aspect of reality, it also provides insight into the problem of interpreting human experience. For Whitehead, there is no detached, discrete "fact" in itself. Every fact is always part of the interrelated complexity of entities. In this statement, Whitehead does not simply mean that propositions require metaphysics. He means that all propositions already *imply* a metaphysics. Therefore, philosophical assertions are not simple, objective, detached descriptions of objects or of the external world. They are already enmeshed in a presupposed context that defines them and their usage. Since all propositions presuppose a system and context, it is impossible to reduce linguistic assertions to a simple, definite signification of reality. Thus, Whitehead writes that "language is thoroughly indeterminate by reason of the fact that every occurrence presupposes some systematic type of environment" (PR, 12).

The meaning of particular propositions depends upon their particular contexts, and thus varies from one context to another. As a result, we cannot assume that there are any self-evident, unprejudiced philosophical arguments that do not presuppose some interpretive context and worldview. In rejecting the possibility of a detached and disinterested philosophical description, Whitehead moves away from the core of modernism and opens the way for the deconstruction that also marks Derrida's work. This implication already reflects a "postmodern" bent in that it does not presuppose a singular, "universal" metaphysical context. Rather, it presupposes a multitude of contexts: a multiverse.

Derrida also recognizes the impossibility of the philosophical presumption of attaining precision and accurate representation in a philosophical language. In his reflections upon Paul Valéry's work, Derrida contends that the philosopher gives a formality to philosophical language by forging a connection with natural language that allows mere ciphers to resemble the thing in itself (MP, 293). As a result, philosophy can only pretend to escape the vagueness and metaphoric nature of its language, despite its pretense at formality and precision (MP, 292). All philosophical assertions necessarily rest upon a previously assumed context that provides those assertions with meaning, preventing the philosopher's escape from the linguistic concepts the language presupposes.[13] As philosophy's logocentric bias, prejudices, and intentionality become evident, the door to deconstruction is opened.

Whitehead and Derrida present us with similar concerns about language and its relationship to philosophy. These concerns force philosophers to explore both the manner in which philosophy uses language and the impossibility of escaping the abstractive, interested, and contextual nature of language and its interpretive play. While Derrida concerns himself primarily with writing and its liberation from logocentrism and ontotheological claims, Whitehead concerns himself with language and its role in the interpretation of experience. Nevertheless, they both reject the representational role of language, as simply conforming to some external reality, and they both reject static and self-evident notions of language. Any utterance or symbol is already an interpretive activity.

Meaning and Contextuality

The contextual and interrelated nature of language leads Derrida and Whitehead to recognize both the interrelated nature of the signifier to its context and the dependence of meaning upon their interplay. Meaning is the result of an interplay of differences and similarities. It is not the result of a correlation to an ultimate reality. For instance, to arrive at the notions of *différance* and play, Derrida builds upon Ferdinand de Saussure's maxim that language is a complex network of differences placed in relation. In the context of language, meaning does not occur as ontological presence. Neither is meaning dependent upon nor constituted by an essential substance to which linguistic expressions approximate themselves (OG, 31-32; MP, 24-25). In other words, we do not derive meaning from being nor from a symbolic correlation to being. Instead, meaning and value come from the interplay of differences and deference that Derrida hopes to capture in coining the word *différance* (OG, 50-57).

According to Whitehead, the interrelated nature of meaning allows for the differences in meaning that can occur between the speaker and the hearer, and more importantly, between the writer and the reader. Our language, both spoken and written, allows us to abstract particularities from their immediate context. As a result, we are able to place them in different contexts that give those particulars new meaning. Due to the differentiation of contexts, both in speech and in writing we are able to arrive at different conclusions even though we share a certain identity of meaning for a given word. For instance,

Whitehead notes wisely that the expression "a warm day" is "very different for speakers in Texas, or on the coast of England bordering the North Sea" (MT, 39). The words *a warm day* might share certain common meanings, but convey different feelings for the speakers in these different climates. In the case of a book, this goes even further since the book can be far removed from the context in which it is written, conveying different feelings and moods to different readers. As a result, language bears an elliptical character in which there is a hermeneutical play between the interpreter and the originator of a proposition (CN, 1-25).

The contextual nature of language leads Whitehead to conclude that there are "no brute, self-contained matters of fact, capable of being understood apart from interpretation as an element of a system" (PR, 14). Like Derrida, Whitehead recognizes that meaning results from a complex interplay of differences and contrasts that distinguish one thing from another, even if that play is not limited to language. As early as 1917, Whitehead begins to explore the necessary connection between context and meaning. As a result, he concludes that the fragmentary nature of experiences requires an interrelated context from which they can derive meaning (MT, 217). Later, Whitehead argues that meaning and value emerge from the interplay between the infinite relatedness of things and their concrete embodiment (MG, 674-675). In the development of his philosophy, Whitehead concludes that in the processes of exclusion and differentiation things acquire their identity and uniqueness (MT, 50-54, 57-63). In the process of differentiation, which renders "things" concrete, meaning can also emerge. For Whitehead, meaning is never the result of an infinite universal essence. Instead, it is the result of an "interplay" of differentiations and inclusions within a particular concrete entity in relation to other concrete entities. Unfortunately, as Whitehead notes, the "history of thought is a tragic mixture of vibrant disclosure and of deadening closure" (MT, 58). These assumptions of closure and certainty in knowledge are the "anti-Christ of learning" and "dogmatism" that Whitehead rejects (MT, 58).

The Fallacy of Misplaced Concreteness

Another area that demonstrates how Whitehead's postmodern concerns develop alongside his metaphysical concerns is in the development of what he calls "the fallacy of misplaced concreteness." In developing his argument against this fallacy, Whitehead's philosophy moves away from modernity's logocentric assumptions of an underlying ontological reality to which linguistic expressions conform. His metaphysics and his hermeneutics coincide in noting this fallacy. According to Whitehead's philosophy, reality is a fluid interplay of relations between concrete actualities and infinite possibilities. As a result of its dynamic and interrelated nature, reality cannot be limited to any given static or fixed concept without reducing its fluid nature to a rigid abstraction. Linguistic expressions are necessarily abstractions from reality, and hence, interpret actual entities by defining only certain aspects. These abstractions, taken as full representations of actual entities, would both distort and pose as the final reality (MT, 18). In addition, Whitehead's actual entities are ontologically the equivalent of Descartes's *res vera,* with one exception: their substantial self-sufficiency (PR, xiii, 59, 205). Thus, the particular spatio-temporal self-determinations of actual entities prevent the conveyance of their full "ontological presence" in any linguistic expression.

Whitehead understands each experience as being particular in nature and confined to its own universe (PR, 43). Experience is both finite and interrelated to its context. As a result, he argues that there is no singular absolute universal expression of truth (MT, 69-70). All truths are ultimately relative to certain given presuppositions, abstractions, and exclusions (AI, 241-242). Truth depends partially upon the unique perspective and standpoint of the interpreter. In this respect, Whitehead's philosophy parallels theories of relativity in physics. What is true for one observer may not be true for another observer, even if they are talking about the same event. This does not mean that truth is reduced to an utter relativism. Instead, Whitehead allows for the "verification" of truth by its correspondence to the actual state of affairs (PR, 186-191). In other words, truth is not determined by its identification with an absolute universal. Rather, it is determined by how well it depicts and describes a particular state of affairs in a given context from a given perspective.

The recognition of both our perspectival limitations and the interrelated nature of reality leads Whitehead to argue, similarly to Peirce and James, for an open metaphysical system that continually seeks "better" descriptions of the whole of reality. But, unlike them, he does not share the belief that a final and ultimate description of reality is possible. Instead, Whitehead offers an open system that allows for the continual development of new interconnections and meanings.

According to Whitehead, science and philosophy abstract their data from the complex and dynamic interrelatedness of reality. What they abstract also depends on the particular interests and perspectives of the disciplines. Because scientists and philosophers abstract data based on particular interests, the objective philosophical and scientific precision craved by the rationalism of modernity is impossible. There is always a creative or vested interpretation of reality involved. The fallacy occurs when these disciplines forget that their concepts are particular abstractions from reality and thus function as if their concepts were actual universal representations of reality. The danger of the fallacy of misplaced concreteness is the pretense that a given abstraction is the actual reality it purports to represent. According to Whitehead, this pretense leads to the mechanistic views of the universe that have pervaded modernity (SMW, 76).

Interestingly enough, Whitehead arrives at the notion of the fallacy of misplaced concreteness through his reading of Bergson's critique of simple location and the spatialization of things (SMW, 50), a critique also familiar to Derrida (MP, 37, 227). The extent to which Bergson serves as a common denominator for Whitehead and Derrida is minor, but not insignificant. Whitehead "deconstructs" the modern fallacy of simple location and the spatialization of reality, thus critiquing the representational assumptions of philosophy. He moves away from any understanding of linguistic abstractions as able to offer "immediate representations" that are unaffected by temporality (PR, 8). Like Bergson and Derrida, Whitehead desires to open the way for including temporalization in his philosophy. Without this temporalization, a simple location of reality creates a false representation that excludes the fluidity of temporal relations (SMW, 51).

Whitehead suspects "modern scientists" who claim to explain every element of the universe by means of a theory. He suspects them because scientific theoretical methods involve certain presuppositions and contextual experiences (PR, 42). Thus, Whitehead prefers that different interpretative methods coexist. He wants to unmask the scientific and philosophical desire to abstract and fix reality in a singular expression. Similarly, Derrida wants to unmask the "pretense" of modernity that attempts to fix the meaning of the flux of experience in singular monolithic assertions. In their tasks they share a common vision that recognizes both the fluidity of human experience and the futility of our attempts at systematizing them into rigid and monolithic systems.

In addition, Whitehead did not think that human sense perception itself is a simple enterprise. Rather, it is the juncture of two modes of experience: presentational immediacy and casual efficacy. Together, these forms of experience form "symbolic reference" (PR, 168 ff.). Our perception internally combines a multitude of sense experience into a manageable whole that we project to a particular location that might be either internal or external to ourselves (S, 30-59). Through "presentational immediacy," Whitehead distinguishes between the manner in which "things are *objectively* in our experience and *formally* existing in their own completeness" (S, 25). As a result, Whitehead concludes that objectification is an abstraction that does not objectify the actual entity in its entirety (S, 25). The "symbolic" nature of sense perception and experience prevents the ontological fullness of being to be captured by either language or philosophy.[14]

Not only do we fail to recognize our epistemological limits by generalizing abstractions, we also unconsciously generalize our individual finite perspectives into an infinite universal reality (MT, 42-43). Human experience "atomizes" the interrelated continuum of time and space into manageable bits that are conditioned by our perspective (PR, 67). While this segmenting of time and space facilitates our understanding and perception of the whole of "reality," it also places limitations on our perspective. Ultimately, any meta-physics is limited by its unique perspective and its unique standpoint (MT, 67). These limitations imply that our understanding is primarily "abstract" in nature, limiting our ability to know the significance of something in relation to all possible environments (MT, 60).

Intertextuality and the Dissolution of the Subject-Object Dichotomy

One of the strongest moves that Whitehead makes toward a postmodern stance is his critique of the Cartesian separation of the subject from the object. The detached rationality characterizing the Enlightenment project is an impossibility for Whitehead. According to Cobb, Whitehead overcomes the epistemological and metaphysical dualism of the subject and the object while preserving a distinction between them. As a result, Whitehead moves away from the epistemology of modernity, and accords to all things a certain level of subjective agency.[15] Furthermore, according to William Dean, the empiricism of Whitehead's philosophy not only destroys the dualism of the subject and object, but also other traditional dualisms, such as those of spirit-matter and human-nonhuman, in a manner that transcends even Derrida's works.[16] Whitehead accomplishes this task in several ways. First, his panpsychism prevents the privileging of human experience above that of other entities. As a result, no actual entity is purely objective. Second, the role that perspective plays in constructing our experience allows Whitehead to assert that both subjects and objects are the same actual entities conceived from different spatiotemporal perspectives.[17]

Third, Whitehead recognizes a subjective bias in Descartes's philosophy. According to Whitehead, Descartes gives primacy to the experiencing subject over the object of experience, thus shifting the focus to the subject as the primary source for philosophical reflection. Although Whitehead agrees with certain beneficial aspects of Cartesian philosophy, he argues that Descartes and his successors missed the extent of their discovery due to their understanding of experience in terms of "substance-quality categories" (PR, 159). Ultimately Whitehead articulates what he calls "the revised subjectivist principle": "that apart from the experiences of subjects there is nothing, nothing, bare nothingness" (PR, 167). Whitehead rejects any notions of primary substances underlying sense perception, as well as the harsh subject-object division of experience. Instead of a simple bifurcation of mind and nature, Whitehead recognizes with the onset of the new developments of physics, that the subject as active and the object as passive is not an accurate depiction (CN, 27). Attempts at reducing the world to subjects and objects inevitably fail because they do not recognize that we are hopelessly interrelated with the world that we experience (PR, 49-50; SMW, 129). The subject cannot be removed from the object nor can the object be removed from the subject. On the contrary, Whitehead argues for their mutual constitution of one another.

In Derrida's case, this issue plays itself out in the realm of language and philosophy. Derrida, like Whitehead, also seeks to overcome what he terms the *illusion* of a singular, objective present that dominates language and philosophy in favor of the interwoven play of meanings and differentiation (MP, 12-13). Rather than a fixed meaning that conforms to some objectively verifiable exterior reality, Derrida acknowledges the interrelated nature of language itself, and rejects the presumed fixed meaning of abstractions and objective data. In Whitehead, the interrelated and fluid nature of *reality* prevents rigid fixed meanings that objectively depict reality in its fullness. In Derrida, it is the interrelated and fluid nature of *language* that prevents it. Nevertheless, the results are remarkably similar. Since Derrida rejects the possibility of a purely objective philosophical language that corresponds to reality, he also rejects the radical subject-object duality that pervades modern philosophy.

Temporalization, Iterability, and the Present

Whitehead's and Derrida's shared postmodern concerns also undergird the development of their philosophies. For instance, in Derrida's philosophy, temporality plays a crucial role as an element of the radical otherness of *différance,* as well as in the iterability of the sign. For Derrida, signification can occur only if

> each so-called "present" element . . . appearing on the scene of presence, is related to something other than itself, thereby keeping within itself the mark of the past element, and already letting itself be vitiated by the mark of its relation to the future element, this trace being related no less to what is called the future than to what is called the past, and constituting what is called the present by means of this very relation to what it is not. . . . (MP, 13)

As a result, he understands the "present" of presence as an irreducible synthesis of traces "of retention and protensions," which he eventually terms *différance.* The temporalization of presence recognized by Derrida bears a strong similarity to the constitution of an actual entity's concrescence in Whitehead's philosophy. Both are inescapably interrelated, temporalized, and constituted by relations and differentiations to the past (givenness) and the future (possibility).

For Derrida, the basic nature of anything that can be termed as *presence* is already constructed by the dynamic interplay, interrelation, and differentiation of *différance*. As a result, Derrida concludes that any kind of ontological presence, if it is to be "known," is necessarily mediated by signs (MP, 316-319). Since the temporalization of the present requires the separation of an interval to differentiate the present from what it is not, then only in the temporal deferral of a sign can one encounter the mediation of presence. For Derrida, only signs are repeatable and objectifiable. In a sense, the sign bears a similarity to the eternally objectified superject that allows the closure and repeatability of objectified actual entities in other actual entities that are no longer their temporal contemporaries.

In addition, Derrida's notion of *différance* serves as the "constitutive, productive, and originary causality" that grounds the very possibility of rationality (MP, 6). Linguistically, *différance* is a productive activity or movement that serves as the ground of what can be said.[18] Whitehead understands creativity as the originary creative activity or principle that unites the disjunctive many into one, which then becomes part of the disjunctive many once more, as well as the ground of reason itself (PR, 21). Similarly, Derrida understands *différance* to be the originary ground of language and reason. In addition, Derrida expressly argues that *différance* is not to be equated to either a being or God. This distancing of *différance* from both being and God remarkably resembles Whitehead's differentiation of creativity from both actual entities and God. The similarities between these concepts are apparent. In part, these similarities may be due to their shared concern with temporality and their shared critique of modernity. Regardless, these similarities merit further consideration beyond the scope of this chapter.

Conclusions?

The very act of arriving at any conclusions is a risky enterprise that attempts to fix and give closure to the very openness of the system that both Whitehead and Derrida recognize. However, in the juxtaposition of their ideas and concerns, a new possibility for dialogue and openness emerges. Rather than hiding Whitehead in the shrouds of an arcane modern world view, we can achieve a greater appreciation for his work. We may be unable to detach Whitehead from his own particular context at the end of modernity, but at the same time we should not cover him over with the presumptions of a dead metaphysics. When we place Whitehead in a new relationship with a postmodern worldview, we realize that what some would claim to be the arcane ravings of an old philosopher may actually prophesy the coming of a new age.

Underlying both Whitehead and Derrida are radically similar concerns that recognize the limits of language and philosophy while deconstructing many of the presuppositions of modernity. Even more, both Whitehead and Derrida share a dynamic and interrelated view of reality. And while Derrida's "reality" is limited to the interplay of language, for Whitehead, the interplay of relations, contrasts, and differences is *both* linguistic and at the base of all experience.

Although we might be tempted to ignore Whitehead's contribution to the deconstruction of a modern worldview, we should not do so. We should no longer ignore Whitehead as a potential contributor to, and predecesor of, our current postmodern philosophers. Nor should we limit our postmodern analysis of Whitehead to his constructive metaphysical system. Instead, we need to recognize the full scope of his philosophical task, which includes both a critical deconstruction of the presuppositions of modernity and a reconstruction of hermeneutical and metaphysical systems to interpret all aspects of human experience.

If we would take seriously both Whitehead's and Derrida's critiques of the presumptions of detachment, abstraction, permanence, and exclusivity inherent to modernity, we would pave the way for a radically new approach to human interaction and scholarly reflection. The detachment and isolation engendered by modernism could be replaced by a greater appreciation for the interconnected nature of all reality. This would help us to overcome the dichotomies that separate us and thrust us against each other, as well as against all of creation. A recognition of the creative interplay of both language and reality might impart a greater appreciation for the role they play in our thoughts and in the construction of our ways of experiencing reality. Rather than the domination of absolute, unchanging truths and ideologies, an appreciation for change and diversity could create an openness toward different perspectives.

The dominance of Western philosophical views in scholarly circles often reduces Third World perspectives to an inferior status. Theologies and philosophies that deny the possibility of detached critical reflection are still viewed with suspicion and relegated to a marginal status. However, both Whitehead's and Derrida's critiques of modernism present noble and exciting possibilities for decentering the domination and absolutist claims of modernity, opening the way for other philosophical perspectives without necessarily falling prey to a radical relativism.

Notes

1. Derrida makes several references to Charles S. Peirce's semiotics going as far as noting that Peirce takes the irreducibility of the sign's "becoming-unmotivated" more seriously than Saussure. He also notes Peirce's rooting symbols and signs upon the "play" that relates them to other symbols and signs, demonstrating his familiarity with precursors of process thought.

2. See David Ray Griffin et al., *Founders of Constructive Postmodern Philosophy* (Albany: State University of New York Press, 1993), 1–42.

3. See John B. Cobb Jr.'s "Alfred North Whitehead" in *Founders of Constructive Postmodern Philosophy,* 167–187.

4. Ibid.

5. Robert C. Neville argues in *The High Road Around Modernism* (Albany: State University of New York Press, 1992) that Whitehead's thought is neither modern nor postmodern. While Neville's argument is compelling, I still think one can make an argument that shows that Whitehead was *postmodern* in the broadest sense of the term. This form of "postmodernism" (if this is what we shall call it) foreshadows many of the concerns of contemporary postmodern theorists, while arriving at constructive solutions.

6. Griffin et al., *Varieties of Postmodern Theology* (Albany: State University of New York Press, 1989), 31, 41.

7. Ibid.

8. William Dean, "Deconstruction and Process," *Journal of Religion* 64 (1984), 1–19.

9. Stanley Grenz addresses this issue in *A Primer on Postmodernism* (Grand Rapids: Eerdmans, 1996), 142. This compares to Whitehead in *Process and Reality,* 11–12.

10. Christopher Norris notes this aspect of Derrida's philosophy in *Derrida* (Cambridge: Harvard University Press, 1987), 23.

11. Derrida avoids this problem through the recognition that any mark that is left retains the iterability that makes it decipherable to a third party through its bearing of a relation (MP, 315).

12. Marjorie Hewitt Suchocki, *American Journal of Theology and Philosophy* 11 (May 1990), 133–142.

13. Derrida emphasizes this point by citing the following from Paul Valéry: "The strongest of them [philosophers] have worn themselves out in the effort to *make their thoughts speak.* In vain have they created or transfigured certain words; they could not succeed in transmitting their inner reality. Whatever the words may be—Ideas or Dynamis or Being or Noumenon or Cogito or Ego—they are all *ciphers,* the meaning of which is determined solely by the context. . . ." (MP, 292).

14. For an extensive discussion of Whitehead's understanding of language, symbolism, and abstractions see Stephen T. Franklin's book, *Speaking from the Depths: Alfred North Whitehead's Hermeneutical Metaphysics of Propositions, Experience, Symbolism, Language, and Religion* (Grand Rapids: Eerdmans, 1990).

15. In Griffin et al., *Founders of Constructive Postmodern Philosophy,* 174–178.

16. Dean, "Deconstruction and Process," 8.

17. Cobb in Griffin et al., *Founders of Constructive Postmodern Philosophy,* 174–175.

18. Derrida makes this clarification in the discussion ensuing his original presentation of his article on *différance,* as recorded in *Derrida and Différance,* David Wood and Robert Bernasconi, eds. (Evanston, IL: Northwestern University, 1988), 85.

4

Whitehead and the Critique of Logocentrism

JOSEPH A. BRACKEN, S.J.

The theme of "otherness" is prominent in academic circles within the United States and Western Europe at present. Here the influence of Emmanuel Levinas with his groundbreaking work *Totality and Infinity* is clearly evident. That is, the drive within classical metaphysics toward "totalizing" schemes in which individuality is sacrificed to the logical exigencies of a set of universal concepts, in Levinas's view, must be countered by a heightened awareness of the "infinity" present in the "face" of the other.[1] Intersubjectivity, in other words, would seem to privilege a strong sense of otherness over the classical notion of sameness even while somehow maintaining their dialectical relationship. Within the philosophy of Alfred North Whitehead, for example, "actual occasions" as momentary subjects of experience are invariably different from one another since each is a unique self-creation out of data perspectively available to it alone (PR, 65). Yet paradoxically, at any given moment each actual occasion and its contemporaries help to constitute what Whitehead calls "the extensive continuum," namely, "a complex of entities united by the various allied relationships of whole to part, and of overlapping so as to possess common parts, and of contact, and of other relationships derived from these primary relationships" (PR, 66). Moreover, within the interpersonal context referred to by Levinas, it is clear that human beings regularly bridge the "infinity" that separates them from one another as different subjects of experience through language and various other forms of communication. Hence, within a theoretical scheme based on intersubjectivity, while the focus has to be more on otherness than on sameness, yet, as just noted, commonalities (for human beings, affinities in the form of shared patterns of thought and behavior) must likewise be present as a check against a Leibnizian atomism in which each monad or self-enclosed subject of experience would be in effect a world unto itself.

91

To provide theoretical justification for my proposal here, I will in the first part of this chapter carefully analyze some of the key terms in the philosophy of Jacques Derrida so as to indicate how they make better sense in the context of a possible metaphysics of intersubjectivity than in the context of the classical metaphysics of being, which Derrida evidently had in mind in mounting his critique of the Western philosophical tradition. In particular, I will focus on his key notion of *différance* as the systematic play of differences, and indicate its affinity with Whitehead's notion of creativity as that principle whereby "[t]he many become one, and are increased by one" (PR, 21).[2] In both cases, Whitehead and Derrida were trying to verbalize the elusive dynamism of becoming, the moment of creative advance.[3] Then in the second part of the chapter, I will make clear how process-relational metaphysics still runs the risk of what Derrida calls the "logocentrism" implicit in the entire Western philosophical tradition. But I will at the same time indicate how this charge of logocentrism can be deftly avoided if one gives closer attention to the logical consequences of the notion of "society" within Whitehead's conceptual scheme. That is, I will set forth my own understanding of how a democratically organized society of actual occasions can be understood as a network of interrelated differences that exist in virtue of creativity but that for the same reason operate without a logical centerpoint or Logos precisely in the sense deconstructed by Derrida.

Différance *and* Creativity *Compared*

In an essay simply titled *"Différance"* Derrida lays forth at some length his understanding of this key term in his philosophy. He begins by noting that his neologism, *différance,* when spoken aloud, is indistinguishable from the conventionally spelled French word, namely, *différence* (MP, 3-5). He then adds that *"différance is not,* does not exist, is not a present-being *(on)* in any form" (MP, 6). Thus "it has neither existence nor essence. It derives from no category of being, whether present or absent" (MP, 6). This is remarkably similar to Whitehead's description of *creativity* as that which is actual in terms of its accidents or instantiations: "It is only then capable of characterization through its accidental embodiments, and apart from these accidents is devoid of actuality" (PR, 7). In both cases, we are dealing with something that may be seen as a principle of activity rather than as an entity.[4] Both *différance* and creativity, therefore, empower entities to be themselves, in effect, to make a difference in a world of individual entities.

This is not to ignore, of course, that the overall thrust of the philosophy of Derrida is quite different from that of Whitehead. Derrida's focus is on detecting subtle differences of perspective within established identities so as to set free a creative questioning of those same identities. Deconstruction, he says, insists "not on multiplicity for itself but on the heterogeneity, the difference, the disassociation, which is absolutely necessary for the relation to the other. What disrupts the totality is the condition for the relation to the other."[5] Whitehead, on the other hand, as a metaphysician, is focused on principles of order and continuity within the creative process. Yet both thinkers, as just noted, have tried to capture the creative moment when something new emerges from the old without cutting off all sense of continuity with the old. As I will indicate later in this section, the notion of "trace" and the dialectic of presence and absence, which are so prominent in Derrida's philosophy, likewise have their counterpart in the philosophy of Whitehead.

In the meantime, however, note should be taken of still another feature of *différance* in Derrida's philosophy that can be matched with Whitehead's understanding of creativity. Derrida points out that the notion of *khora* (receptacle) in Plato's *Timaeus* is basically incompatible with the so-called philosophy of Plato with its emphasis on a graded hierarchy of forms up to and including the Idea of the Good as the Form of Forms.[6] But Plato, after all, must have had some reason for discussion of this term in the *Timaeus* even if he did not make clear his intention in the text itself. Since *khora* represents for Plato simply a receptacle devoid of any determinations apart from the entities to be found within it, in my judgment, it is Plato's expression for the principle of pure potentiality that stands in necessary opposition to the Idea of the Good as the principle of pure actuality in his philosophy. Yet, like Aristotle with his term *hyle,* Plato conceived *khora* or the "receptacle" as a purely passive reality, namely, that which receives forms (as opposed to that which produces forms). Derrida, on the other hand, thinks of *khora* in active terms as linked to *différance,* the systematic "play" of differences; "*khora* is its surname."[7] In a strikingly parallel move, Whitehead notes that creativity "is another rendering of the Aristotelian 'matter,' and of the modern 'neutral stuff.' But it is divested of the notion of passive reception, either of 'form,' or of external relations; it is the pure notion of the activity conditioned by the objective immortality of the actual world" (PR, 31).

Thus what both Derrida and Whitehead seem to be getting at here is the way in which the relation between the principles of potentiality and actuality is curiously reversed when one switches from a metaphysics of Being to a metaphysics of Becoming. Within a metaphysics of Being the principle of actuality is active "from the top down," so to speak, with the principle of potentiality as the necessary receptacle for the play of forms within it. Within a metaphysics of Becoming, on the other hand, the principle of potentiality is active "from the bottom up," producing as effects of its activity the various actualities encountered in the world. For basically the same reason, neither Derrida nor Whitehead want to associate *différance* or creativity with the actuality of a God understood as the Supreme Being.

Derrida, for example, is emphatic that *différance* is not to be identified with God, even the God of negative theology, since negative theologies "are always concerned with disengaging a superessentiality beyond the finite categories of essence and existence, that is, of presence, and always hastening to recall that God is refused the predicate of existence, only in order to acknowledge his superior, inconceivable, and ineffable mode of being" (MP, 6).[8] Similar to Derrida, Whitehead declares that God and creativity are not to be identified, but rather that "God is its [creativity's] primordial, non-temporal accident" (PR, 7). God is an instance of the operation of creativity, not the transcendent source of creativity. Within my own conceptual reworking of Whitehead's metaphysical scheme, to be sure, I modify Whitehead's understanding of creativity so as to avoid the otherwise inevitable consequence of two Ultimates, God and creativity.[9] That is, I propose that creativity is the nature or principle of activity first for God and then by a free decision on God's part likewise for all creatures.[10] But even within my trinitarian scheme creativity is not operative from above, but, properly understood, from below. That is, within God creativity can be described as the *underlying* principle for the existence and interrelated activity of the three divine persons of orthodox Christian belief. Likewise, within creation, creativity is the *underlying* principle for the existence and interrelated activity of all creatures. Hence, even though coeternal with God as the Supreme Being, creativity is immanent within creatures rather than transcendent to them. It may be aptly described as the "divine matrix" within which the three divine persons and all their creatures exist in dynamic interrelation.[11]

Later in his essay, Derrida notes that *différance,* like the Latin *differre,* has two meanings. The first, less common, meaning is to put off until later or "to temporize": "to take recourse, consciously or unconsciously, in the temporal and temporizing mediation of a detour that suspends the accomplishment or fulfillment of 'desire' or 'will,' and equally effects this suspension in a mode that annuls or tempers its own effect" (MP, 8). The second, more common meaning of *différance* or *differre* is "to be not identical, to be other, discernible, etc." (MP, 8). Here I would argue that a precise analog to these two meanings is to be found in Whitehead's creativity as the metaphysical principle whereby "[t]he many become one, and are increased by one" (PR, 21). That is, in virtue of creativity a new actual occasion is created that is different from its predecessors but whose ultimate identity lies not in itself but in the nexus or social configuration of actual occasions out of which it arose and to which it contributes its own momentary pattern of intelligibility even as it passes out of existence. No single actual occasion taken by itself has, therefore, any enduring significance; its real significance lies in its being the latest member of a temporally ordered nexus or "society" of actual occasions. In Derrida's terms, its ultimate meaning is "deferred" to the ongoing context of the society to which it belongs. As Whitehead notes in *Adventures of Ideas,* a society "enjoys a history expressing its changing reactions to changing circumstances. But an actual occasion has no such history. It never changes. It only becomes and perishes" (AI, 204).

Derrida also notes that *différance* designates "a constitutive, productive, and originary causality, the process of scission and division which would produce or constitute different things or differences" (MP, 9). But is not creativity also a "constitutive, productive, and originary causality" whereby "the many become one, and are increased by one?" Furthermore, perhaps even more than Derrida's notion of *différance,* Whitehead's category of creativity makes clear that, even though each actual occasion is different from its predecessors and successors, an unmistakable affinity between these separate actual occasions is likewise present in that they are all instantiations of a shared causative principle of activity or becoming. As just noted, differences only make a difference when there is a dialectical connection between the individuals thus distinguished from one another. At the same time, postulating this underlying unity does not in and of itself imply a covert return to "logocentrism" where all differences are ultimately dissolved into an undifferentiated sameness. For everything depends upon how one conceives this sameness: namely, as the sameness of an immanent activity or the sameness of a transcendent entity. Only in the latter case, as I see it, can one raise the question of logocentrism. For, an activity that is immanent in various entities so as to enable them to exist as quite distinct individuals must by definition operate somewhat differently in each entity. Hence, creativity is paradoxically the principle of otherness or separateness within these entities even as it simultaneously functions as the principle of unity between them.

Derrida also proposes that *différance* as "temporizing" involves temporalization and spacing, "the becoming-time of space and the becoming-space of time" (MP, 8). His argument here is somewhat convoluted since he begins with an analysis of language rather than an analysis of extramental reality in which space and time are key coordinates.[12] His initial reference, therefore, is to Ferdinand de Saussure's celebrated hypothesis that language is an arbitrary system of signs whose significance is determined by their relation to one another rather than by their common relation to an external reality (MP, 10).[13] Derrida then continues, "The first consequence to be drawn from this is that the signified concept is never present in and of itself, in a sufficient presence that would refer only to itself. Essentially and lawfully, every concept is inscribed in a chain or in a system within which it refers to the other, to other concepts, by means of the systematic play of differences" (MP, 11). Almost the same statement can be made about an actual occasion as a member of an ongoing social nexus or "society." Its coming-to-be has meaning and value only in terms of the society to which it belongs. The key difference, of course, is that while Derrida refers to *différance* as the "systematic play of differences" within language, Whitehead's notion of creativity is operative primarily within extramental reality to insure the *ordered* sequence of actual occasions whereby one group of actual occasions with its "common element of form" or shared pattern of intelligibility can be distinguished from another group of actual occasions with still another shared pattern of intelligibility (PR, 21, 34-35). Yet Derrida is not insensitive to the possibility that there is more at work in language than simply language itself. For he immediately adds the following note to this remark: "Such a play [of differences], *différance,* is thus no longer simply a concept, but rather the possibility of conceptuality, of a conceptual process and system in general" (MP, 11). This reference to "the possibility of conceptuality" and of "system in general," as we shall see later in this section, will eventually lead Derrida into more overtly metaphysical reflection by way of explanation for the reality of *différance.* Here it is sufficient to note that creativity for Whitehead, like *différance* for Derrida, is not in itself the actuality of conceptual process, system, or any other determinate reality, but rather its ontological possibility.

Derrida's second conclusion from Saussure's hypothesis runs as follows:

> It is because of *différance* that the movement of signification is possible only if each so-called "present" element, each element appearing on the scene of presence, is related to something other than itself, thereby keeping within itself the mark of the past element, and already letting itself be vitiated by the mark of its relation to the future element, this trace being related no less to what is called the future than to what is called the past, and constituting what is called the present by means of this very relation to what it is not: what it absolutely is not, not even a past or a future as a modified present. (MP, 13)[14]

Once again, the parallel with Whitehead's notion of an actual occasion is remarkable. An actual occasion always bears the mark of its past in that it is largely constituted out of "prehensions," both physical and conceptual, of its predecessor actual occasions. Likewise, it anticipates the impact that it as a "superject" or completed actual occasion will have on its successors, above all, within the same society of actual occasions. Hence, it is in a very real sense constituted here and now by its (anticipated) future. Thus an actual occasion, like an "element" in the quotation from Derrida, is never really present to itself but always in transition from past to future.

Finally, Derrida arrives at an explanation of what he just referred to as "the becoming-space of time" and "the becoming-time of space":

> An interval must separate the present from what it is not in order for the present to be itself, but this interval that constitutes it as present must, by the same token, divide the present in and of itself. . . . In constituting itself, in dividing itself dynamically, this interval is what might be called *spacing,* the becoming-space of time or the becoming-time of space *(temporization).* And it is this constitution of the present, as an "originary" and irreducibly nonsimple (and therefore, *stricto sensu*

nonoriginary) synthesis of marks, or traces of retentions and protentions
. . . that I propose to call archi-writing, archi-trace, or *différance.* Which
(is) (simultaneously) spacing (and) temporization. (MP, 13)

Here, too, there seems to be a significant parallel with Whitehead's account of
the self-constitution of an actual occasion. It must separate itself from its
predecessors on which it heavily depends for its self-constitution in order to
be itself. Likewise, it must somehow distinguish itself from its successors in
order to assess its anticipated impact upon those same successor actual occasions. In the process, the actual occasion together with its predecessors and
successors sets up a space-time system governing the society as a whole. That
is, the Whiteheadian society does not exist in space and time but creates its
own space-time parameters in virtue of the ordered succession of its member
actual occasions (PR, 92).[15]

The point of this extended comparison of Whitehead's concept of creativity and Derrida's notion of *différance,* of course, is not to suggest that Derrida was somehow dependent upon Whitehead's philosophy for his own
understanding of the nature of language, but rather to insinuate that Derrida is
perhaps more of a metaphysician than he himself is prepared to admit. That
is, even though he sees himself as working within the tradition of classical
metaphysics only in order to deconstruct it, that is, to set it free from its own
rigidified presuppositions,[16] his own more positive efforts to understand the
nature of language, when systematically organized, themselves seem to presuppose an inchoate metaphysics, a new way of understanding not only
human language but reality as a whole. In this respect, the sage remark of
Etienne Gilson to the effect that philosophy buries its undertakers,[17] may be
vindicated once again. That is, one cannot think systematically without explicitly or implicitly making certain claims not only about one's specific subject matter but also about how one's subject matter fits into the broader
scheme of things, that is, in the end, the nature of reality.

Derrida seems indirectly to confirm this observation with his remarks
about language and self-consciousness in the second half of the article on *différance.* He begins by citing Saussure once more to the effect that language is
not an effect of the speaking subject but rather that the speaking subject is a
function of language: "the subject (in its identity with itself, its self-consciousness) is inscribed in language, is a 'function' of language, becomes a
speaking subject only by making its speech conform . . . to the system of the
rules of language as a system of differences, or at the very least by conforming to the general law of *différance*" (MP, 15). He then cites Friedrich Nietzsche, Sigmund Freud, and Martin Heidegger in support of his basically metaphysical claim that consciousness is a function of language rather than an
entitative reality in its own right, that is, the self-presence of the subject to
itself "before distributing its signs in space and in the world" (MP, 16).

Nietzsche, for example, argued that consciousness is the effect of unconscious forces within the psyche. Derrida comments, "Force itself is never present; it is only a play of differences and quantities. There would be no force in general without the difference between forces" (MP, 17). For that matter, as Derrida sees it, Nietzsche's entire philosophical project is an implicit affirmation of *différance* when the latter is understood as "the displaced and equivocal passage of one different thing to another, from one term of an opposition to the other" (e.g., for Nietzsche, from the sensible to the intelligible, from nature to culture, etc.) (MP, 17).

Likewise, within Freudian psychological theory the two notions of differing and deferring are inextricably tied together:

> A certain alterity—to which Freud gives the metaphysical name of the unconscious—is definitively exempt from every process of presentation by means of which we would call upon it to show itself in person. In this context, and beneath this guise, the unconscious is not, as we know, a hidden, virtual, or potential self-presence. It differs from, and defers, itself; which doubtless means that it is woven of differences, and also that it sends out delegates, representatives, proxies; but without any chance that the giver of proxies might "exist," might be present, be "itself" somewhere, and with even less chance that it might become conscious. (MP, 20-21)

The parallel with Whitehead's notion of consciousness is once again quite striking. For Whitehead, too, consciousness is not the permanent presence of the human subject to itself, but a varying function of mental processes, most of which are not conscious. That is, for Whitehead consciousness arises only at an advanced stage in the "concrescence" of some (but by no means all) actual occasions when "intellectual feelings" provide a contrast between actuality and potentiality, that is, a "contrast between a nexus [of actual occasions] which *is,* and a proposition which in its own nature *negates* the decision of its truth or falsehood" (PR, 261).[18] Strictly speaking, a Whiteheadian "proposition" or imaginative possibility does not "negate" the decision of the truth or falsehood of a given set of actual occasions. Rather (in Derrida's terms), it "defers" a decision as to truth or falsehood until that moment when an actual occasion has to decide whether or not to actualize that new possibility. In any event, Whitehead is clear that consciousness as such varies in intensity: "[C]onsciousness flickers; and even at its brightest, there is a small focal region of clear illumination, and a large penumbral region of experience which tells of intense experience in dim apprehension" (PR, 267). Finally, for Whitehead as well as for Derrida, language plays a key role in the emergence of consciousness. For, while nonhuman animal species exercise consciousness to some degree, their inability to communicate with one another by means of language severely restricts the range of possibilities available to them in consciousness. Language, in other words, elicits in human beings these "intellectual feelings" that even prior to conscious awareness propose a variety of new possibilities for what is perceived to exist and thus add notably to the intensity of consciousness here and now.[19]

My purpose, once again, in this extended comparison between Whitehead and Derrida on various topics is to suggest that Derrida is indirectly constructing a new metaphysics even as he seeks systematically to deconstruct the implicit presuppositions of classical Western metaphysics. Yet, insofar as the informal metaphysics of Derrida appears to have a natural affinity with the metaphysical system of Whitehead, one is further led to surmise that, if Derrida himself or one of his disciples were more thoroughly to systematize his reflections on the nature of language, this resemblance might well be even more striking.[20] Derrida, in other words, however tentatively, seems to be at work on a metaphysics of becoming, above all, in the sphere of human inter-subjectivity, which resonates deeply with Whitehead's fundamental insights both in *Process and Reality* and elsewhere. My surmise here is, I believe, unexpectedly confirmed when one reviews in the final pages of *"Différance"* Derrida's comments on the philosophy of Heidegger and the latter's key insight into the ontological difference between Being and beings.

Derrida begins by noting the alterity of past and future to the present. That is, there is a past that has never been present and a future that never will be present (MP, 21). Time, in other words, is not a succession of "nows" that move uniformly out of the future into the present and thence into the past. Rather, much akin to what Whitehead says about the self-constitution of an actual occasion, Derrida says that the present moment always contains the "trace" of the past and the "trace" of the future. The specific content of what is meant by past and future may vary from moment to moment, but the relation of past and future to the present moment never varies. In similar fashion, the meaning of Being is not exhausted by the beings, particular entities, which it empowers to exist here and now in the present. Thus, while in one sense *différance* can be understood as "the historical and epochal *unfolding* of Being or of the ontological difference," from another angle *différance* is "'older' than the ontological difference or than the truth of Being" (MP, 22). For the latter terms are simply historical manifestations of the deeper reality of *différance* or "the trace": "[a]lways differing and deferring, the trace is never as it is in the presentation of itself" (MP, 23).

Derrida illustrates this point by reference to a text of Heidegger, *Der Spruch des Anaximander* ("The Anaximander Fragment), in which Heidegger first distinguishes between what is present and the act of "presencing" and then indicates that the nature or essence of this act of "presencing" and the relation of the act of presenting to what is present still remain hidden (MP, 23). As Derrida comments, the difference between Being and beings has disappeared without leaving a trace. For, when the activity of "presencing" appears as something present, indeed, as the highest being present *(in einem höchsten Anwesenden),* then "erasure" belongs to the reality of the "trace." That is, not only can the "trace" be regularly erased, but in fact it is constantly being erased (MP, 24). Only thus can one explain the historical oblivion of the distinction between Being and beings from the beginning of Western philosophy. At the same time, as Heidegger also notes, the trace curiously remains in the very language that is used to talk about Being (MP, 25).[21]

Pursuing this last point further, Derrida calls attention to Heidegger's translation of Anaximander's word *(to khreon)* as *Brauch* (usage), that which primordially discloses and conceals the reality of Being (MP, 25). As Derrida sees it, Heidegger's *Brauch* is equivalent to his own term *différance;* but for that same reason he questions whether Heidegger or anyone else can through reflection on *Brauch* (or *différance*) arrive at a knowledge of the essence of Being *(Wesen des Seins).* "There is no essence of *différance;* it (is) that which not only could never be appropriated in the *as such* of its name or its appearing, but also that which threatens the authority of the *as such* in general, of the presence of the thing itself in its essence" (MP, 25-26). Grammatically speaking, *différance* is a noun, a name for a thing; in this case, however, it does not refer to an object but rather to an activity that "unceasingly dislocates itself in a chain of differing and deferring substitutions" (MP, 26). Heidegger's search for a single, unique word to describe the reality of Being is, in Derrida's view, a remnant of metaphysical thinking in Heidegger's reflections. Yet Derrida shares with Heidegger the nostalgic desire or perhaps even hope that in language Being or *différance* will "always and everywhere" somehow make itself felt (MP, 27).

Derrida's focus, accordingly, here at the end of his essay on *différance,* is still on the deconstruction of the classical metaphysics of Being in which Being is given a name and thus assigned a place within a hierarchically ordered metaphysical scheme. But in my judgment, he is setting forth inadvertently a new metaphysics of becoming with *différance* as its archetypal principle. That is, while his preferred subject matter is the elusive character of language as an ongoing play of differences, he affirms with Heidegger that something more is at stake in language than language itself. *Différance* is somehow descriptive of Being (in the sense of universal Becoming) as well as of language. In that respect, there is a deep, even if somewhat oblique, affinity of Derrida's philosophy with that of Whitehead. That is, the basic metaphysical instincts of both men flow in the same direction: namely, an affirmation, on the one hand, of the universal fluidity of reality and, on the other hand, of the interconnectedness of everything with everything else as a result. Whitehead is clearly the more systematic thinker, but Derrida may be more insightful with respect to the issue of "logocentrism." As I shall indicate in the next section, Whitehead's notion of the God-world relationship is somewhat ambiguous and the efforts of his disciples, notably Charles Hartshorne, to clear up these ambiguities have resulted in what appears to be a subtle form of logocentrism. But, as I will further explain, there should be a way for other disciples of Whitehead to remedy that oversight in conventional process-relational metaphysics and at the same time to remain faithful to Whitehead's own deeper impulses in terms of the God-world relationship.

Overcoming Residual Logocentrism in
Process-Relational Metaphysics

In the final chapter of *Process and Reality,* Whitehead discusses what he means by the "consequent nature" of God as opposed to the "primordial nature" of God. In virtue of the divine primordial nature, God "is the unlimited conceptual realization of the absolute wealth of potentiality" (PR, 343). That is, in one comprehensive valuation God brings order and coherence out of the vast plurality of eternal objects or patterns of intelligibility pertinent to the world of creation. But this nontemporal conceptual prehension of possibilities on God's part must be then linked with God's physical prehension of the actual course of events within creation. This is accomplished, in Whitehead's view, through the divine consequent nature that is as a result the objectification of the world in God. God thus "shares with every new creation its actual world; and the concrescent creature is objectified in God as a novel element in God's objectification of that actual world. This prehension into God of each creature is directed with the subjective aim, and clothed with the subjective form, wholly derivative from his all-inclusive conceptual valuation" (PR, 345). Like all other actual entities, therefore, God is dipolar in nature. But whereas a finite actual entity begins its concrescence with the physical prehension of past actual occasions and then adds from a variety of sources conceptual prehensions pertinent to its own self-constitution, God begins with an unlimited conceptual prehension of possibilities and then adds physical prehensions or physical feelings to that all-embracing conceptual vision in line with actual events taking place in the world.

Thus far Whitehead's concept of the God-world relationship is consistent with his overall theory for the self-constitution of actual entities. What is not clear, however, is whether or not God as a result equivalently constitutes the transcendent ground or ontological principle of unity for the cosmic process from moment to moment.[22] For, even though each actual entity unifies the physical and conceptual data proper to its world, and even though subsequent actual entities can prehend the actual world(s) proper to their predecessors (PR, 230), the actual worlds of all these finite actual entities are strictly perspectival. They are limited, in other words, by what Whitehead calls their "subjective aim" at internal self-constitution in one way rather than another (PR, 25).[23] Only God has a nonperspectival vision of the wealth of conceptual possibilities in virtue of the divine primordial nature; and only God has a nonperspectival physical prehension of the events taking place in the world of creation. Thus it would appear that if the world has an objective unity, if it in effect constitutes a single all-comprehensive process, then only God in virtue of the divine consequent nature is able to give it that all-embracing unity and order. As Whitehead comments with respect to the completeness of the divine consequent nature, "[i]n it there is no loss, no obstruction. The world is felt in a unison of immediacy" (PR, 346).

But is there not a perspectival character even to God's unification of the world process within the divine subjectivity? For, as Whitehead notes further, "[t]he revolts of destructive evil, purely self-regarding, are dismissed into their triviality of merely individual facts; and yet the good they did achieve in individual joy, in individual sorrow, in the introduction of needed contrast, is yet saved by its relation to the completed whole" (PR, 346). Thus, to achieve the harmony proper to the divine being, God must downplay the immediate significance of certain events taking place in creation and give considerably more significance to those same events from a long-range perspective. As a result, there is an inevitable selectivity present even in God's prehension of the unity of the world process. God's consequent nature is equivalently God's judgment on the world, losing nothing that can be saved (PR, 346). But presumably there are events, or in any case dimensions of events, which cannot be saved.

Furthermore, as Whitehead also makes clear in the final paragraphs of *Process and Reality,* "God and the world are the contrasted opposites in terms of which Creativity achieves its supreme task of transforming disjointed multiplicity, with its diversities in opposition, into concrescent unity, with its diversities in contrast" (PR, 348). From this perspective, there would seem to be no possibility of residual logocentrism in Whitehead's notion of the God-world relationship since God and the world are juxtaposed to one another within the cosmic process with no hint of the world being thereby subordinated to God. But there still remains the speculative question whether or not the world possesses an objective unity and cohesiveness in itself over and above God's subjective prehension of it from moment to moment. Here the ambiguity in Whitehead's conception of the God-world relationship becomes apparent, for the consequent nature of God does indeed appear to be the unifying principle for the events taking place in the world within one key passage out of *Process and Reality.*

Whitehead begins with the comment that there are "four creative phases in which the universe accomplishes its actuality": The first phase is that of "conceptual origination, deficient in actuality, but infinite in its adjustment of valuation." Presumably this phase has reference to the primordial nature of God that is, as just noted, God's initial valuation of all the eternal objects pertinent to the world process. The second phase is that of "physical origination, with its multiplicity of actualities." This phase evidently has to do with the sheer multiplicity of finite actual entities concrescing within the world process at any given moment. As Whitehead notes, "[i]n this phase full actuality is attained; but there is deficiency in the solidarity of individuals with one another" (PR, 350). As a result, a third phase is needed "in which the many are one everlastingly, without the qualification of any loss either of individual identity or of completenesss of unity" (PR, 350-351). The reference to "everlastingness" implies that the multiple finite actual entities find their unity with one another within the divine consequent nature; hence, the objective unity of the world process would seem to be from moment to moment contained within the divine consequent nature. This impression is confirmed by the fourth and last phase of the world process in which "the perfected actuality [of the world process and/or the divine consequent nature at any given moment] passes back into the temporal world, and qualifies this world so that each temporal actuality includes it as an immediate fact of relevant experience" (PR, 351). The unity of the world process thus achieved from moment to moment within God serves as the basis for the divine initial aims to initiate the process of self-constitution for the next set of creaturely actual entities.

From the perspective of Derrida and other deconstructionists, accordingly, this might well be interpreted as an instance of logocentrism whereby the One as a transcendent reality serves as the principle of unity for the empirical Many. There is, however, as I see it, a relatively easy way in which to deflect possible criticism of Whitehead's thought on this point by contemporary deconstructionists, and at the same time to clear up the residual ambiguity in his thought, as just noted, in which the *objective* unity of the world process appears to be constituted, albeit somewhat ambivalently, by the strictly *subjective* unity of the divine consequent nature.

For Whitehead seems to have not specified carefully enough the need for some kind of objective unity for societies as ontological totalities that are more than the sum of their constituent parts or members. He distinguishes, for example, between social and nonsocial nexuses of actual entities. Societies are social nexuses in that they perpetuate a "common element of form" among their constituent actual entities from one moment to the next (PR, 34). Likewise, he distinguishes between personally ordered societies of actual entities whose constituent actual entities carry forward a "character" or "common element of form" from one moment to the next and corpuscular societies that are made up of "strands of enduring objects," namely, subordinate personally ordered societies of actual entities (PR, 34-35). But what remains unclear therewith is the extent to which personally ordered societies and, even more so, corpuscular societies are ontological totalities greater than the sum of their parts, that is, their constituent actual occasions. Especially since Whitehead likewise claims in the same chapter of *Process and Reality* that "the ultimate metaphysical truth is atomism" (PR, 35), the exact ontological status of such societies in Whitehead's philosophy is ambiguous. Societies as "Public Matters of Fact" evidently exist (PR, 22). But are they ultimately reducible to the interplay of individual actual occasions or do they in some sense constitute an objective reality over and above those same occasions?

Hartshorne provided for most Whiteheadians the standard resolution for this philosophical issue many years ago with his proposal that a distinction should be made between compound and composite individuals in commonsense experience.[24] Compound individuals are those complex or "structured" societies of actual occasions that are governed by a regnant subsociety of actual occasions. This regnant subsociety of actual occasions gives an objective unity and coherence to all the other subsocieties of actual occasions within the structured society that is the compound individual entity at the level of commonsense experience (e.g., a human being or any other higher-order animal organism). All other more democratically organized "structured" societies, in which there is no regnant subsociety of actual occasions, are to be regarded in Hartshorne's view as composite individuals or "virtual aggregates" of actual occasions (e.g., the societies of actual occasions making up rocks and other strictly inanimate objects in the macroscopic world).

My counterargument is that most Whiteheadian societies are not governed by a regnant subsociety. Both in the suborganic world of atoms and molecules and in the supraorganic world of communities and environments, Whiteheadian societies are best understood as democratically organized and thus as without a regnant subsociety to give them some kind of objective unity. Accordingly, I propose that Whiteheadian societies without exception are the product of the coordinated activity of all their subsocieties and constituent actual occasions. Where a regnant subsociety is present, naturally it exercises a predominant influence on the functioning of the structured society as a whole; but all the other subsocieties likewise play a role in the overall functioning of the structured society. Hence, even though a Whiteheadian structured society does not exercise agency except in and through its subsocieties and their constituent actual occasions, it is nevertheless an objective ontological unity in its own right through the dynamic interplay of those same subsocieties and constituent actual occasions. Together, in effect, they make some macroscopic reality (e.g., a human being or some other higher-order animal organism) to be what it is at any given moment, namely, a whole greater than the sum of its functioning parts.

Most important for our discussion here, however, is that this understanding of Whiteheadian structured societies is quite consciously nonlogocentric. Within a Whiteheadian structured society, whether it be monarchically organized in terms of a regnant subsociety or democratically organized as the by-product of subsocieties in strictly coordinate interaction, there is no single unifying center of activity but instead an ongoing interplay of multiple centers of activity that together constitute the objective ontological unity of some macroscopic reality. Furthermore, if one grants the legitimacy of this extension of Whitehead's thought on the nature of societies, one can clear up the ambiguity surrounding his presentation of the God-world relationship in *Process and*

Reality. That is, one can say that the world as an all-embracing structured society of a myriad number of societies and constituent actual occasions possesses its own ontological unity even prior to its prehension by God into the divine consequent nature. God's prehension of the world from moment to moment is needed, to be sure, in order to provide an objective basis for the divine initial aim to initiate the process of self-constitution for the next set of actual occasions. But God's prehension of the predecessor actual occasions is not needed to give the world an objective unity that it otherwise would not have. Thus there is no question of logocentrism either within the world as a complex social reality in its own right or between God and the world in terms of God's unification of the multiple actualities of the world at any given moment through incorporation into the divine consequent nature.

The importance of this modest further specification of Whitehead's categoreal scheme is even more apparent when one compares it with Hartshorne's attempt to clarify Whitehead's understanding of the God-world relationship. In line with his understanding of a Whiteheadian structured society as a "compound individual," Hartshorne suggests that the God-world relationship is best presented in "soul-body" terms.[25] That is, the world is the "body" of God, the physical component of the divine being; and God is the soul of the world, its inner animating principle. Yet this analogy, as I see it, is clearly logocentric. For God as a transcendent individual entity is evidently the unifying principle for the world as an aggregate of societies and their constituent actual occasions.

On the other hand, if, as I have argued elsewhere,[26] God be understood in trinitarian terms as a community of three interrelated divine subjects of experience, then the prevailing image of the God-world relationship is not that of an organism with God as its unifying principle. It is rather the image of an all-comprehensive society in which the three divine persons of the Christian doctrine of the Trinity are indeed the primordial members, but in which all creatures are likewise members adding their specific pattern of intelligibility to the overall shape or structure of the cosmic society as an objective ontological reality. Thus there is no single focal point for the understanding of the operation of this cosmic society. The Logos or ontological principle of unity is distributed among its members, both divine and creaturely, in terms of their dynamic interrelation to one another and their collective contribution to the order and well-being of the whole. "The One," therefore, is not a transcendent entity but a unifying *activity,* namely, Whiteheadian creativity insofar as it first constitutes the tripersonal reality of God as a divine community and then the ongoing reality of creation as a subcommunity within the divine communitarian life, that is, a comprehensive "structured society" of subsocieties and their constituent actual occasions in dynamic interrelation.[27]

This is not to deny, of course, that God is necessary to the world in a way that the world is not necessary to God. For, even within a radically communitarian understanding of the God-world relationship, the world shares in the divine communitarian life only through the gracious free decision of the divine persons. But, as I see it, the key point in the charge of logocentrism, namely, that the One as a transcendent entity effectively orders and controls the relations of the empirical Many to one another, is thereby countermanded. For reality is no longer understood in terms of a graded hierarchy of individual entities up to and including God as a strictly transcendent entity. Rather, reality is set forth as a network of social totalities or interacting "systems" with individual entities or subjects of experience as their constituent parts or members. The Logos, as just noted, is therefore not concentrated in an individual entity but instead distributed among all the members of a given social totality or system in terms of their dynamic interrelation. The net result, accordingly, is a specifically social understanding of reality in which individual entities, on the one hand, are ontologically subordinate to the social totalities of which they are members but yet, on the other hand, are naturally equipped by their dynamic interrelation to modify the ongoing character or structure of those same social totalities.

To sum up, then, in this chapter I have attempted to show how Derrida in his efforts at a systematic deconstruction of classical metaphysics is consciously or unconsciously at work on a new metaphysics of becoming. Furthermore, if my extended analysis and comparison of Derrida's *différance* and Whitehead's notion of creativity has any logical plausibility, then it would appear that Derrida's implicit metaphysics of becoming bears a strong affinity with the basic insights of Whitehead's process-relational metaphysics: namely, the overall fluidity of reality and yet for the same reason the interrelation of everything with everything else in the forward movement of the cosmic process. As I indicated in the second half of the chapter, however, there seem to be residual elements of the classical metaphysics of being in contemporary process-relational metaphysics. Above all if one subscribes to Hartshorne's distinction between compound and composite individuals for the unity of structured societies of actual occasions and to his rethinking of the God-world relationship within Whitehead's philosophy along the lines of a soul-body analogy, a subtle form of logocentrism may be present.

At the same time, as I indicated, there is a relatively easy way in which to meet the potential objections of contemporary deconstructionists to this feature of process-relational metaphysics. That is, by allowing for the objective unity of Whiteheadian societies in virtue of the coordinated activity of their constituent actual occasions, one can convert process-relational metaphysics into a more thoroughgoing social ontology in which the necessary emphasis on the autonomy of individual actual occasions is balanced against an equally important emphasis on the objective reality of the societies of which they are constituent members. Thus, as just noted, the Logos or ontological principle of unity for the cosmic process is not located in a transcendent entity but rather in a transcendent activity, namely, what Derrida calls *dif-*

férance and what Whitehead calls "creativity." Furthermore, as just indicated, *différance* and creativity thereby play a dual role in the philosophies of Derrida and Whitehead, respectively. That is, each serves both as the principle of differentiation and as the principle of unity for all the particular entities of this world. What makes entities different from one another thus paradoxically links them together in ongoing patterns of dynamic interrelation.

Notes

1. Emmanuel Levinas, *Totality and Infinity: An Essay on Exteriority,* Alphonso Lingis, trans. (Pittsburgh: Duquesne University Press, 1969), 50–51.

2. Cf. also Luis G. Pedraja in this volume and in "Whitehead, Deconstruction and Postmodernism," *Process Studies* 28 (1999), 68–74, esp. 75, 82-83. Pedraja's reflections on the relation between Whitehead and Derrida in the matter of postmodernism are remarkably similar to my own even though neither of us was antecedently aware of the other's work on the same theme.

3. More than Whitehead, Derrida focuses on the future as the unexpected, as that which would seem to be impossible from the vantage point of the past (cf. John D. Caputo's commentary on "A Conversation with Jacques Derrida," in *Deconstruction in a Nutshell,* John D. Caputo, ed. [New York: Fordam University Press, 1997], 117–118: "History, thus, is not a course set in advance headed toward its *telos* as toward a future-present, a foreseeable, plannable, programmable, anticipatable, masterable future. History means, rather, to set sail without a course, on the prowl for something 'new.' Such an open-ended, nonteleological history is just what Derrida means by 'history,' which means for him that something—an 'event'—is really happening, e-venting [*é-venir*]"). At the same time, Whitehead's notion of the self-constitution of an actual occasion is that, while clearly dependent upon its past, it is, at least in principle, a new and original moment in an ongoing process. Hence, Whitehead like Derrida is opposed on principle to the teleological mind-set of classical metaphysics, which subtly undercuts any real possibility of evolution in the sense of unplanned change.

4. Mark C. Taylor, *Deconstructing Theology* (New York: Crossroad, 1982), 100–101: "Saussurean *différence* and Derridean *différance* are variations of Hegel's notion of negativity. . . . When negativity is adequately grasped in its infinity and absoluteness, it reveals itself to be the essence, the *Wesen* or *Inbegriff* of everything. Essence is pure negative activity that relates itself to itself in otherness. . . . Essence realizes itself through active self-negation in which it posits itself as other, that is, as determinate being, and returns to itself from this otherness by negating its own negation." Common to Saussure, Derrida, Hegel, and Whitehead, therefore, is the insight that an infinite activity underlies all the finite determinations to be found in this world. It is this necessarily indeterminate activity that establishes the dynamic identity-in-difference of all determinate individual entities with one another.

5. Derrida, "Conversation with Jacques Derrida," 13.

6. Ibid., 9. Cf. also Derrida, "Khora," *On the Name,* Ian McLeod, trans., Thomas Dutoit, ed. (Stanford, CA: Stanford University Press, 1995), 87–127.

7. Ibid., 126. Derrida does not explicitly use the term *différance* here, but I rely upon the judgment of Caputo that *différance* is what is intended with Derrida's reference at this point to "a necessity which is neither generative nor engendered" (cf. Caputo, *Deconstruction in a Nutshell*, 96–105).

8. Cf. also Caputo, *The Prayers and Tears of Jacques Derrida: Religion without Religion* (Bloomington: Indiana University Press, 1997), 1–19. Caputo is emphatic that deconstructionism and negative theology of God are not to be conflated. "*Différance* does not settle the God question one way or the other; in fact, the point is to unsettle it, to make it more difficult, by showing that, even as we love the name of God, we must still ask what it is we love" (13).

9. Cf., e.g., Whitehead, *Science and the Modern World* (New York: Free Press, 1967), 178–179.

10. Cf., e.g., Joseph A. Bracken, S.J., *Society and Spirit: A Trinitarian Cosmology* (Cranbury, NJ: Associated University Presses, 1991), 123–139.

11. Cf. my recent book, *The Divine Matrix: Creativity as Link between East and West* (Maryknoll, NY: Orbis Books, 1995), esp. chapter 4.

12. "Let us start, since we are already there, from the problematic of the sign and of writing" (MP, 9).

13. "Whether we take the signified or the signifier, language has neither ideas nor sounds that existed before the linguistic system, but only conceptual and phonic differences that have issued from the system" (MP, 11). Here I follow Whitehead in arguing that language does have an extramental reference, but on the level of feeling in terms of causal efficacy rather than on the level of presentational immediacy in terms of perceptions or concepts. Hence, within the limits of what is immediately present to consciousness by way of perceptions or concepts, Saussure is correct in proposing that language is a self-enclosed system of signs without reference to extramental reality.

14. Cf. also on this point Pedraja, "Whitehead, Deconstruction and Postmodernism," in this volume.

15. "Thus the physical relations, the geometrical relations of measurement, the dimensional relations, and the various grades of extensive relations involved in the physical and geometrical theory of nature, are derivative from a series of societies [of actual occasions] of increasing width of prevalence, the more special societies being included in the wider societies" (PR, 92).

16. Cf., e. g., Derrida, "Conversation with Jacques Derrida," 6: "That is what deconstruction is made of: not the mixture but the tension between memory, fidelity, the preservation of something that has been given to us, and, at the same time, heterogeneity, something absolutely new, and a break."

17. Etienne Gilson, *The Unity of Philosophical Experience* (Westminster, MD: Four Courts Press, 1982), 306.

18. Cf. also Stephen T. Franklin, *Speaking from the Depths: Alfred North Whitehead's Hermeneutical Metaphysics of Propositions, Experience, Symbolism, Language and Religion* (Grand Rapids: Eerdmans, 1990), 27–29.

19. Cf. ibid., 245–246.

20. Cf. on this point Caputo's commentary on Derrida's style of writing: "So, if Derrida has a style, a signature, a dominant tone, a unity of purpose, if his works weave a certain fabric, it is up to someone else to trace that signature out later on, to countersign it for him. It is not his business and it would be stultifying for him to have to obey any such internal imperative, to censor himself, to pursue such an image, to abide by a contract that has been signed for him without his consent" (Caputo, *Deconstruction in a Nutshell,* 46). By the same token, of course, a systematization of Derrida's thought along the lines that I have suggested in this chapter is not out of place.

21. Derrida quotes from Heidegger (*Holzwege,* 6th ed. [Frankfurt am Main: V. Klostermann, 1980], 317–368; see also *Early Greek Thinking,* David Ferrell Krell and Frank A. Capuzzi, trans. [New York: Harper, 1975]): "However, the distinction between Being and beings, as something forgotten, can invade our experience only if it has already unveiled itself with the presencing of what is present *(mit dem Anwesen des Anwesenden); only if it has left a trace (eine Spur geprägt hat)* which remains preserved *(gewahrt bleibt)* in the language to which Being comes" (MP, 25).

22. This, of course, presumes that the cosmic process has an objective unity, that is, that it constitutes a universe rather than a number of loosely related "pockets of order" (cf. Robert C. Neville, *The High Road Around Modernism* [Albany: State University of New York Press, 1992], 119). In line with my field-oriented approach to Whiteheadian societies, I assume here that the physical universe even with its myriad subdivisions is a single all-comprehensive structured field of activity for the events taking place within it. Likewise, I presume that changes take place in the field as a result of these events instantaneously rather than simply at the speed of light as prescribed by Einstein's theories of special and general relativity. Hence, from moment to moment there is an objective state of affairs in the universe that has been effected by the subjective agencies of all actual occasions in existence up to that point. I recognize the controversial character of this presupposition. But, as far as I know, it has not been refuted by discoveries in the natural sciences; in fact, within the thought-world of quantum mechanics as a result of the empirical refutation of the Einstein-Podalsky-Rosen *Gedankenexperiment,* there have been cautious proposals along these same lines about the "nonlocality" of interrelated quantum-events separated from one another by a distance greater than the speed of light (cf. Ian Barbour, *Religion and Science: Historical and Contemporary Issues* [San Francisco: HarperCollins, 1997], 175–177).

23. "The 'subjective aim,' which controls the becoming of a subject, is that subject feeling a proposition with the subjective form of purpose to realize it in that process of self-creation" (PR, 25).

24. Charles Hartshorne, "The Compound Individual," in *Philosophical Essays for Alfred North Whitehead,* F. S. C. Northrup, ed. (New York: Russell and Russell, 1936), 193–210.

25. Cf., e.g., ibid., 218–220; likewise by the same author, *Man's Vision of God and the Logic of Theism* (Hamden, CT: Archon Books, 1964), 174–211.

26. Cf., e.g., Bracken, *Society and Spirit,* 140–160.

27. Anselm Kyonsuk Min has argued in a recent article that the proper metaphor, at least within a Christian context, for expressing the solidarity of individuals with one

another even as one likewise acknowledges their basic "otherness" to each other should be the scriptural term *Body of Christ*: cf. Min, "Solidarity of Others in the Body of Christ: A New Theological Paradigm," *Toronto Journal of Theology* 14 (1998), 239–254. While this might initially seem to be related to Hartshorne's notion of the world as the "body" of God, Min is careful to place the notion of the Body of Christ within an explicitly trinitarian context. As Min notes, "[t]he Holy Spirit creates, redeems and re-creates all things by bringing them together in Christ as the primordial model of the creature created in the image of God. If Christ is the model of solidarity, the Holy Spirit is the agent of solidarity, and God the source of solidarity" (250). In this way, Min moves away from the inevitable limitations of an organic model for the understanding of the God-world relationship toward the societal model advocated in this chapter.

5

Unconforming Becomings
The Significance of Whitehead's Novelty and Butler's Subversion for the Repetitions of Lesbian Identity and the Expansion of the Future

CHRISTINA K. HUTCHINS

In all the futures I have walked toward
I have seen a future I can hardly name.

—Muriel Rukeyser, *Body of Waking*

Vital then, that we widen the "I" that we are as much as we can. . . .

—Jeanette Winterson, *Art Objects*

*Inclusivity, Categorization, and the Discourse on
Gays and Lesbians in Churches and Society*

At the turn of the millennium in the United States, many Christian churches are theologically positioning themselves in relation to, or reaction against, various considerations of lesbian and gay lives in social and religious institutions. The wrenching emotional and ecclesial turmoil characterizing the debates suggests that far more than academic abstractions are at stake in the shiftings of cultural concepts of identity and the relational construction of the subject. Drawing on theoretical interactions of process and deconstructive postmodernisms, this chapter points to the importance of understanding identities as processes of becoming that can open novel possibilities for the future of Christianity and of humanity itself.

In the past decade, rifts have widened between those who believe that lesbians and gay men should be fully included in religious, social, and political life and those who oppose the full humanity and participation of "practicing" homosexuals.[1] An extreme of the latter position, the Religious Right, attempt simultaneously to regulate the heterosexual nuclear family *and* access to God and political power, by fixing the "naturalness" of heterosexuality onto a Christian identity defined in binary opposition to "homosexual" identity.[2] Yet even those who risk a great deal to work for the full inclusion of gays and lesbians, including many queer[3] people, often attempt to regulate terms of the debate in ways that can be understood as heteronormative (displayed, e.g., by the increasing focus on "gay marriage"); that is, they often "fix" the identity of lesbians and gay men in binary opposition to heterosexuality, citing the genetic, biological origin of same sex orientation, with the unwitting effect of reifying dominant cultural categories. By utilizing essentialist arguments in the debate surrounding lesbian and gay lives in religious and social institutions, do even progressive positions threaten to narrow social and sacred possibilities for our shared and open-ended future?

As a member of the United Church of Christ, a liberal denomination marked by a prominent and public stance of affirmation of gay and lesbian persons and relationships, I am both grateful for, and troubled by, the terms of discourse surrounding the inclusion of gay, lesbian, bisexual, and transgendered persons in church and society. I am grateful, because as an "out" lesbian and an ordained minister, I can inhabit a still-too-rare space of voice, visibility, and community. I am troubled, however, because positions of inclusivity increasingly rely on essentialist arguments and heteronormative constructions of social and religious acceptability.[4]

Essentialist arguments depend upon and reify an ontology based on the metaphysics of substance as the hermeneutical lens for interpreting human identity. Therefore they reinforce the Cartesian subject/object split and the subsequent binary oppositions of "self" and "other," exemplified by the sentence, "I am _____ because I am not _____." Such binary oppositions inevitably fund culturally oppressive dualisms, since even nonhegemonic identities are implicated in, enforced, and created by the same repressive regimes that they may be seeking to resist. In other words, when the second blank space in this sentence is occupied by a hegemonic identifier such as "white, man, straight, wealthy, physically able, or Christian," the first blank space becomes dependent upon its opposition to the second for its own self-definition. In such a way, nonhegemonic identities may be understood not as essential differences, but as cultural constructions, which even when used in resistant ways, may continue to reify hegemonic powers of definition and binary categorization, reinforcing the universalizing tendencies of dominant positions. Thus, essentialist positions, utilized by those arguing for greater inclusion of lesbians and gay men in churches, however progressive in comparison with the overt exclusion of the Religious Right, do not escape the heteronormatively privileged straight/gay binarism. Such binary oppositions limit the possibilities of the future and replace the concrete reality of the complexities and dynamisms of human relationships with abstracted categories constructed as dualistic opposites. The naturalization of cultural categories, the placing of man/woman and gay/straight as *opposites* becomes one characteristic of what Judith Butler calls the "fiction of compulsory heterosexuality." For Alfred North Whitehead, such a substitution or act of mistaking of abstract categories of thought and social construction for the relational dynamisms of actuality commits the gravest of philosophical errors, the "fallacy of misplaced concreteness."[5] The immensity of the error cannot be underestimated, because when we believe that the categories have more concrete reality than the creative motion of actuality, we narrow the possibilities of and for the future. To mistake constructed categories, such as the heteronormatively privileged straight/gay binarism in church conversations on lesbian and gay inclusion, for actuality or "nature," limits the freedom and power of love that Christianity claims as its raison d'être and narrows the possibilities for future human relationships in general.

This chapter explores identity understood as ongoing, creative process(es) in which "the subject" always exists only in relation to, and as a result or effect of, the event of her own becoming, an event that is at once *both* freely shaped by the becoming subject *and* limited, formed, and deformed by its context. In order to personalize and concretize an otherwise abstract exploration, I offer an example of a recent denominational gathering in which, as a participant, I found myself wondering what it means to "be" a lesbian, a question that problematizes issues of representation, identity, and categorization that are often obscured in the debate surrounding lesbian and gay lives in religious and social institutions. After a brief extension of categorization and identity politics into the more philosophical questions of essence and ontology, the essay proceeds by way of an active juxtaposition of ideas from the process metaphysics of Whitehead[6] with insights of Butler on performativity and the fluid, always-in-process, iterating subject.[7] I analyze the relationships between repetition and novelty (Whitehead) and repetition and subversive resignification (Butler) and conclude by addressing the political effectiveness and religious significance of the dynamic insights generated by the interplay of Butler's and Whitehead's thought. My thesis is that an emphasis on the "unconformity" (nonconformity + unconventionality) by which the repetitions of lesbian identity are performed destabilizes the very institutions and cultural categories in and by which that identity is shaped. Such destabilizations open and broaden the public space for future becomings, expansions that carry religious significance, as does the manner in which such destabilizations act as lures for increasing the experiential richness, dynamism, and intensity of human existence.

Some Discursive Problems with Representation, Identity, and Categorization

One sunny Saturday morning in May of 1997, members of the United Church of Christ (UCC) in northern California entered into deliberate conversation about multiculturalism and identity in the UCC and in our wider society. Each participant had been carefully selected to represent a particular identity group.[8] I was asked to "be" the "lesbian."

I had agreed to be present, but nonetheless remained uncomfortable at being asked to *represent* "lesbians" as an identity group and at how that act necessarily would exclude from view or voice those who may not live out or understand that identity as I do. Any attempt to speak *for* lesbians carries in it an assumption that there is some essential character that we commonly share. I was aware of my own privilege in being a part of the conversation and of a heavy and impossible responsibility to those not present.[9] I was also disturbed at the idea of fixing *my own identity* in a primary way to the category of "lesbian." Not only has my own sexuality been fluidly expressed in a variety of ways over my lifetime, but by naming myself within the category of "lesbian," I was defining myself *as a fixed identity* (and perhaps a rather reductively sexualized identity), rather than as a subject *in ongoing, multiple processes of becoming.* In addition, the fixed identity of "lesbian" is a category that has been named and projected with attributes and values by the hegemonic position of compulsory heterosexuality in the discourse of our culture and religious traditions. While the planners of the multicultural discussions had some sensitivity to issues of race, sexual orientation, and other "isms," the fact was that while there were a designated "gay" and "lesbian," there was no "heterosexual" representative. All other participants of various ethnic and social categories were presumed to be heterosexual,[10] an unexamined operation of heteronormativity in which gay men and lesbians were being defined as "Other." By using the category, lesbian, how would I be allowing that category, and thus the dominant view or hegemonic norm, to define me? By doing so, would I be actively reinforcing the binary terms of the dominant discourse? How would I be affecting and perhaps foreclosing relational possibilities in, for, and of the future?

Each participant was asked to state in a single sentence the most important gift that our "identity group" brings to the wider gathering of the United Church of Christ. When my turn came, I said, "My name is Christina Hutchins, and I was asked to participate as a lesbian." As soon as the word *lesbian* was pronounced, I noticed an instant hush in the room, a kind of snapping into a deeper listening. That word certainly claims people's attention. Feeling that tiny and vast pause, I tried to discern what might be the most politically effective and religiously significant response to the question that we'd been asked. I actually ended up voicing *two* gifts that I think lesbians particularly bring to the larger church: (1) an insistence on an embodied faith;[11] and (2) a sense that identities are culturally constructed rather than natural, fluid rather than fixed or given, and that the categories themselves and acts of categorization, while often helpful, are also restrictive. The remainder of this chapter is an expansion of the second statement: that the *destabilization* of identity categories is a gift that lesbians[12] bring to the wider church.

Essentialism and Ontology

Questions and concerns about identity, inclusion, exclusion, subjectivity, representation, and categorization are relevant to dilemmas surrounding what it means to be a representative subject. When we make "I am" statements, such as "I am a woman," "I am a lesbian," "I am a feminist" or "I am a Euro-American" (an identifier which, by the way, is usually used as an adjective rather than as a substantive noun like "lesbian"), we are usually making particular claims, not only about what categories we "belong to," but also about what it means to *essentially be* who we are. To begin to question one's identity categories also initiates a critique of one's *essentialism* and one's *ontology*. Essentialism is the notion that one has or can be primarily defined by a central characteristic or "core" shared with all others "within" a category, such that I might have a shared "essence" as a woman, a white person, a lesbian, or even as a human being.[13] *Ontology* involves the underlying way(s) in which culture defines what it means "to be" or to exist as a human being.

While drawing on a supposed common "essence" has often been useful for feminists and for gay men and lesbians in particular political contexts, including many church contexts, it is important to ask what (and *who*) such essentialism obscures, invisibilizes, and excludes. When a person is asked to define herself by a single, defined category, such as "lesbian," in the situation above, she is being asked to choose *between* parts of herself, to claim that one identifying characteristic or behavior, such as sexual orientation, is more *essential* to her being than another, such as race, age, class, income, or educational level.[14]

The feminist theorist Jane Flax points out a different problematic face of essentialism: "Man and woman are posited as exclusionary categories. One can be only one gender, never the other or both. . . ." Likewise, categories of sexuality are oppositionally defined, creating a problem not only for bisexuals but in and for the freedom of expression of sexual desire in general. Flax continues: "gender relations have been (more) defined and (imperfectly) controlled by one of their interrelated aspects—the man."[15] Not only is "woman" set in essential opposition to "man," and "homosexual" defined only in mutual oppositional relation to "heterosexual," but the exact nature of the oppositions and the various facets of the "essential nature" of "woman" or "homosexual" have been constructed in service of more or less conscious purposes of domination.[16]

Often either "God" or "nature" (or both, as is the case with some religious conservatives) are named as authorities in the definitive act of essentialist claims. In secular and political arenas, many thinkers, as well as our mass media, draw upon "nature" in the form of biological and/or psychological theories of origin/archetypes to justify definitions of essentialism. The historian Thomas Laqueur describes well our current two-sex model undergirded by a widespread biological essentialism of "hormones and other chemicals that are meant to serve as a sort of ontological granite for observable sexual differences."[17] In broad-based political discussions of gay/lesbian identities, whenever questions of "the cause" of homosexual behaviors come up (questions that are themselves hegemonically generated), it is amazing how much more "accepting" many people *seem* if they can be assured that such behaviors result from genetically determined, biological essentialism, rather than from an indeterminate number of factors, including free choice and cultural construction. While often politically useful, the reliance on biology in justifying homosexual behaviors omits so much of what it is to be queer: layers of history carried in/on the body, freedoms to relate sexually and otherwise in noncoercive ways as one *chooses* and finds joy and satisfaction in a relationship.[18] Is it possible that we are constraining ourselves *politically* and *religiously,* as well as personally, by allowing acceptance to revolve around biological essentialism rather than a more creative way of being human? Is it possible that by utilizing essentialist arguments we are narrowing social and sacred possibilities, doing irreparable damage to our shared and open-ended future?

Teresa de Lauretis offers several helpful definitions of "essence": "1. Absolute being, substance in the metaphysical sense; the reality underlying phenomena. 2. That which constitutes the being of a thing, that 'by which it is what it is' . . . Objective character, intrinsic nature as a 'thing-in-itself.'"[19] She reminds us that questions of essentialism are related to those of ontology and the metaphysically fixed subject. In fact, it is through philosophical questions and critiques of ontology that the problematic limitations of essentialism may be most profoundly and clearly addressed. Most modern philosophies, ethical theories, and theologies have assumed an ontologically fixed subject as a starting point for philosophical thought, human agency, and divine relation: a "doer" precedes her (actually, it's usually *his*) deeds and processes of relation. Certainly, the UCC leadership who set up the categories at the denominational multicultural event I attended, assumed that the "selves" who *fit* into a particular *identity group* would do so from basically fixed subject positions. However, with deconstruction, the "fixed" or "foundational" nature of the choosing subject loses its authority as an automatic assumption or starting place for thought or action. In fact, the "subject" falls to pieces; the "subject" becomes *subjectivity,* a shifting, fully contextualized, nonunified perspective inseparably related to its world. Chris Weedon expresses this shift quite clearly:

> Subjectivity is produced in a whole range of discursive practices—economic, social and political—the meanings of which are a constant site of struggle over power. . . . Moreover for poststructuralism, subjectivity is neither unified nor fixed. Unlike humanism, which implies a conscious, knowing, unified, rational subject, poststructuralism theorizes subjectivity as a site of disunity and conflict, central to the process of political change and to preserving the status quo.[20]

In other words, "being" a subject no longer exists; rather, one is always in the act of "becoming" a subject: subjectivity is a process. "Against [the] irreducible humanist essence of subjectivity, poststructuralism proposes a subjectivity which is precarious, contradictory and in process, constantly being reconstituted in discourse each time we think or speak."[21] Whitehead and Butler each offer philosophical insights that reach toward a nonessentialist subjectivity. In the sections that follow, their approaches are analyzed in terms of politically and religiously significant insights for reconstituting discourse and opening a relational future less constricted by the fixing grip of normative categories defined and regulated by the status quo.

Metaphysics and Deconstruction; Universals and Antifoundational Thought

Bringing Butler and Whitehead together itself suggests a fairly unconventional academic practice. Butler is widely recognized as representing the contemporary deconstructive "edge," her work informed in primary ways by Friedrich Nietzsche, Jacques Derrida, Michel Foucault, and the poststructuralist unfastenings of the rational, universalizing foundations of modernist discourse. Whitehead, on the other hand, the author of the 1928 *Process and Reality,* is often understood primarily as having created a "metaphysics," a massive construction that attempts rationally and universally to account for experience through systematic claims. However, this difference between the two may not mark as wide a gap between them as an oversimplification of each of their positions might make it appear. In the sections that follow, in addition to enhancing the reach of both thinkers in relation to the social and religious significance of fluid subjectivities, I hope to demonstrate some general affinities between poststructuralist claims and process thought. While I propose neither to *apply* the entire metatheory of process metaphysics to Butler's thought, nor to comprehensively *critique* process thought using the work of Butler, I do want to utilize places of overlap or affinity between the two. Therefore, the tensions or contrasts between Whitehead's metaphysics and Butler's deconstructive antifoundationalism warrant a brief examination.

Whitehead's development of process thought (or "philosophy of organism," as he called it) in many ways qualifies as a metaphysics, based as it is in part on observations of post-Newtonian physics: the basic notion that what *seems to be* substantive matter can be understood as dynamic interplays of energy. Though Whitehead's philosophy does attempt to explain the totality of the universe through the notion of creative acts of becoming, it also understands itself as historically generated and conditioned. For Whitehead and other process philosophers, the cosmos is composed of open-ended, plural processes, as is, necessarily, the *ongoing* philosophical task. Whitehead writes, "In philosophical discourse, the merest hint of dogmatic certainty as to finality of statement is an exhibition of folly" (PR, xiv). This whimsical admission of uncertainty, along with Whitehead's methodological commitment to begin and end each philosophical thinking-act in the particularities of experience, loosens up much of what might otherwise now be read as an oppressive metatheory. Not only is there nothing absolute in his claims,[22] but "hermeneutical scheme" might be a better phrase than "metaphysics" for characterizing Whitehead's attempt to provide "generic notions that add lucidity to our apprehension of the facts of experience" and a frame of "general ideas in terms of which every element of our experience can be interpreted" (PR, 10, 3).[23] In fact, what Whitehead calls "metaphysics" "is nothing but the description of the generalities which apply to the details of practice" (PR, 13).

In addition, the concern and content of Whitehead's endeavor is a deliberate departure from the metaphysics that so much postmodern thought also attempts to abandon. Poststructuralist and process critiques of "metaphysics" share the distinction of aiming their reformulations primarily at the metaphysics of *substance*. Butler, for instance, describes her task in *Gender Trouble* as "the challenge for rethinking gender categories outside of the metaphysics of substance" (GT, 25). Likewise, when Foucault, whose genealogical method Butler takes up and expands, distances himself from "metaphysics," he attacks the same metaphysical system that Whitehead is concerned with unhinging: the metaphysics of substance, which limits itself to singular origins and linear relations of cause and effect: "If interpretation were the slow exposure of the meaning hidden in *an* origin, then only metaphysics could interpret the development of humanity. . . . The development of humanity is [instead] a series of interpretations. . . . They must be made to appear as events on the stage of historical process."[24] In outlining the role of genealogy, Foucault describes a method and worldview that resonate in many ways with a process-oriented metaphysics. In fact, Whitehead's project can be understood as a motion from a substance-oriented metaphysics, with its Cartesian subject/object split and singular cause and effect relations, to a more postmodern worldview, an interrogation of *how* "interpretations . . . appear as events on the stage of . . . process."

Butler's clear developments and extensions of poststructuralist figurings of identities as constellations of multiple and unstable positions create potential tensions with Whitehead's stretch toward metaphysical universalization. However, while Butler explicitly distances herself from any task "which would articulate a comprehensive universality," she does not undo the category of "the universal" altogether. Perhaps because realities *are* shaped and constrained by foundationalist claims, which attempt to totalize and thus "shut down rather than authorize . . . unanticipated claims," she understands "the universal" as a category that must be left "permanently open, permanently contested, permanently contingent, in order not to foreclose in advance future claims for inclusion" (CF, 8).[25] Because the primary universal in Whitehead's metaphysics is "creativity," which by definition is open-ended, plural, and unfixed, as well as always contingent and conditioned, it is interesting to place Whitehead's "universal," the "principle of *novelty*" (PR, 21),[26] in direct conversation with Butler's urgent stance that the very category of the "universal" must be "a site of insistent contest and resignification" (CF, 7). While Butler hopes that her work has "no normative ground," she does admit to a "normative direction," a motion of expanding and complexifying the views of what categorical identities might be, "without filling in the content of what that's going to be" (GP, 125).

In terms of "the universal," she writes, "I am not trying to do away with the category, but trying to relieve the category of its foundationalist weight in order to render it as a site of permanent political contest" (CF, 8).[27] In order to do so, she suggests that we "pursue the moments of degrounding, when we're standing in two different places at once; or we don't know exactly where we're standing; or when we've produced an aesthetic practice that shakes the ground. That's when resistance to recuperation happens" (GP, 122). Thus, Butler's antifoundationalism occurs in her unwillingness to fix, purify, or totalize the meaning or content of a particular category in comprehensive ways, which would foreclose future possibilities. She is not saying, however, as her detractors often claim, that *there are no* foundations; rather, she claims "that wherever there is one, there will also be a foundering, a contestation" (CF, 16). For those parts of each of us and of our social relations existing "outside" of hegemonic norms, such founderings and contestations are a way of life, a survival mechanism. I suggest that such contestations also expand future human relational possibilities, in general, and that such dynamic expansions are motions of the holy.

In exploring lesbian identity as (an) ongoing process(es) of becoming in the sections that follow, I hope to convey a sense of motion which Butler and Whitehead each reach toward but have difficulty expressing in a grammar that is still based on a metaphysics of substance. The notion of "becoming" is an apt point of linkage between the two thinkers. Not only does it refer back to Nietzsche's metaphor of becoming,[28] which both thinkers invoke, but "becoming" carries an inarticulable sense of motion, of the possibilities of an unknown future.

Whitehead: Process Thought

Whitehead's philosophy of organism is perhaps most succinctly expressed by Whitehead in the statement, "Process is the becoming of experience" (PR, 166). Whitehead, along with certain other American philosophers, for example, Charles S. Peirce, William James, John Dewey, and Charles Hartshorne, attempted to develop a philosophy, cosmology, or hermeneutical system that would begin not with transcendental reason, but with the dynamism of experience and a view of reality as social process.[29]

Process thought reconceives of matter as process, act, or event. "Actual entities," which are also called "actual occasions," "are the final real things of which the world is made up. There is no going behind actual entities to find anything more real" (PR, 18). Actual entities are events, or moments of "concrescence," of the *becoming* of a "subject." They are atomistic becomings, blips, noncontinuous moments, drops of existence, and they "perish" as soon as they have fully "prehended" their universe. Prehension involves an occasion's taking into its "becoming," by the act of valuing either positively or negatively, the contents of its context, the past occasions, and then integrating the felt content of that context (those occasions) into the shape of its own becoming. A "prehension . . . involves emotion, and purpose, and valuation, and causation" (PR, 19) so that the "becoming" of a moment of subjectivity is a moment of *feeling* every other entity in its universe. Process thought can be understood as a metaphysic of feeling, of felt valuation, a hermeneutic both aesthetic and ethical, because acts of prehension are decisions, never neutral, always involving value judgments of inclusion and exclusion. In this way, all events, or actual occasions, are self-creative, though our language is problematic, since that "self" is only apparent in the event itself.[30] "*How* an actual entity becomes determines *what* that actual entity *is* . . . Its 'being' is constituted by its 'becoming.' This is the 'principle of process'" (PR, 23).

This process is always "atomistic": the act of becoming is also an act of perishing. Since "'becoming' is the transformation of incoherence into coherence, and in each particular instance ceases with this attainment" (PR, 25), existence is discontinuous. The observed world has a more or less seeming continuity or coherence only because there is a constant unfolding of infinite acts of self-determination. This self-creative process is shared, in Whitehead's view, by the tiniest atoms and subatomic energy particles, stars, galaxies, trees, God, rocks, and humans. In the case of humans and rocks (and, for Whitehead, God), there are "real individual facts of the togetherness of actual entities, which are real, individual and particular. . . . Any such particular fact of togetherness among actual entities is called a 'nexus'" (PR, 20). When such a nexus is related temporally, that is, "forms a single line of inheritance of its defining characteristic," it is called an "enduring object." It "enjoys a personal order" and is a "society" (PR, 34).[31] Every human embodies or conjoins a complex "society" or "nexus" composed of countless, multiple becomings, related both temporally and spatially. As humans we can say that we *are* or *have* consciousness, corporate feelings, a body. We *become* bodily, both unconsciously and consciously: "It is by reason of the body, with its miracle of order, that the treasures of the past environment are poured into the living occasion. . . . It receives from the past; it lives in the present" (PR, 339).

Repetition plays a crucial role in process thought. Enduring objects result from multiple repetitions of occasions that occur with more or less exactness or variety. For a rock or a table, fewer and smaller variations happen in and between repeated acts of becoming than for a living tree or a human woman. Repetition acts as a means by which feelings are intensified to the point of physical sensations and consciousness. The body concentrates the past, moving related past occasions toward consciousness. "Intensity," which Whitehead believes characterizes the direction into which the universe (*multiverse* might be a more accurate term) is increasing and moving, arises "from the force of repetition" (PR, 253). When repetitions occur with a sense of what Whitehead calls "width," which is both an aesthetic and ethical term for positively prehending with greater depth, breadth, and clarity the possible contrasts in any particular act of becoming, greater complexity and intensity are expressed in the acts of becoming. The responsibility of *how* we become, of determining *who* we become, moment by moment, is ethically and aesthetically informed by how deeply and clearly we feel the complexities, the contrasts of the contexts or universe that surround and enter into those becomings. "The savouring of the complexity of the universe can enter into satisfaction only through the dimension of width . . . the function of width is to deepen the ocean of feeling" (PR, 166).[32] Increases in complexity and intensity of acts of becoming open more possibilities for future becomings.

And yet, though concrescence, or becoming, is a self-creative act, in that it carries the responsibility for how and therefore what/who it becomes, "the character of an actual entity is governed by its datum" (PR, 110). We are limited, constrained in the repetitions of our becoming by what Whitehead calls "stubborn fact." Thus, process thought simultaneously develops *both* a kind of artistic freedom for the creative play of self-shaping of the becoming subject *and* a kind of determinism, a sense of limitation—inscribed upon and into the act of becoming—by the reality of that which already exists.

In terms of the problems raised by categorically defined identities, Whitehead effectively addressed some of the issues of essentialism and fixed ontology by positing, like poststructuralist views half a century later, a subjectivity in process. Whitehead writes, "The philosophies of substance presuppose a subject which then encounters a datum, and then reacts to the datum. The philosophy of organism presupposes a datum which is met with feelings, and progressively attains the unity of a subject. But with this doctrine, 'superject' would be a better term than subject" (PR, 155). "Subject," because it implies stasis, or something fixed, is problematic for Whitehead. By using "superject" he conveys the motion of efficient causation: the completed and perished "becoming" of one "subject" affects subsequent "becomings." The "subject" is always a subject arising out of the process of prehending its past, its context, *and,* having perished, affecting other, future processes of becoming by being prehended by those concrescing others.

Performativity and the Deconstruction of Fixed Identity

Butler begins her article "Imitation and Gender Insubordination" with a complaint that "being" is too fixed of a category for her comfort. She writes, "[t]he prospect of *being* anything, even for pay [she has a great sense of humor], has always produced in me a certain anxiety, for 'to be' gay, 'to be' lesbian seems to be more than a simple injunction to become who or what I already am" (IGI, 13). Part of the discomfort comes in the realization that "identity categories tend to be instruments of regulatory regimes," such that Butler says she is "permanently troubled by identity categories, consider[s] them to be invariable stumbling-blocks, and understand[s] them, even promote[s] them as sites of necessary trouble" (IGI, 13, 14). She would like it to remain "permanently unclear" precisely what is being signified by a sign that says "Lesbian" under which she is willing to stand at a political occasion. In addition, she claims that "pleasure" is produced for her by the instability of the category.

For Butler, what we experience are performative moments of identity, which share some affinities with Whitehead's actual occasions. She writes playfully about being invited to a public speaking event *as* a lesbian:

> When and where does my being a lesbian come into play, when and where does this playing a lesbian constitute something like what I am? To say that I "play" at being one is not to say that I am not one "really"; rather, how and where I play at being one is the way in which that "being" gets established, instituted, circulated, confirmed. This is not a performance from which I can take radical distance, for this is deepseated play, psychically entrenched play, *and this "I" does not play its lesbianism as a role.* Rather it is through the repeated play of this sexuality that the "I" is insistently reconstituted as a lesbian "I." . . . (IGI, 18)

There are several key ideas packed into this description. First of all, identity is *performative,* which for Butler means "constituting the identity it is purported to be. In this sense, gender [and sexual orientation] is always a doing, though not a doing by a subject who might be said to preexist the deed" (GT, 25). Thus, when Butler "plays at being lesbian," this play constitutes the *reality* of her being lesbian. She is always becoming. This is serious play, because it determines not only *who* she is and will become, but affects the future possibilities of the cultural discourse in which it takes place. She plays "with" and "in" the mechanisms or motions by which categorical identity is established, instituted, and circumscribed. Cultural discourse takes place not only—or even primarily—*within* her, but by her act of playing with/out the ways in which she is externally, culturally inscribed. Butler continues by exploring this "play" as a process of repetition:

> paradoxically, it is precisely the *repetition* of that play that establishes so well the *instability* of the very category that it constitutes. For if the "I" is a site of repetition, that is, if the "I" only achieves the semblance of identity through a certain repetition of itself, then the "I" is always displaced by the very repetition that sustains it. In other words, does or can the "I" ever repeat itself, cite itself, faithfully, or is there always a displacement from its former moment that establishes the permanently non-self-identical status of that "I" or its "being lesbian"? (IGI, 18)

Any sense of a "stable" identity results from, is an effect of repetition, as is the "instability" of the category itself. *Becoming* involves *repetition,* because each performative instance is both discrete, displacing the "former moment," and delimited, shaped by, and inseparably related to that former moment and to the constraints that preceded and shaped its relation with its context. *Citation* is the act of this repetition within the relational dynamism of the process, and because of the dynamism, repetitions never happen with exact uniformity or sameness. In *Bodies that Matter,* Butler writes, "let us remember that reiterations are never simply replicas of the same" (BTM, 226). The sense that an identity, such as that of lesbian or woman, is fixed, stable, *like* an essence, comes about through the "sedimentation" of these repetitions over time within particular power dynamics. "The process of that sedimentation or what we might call *materialization* will be a kind of citationality, the acquisition of being through the citing of power, a citing that establishes an originary complicity with power in the formation of the 'I'" (BTM, 15). This means that while Butler retains and amplifies deconstruction's critique of essentialism, she also opens a way of understanding and still being able to speak from subject positions: We can say "I am a woman" or "I am a lesbian." The idea of sedimentation allows for the feelings and intimations we experience *as* essences, norms, and continuities within hegemonic culture. Without sacrificing the iterated dynamism of performativity, sedimentation allows us to talk about and form experienced categorical identities without drawing on a metaphysics of substance that philosophically naturalizes those identities as essences. Identity can be understood as provisional, as culturally constituted and constrained, and an identity category can be viewed as a repeated site of relational dynamism:

> The repetition of one's subjectivity is not a choice. Nor can it be stopped: The subject is not *determined* by the rules through which it is generated because signification is *not a founding act, but rather a regulatory process of repetition* that both conceals itself and enforces its rules precisely through the production of substantializing effects. In a sense, all signification takes place within the orbit of the compulsion to repeat: 'agency,' then, is to be located within the possibility of a variation on that repetition. (GT, 145)

Not unlike process thought, both the inevitability of the repetition and the limitations of the datum, "stubborn fact" for Whitehead or "rules of signification" for Butler, confine the possibilities of becoming. However, there is still the notion that *how* one becomes affects *what* and *who* one becomes and the wider future of discourse itself. To be constituted by discourse is not necessarily to be determined by discourse. Though inscription is relational and societal, and though iteration happens under and through the force of prohibitions, there is nonetheless a self-creativity or agency possible *in the activity of varying the repetitions.*

Butler focuses this creativity of variation in and through the example of "drag." In the inevitable process of repetition, compulsory heterosexuality has set itself up as an "original way of being" or "the essence of identity," a regulatory norm that is to be copied moment by moment and generation by generation. Butler calls it "the regulatory fiction of heterosexual coherence" because it is a "fabrication manufactured and sustained through corporeal signs [like clothing and bodily gestures] and other discursive means,"[33] and is widely believed to be the only "coherent" way to put a life together. By performing "drag," a lesbian, gay, or transgendered person not only replicates the culturally constructed heterosexual compulsory repetition in a way that parodies those constructs, but s/he also *resignifies* those constructs, becoming a *de-instituting* repetition. By bringing "into relief the utterly constructed status of the so-called original," the resignification of drag shows that "heterosexuality only constitutes itself as the original through a convincing act of repetition. The more 'act' is expropriated, the more the heterosexual claim to originality is exposed as illusory" (GT, 31). Parody becomes a strategy of resistance;[34] drag—playing between or with "mismatches" of gender—becomes a practice that in imitating gender implicitly reveals the imitative structure of gender itself and draws attention to those processes that consolidate identities. In other words,

> drag enacts the very structure of impersonation by which *any gender* is assumed. Drag is not the putting on of a gender that belongs properly to

some other group. . . . Drag constitutes the mundane way in which genders are appropriated, theatricalized, worn, and done; it implies that all
gendering is a kind of impersonation and approximation. If this is true,
there is no original or primary gender that drag imitates, but *gender is a
kind of imitation for which there is no original.* (IGI, 21)[35]

For Butler, subjectivity *is* performative. Identity and identity categories
are neither essential nor fixed, nor the outcome of some inner substance of
who we are, waiting for fulfillment. Rather, identity is formed *in moment by
moment activity,* an activity that requires and creates/constructs a body and is
sedimented through time.[36] In the introduction to *Bodies that Matter,* Butler
claims that a part of her project is

> a rethinking of the process by which a bodily norm is assumed, appro-
> priated, taken on as not, strictly speaking, undergone *by a subject,* but
> rather that the subject, the speaking "I," is formed by virtue of having
> gone through such a process of assuming a sex; and a linking of this
> process of "assuming" a sex with the question of *identification,* and
> with the discursive means by which the heterosexual imperative enables
> certain sexed identifications and forecloses and/or disavows other iden-
> tifications. (BTM, 3)

To the extent that she has found a way to understand the "subject" as constituted or occasioned by the performative process, and the subject's particular
cultural "identity" as an effect or occasion of that process, Butler offers a
wonderful tool for deconstructing identities as belonging to fixed categories.
The object is not to do away with categories or coalitions all together, but to
understand them as *permanently unfixed, open sites of becoming and cultural
valuation,* where individuals and culture itself are constantly reified, redefined, and redefining. In Butler's words,

> The antifoundationalist approach to coalitional politics assumes neither
> that "identity" is a premise nor that the shape or meaning of a coalitional
> assemblage can be known prior to its achievement. Because the articu-
> lation of an identity within available cultural terms instates a definition
> that forecloses in advance the emergence of new identity concepts in
> and through politically engaged actions, the foundationalist tactic can-
> not take the transformation or expansion of existing identity concepts as
> a normative goal. (GT, 15)[37]

In addition, Butler hints that lesbians, in particular, inhabit a unique site
within cultural discourse. Because lesbians experience oppression partly
through being considered "a domain of unviable (un)subjects—*abjects,* we
might call them—who are neither named nor prohibited within the economy

of the law," who inhabit a "domain of unthinkability and unnameability," we perhaps embody or perform unique possibilities for rendering ourselves "visible" beyond "existing regulatory regimes. . . . Lesbianism is not explicitly prohibited in part because it has not even fully made its way into the thinkable, the imaginable, that grid of cultural intelligibility that regulates the real and the nameable. How, then, to 'be' a lesbian in a political context in which the lesbian does not exist?" (IGI, 20).[38] Though Butler's 1988 suggestion that the lesbian does not exist may not now be quite so uncontested (after "Ellen" has come out on prime-time TV and all), I think it is still relevant. Her further question, "Can the exclusion from ontology itself become a rallying point for resistance?" (IGI, 20)[39] remains with me as a very hopeful possibility. Butler's question suggests that an exclusion from cultural intelligibility may also involve an exclusion from the tyranny of the fixed subject and, thus, from the metaphysics of substance. Each day people throughout the world are killed and kill each other in the name of identity politics. How might our visions, parameters, and worldviews shape human relations if we based those visions and worldviews not on fixed subject positions and identities, but on the creative and fluid acts of multiple becomings? How do we imagine, discover, and perform such politics, ethics, and theologies into existence? How might insights drawn from nonfixed identity subjectivities move into our existing, identity-based habits of relating, thinking, and believing, in ways that heal and liberate human relations in academic institutions, in the broad social institutions of media and government, and in the various religious organizations we rely upon to emancipate and vivify our lives?

The Importance of Repetition
and of "Resignification" or "Novelty"

Though the two projects differ in purpose, method, and proposed scope, I believe that Judith Butler's well-nuanced development of social identities as effects of hegemonic discourse displays several shared affinities with Alfred North Whitehead's process thought. Both share a sense of a fluid, creative subjectivity that shapes and is shaped by the activity of becoming a "subject" in relation with the confines of the repetitions of the "subject's" context or past reality. These dynamic models abandon the metaphysics of substance in order to understand matter itself as a process,[40] and to characterize the "subject" as an *effect* of performativity (Butler) or as a concrescent *event* (Whitehead).

Each mode of thought also develops both complex, nondualistic relations between the reality of being conditioned and constrained by the world (discourse or datum) that is inescapably inscribed into/onto our becoming *and* the agency of the self- and future-creating activity of performance or concrescence. In Whitehead's philosophy, which involves not only cultural inscription, but the inscription of the entire universe, each actual occasion is both determined ("the datum both limits and supplies" [PR, 110]) and free ("each concrescence is to be referred to a definite free initiation and a definite free conclusion" [PR, 47]). Butler, too, unhinges the oppositional "either/or" between agency and cultural constructedness and constraint. Near the end of *Gender Trouble,* she writes, "the feminist discourse on cultural construction remains trapped within the unnecessary binarism of free will and determinism. Construction is not opposed to agency; it is the necessary scene of agency, the very terms in which agency is articulated and becomes culturally intelligible" (GT, 147).[41] For Butler, the fluidity of subjectivity means that we simultaneously and inseparably are *interpolated into* systems that preexist us (a notion she uses from Foucault) *and* we have to actively *become* moment by moment, reminiscent of Simone de Beauvoir's notion of becoming a woman: "One is not born a woman, but rather becomes one."[42]

The necessary, inescapable repetition of becoming, for both Whitehead and Butler, carries in itself hope of and for the future, because repetition is the way in which *novelty* (Whitehead) or *subversive resignification* (Butler) can enter into the ongoing processes of discourse in the world. Butler writes,

> for if the performance is "repeated," there is always the question of what differentiates from each other the moments of identity that are repeated. And if the "I" is the effect of a certain repetition, one which produces the semblance of a continuity or coherence, then there is no "I" that precedes the gender that it is said to perform; the repetition, and the failure to repeat, produce a string of performances that constitute and contest the coherence of that "I." (IGI, 18)[43]

For Butler, it is the "string of performances" that both "constitute and contest the coherence" of the subject that creates a space for the creative activity of subversively resignifying the self and the categories of discourse themselves. This is perhaps the clearest and most vivid and crucial of the affinities between Butler and Whitehead. Whitehead writes,

> Thus an enduring object gains the enhanced intensity of feeling arising from contrast between inheritance and novel effect, and also gains the enhanced intensity arising from the combined inheritance of its stable rhythmic character through-out its life-history. It has the weight of repetition, the intensity of contrast, and the balance between the two factors of the contrast. (PR, 279)[44]

For Whitehead, the experience of the contrast between inheritance and novelty, or using Butler's words, between constituting and contesting the coherence of the enduring "I," is "an intense experience of aesthetic fact" (PR,

279). The experienced contrasts increase the intensity of experience, and are thus *aesthetically and ethically* valuable: "All aesthetic experience is feeling arising out of the realization of contrast under identity" (PR, 280). I find this insight of Whitehead's returning me to Butler's sense of the trouble and the pleasure of working with and from identity categories. "In fact if the category [of lesbian] were to offer no trouble, it would cease to be interesting: it is precisely the *pleasure* produced by the instability of those categories which sustains the various erotic practices that make me a candidate for the category [of lesbian] to begin with" (IGI, 14). Identity categories, then, can be sites in which to experience the *intensity* of feeling and the aesthetic *pleasure* of creating ways of subverting those very categories. Finally, in the dance between the two, Butler's Foucaultian invocation of the *pleasure* of troubling categories turns toward the esteemed place *enjoyment* holds in Whitehead's endeavor. Becoming itself is enjoyment.[45] And particular enjoyment floods from the prospect of broadening future relational possibilities through the realization of increased contrasts in one's present becoming. "The function of being a means is not disjoined from the function of being an end. The sense of worth beyond itself is immediately enjoyed as an overpowering element in the individual self-attainment" (PR, 350).[46]

For both Whitehead and Butler, the deep-seated play of contrasts is both aesthetically pleasurable, a felt enjoyment of efficient causation (Whitehead), and an ethical responsibility. The future opens outward: its possibilities and its limitations open out from the playful juxtaposition of contrasts and affinities in the becoming of the present moment. In a sense, for both thinkers, we live both for and into ourselves, and at the same time, for and into an undetermined future where the activity of our becoming will deeply and irrevocably affect the possibilities of future becomings. The actions of our performativity *matter.* They have no purely private meaning or value, but extensively effect and affect one anothers' futures.

The past flows into the present through the becoming occasion from which particular future possibilities will be rendered. Whitehead calls this effective motion "creativity." It is *the* "universal" in his metaphysics. "'Creativity' is the principle of *novelty.* . . . The 'creative advance' is the application of this ultimate principle of creativity to each novel situation which it originates" (PR, 21). For Whitehead, creativity means not only that the universe and the possible increase of intensity, complexity, and plurality expand endlessly, but that the ongoing, multiple unfoldings of reality are uncontrolled, uncontrollable, and the future is unknowable and fully open. He writes, "Thus, if there is to be progress beyond limited ideals, the course of history by way of escape must venture along the borders of chaos" (PR, 111). Butler shares with Whitehead this sense of excitement and trepidation at the realization of the dynamism of the processes in which we participate. If there is no closure on the category (and there can never be complete closure), a category can and will be a site spawning unexpected and uncontrollable permutations. While Butler writes not of "novelty" but of "resignification," strong affinities surface between Whitehead and her far more developed notion of power relations:

> The effects of performatives, understood as discursive productions, do not conclude at the terminus of a given statement or utterance, the passing of legislation, the announcement of a birth. *The reach of their significance cannot be controlled by the one who utters or writes, since such productions are not owned by the one who utters them.* (BTM, 241, my emphasis)[47]

In other words, "[t]he incalculable effects of action are as much a part of their subversive promise as those that we plan in advance" (BTM, 241).[48] We live with both the risks and the promise, as well as the relief, of not being able to control the unknowable reaches of our resignifying activities of creatively subverting the hegemonic norms, the novelty of our own becomings entering the world.

Toward Some Conclusions: Unconforming Becomings

So, then *what,* in the midst of these provocative connections that remain speculative and abstract, unless connected to particular, embodied, contextual events, might carry *political effectiveness and religious significance* in the world in which we come into being? How might we utilize categories of identity in ways that subvert their hegemony and open novel possibilities for human relationship? What *matters* here and how? For instance, what, in the debates over inclusion of gay men and lesbians, do churches *miss* when conversations are focused and limited by heteronormative essentialism and a metaphysics of substance? How might such debates obscure particular and ongoing creative revelations that queer relationships embody and engender within communities of faith? And, if we do not deliberately question our ontological assumptions, How might the vivifying pulse or motion of the holy, which the Christian faith claims as its raison d'être, be obscured or even diminished by notions such as the binary opposition of genders, of hetero/homosexualities, and of the divine and the human, by assumptions of the fixed essence of the human person, and by declarations of Christian identity claiming an essential unity of all who are "one" in Christ?

I return to the denominational gathering where, as the representative "lesbian," I said that identity is more fluid than the stated categories, and that however useful or helpful those categories, they also confine and restrict us. As soon as I voiced that thought aloud, most of the people in the room, including the planners of the event, who were four straight, white clergy males in their sixties (an interesting group to be planning multicultural discussions and creating a list of categories with which nonhegemonic others are to "self-identify," though the fact is, it was through their commitment that the event occurred at all), said, "yes, yes, yes, you're right." One of the members of the planning team added, "Yes, these categories are, after all, just categories. We are, after all, all human together. We are all *one* in Christ." Inwardly, I immediately asked, "*Whose* definition of 'we,' of 'after all,' of 'all,' of 'human,' of 'together,' of 'one,' of 'Christ' . . . *yours*?" Why did those who, though not necessarily less progressive ideologically, but who nonetheless benefit most from hegemonic norms, so quickly agree that categorical identities are transcendable and perhaps disposable? Why the hurry to move to a sense of *unity*, of being *one* together? Why can't we just remain *many* together: many people, many Christianities, many ways, without foreclosing the conversations that might, over time, reveal the effects of our power relations on the very real differences between us?[49] And what are the possibilities of *using* our differences to effect change on those power relations? Is it possible that the categories are necessary sites for undoing the very binary oppositions that define and reify them?

In that situation, I immediately regretted having spoken of the fluidity of identity from a site that people who comfortably live the hegemonic norm of compulsory heterosexuality would rather not have to acknowledge after all. If hegemonic society functions by co-opting the energies, creative insights, and discourses of nonhegemonic positions, why should it be any different with ideas of a fluid, becoming subject, which arrive on the scene just when the category of lesbian (as with categories of race and gender) is becoming a problematic, disruptive voice, and thus a *reality* in the dominant discourse?[50] But, if having only my single sentence or two, it was not expedient to bring up the fluidity of identity and the problem of categorization, without being able to more fully explain how radical antifoundational thought undercuts the essentialist, ontological assumptions of the dominant discourse, what might I have said instead?

If we are, as humans, fluidly and necessarily repeating (performing) whatever cultural categories we live and are defined by, it is in the *unconformity* (nonconformity + unconventionality) *within the forcefield of expectations of compulsive and compulsory repetition* that the creative power of novelty (Whitehead) and subversive activity of resignification (Butler) reside. And it is in *emphasizing* that aspect of our fluid identities, by publicly articulating the *nonconforming, unconventional* character of our repetitions, that we have the most effectiveness in destabilizing the hegemonic assumptions that underlie the categories of identity politics. The subtlety of emphasis in Butler's work is on the subversiveness, and in Whitehead's aesthetically informed metaphysic, the ethical impulse finds expression in the "width" produced by including increased contrast within and by performative iterations. At this time and place it does not seem expedient (or possible) to do away with the category "lesbian" itself and to collapse into the cultural invisibility and lack of voice of a hegemonic "one." Nor is that the intent of Butler's antifoundationalist approach. She *does* seek to undermine and complexify the understanding of "lesbian" as stable, unified, or fully defined within and by available cultural terms. She writes, "The assumption of its essential incompleteness permits [the] category to serve as a permanently available site of contested meanings. The definitional incompleteness of the category might then serve as a normative ideal relieved of coercive force" (GT, 15).[51] If categorical identities remain in a sense inescapable, never merely descriptive, but always normative and therefore exclusive, the work of becoming focuses on making those categories sites of permanent openness and instability. Increased agency only becomes possible in the midst of the dynamic unfixing and expansion of the categories that constrain.[52] For a lesbian involved in the ongoing processes of becoming in, by, and in resistance to the effects of compulsory heterosexuality, what matters are *how* the iterations carry and reveal contrasts and thus can begin to differ from that which is expected. Rather than citing iterations that seek unobtrusively to increase cultural coherence or to slip into adapted cultural universals, it is the active, playful, parodic citations, those that refuse to unproblematically conform to conventional binarisms of sexuality and gender, which reveal the confines of the norms that seek to prohibit human difference and relational complexification. The intense, powerful, beautiful play of embodied, seemingly unresolved contrasts opens new ethical and aesthetic dimensions. The novel conjunctions and disjunctions of such iterations dissolve the hegemonic binary oppositions that numb and limit social relationality, and they trouble the categories of woman and man, feminine and masculine, gay and straight, human and divine. In other words, effecting structural change politically and religiously requires that the *differences* by which we are differently inscribed and make ourselves differently than the expected norms *be made visible, audible.*

I wish I'd said at the denominational gathering that lesbians bring not only a willingness to break silence and step into visibility, but that we do so in ways that by their *unconforming becomings* constantly stretch and redefine the very institutions and categories in which we reside, thus revealing their permanent incompleteness. This is a gift that those persons and relationships "outside" of hegemonic norms bring to the wider churches and to the wider culture. When novelty and subversion enter and (re)form the experiential processes of identity formation, the creative space or freedom (future possibilities) for all human becoming expands. The *public articulation of unconformity* enables its disruptive and creative power to enter into the *conscious* discourse of social change, reminding us that public space for social change lives always already right in our midst.[53] The space of becoming resides in the instability and incompleteness of the categories we live by, always shrinking or expanding according to the ways in which we iterate and articulate our becomings. The expansion of public space for the discourse of becoming carries significance for and beyond the political. In the language of religious intuition, such expansion embodies the motion of the holy.

To articulate those becomings that *unconform* hegemonic or dominant norms *expands* the future space of and for becoming. More possibilities become available for prehension by future occasions, and those possibilities carry within them a greater degree of contrast or width and thus a capacity for more—and more intense—internal relations with other possibilities in future becomings. Butler characterizes this as the work of "assisting a radical resignification of the symbolic domain, deviating the citational chain toward a more possible future to expand the very meaning of what counts as a valued and valuable body in the world" (BTM, 22).[54] For Whitehead, the expansion involves an extension of and into future potentialities, of and for dynamic interconnections in the world.[55] To contribute to an expansion of future relational possibilities is an act of hope, of resistance to the tyranny of compulsory heterosexuality, in particular, and to the metaphysics of substance, in general, and the reliance of that metaphysics on binary oppositions that function culturally as hierarchical dualisms. Because hegemonic forms remain dominant by actively seeking to narrow down possibilities available for the becomings of the future, the sense of expansion, of breaking open space for the future is particularly important for gay/lesbian/queer persons and for others who live at the "margins" or "beyond the borders" of dominant cultural paradigms.[56]

To enter into the expansive motion of creativity, by subversive resignification or by becoming *differently*, with a greater degree of width, and thus more novelty, even (and especially) among and within and limited by the repetitions of the dominant society, is to participate in and with a *holy motion*. The interplay between Butler's and Whitehead's dynamic insights is extremely useful in the articulation of this experiential process, an articulation that allows the process and its invaluable, subversive, and creative power to enter into the conscious discourse, the speech acts, and actual world of social change.

The Expansion of the Future:
Divinity and Excess, Responsibility and Hope

Whitehead's concept of divinity offers one way of connecting the motion of expanding relational possibilities with that which is holy. Whitehead's God can be understood as the motion of creativity characterized into its primordial and consequent trajectories, lure and memory. "Viewed as primordial," God "is the unlimited conceptual realization of the absolute wealth of potentiality . . . the lure for feeling, the eternal urge of desire" (PR, 343-344). The primordial nature is not *before* act(s) of creation, but is *with* creation; likewise, the consequent nature is not *after*, "but in unison of becoming with every other creative act" (PR, 345). The consequent character reflects a reaction of the world on God, on/into the reservoir of future possibility: "This final phase of passage in God's nature is ever enlarging itself" (PR, 349), a motion that expands the "wealth of potentiality" for the primordial trajectories. I understand this motion of the expansion of future relational possibilities as holy, as the freedom and power of love, a revelation that Christianity claims and embodies, yet too often has obscured by the "fallacy of misplaced concreteness," by categorical imperialisms that reify a metaphysics of substance, and by the violence of attempting to contain and control the always plural dynamism of creative love breaking open new possibilities.

In addition to opening future relational possibilities, unconforming repetitions can be viewed as politically powerful and religiously significant, *holy,* partly because, by their *intensity,* they act as lures for further felt experiences. In a society and in religious institutions where uncritical, automatic repetitions within hegemonic norms predominate, conforming becomings (assuming dominant cultural habits of prehension or signification) may be experienced as confining, as dreary and "unfulfilling," however thoroughly those losses are concealed. Whitehead writes of the "tedium arising from the unrelieved dominance of fashion in [European] art" (PR, 339). A kind of cultural fatigue and listlessness result from repetitions that lack "width," variety, subversion, critical novelty, from repetitions that gradually shrink public spaces of becoming. The limitations iterated into human becomings by the unrelieved dominance of binary gender norms and compulsory heterosexuality, and by the assumption that categories and institutions are definitionally complete, are experienced as such "tedium." In the midst of that "tedium," often unacknowledged needs and yearnings pulse, barely discernible: longings for new and creative ways to experience deepened aesthetic pleasure and conscious ethical commitments, desire for active participation in the critical reshaping of relational possibilities for society and our own lives. Voiced differences of unconforming becomings reveal themselves as politically powerful and religiously vital *tools,* as well as experiences, because the creation of novel conjunctions not only embodies the motion that expands our universe, but also acts as a *lure for further engagement.* By presenting novel possibilities for creativity's further conditioning, unconforming becomings respond to the pulse of a world yearning for intensity. While novelty in itself is neither life-giving nor destructive, it opens future possibilities that are necessarily disruptive, uncontrollable, and multiple, and therefore intensely terrifying, interesting, and exciting. The possibilities presented by novelty draw forth, elicit in human becoming, both the aesthetic pleasures and the ethical commitments of further creative, subversive, constructive activity.

Finally, in addition to utilizing Butler and Whitehead to demonstrate some general affinities between poststructuralist claims and process thought,

I claim that the intensities created by novel categorical constructions, which arise through iterated contrasts between genders, sexual desires, and behaviors of lesbians, not only act as lures for further felt experience of contrasts, but open a broader future. When novelty and subversion (re)form the experiential processes of identity formation, the creative space or freedom for all human becoming expands. In this expansion we might recognize a motion of the holy. In particular, for Christians, the motion of perpetual categorical remaking, opening, dissolving, breaking, and expansion characterizes the discipleship that Jesus of Nazareth taught and lived. Such ongoing expansion of the relational future is a call that institutional churches, in fixing creeds and scripture, in regulating marriage, ordination, and conditions of membership, and perhaps most of all, Christian identity as primarily gendered and heterosexual—thus establishing both human and divine identities as essentially separate, culturally independent, and complete—have sadly, hugely failed. The attempt to fix, confine, control, or entomb the creative motion of love that expands the relational future characterizes the concept of idolatry. To seek to free the ever-expanding relational performativities of love characterizes a holy motion that forms, informs, and reforms human and divine lives.

In conclusion, the juxtaposition of Butler and Whitehead offers two connected directives: responsibility and hope. Both remind us of *the responsibility involved in our own activities of becoming.* Whitehead writes of "the insistent craving that zest for existence be refreshed by the ever-present, unfading importance of our immediate actions, which perish and yet live for ever more" (PR, 351). And Butler asks, "[i]f repetition is bound to persist as the mechanism of the cultural reproduction of identities, then the crucial question emerges, What kind of subversive repetition might call into question the regulatory practice of identity itself?" (GT, 32). How might we turn each of the categorical sites in which we repeat our lives into a perpetual site of dynamic complexification? How might we ask ourselves, "What kind of subversive repetition might call into question the present and future constraints set into this moment of becoming?" Agency happens in pursuing and naming the moments of unconforming becoming, moments that exceed and thereby shift the categorical limitations we live in and by. Responsibility involves a constant carrying along with us—in the ongoing activities of our becomings— something like Whitehead's awareness of the "unfading importance of our immediate actions" and Butler's continual question, "What kind of subversive repetition might call into question" the very regulatory practices we live by?

Hope resides in the process(es), in the multiplicities and excesses of becoming. This contextualized, process-oriented critique of culturally imposed dominance contains and offers a possibility of trusting in the process itself. In addition to underlining the responsibility involved in ongoing creation, Whitehead suggests relaxing into what he calls "the multiple freedom of actuality" (PR, 349). He writes,

The social history of mankind exhibits great organizations in their alternating functions of conditions for progress, and of contrivances for stunting humanity. The history of the Mediterranean lands, and of western Europe, is the history of the blessing and the curse of political organizations, of religious organizations, of schemes of thought, of social agencies for large purposes. The moment of dominance, prayed for, worked for, sacrificed for, by generations of the noblest spirits, marks the turning point where the blessing passes into the curse. Some new principle of refreshment is required. . . . Life refuses to be embalmed alive. The more prolonged the halt in some unrelieved system of order, the greater the crash of the dead society. (PR, 339)

Life's refusing "to be embalmed alive" resonates with Butler's notion of the "excess that necessarily accompanies any effort to posit identity once and for all" (GT, 143). Butler, too, in addition to pointing to the necessity of the play, work, and responsibility involved as our identities are continually reiterated, relates a trust in the process itself. "Excess" is characterized by that which exceeds, disrupts, or cannot be contained or expressed within, by or through categorical "sites" of identity such as gender, race, or sexual orientation. Excess describes that which cannot be expressed in or by any single performative category, binary opposition, or act of identity, yet despite all regulatory regimes and institutional powers, persists. If Whitehead's language about God offers one way of characterizing and valuing the motions of expanding relational possibilities into and for the future, I believe that Butler's invocation of excess is another way of naming those motions as sacred or holy, though Butler does not do so. For Butler, excess is that which is systematically denied by the traditional philosophical notion of a fixed, volitional subject and by the habitual processes of categorization that characterize our thought, language, and ways of relating with one another. Excess orients itself toward and into the open and unknowable future: "the effects of an action always supersede the stated intention or purpose of the act" (CF, 10).[57] I characterize excess as that which no site can fully contain, as a holy motion that broadens public space, a catalyst on which future freedoms depend. The "gaps and fissures" that bear the promise of the future are opened by "that which exceeds the norm . . . that which cannot be wholly defined or fixed by the repetitive labor of that norm" (BTM, 10).[58] In this spilling toward the future, Butler implies a guarded hope:

How then to expose the causal lines as retrospectively and performatively produced fabrications? . . . Perhaps this will be a matter of working sexuality *against* identity, even against gender, and of *letting that which cannot fully appear in any performance persist in its disruptive promise.* (IGI, 29, my emphasis)

And what exactly *is* "that which cannot fully appear," but "persists" in its "disruptive promise?" Is it power, the invisible, the holy? Perhaps "that which cannot fully appear" both obscures and points, not toward an "it," not to a metaphysical substance, but to the motion(s) of a *how*. If so, that which "refuses to be embalmed alive" and "cannot be fully known" is no *noun*, but a *verb*, the creative process itself, the bursting open, the novel connecting, the queering, dissolving, fracturing, and excessive blooming, the expansion of social and sacred possibilities for our shared and open-ended future. If we participate in the blooming and queering, the fracturing and novel connecting, if we unconform our own becomings, we will participate in the relational expansion of an undreamable future. Perhaps in the midst of the pleasure of that conjoined responsibility and hope, we might name the motion, that verb, which cannot fully appear: love . . . or might it be play?

Notes

1. I use "gay," "lesbian," and "homosexual" deliberately here, aware that I am excluding bisexual, transgendered persons, and other sexual minorities from "the debate." But I do so not because I want to simplify the terms or contestability of the conversations. On the contrary, I hope to demonstrate that it is precisely the degree to which a straight/gay binarism operates as definitional—thereby reifying a metaphysics of substance—that reiterates and conserves the "simplifying" norms of compulsory heterosexuality, constraining broader relational possibilities.

2. See Kathy Rudy's helpful exposition, *Sex and the Church: Gender, Homosexuality, and the Transformation of Christian Ethics* (Boston: Beacon, 1997). Rudy analyzes the Christian Right's commitment to re-create the gendered theology of the nineteenth century's Cult of Domesticity, in which access to God depended on the binary opposition of gender. Rudy also explores, not whether gay people should be allowed to "fit" into churches, but which historically gay practices, including gay male promiscuity as a model for Christian community, might renew and invigorate contemporary churches.

3. I occasionally use the word *queer* in this chapter, a term that seeks to play off of the energy of reversal from its common derogatory usage. Queer, according to Annamarie Jagose, "describes those gestures or analytical models which dramatize incoherences in the allegedly stable relations between chromosomal sex, gender and sexual desire. . . . Queer locates and exploits the incoherences in those three terms which stabilize heterosexuality" (Jagose, *Queer Theory: An Introduction* [New York: New York University Press, 1996], 3).

4. For example, essentialist views often come into play when tolerance is based on assertions of biological or genetic determinism, being "born that way." Tolerance or acceptance based on essentialist views tends to be inclusion "into" heteronormativity. That "acceptable" lesbian and gay lives must be heteronormatively constituted is exemplified by the UCC's 1997 General Synod statement on "fidelity in covenant." While not using the phrase "heterosexual marriage" (in deference to the 1985 state-

ment of affirmation of gay and lesbian persons), the 1997 statement affirms only covenanted, monogamous, partnered relationships. Thus the "otherness" of the binarism is not undone, but simply shifts to "other" nonhegemonic relations or identities, such as nonmonogamy, promiscuity, and excessive gender blurring. "Inclusion" then becomes not about the free motion of love, but about being heteronormative.

5. Whitehead calls "the fallacy of misplaced concreteness" an "overstatement" of generalization: "This fallacy consists in neglecting the degree of abstraction involved when an actual entity is considered merely so far as it exemplifies certain categories of thought" (PR, 7-8).

6. Process insights are drawn primarily from Whitehead's *Process and Reality*.

7. In this chapter I draw primarily from Butler's article, "Imitation and Gender Insubordination" in *inside/out: Lesbian Theories, Gay Theories*. I also use insights drawn more broadly from "Gender Trouble, Feminist Theory and Psychoanalytic Discourse," in *Feminism/ Postmodernism*, Linda J. Nicholson, ed. (New York: Routledge, 1990) and other major works by Butler concerning the deconstruction of fixed gender identity.

8. Identities included in the conversation were Samoan, Filipino/American, African-American, Commonwealth Countries, Native American-Hawaiian, Congregational Christian, Seniors, Youth, Gay, Lesbian, Urban, Multiracial, Rural, Other Protestant, Catholic, Asian-American, Metropolitan (between suburban and urban), Small Town, Suburban, and Euro-American.

9. An interview between Gayatri Chakravorty Spivak and Sneja Gunew in *The Cultural Studies Reader,* Simon During, ed. (New York: Routledge, 1993) contains an interesting discussion of, among other things, representation. Spivak says, "this question of representation, self-representation, representing others, is a problem . . . constructing the Other simply as an object of knowledge, leaving out the real Others because of the ones who are getting access into public places due to these waves of benevolence and so on. I think as long as one remains aware that it is a very problematic field, there is some hope" (198).

10. Being able to "choose" or be representative of only *one* identity group is particularly difficult for people who "fit" more than one nonhegemonic category. A forced choice of "which identity is primary" often ensues, and usually the primary identity is that category that is experienced as most oppressed by, or oppositional to, hegemonic norms. The person with many nonhegemonic traits or characteristics is split into various facets and forced choices between identity-based alliances, while the person with many hegemonic traits is able to be "whole" and does not feel tension or conflict between categorical identifiers such as race, ethnicity, class, gender, sexuality, able-bodiedness, education level, or income level. In such a way, hegemonic norms remain both powerful and obscured.

11. That lesbians may bring a "gift" of a faith or spirituality that cannot ignore the body or its behaviors and desires, reflects an insistence partly enforced through a history of exclusion/invisibility from/within the church due to the judgment of lesbian bodies and acts as "deviant." The sense of the sacred as embodied may also partly come from those bodies in the joyful, pleasurable acts of sexual relations.

12. In claiming destabilization as a gift that "lesbians" bring, I do not mean to

imply that others can and do not bring that gift, too! Rudy is excellent on this point: "From a Christian perspective, gay and lesbian people are good for the entire church because they can lead us all closer to God. (This is something like an extreme liberationist perspective of God's 'option' for the oppressed.) This line of argument is extremely dangerous. I resist the narrative that gays, lesbians, and other sexual minorities are spiritually oriented in a way that straight or celibate people are not, because such an assertion relies on the very distinctions I am trying here to challenge. That is, the major mistake of homophobic Christianity has been to think that solely because of their sexual preference, lesbian and gay people have nothing to contribute to the church. However, the reverse proposition, that gays, lesbians, bisexuals, and transgendered people—as a result of their natures—inherently have a special connection to God, is equally essentialist and problematic" (122–123).

13. For an essentialist thinker, identity is natural, fixed, innate, culturally independent, and intrinsic; identity is an empirical category. For a social constructionist, identity is culturally dependent, relational, an effect of processes of identification.

14. When faced with opportunities to self-select or self-name the cultural category(s) to which we "belong" or have affinities, we often "choose" those categorical assertions in and by which we experience or *feel* the most pain of exclusion, violence, and oppression. Perhaps we gain awareness of the power of the culture's dominance at those categorical sites where we are at odds with its hegemonic assumptions. In fact, those places where we rub up against culture in our nonhegemonic traits (rather, where culture rubs up against *us* in those places) may be the *only* windows we have into the mechanisms and structures of our culture, the only places we experientially *feel* and are *aware* of the power of discourse in culture at all. In the UCC multiculturalism/ identity conversations, I would guess that I was chosen as a "representative" or "token" lesbian because my other identities, particularly race and class, "fit" easily into the hegemonic norms of the dominant discourse. It is easier to abstract "lesbianism" as my essence, because I am not as "complicated" by other nonhegemonic identities. By so doing, however, the categorical essence of "lesbian" becomes defined in that discourse in ways that exclude and obscure the heterogeneity both within and breaking beyond that category. Butler, discussing the category of "woman," makes a similar comment. She claims that when we rely on an identity category in a fundamental way, it "becomes normative in character and, hence, exclusionary in principle," and "the category effects a political closure on the kinds of experiences articulable as part of a feminist discourse" (Butler, "Gender Trouble," in *Feminism/Postmodernism*, 325).

In contemporary feminisms, the question of essentialism, the question of whether there *is* an "essence of *woman*," of whether you and I speak *primarily* "as women," is becoming ever more clearly articulated as it becomes more crucial to the ways in which we understand each other and ourselves. Elizabeth Spelman describes the problem well: "I try to show that the notion of a generic 'woman' functions in feminist thought much the way the notion of generic 'man' has functioned in Western philosophy: it obscures the heterogeneity of women and cuts off examination of the significance of such heterogeneity for feminist theory and political activity (Spelman, *Inessential Woman: Problems of Exclusion in Feminist Thought* [Boston: Beacon, 1988], ix). Linda Nicholson echoes Spelman's concern: "In so far as the category is given substantive, cross-cultural content, there arises the possibility that it becomes totalizing and discriminating against the experiences and realities of some" (Nicholson, Introduction to *Feminism/Postmodernism,* 15).

15. Jane Flax, "Postmodernism and Gender Relations in Feminist Theory," in *Feminism/Postmodernism,* 45.

16. That "essential woman" has been culturally constructed as a tool of hegemonic discourse is startlingly apparent in a book that I recently happened to pull (nearly at random; I was attracted by the age of its cover) from a shelf in the feminism section of the Graduate Theological Union library. In *The Mirror of True Womanhood: A Book of Instruction for Women in the World,* 18th ed. (New York: P. J. Kenedy, 1877), the author, the Reverend Bernard O'Reilly, L.D., writes, "[i]t is precisely because women are, by the noble instincts which God has given to their nature, prone to all that is most heroic, that this book has been written for them." It is not insignificant that most of the essentially feminine traits that the author reveres as God-given "nature" are actually husband-benefiting *behaviors,* revealed by chapter headings such as, "Generosity in Forgetting One's Pain, to Please Others" (3, 229). In an achingly common move, both God and "nature" are invoked to justify the author's hegemonic definition of essential woman.

17. Thomas Laqueur, *Making Sex: Body and Gender from the Greeks to Freud* (Cambridge: Harvard University Press, 1990), 21.

18. In suggesting that acceptance avoid biological essentialism, I have no intention of denigrating gay, lesbian, bisexual, or transgendered persons, nor well-meaning heterosexual allies who have utilized such arguments in their courageous commitments toward opening political rights and religious freedoms. On the contrary, I carry deep gratitude and daily benefit from such commitments. However, I *am* critiquing the habits of thought that fund biological and other essentialisms. By utilizing unexamined habits of thought, depending on heterosexually sedimented arguments to buttress g/l/b/t rights, we may end up forfeiting the extraordinary opportunities queer lives open for the dynamic rethinking and shaping of human lives, relations, and patterns of thought.

In addition, I am not suggesting here that sexual identities are necessarily chosen. Rather, I suggest that a tendency on the part of progressives to shun the view that sexual relationality may be at least partially fluid or chosen inadvertently reinforces heteronormative habits of thought. Thus I advocate that g/l/b/t and well-meaning heterosexuals *refrain from* using biological determinism—or any single *cause—as a condition for the acceptability* of queer lives and relations. I share theorist Eve Kosofsky Sedgwick's view that the concept of ontogeny itself, the question of "the cause" of homosexuality, has developed through "gay-genocidal nexuses of thought," and that queer-affirmative work "does well when it aims to minimize its reliance on any particular account of the origin of sexual preference and identity in individuals." (*Epistemology of the Closet,* Berkeley: University of California Press, 1990, 40.) (For more on the critique of "cause" see Christina Hutchins, "Holy Ferment: Queer Philosophical Destabilizations and the Discourse on Lesbian, Gay, Bisexual and Transgender Lives in Christian Institutions," *Theology and Sexuality,* 2001. For a study, including extensive interviews, exploring the possibilities of chosen homosexualities, see Vera Whisman, *Queer by Choice: Lesbians, Gay Men, and the Politics of Identity,* New York: Routledge, 1996).

19. Teresa de Lauretis, "Upping the Anti [sic] in Feminist Theory," in *The Cultural Studies Reader,* Simon During, ed. (New York: Routledge, 1993), 76.

20. Chris Weedon, *Feminist Practice and Poststructuralist Theory* (Cambridge: Blackwell, 1987), 21.

21. Ibid., 33.

22. "Philosophers can never hope finally to formulate these metaphysical first principles . . . however such elements of language be stabilized as technicalities, they remain metaphors mutely appealing for an imaginative leap" (PR, 4). Not only does Whitehead understand the lack of the absolute in philosophy as a problem of language, but of the philosophical enterprise itself: "There is no totality which is the harmony of all perfections. Whatever is realized in any one occasion of experience necessarily excludes the unbounded welter of contrary possibilities. There are always 'others,' which might have been and are not. . . . This doctrine is commonplace in the fine arts. It also is—or should be—a commonplace of political philosophy" (AI, 276).

23. For Whitehead, "the primary method of philosophy is descriptive generalization" (PR, 10). I am indebted to Luis G. Pedraja's excellent treatment of the topic for the phrase "hermeneutical scheme." He writes, "[a]lthough it may not seem evident, Whitehead does not want to establish an absolute metaphysical scheme. What he wants is to develop a comprehensive hermeneutical scheme to serve as an interpretive context in which individual experiences can acquire meaning" (chapter 3 in this volume). And the possibility of utilizing a relative metaphysics offers novel possibilities for contemporary feminist and critical theory. Catherine Keller writes, "[t]his emerging feminist vision requires something like metaphysical sensibility, because such vision drives beyond the sphere of the interpersonal, seeking a broader context in which all relations may be reassessed" (Keller, *From a Broken Web* [Boston: Beacon, 1986], 158).

24. Michel Foucault, "Nietzsche, Genealogy, History," in *Language, Counter-Memory, Practice,* D. F. Bondchard, ed. (Ithaca: Cornell University Press, 1977), 151–152. Butler further supports the view that Foucault's genealogical method of exposing "causes" as "effects" of regulatory regimes overtly critiques the metaphysics of substance: "The strategic displacement of that binary relation and the metaphysics of substance on which it relies presuppose that the categories of female and male, woman and man, are similarly produced within the binary frame. . . Foucault's genealogical inquiry exposes this ostensible 'cause' as 'an effect,' the production of a given regime of sexuality that seeks to regulate sexual experience by instating the discrete categories of sex as foundational and causal functions within any discursive account of sexuality. . . . [H]is analysis implies the interesting belief that sexual heterogeneity . . . implies a critique of the metaphysics of substance as it informs the identitarian categories of sex" (GT, 23–24).

Whitehead also shares affinities with Derrida (and through Derrida with Butler) on the ways in which the very grammar of our language constrains and is constrained by a metaphysics of substance, making it difficult to conceptualize, write or speak in/through an alternative metaphysical hermeneutic. Substance metaphysics is *sedimented* into our language *structures* in which a *subject* is followed by a verb in the *predicate,* indicating a preexisting, fixed subject that subsequently acts or is acted upon. Both Whitehead and Butler struggle with how to use language without further foreclosing the dynamism of reality.

25. Later in the same essay, Butler addresses a common misconception about deconstruction: "To deconstruct is not to negate or to dismiss, but to call into question and, perhaps most importantly, to open up a term, like the subject, to a reusage or redeployment that previously has not been authorized" (CF, 15).

26. For Whitehead, each concrescent occasion unifies its universe, such that "the many become one and are increased by one" (PR, 21). However, each universalizing moment of concrescence is only a moment, and it ceases with its attainment. In addition, though each occasion concresces as a universalized *one,* the *many* always remain. Because all unification is momentary, the fragmentation and plurality of the universe are neither erased nor diminished, but rather increased. In this way, Whitehead unhinges the potential dualism between the one and the many.

27. Elsewhere Butler suggests that what is needed "is a dynamic and more diffuse conception of power, one which is committed to the difficulty of cultural translation as well as the need to rearticulate 'universality' in non-imperialist directions" (GP, 125).

28. Nietzsche wrote, "What does your conscience say? 'You should become him who you are'" (Nietzsche, *The Joyful Wisdom,* in *The Complete Works of Friedrich Nietzsche,* Oscar Levy, ed. [New York: Russell and Russell, 1964]). Butler explicitly invokes Nietzsche: "The challenge for rethinking gender categories outside of the metaphysics of substance will have to consider the relevance of Nietzsche's claim in *On the Genealogy of Morals* that 'there is no 'being' behind doing, effecting, becoming; 'the doer' is merely a fiction added to the deed—the deed is everything'" (GT, 25). In my referring "becoming" to both thinkers, it is important to point out that Whitehead never developed a concept of the "self"; rather, "becoming" was always ontological and cosmological. Yet Keller, along with others, has utilized very effectively Whitehead's notion of concrescence, bringing it into conversation with feminist thinkers, in order to interrogate selfhood and subjectivity: "Self is an event, a process, and no fixed substance, no substantive" (194). Cf. chapter 4, "The Selves of Psyche."

29. In addition, process metaphysics have been used to develop "process theologies" by John B. Cobb Jr., David Ray Giffin, Rita Nakashima Brock, Marjorie Suchocki, and others, as well as used in conjunction with fields such as environmental ethics (Jay McDaniel) and feminist philosophy and ethics (Keller).

30. See note 24. Grammatical structuring of the sentence is based on and further sediments metaphysics of substance.

31. Whitehead continues: "[T]hese enduring objects and 'societies,' analyzable into strands of enduring objects, are the [comparatively] permanent entities which enjoy adventures of change through time and space" (PR, 34).

32. In addition, "width," or the inclusion of contrasts in the act of concrescence, enhances the permanence of an occasion, the durability of its ability, upon perishing, to affect future becomings (PR, 163).

33. Butler, "Gender Trouble," in *Feminism/Postmodernism,* 336.

34. I cannot resist bringing a bit of Whitehead into conversation here with Butler's use of parody as a strategy of resistance to the conventions of gender consolidation. Whitehead writes, "The last flicker of originality is exhibited by the survival of satire. Satire does not necessarily imply a decadent society, though it flourishes upon

the outworn features in the social system . . . [when] there remains the show of civilization, without any of its realities" (AI, 277–278).

35. In a conversation, Mary Ann Tolbert pointed out an important critique of Butler's use of "drag." When discussing the activity of "drag," Butler does not address the difference between male to female and female to male drag in our society. Due to power imbalances, male to female drag is a more shocking, playful, and subversive act—a giving up or turning over of power—while female to male drag may involve an active complicity with existing power relations. There are also complexities and differences within the activities of female to male drag. For instance, a woman who puts on a "power suit," stylized after men's clothing but tailored specifically for a woman, is performing something different than a lesbian butch who wears "real" men's clothes.

36. An example of how repetitions of becoming actively consolidate, sediment, or *matter,* might be a body builder: a person who lifts weights repetitively over months or years, literally (re)shaping her body under/within cultural norms, and further reifying or resisting hegemonic norms (depending perhaps on whether the body builder is a man or a woman, and/or which muscles are worked, emphasized, delineated, etc.).

37. Butler continues, "An open coalition, then, will affirm identities that are alternately instituted and relinquished according to the purposes at hand; it will be an open assemblage that permits of multiple convergences and divergences without obedience to a normative telos of definitional closure" (GT, 16).

38. The word *abject* describes a domain that is neither subject nor object, that which cannot be known by its opposition to another. Butler relates the word to "lesbian unthinkability" because if, following de Beauvoir, "man" has named himself Self, subject, active, and so forth, and woman as the Other, object, passive, and so forth, and defined the two in opposition to one another, then the active relation of one woman with another problematizes the opposition, because an "object" cannot actively have or possess another "object," nor is she a "subject," living out a relation with an opposite, an "object," who defines her "subject" status. "Abject," as that which cannot be fully named or thought, implies a lack of the content of either object or subject (or perhaps the presence of the content of both at once). And because the boundaries of a subject or an object are defined and constrained by the act of naming, abjects are not limited by the boundedness, fixity, ontological weight, or "being-ness" of a subject, nor by the static passivity of an object.

By developing some of the exclusions from the binary opposition of "sex," Monique Wittig, a French anti-essentialist materialist feminist, claims "lesbian" as a concept beyond the categories of sex (woman and man). Because for Wittig, "women" only expresses meaning in heterosexual systems of thought (and economic arrangements), lesbians are not women. In fact, for Wittig, lesbians, by breaking out of the binarism of sex, demonstrate that "women" are not a natural group or an essential category. It is interesting to note that Wittig engages in essentialist thinking in the act of trying to discredit it—by homogenizing lesbians into a single harmonious group. (See Wittig, *The Straight Mind and Other Essays* [Boston: Beacon, 1992].)

39. Lesbian "unthinkability" certainly remains an issue. The *Ellen* show was pulled off the air within a year of April 1997, when both the television character and "real life" Ellens "came out." One reason given by an ABC executive was that the show had "too much" lesbian content. Ellen Degeneres's portrayal of the daily life and

relational issues that would be considered mundane on a "heterosexual" show were too much of a challenge to the popular unthinkability of lesbianism. Another, more personal example: When my partner and I hold hands in public or simply do errands, stand in line together, and so forth, we are very often asked, "Are you two sisters?" If one of us replies, "actually, we're lovers," the response is often either silence or, occasionally, an insistent, "No, you're sisters!"—a blatant refusal or inability to *see,* to *hear,* to perceive the "nature" or name of our relation.

40. In BTM, Butler writes, "What I propose in place of these conceptions of construction [in which there is no self-creative power] is a return to the notion of matter, not as site or surface, but as *a process of materialization that stabilizes over time to produce the effect of boundary, fixity, and surface we call matter*" (9). Butler uses the word *matter* to convey not only *whose* bodies are important (all bodies and potential bodies), but that bodies *are mattering,* that is, coming into existence through a discursive, metaphysical process of continual resignification. In several places, Butler comes quite close to Whitehead's notion of concrescence in her characterizations of performativity: "It is not simply a matter of construing performativity as a repetition of acts, as if 'acts' remain intact and self-identical as they are repeated in time, and where 'time' is understood as external to the 'acts' themselves. On the contrary, an act is itself a repetition, a sedimentation, and congealment of the past which is precisely foreclosed in its act-like status" (BTM, 244 n.7).

41. In CF Butler explicitly notes that it is the contingency of the subject that engenders or preconditions its agency: "We may be tempted to think that to assume the subject in advance is necessary in order to safeguard the *agency* of the subject. But to claim that the subject is constituted is not to claim that it is determined; on the contrary, the constituted character of the subject is the very precondition of its agency" (12).

42. Simone de Beauvoir, *The Second Sex* (New York: Bantam, 1952), 249.

43. Note that for Butler, the "failure to repeat" refers to the inability to perfectly or exactly repeat an "original" (or "get it right")—an impossibility because there *is* no original. For Whitehead, exact repetition is also impossible (and undesirable), nor are actual occasions "originals" for the becoming of subsequent occasions, though they do shape/effect future occasions. In terms of "societies," "there is disorder in the sense that laws are not perfectly obeyed, and that the reproduction is mingled with instances of failure. There is accordingly a gradual transition to new types of order. . . ." (PR, 91).

44. What a dance when these words of Whitehead's are placed in conjunction with Butler's double movement of invoking a category and opening it as contested! "To ameliorate and rework [the specific violences that a partial concept enforces], it is necessary to learn a double movement: to invoke the category, and hence provisionally to institute an identity and at the same time to open the category as a site of permanent political contest" (BTM, 222). Agency is that double movement (BTM, 220).

45. "The experience enjoyed by an actual entity" is "what the actual entity is in itself, for itself" (PR, 81).

46. Whitehead's *enjoyment* may be even closer to the particularity of Butler's *pleasure* in "troubling," disturbing, or destabilizing categories. A few sentences later, after noting the enjoyment of efficient causation ("It is in this way that the immediacy of sorrow and pain is transformed into an element of triumph"), Whitehead specifically

relates this enjoyment to the redemptive value of *discord,* of which a "very minor exemplification" is "the aesthetic value of discords in art" (PR, 350).

47. This passage is preceded by a clear description of agency: "This *resignification* marks the workings of an agency that is (a) not the same as voluntarism, and that (b) though *implicated* in the very relations of power it seeks to rival, is not, as a consequence, reducible to those dominant forms (BTM, 241). "Performativity describes this relation of being implicated in that which one opposes, this turning of power against itself to produce alternative modalities of power, to establish a kind of political contestation that is not a 'pure' opposition, a 'transcendence' of contemporary relations of power, but *a difficult labor of forging a future from resources inevitably impure. . . .*" (241, my emphasis). It is important to note that since there can never be complete closure on a category or site of a performative event (Butler's notion of excess), any attempts at closure will necessarily produce other subversive constructions. However, categorical subversion or agency may be enhanced by deliberately utilizing the process of resignification against itself.

48. In "Gender as Performance" Butler says, "You can't plan or calculate subversion. In fact, I would say that subversion is precisely an incalculable effect."

49. Here I critique an emphasis on "Christian unity" as over/against fragmentation, multiplicity, and ruptures of difference. My argument is against a hegemonic "one" that erases, obscures, or excludes non-normativity, even as such a "one" *produces* the non-normative. My intention is not to belittle or weaken contemporary avowals of the commitment that all persons should enjoy common rights and freedoms. In fact, it is the *need* for such common freedoms that elicits my own provisional appeal to Whiteheadian creativity as a universal and to a Butlerian view of human capacities and characteristics as relationally constituted (and constrained) processes of becoming.

50. A far more disturbing instance of the use (abuse) of the "fluidity of identity" notion is being propagated by conservative Christian organizations in the "transforming movement" of "ex-gay ministries" in which "homosexuals" learn to be attracted to the "opposite sex" so they can enter into heterosexual marriage. An example of this was a full page advertisement in the July 13, 1998 *New York Times* that read, "Thousands of ex-gays like these have walked away from their homosexual identities. While the paths each took into homosexuality may vary, their stories of hope and healing [from nonheterosexual identities] through the transforming love of Jesus Christ are the same. Ex-gay ministries throughout the U.S. work daily with homosexuals seeking change, and many provide outreach programs to their families and loved ones." It is important to notice that for the Radical Right, the "transformation" never goes in the *other* direction: from heterosexuality into and toward homosexuality. The motion is rather always toward the conventional, the status quo, *toward and into* compulsory heterosexuality and hegemonic power relations, which stabilize what for the Radical Right *is* a fixed, stable, enforced category: *gender.* (For an excellent discussion of this see Rudy, *Sex and the Church.*) In this sense, though there is "motion," and the word *transformative* is being used, there is very little "novelty" or "subversion"; future relational possibilities are not being widened, but further confined.

51. Note that Butler is speaking in *Gender Trouble* of the category "woman," and I have related the quotation here to the context of "lesbian." It is important to make

clear that categorical incompleteness, disruption, and the resulting expansion of relational possibilities are not limited to the category "lesbian"; there is no *one* site from which to resist hegemonic namings and to recreate relational possibilities effectively. Such sites are always multiple and surprising.

52. Butler writes about this in terms of "women": "to authorize or safeguard the category of women as a site of possible resignifications is to expand the possibilities of what it means to be a woman and in this sense to condition and enable an enhanced sense of agency" (CF, 16).

53. This is reminiscent of Jesus' teachings about the realm of God, which is "always in the midst." The realm of God, characterized in Jesus' parables of the mustard seed or leaven hidden in measures of dough, is also a metaphor about expanding the future, breaking open the containers that constrain the present through the very power of novel becoming that relationally resides in them. (Cf. Matt. 13: 31–33.)

54. In *Gender Trouble,* Butler points to subversive citations within established norms of continuity as "critical opportunities to expose the limits and regulatory aims of that domain of intelligibility and, hence, to *open up within the very terms of that matrix of intelligibility rival and subversive matrices* of gender disorder" (17).

55. "The extensiveness of space is really the spatialization of extension" (PR, 289).

56. While expanding or opening space for the relational future is both a necessity and an act of resistance for queer lives, it is imperative that the *self-creativity* of this event be emphasized. I am not advocating the forcible breaking of another's boundaries as happens in events of sexual violence or in the inappropriate "outing" by others, especially by those who iterate within more dominant categories, of a queer person or act.

57. Here Butler explicitly draws on Foucault. The idea of effects that "supersede" the purpose of the act also carries affinities with Whitehead's notion of the "superject," which is the public trajectory(ies) created by an act of becoming: "An actual entity considered in reference to the publicity of things is a 'superject'; namely, it arises from the publicity which it finds, and it adds itself to the publicity which it transmits. It is a moment of passage from decided public facts to a novel public fact" (PR, 289).

58. I am aware that I am utilizing Butler's insights, particularly in this discussion of excess, not only in ways that she does not herself do, but in ways that move in the hegemonic direction that has been all too familiar in Western history: supersessionism of the work of Jewish persons by and for Christian constructions. I can only hope that my purpose is sufficiently subversive—opening cultural categories that have become sedimented in violently constraining ways by Christian institutions, habits, and ways of thought, and that affect and confine secular as well as religious life.

6

Figuring Subjectivity for Grounded Transformations

A Critical Comparison of Rosi Braidotti's and John Cobb's Figurations

ANNE DANIELL

> There are two principles inherent in the very nature of things, recurring in some particular embodiments whatever field we explore—the spirit of change, and the spirit of conservation. There can be nothing real without both.
>
> —Alfred North Whitehead, *SMW*

Introduction: Modernity's "Separative Self" and Figurations for Postmodern Subjectivity

If there is some commonality to the great variety of theories claiming the title "postmodern," it might be this: that the Enlightenment-derived ideal of the subject as a "separative self"[1] has helped to foster some of the most severe problems plaguing the modern era, including racism, ethnocentrism, sexism, heterosexism, the unmitigated wasting of the natural environment, and the proliferation of mass weaponry with the capacity to devastate the human and other species of the earth. Built upon René Descartes's seventeenth-century version of the human as a "thinking thing" in contradistinction to a "feeling thing," the modern, Western version of subjectivity has tended to view the human mind as independent of, and hence ultimately separable from, the body's flesh, the terrestrial environment, and the viscous emotions of relationships.[2] The ideal of the separative self denies the interrelational, contextual composition of all identities. Underpinning the hierarchical and dualistic character of Western modernity, the separative-self ideal is grafted with notions of transcendence—not mired in the body, nature, and given cultural contexts—while those subject positions deemed abnormal or "other" are viewed as somehow less able to evade immanence—imprisoned in their bodies, emotions, and cultural and environmental contexts.

Stemming in part from the late-modernist, identity-politics critique of the individualistic, enlightenment self, postmodernists have countered this ideal of *in*dependence with images of plurality, fluidity, and ceaseless motility. The question addressed in this chapter is whether these postmodern images of perpetual change might not also promote a modernist aversion to the earthly, the immanent, and the bodily. Rather than being truly "post"-modern, might they not also advance "hypermodernism"[3]—a state of chronic, capitalistic "development"—at the cost of the more sustainable economic practices of communities that have been characterized by colonial powers as "unchanging" and "primitive?"[4]

To explore this question I compare two postmodern figurations: the feminist and gender theorist Rosi Braidotti's trope of the "female feminist nomadic subject," from her *Nomadic Subjects* (NS) and the theologian John B. Cobb Jr.'s image of christ[5] as the "process of creative transformation," from his *Christ in a Pluralistic Age* (CPA). Expanding upon the work of theorist Gilles Deleuze, Braidotti defines *figurations* as "politically informed images that portray the complex interaction of levels of subjectivity" while instigating "ways out of the phallocentric vision of the subject" (NS, 3–4). Both Braidotti's and Cobb's figurations aim at launching Western thinking beyond its traditional reliance upon essentialist or substantive modes of thinking. Although their rhetoric at times suggests that a mere reversal of emphasis—that is, replacing the stasis and quiescence common to substance language with the fluidity and change prevalent in postmodern language—will suffice to subvert modernist modes of thinking, upon careful analysis we may come to understand how their figurations offer a more complex rendering of the interdependence of change and repetition, movement and rest, evolution and endurance.

Here is the paradox to be explored: The figurations proposed by Braidotti and Cobb, meant as they are to stimulate transition and openness to diversity, are bequeathed with meaning and value from their being "grounded" in specific kinds of communities and identities. In other words, the ideal of transformation has value only in relation to the definiteness or "givenness" of concrete subjects and communities. When we study them carefully, we thus realize that Braidotti's "female feminist nomadic subject" and Cobb's "christ" as the "process of creative transformation" must necessarily represent both differentiantion *and* reiteration, innovation *and* conservation. Since life (at least as we know it, in its conscious, human form) is experienced concretely, images of subjectivity that promote change must at the same time reflect aspects of givenness.

In *Nomadic Subjects,* for example, Braidotti urges more liberating, diverse, and alterable modes of subjectivity for women. Yet the title she chooses for her figuration, the "female feminist nomadic subject," expresses not only motion and change as implied by "nomadic," but also the concreteness of an already existing kind of subjectivity—the "female feminist." While she does not put it in these exact terms, it is clear that the valuing of a particular kind of subject (in this case, the "female feminist" kind) serves as the necessary ground[6] out of which new variations of subjectivity may emerge. Stated differently, it is the persistent instantiation of previous patterns of identity that produces the requisite givenness from which may arise future transfigurations. In similar fashion, Cobb's proposition that christ be recognized as the incarnate "process of creative transformation" entails the reinscription of a certain previously established *Christian* subjectivity, even as it encourages the transformation of one's faith and identity through serious encounter with religio-cultural pluralism. As this chapter will explore further, it is because of given patterns of identity and community that figurations have the capacity to evoke desire for both transfiguration and duration.

How might contemporary notions of subjectivity and ground cease to convey images of immobility, invariability, and *in*dependence and express instead a more complex *inter*dependence of that which endures and that which changes, of the reiteration and divergence of patterns? Whereas Christianized Westerners have traditionally envisaged the divine as immutable—God as the "unmoved Mover"—today it appears to be unfettered mobility, change, and "development"—all qualities characteristic of the global, "free-market" economy—that Westerners (both those who do and do not consider themselves "religious") worship.[7] Moreover, whereas the earth with its ever-burgeoning life and ceaseless decay was at one time defamed precisely because of its association with fluctuation,[8] today's Western ethos is more likely to depict the earth and its nonhuman creation (when the nonhuman is given any consideration at all) as undeveloped, stagnant, inanimate, and hence as not of great significance.

Due to this reversal in attitudes from a premodern worship of the unchanging to a late-modern reverence for unceasing change, I find it important that postmodern figurations do more than simply assert faith in the antithesis of the "unmoved mover." In critically comparing Braidotti's and Cobb's figurations, I therefore draw attention to the ways in which each image, on the surface, may be perceived as promoting a one-sided "change for the sake of change," but then demonstrate how each, when considered more carefully, may be viewed as grasping the interdependency of transformation and duration, variation and stability.

*Grounding Transformation: Braidotti's "Nomadic Subject" and
Cobb's Christ as the "Process of Creative Transformation"*

Braidotti's Nomadic Subject

In *Nomadic Subjects* Braidotti discloses her own identity as an example of
what she terms *nomadic subjectivity:* Having grown up pluri-lingual and pluri-
cultural,[9] she depicts herself as a hybrid composed of various contexts as
opposed to claiming one specific ethnic identity (NS, 9–11). She contends that
similar to nomadic peoples, she does not experience herself as belonging to a
particular place, but views her subjectivity as shaped by the various life-ways
she has encountered (NS, 8–10). She suggests, moreover, that such a nomadic
subjectivity is not a minority position but is pervasive; indeed, all identities—
individual and communal—are always produced in and through a mélange of
multiple and diverse influences. In Braidotti's opinion, acknowledging this
pluralism as a cultural "fact" would help to remove the stigma of hybridity
experienced at many levels of society by those whose identities are more obviously "multi" or "other."

Braidotti defines the nomadic position as "opposed to fixity" and all
universalizing and linear claims, including notions of the "essential self" and
historical progress or teleology (NS, 35). Nomadism, she explains, promotes
a "healthy disrespect for [. . .] conventions," stirring people to "dis-identify"
with all "sedentary" modes of thinking (NS, 30). Concerned about the frequent
romanticization of past identities and places, Braidotti reminds her readers that
no context or identity is ever "pure" (NS, 24–25). For example, no one person
is simply "woman" or "man," "Russian," or "Korean," but every individual
arises from an intertwining of concrete, and hence complex, influences. Furthermore, not only is each subject position different from every other, but
every person has the potential to express a variety of subjectivities; an identity
claim such as "I am a woman" is only partial, and a monolithic view of this
identity may even contradict other partial identities belonging to the same
individual.[10] The figuration of the nomadic subject, therefore, accentuates
both the diversity of subject-types within any given community and the variety of identities belonging to each individual subject.

Nomadism is an image of existence as "a process network of simultaneous power formations," in which subjectivities are produced through what
Braidotti calls "regulative variables"—social and semiotic "axes of identity,"
which include race, class, age, and sexual preference and that work to shape
identity both positively and negatively (98–99). Thus the nomadic subject, as
situated, multifaceted, and alterable, challenges the modernist idea of an
essential or "core" self. For Braidotti, the nomad figuration invokes both
appreciation for, and the desire to, perform subjectivity as a "flux of successive becomings" (NS, 113).

Braidotti's nomadic subject proposes the ideal of perpetual relocation and resistance to a people's (or person's) becoming established in any *one* place or identity (NS, 33). Interpreted from a process-relational perspective, I see the nomadic subject as a motion-infused image emphasizing the processual nature of subjectivity. It conveys the idea that subjectivity is not a given, unchanging thing, but a dynamic, continuous happening, which reproduces and transforms itself by means of its interrelations with other culturally diverse subjects. The nomadic subject is never in a state of completion, but could more aptly be described as an ongoing process of transfiguration. Although stagnancy may at times *feel* like an overwhelming presence in people's lives, to exist is actually to be in a perpetual state of becoming. And yet, as will be further examined, this very relationality, characterized by fluidity and transformation, *also* implies the concrete specificity—based in the repetition of familiar patterns—of one's various communities. In other words, subjects are continually re-created through the dynamic interrelations of their various communities, the "givenness" of which at once provides stability and incites change.

Similar to the work on gender identity of various other feminist poststructuralists (e.g., Luce Irigaray, Donna J. Haraway, and Judith Butler), Braidotti's nomadic subject is meant to help us "think differently about difference" (NS, 78). Braidotti suggests that if we could dissolve modernity's dualistic characterization of difference—the different as "Other" or opposite of the norm—and its accompanying prescriptive force, then difference, indeterminateness, and even hybridity might be perceived as traits that are now *common* to much of humanity. She further contends that if we could recognize differences as necessarily constitutive of individual and communal identities, then we might come to see all subject positions as complex rather than monolithic. Thus, her vision of the subject as a constantly changing process *and* a thoroughly situated identity stretches the boundaries of how subjectivity may be conceived.

Not only a method of academic theorizing, nomadism also suggests everyday ethical praxis. Braidotti describes nomadism as a "path" offering "political hope for a point of exit from phallogocentrism," by which she means the ideology of the rigid, separative self of modern, Western patriarchal societies, who relates to others only externally. A nomadic ethos differs from this modernist paradigm in its desire to foster new facets of subjectivity for changing times and situations. In Braidotti's own words, the nomad does not "tak[e] any kind of identity as permanent" but "makes those *necessarily* situated connections that can help [him/her] to survive . . . never tak[ing] on fully the limits of one national, fixed identity" (NS, 33; my emphasis).

However, while cultivating the talent of adaptation is surely commendable, I wonder whether this ideal of "never becoming fixed" does not also reflect an ultramodern individualism; an ethos of not fully appreciating the interrelational context from which all of our identities emerge; a disposition of never committing to and hence never really belonging to any particular community, relationship, or place. While flexibility according to circumstance is undoubtedly a crucial aspect of survival (not to mention of well-being), should we not also take heed of the apparent human need for community, for being able to live out one's identity deeply (even if not unchangingly), and for being committed to the sustaining of some traditions, places, and relationships, to the conservation of certain environmental niches, for example? According to the way I have thus far described her position, Braidotti's nomadism seems to take seriously only the well-being of the individual and not the survival of the various places and communities out of which an individual's identity takes shape. Surely, if places are to offer needed rest and sustenance, not to mention identity-shaping influences, to the nomadic subject, then there must also be concern for the endurance of particular places/communities. Relatedly, should not the nomad be concerned with how her various sojourns affect, and perhaps help to renew or destroy, such places?

Although her position as discussed thus far would appear to say otherwise, there is an other aspect to Braidotti's nomad that opens space for the valuing of concreteness, including that of particular places and communities. It is, indeed, through her feminist methodology that Braidotti approaches this valuing of the particular, the given, or sustained patterns of identity. Conceiving of women as being contextually shaped in such a manner that they self-identify as members of a sexual *kind*—that is, as women, or as belonging to the category of the female sex—she advocates for a *women-defined* subjectivity of woman. Granted, "woman" remains a rather broad category, referring to many different groups of women, from different ethnicities, races, localities, economic classes, ages, and sexual preferences. Nevertheless, it is this aspect of Braidotti's project—her recognition of this specific pattern of definiteness, the *woman* kind—that reveals how distinctiveness of identity, that is, difference, is partially reliant upon the reiteration of definite, and hence limited, patterns.

As I understand it, Braidotti's nomadic aim is not for subjects to become so boundless that they encompass *all* differences; this, indeed, would erase difference! Rather, a pluralistic society implies that diversity is embodied in specificity, and this means that concrete beings, institutions, and events are never *exactly* alike one another; differences exist because every subject is partial or limited rather than universal. *Actual* subjects, therefore, even if they recognize their own inherent plurality and mutability, are by definition limited. Moreover, the fact that humans *do* recognize differences is due, among other things, to the ongoing repetition of specific patterns of subjectivity. No particular being or event is completely amorphous or all-encompassing; instead, each is uniquely and hence narrowly shaped. As Whitehead put it, "[i]ntensity is the reward of narrowness" (PR, 112).

As a reference to a patterned way of life and to a sociopolitical collectivity, the specific subject position, woman, has the potential in Braidotti's view to foster greater liberty for all those included in this category. This potential will be realized, however, only if those who identify themselves as women aim to consciously and creatively reappropriate this subjectivity. It is this ideal of purposeful reappropriation that makes Braidotti's nomadism a specifically feminist project. She describes her method thus: "'Being-a-woman' as the result of a construction of femininity in history and language *('Woman')*, is to be taken as the starting point for the assertion of the female as subject" (NS, 187). Thus by means of this intentional inhabiting of "woman" as a sociopolitical position, women may work to reinvent notions of femaleness and womanhood in a manner that defies rather than perpetuates a monolithic essentialism and empowers freer modes of agency for all those identified as women.

Braidotti's *female feminist* nomadic subject involves an interplay of transmutation with what I am calling "groundedness." *The* theoretical question for postmodern feminism, Braidotti declares, is "how to reassemble a vision of female subjectivity after the certainties of gender dualism have collapsed" (NS, 99). While conceding that real-life women's experiences and identities differ considerably according to their particular subject-locations, Braidotti believes it is nonetheless critical for women to claim the subject-position "woman"; only in this way will women's actions serve to reformulate what is assumed under this category. Reappropriating "women's identity" may therefore have an impact upon future women's identities and lives.

Thus it is that Braidotti advocates, through her figuration of the "female feminist nomadic subject," for women's deliberate, mindful mimesis of female subjectivity as a method for bringing about change and diversity in women's identities. Although the method of mimesis may seem paradoxical, it is so only when considered within the rationality of substance metaphysics—a metaphysics based on the subject as an unchanging essence. If we instead conceive of subjectivity as process—as multifaceted, in relation to others, and always evolving—mimesis becomes the opportunity for transformation, not for stagnancy. Change *happens* in and through the concreteness of particularity. Hence, a previous pattern of particularity (of gender, ethnicity, race, etc.) must be to some extent renewed in order also to be transformed. The performance of mimesis assumes that there are concrete embodiments of subjectivity—given patterns of identity—that constitute the fertile (or, sometimes not so fertile) grounds out of which future divergences may emerge.

Since according to the nomadic (and process) paradigm there are no absolute substances or essential identities, change need not always be conceived of as a radical breaking away from that which came before. Often, a more resilient kind of change is that which occurs gradually, precisely by means of this mimetic process. If creativity can be presupposed at each moment, in every energy-pulse of becoming (as in a process model), then reiterations of subject positions are never exact repetitions. The riddle of mimesis, then, is the creativity therein: While mimesis is the activity of inheriting and inhabiting patterns from the matrix of interrelationships of which one is a part, every reinstantiation of relational patterns—every moment of becoming—is shaped distinctively. In other words, in the very process of mimesis a space for creativity is opened. This relates to Whitehead's concept of the birth of creativity from interrelationship: "[C]reative action is the universe always becoming one in a particular unity of self-experience, and thereby adding to the multiplicity which is the universe as many" (PR, 57).

Think of a toddler learning to speak, or of an adult learning a new "dance move." As the toddler attempts words and as the adult practices the dance move through observation and repetition, their actions also "become anew"; the learned patterns become their own. Repetition is therefore never strict replication. Not stasis, but becoming, is thus the best way to describe the reiterative performances that engender subjectivity. And when mimesis is performed intentionally, as Braidotti urges, an awareness of the conflicts within a given subjectivity, such as that of "woman," will emerge, enabling discernment, dissatisfaction, and creative cultivation.

A feminist, nomadic politics is therefore based on two suppositions: (1) there is no such thing as a "natural" woman or "essential" female identity outside of ideological discourse; and (2) women's "femaleness," as a concrete, sociopolitical location of identity, is the *ground* (my term) from which further transformations of female subjectivity may develop. The goal of nomadic feminism is not to prove that all women are socially constructed in exactly the same way, nor to insist that all those who self-identify as women must come to some agreement about how to define and change female subjectivity. Rather, the goal *is,* in Braidotti's words, to "speak as a woman in order to empower women, to activate sociosymbolic changes in their condition," this being "a radically anti-essentialist position" (NS, 4). The female feminist nomadic project "mak[es] sexual difference *operational* by bringing about a women-identified re-definition of female subjectivity, of motherhood, and of sexuality" (NS, 55, my emphasis).

The figuration of the nomadic subject has the complexity of what is commonly referred to as the postmodern "both/and": It calls for both change—bringing about diversity—and endurance—valuing that which is "given" (which is not to say *essentially* given) as the living ground sustaining one's life and work. In other words, the adjective *nomadic* insists on dynamism, variety, and transgression—on never getting caught in the snares of the "sanctimonious sacred" (NS, 29); while the noun *subject* implies a concrete, sustaining presence *for whom* the nomadic stance might make a difference.

Cobb's Christ as the Process of Creative Transformation

Cobb's image of christ is strikingly similar to Braidotti's vision of the nomadic subject. As a figuration meant to inspire a certain mode of human subjectivity, christ is conceived by Cobb as the "process of creative transformation," by which he means an omnipresent, creative process involved in all human becoming, and indeed in creation at all levels of existence. Like Braidotti's nomadic subject, which is comprised of both a more universal aspect—the ideal of transformation, including yearning for change and not becoming mired in rigid identities—and a more "grounded" aspect—the previously given specificity of the female feminist subject, Cobb's christ figuration has two facets: (1) the ideal of creative transformation, meant to inspire openness to fluidity and diversity; and (2) the more specific signification of "christ," which reveals an embeddedness in a specific historico-cultural context and identity. In order for the universal aspect of creative transformation (or nomadism) to make any kind of *difference* in the actual world, it must be rooted in the more concrete aspect, christ (or, the female feminist nomadic subject). Thus, even as the christ-symbol is interpreted today in a diversity of ways, these varied interpretations share some common roots in a historical tradition. Cobb puts it this way: "There is an 'existential' dimension to the Christ symbol, namely that its meaning and value are always bound up with actual people, i.e., those who call themselves 'Christians'" (CPA). Without particular, concrete communities for whom the figuration is significant, "christ" would have no meaning or value.

Here, again, is the paradox: An ideal promoting a certain transcendence (creative transformation or nomadism, which signifies an ability to move *beyond* that which came before) is *dependent* for its actualization upon the concrete, upon that which is already established or given. Stated differently, even as creative transformation and nomadism are meant to incite change and variety within subjectivities, they are dependent upon concrete "grounds" or definite modes of identity—"christians" for Cobb and "female feminists" for Braidotti—in order for their meaning and value to take root.[11]

Now I will put some flesh on these rather abstract statements by examining in greater detail what I am calling Cobb's "postmodern figuration": christ as the process of creative transformation. Cobb's interest in the United States' burgeoning cultural and religious diversity was at the cutting edge of mid-1970s social concerns. Growing up in both Japan and the southern United States as the child of missionaries, Cobb (much like Braidotti) experienced his own identity as being shaped by more than one dominant culture. It is not surprising, then, that his vision for a "postmodern"[12] religious praxis entails embracing pluralism, which is at the same time not a reversion to sheer relativism. In a truly pluralistic society, according to Cobb, one's encounter with "the Other" would mean actually grappling with their worldviews and even appropriating some of their "truths," while at the same time not abandoning that which is good and salvific from one's own tradition. In Cobb's view, entering into relationships with people of other religio-cultural traditions should lead one to develop a more mature, complex, and multifaceted subjectivity, uniquely composed of one's past self and influences from "others."

Here we see Cobb applying a famous Whiteheadian axiom: that it is more interesting to transform contradictions into creative contrasts than to leave them as exclusionary contradictions.

The relevance of the christ-symbol in this ever-more pluralistic society, according to Cobb, has to do with its ability to promote nonexclusivist, non-imperialist, diversity-affirming religio-cultural practices. As long as the christ-image is tied to the "absolutization of one pattern of life against others or of one potential center of meaning and existence against others" (CPA, 21), it functions idolatrously, where idolatry means the conferrance of ultimacy upon something culturally specific and hence limited. Cobb similarly uses the term *the sacred* (20–21) to refer to that which becomes stagnant, such as certain creeds, images,[13] and laws. In other words, the *sacred,* as Cobb here uses the term, refers to those rules and institutions that we find ourselves afraid to criticize and work to reform. Such uncritical allegiance to the culturally specific, moreover, often leads to religious exclusivism, that is, to a specific group's claim of their own tradition's superiority.[14]

In large part to counteract such idolatry, Cobb confers upon "christ," the central symbol of Christianity, a meaning intended to stir people's desire for diversity and metamorphosis. Understood as the process of creative transformation, christ need not be limited to Christian experience. Christ refers, rather, to a dynamic, transformative, cosmic force intrinsic to all events and beings. Christ is therefore a potentially universal experience, even if conceptualized and named differently in different religious traditions, or not recognized as ultimate or divine by some traditions. Yet, one of the primary ways for Christians to experience this christ-power, according to Cobb, is by relativizing one's own, specifically Christian truths and practices in light of one's encounters with the truths and life-ways of other religio-cultural groups. In other words, to undergo change because of one's sincere encounter with those of other religious faiths is itself an experience of christ. Christ, as a figuration of transformation, should therefore lead Christians away from claims of superiority and exclusivity and toward yearning for encounters with those of other religio-cultural traditions.[15] In sum, as Cobb understands it, Christians are called through christ to embrace the opportunities present in a pluralistic society, including to profoundly experience diversity and subsequently to undergo change.

Christ, for Cobb, is at one and the same time a culturally constructed concept and the name for a creative and redemptive power immanent to, and interactive with, all of existence. Therefore, although he does appreciate that linguistico-cultural practices shape differently human cultures and the ideas therein, he nonetheless conceives of this cosmic creative process, "christ," as having an ontological reality not completely dependent upon language (CPA, 64–65). Consciously taking part in a historically shaped Christian context, Cobb discerns christ as the concrete manifestation of divinity or the incarnate logos, where logos refers to a "cosmic principle of order" (CPA, 71) and creative force. Yet Cobb also transforms the historical tradition's predominant understanding of christ; he expands the idea of christ beyond God's sole incarnation in one human, Jesus of Nazareth, toward a cosmological incarnation. Christ, for Cobb, plays the role of the "initial aim" in Whitehead's philosophy; christ is that dynamic and relational power that *participates in* the creative evolution of all beings and events through experiencing their reality with them and luring them toward embodying creative new possibilities. Once conceived as the incarnate process of creative transformation, christ reveals that existence *is* creative evolution; everything that exists is part of a vital process of becoming. In Cobb's words, christ's presence can be discerned within all moments of existence as "the not-yet-realized transforming the givenness of the past *from a burden* into a potentiality for new creation" (CPA, 59, emphasis added). As a ubiquitous power, christ is involved in the particular as well as in "the all"; christ is immanent as well as transcendent.[16]

Central to process thought is the idea that life has an indeterminate quality and that the freedom of creativity is therefore present at every moment, within the becoming of every new event. Hence, the human subject should not be viewed as remaining essentially the same over time; the subject, just like every other event, successively "happens" as an ongoing process of (re)creation (CPA, 69–70). Moreover, the way in which the subject continually comes into being is through the evolutions and revolutions of relationships. Accordingly, "the new" does not emerge from nowhere. Rather, novelty is produced through the creative interactions of relationships.

Since christ traditionally has been connected, through the doctrine of the incarnation, with understandings of redemption or salvation, Cobb believes that the christ-symbol has the power to continue to play a significant role in the way Christians view their own developments of identity. Indeed, christ may function as a *figuration,* critiquing and shaping Christians' self-understanding. In Cobb's process vision, there are two general facets to "becoming": (1) the repetition of specific patterns of subjectivity, creating endurance of identity; and (2) the entertaining of new possibilities experienced through relationality, which brings forth change. Embracing subjectivity *as process* could therefore inspire cultivation of identities that seek to incorporate more diversity and complexity than has been common to the modernist, Western view of the self, defined rigidly by discrete identity categories (e.g., being defined stagnantly, throughout one's life, as *either* man or woman, white or black, or heterosexual or homosexual). Cobb's christ-figuration, as the process of creative transformation intrinsic to all events and experienced especially within the interactions of relationships, could thus function to recommend dynamism, evolution, and heterogeneity as a model for the development of subjectivity. Similarly to Braidotti's nomadic subject, then, Cobb's christ could elicit new ways of perceiving and embodying subjectivity.

Beyond Monologism and Hierarchical Dualism: Process as
Grounded Transformation and Transformative Grounding

Yet Cobb's "christ" is similar to Braidotti's "nomadic subject" in another way, as well: both of these figurations, when interpreted one-sidedly, pose serious problems for human becoming, especially concerning humanity's dependence upon a viable terrestrial environment. In *Christ in a Pluralistic Age* Cobb equates "the sacred" with "the stagnant," declaring that in order for liberation to occur, human allegiance to "the given" and "the past as bondage" must be shattered (CPA, 57). Similarly, Braidotti associates "the given" with shackles placed upon those who "settl(e) into socially coded modes of thought and behavior" (NS, 5). Because of the emphasis they each place on the desirability of change and development, these authors' warnings against "settling into givenness" *can* be interpreted as the ideal of change for the sake of change or of novelty for the sake of "the new." Yet we must ask ourselves whether the modern Western association of "the good"—and "goods"—with that which is fast-paced, always-developing, and forever changing isn't what leads us at the same time toward a reckless consumption and poisoning of the natural environment, and consequently the destruction of ourselves. There appears to be a postmodern *fear* of "ground"—literally, as the earth, and figuratively, as an established, "given" social location or identity—so culturally ingrained that it may now be too late for humans to evade massive destruction of the biosphere. Is this not due to our relentless modern practices of "developing" lands and, upon depleting them of their nourishing elements, "moving on?" Does this not sound rather like Braidotti's description of nomadic subjectivity as "only passing through" and Cobb's description of christ as the power that abolishes all allegiances to "the given?" This, I believe, is a one-sided interpretation of these authors, and not their intent. Nonetheless, due to our present culture's overwhelmingly high valuation of economic "development" and "post"-everything, it must be recognized that such an interpretation is possible, as my own initial reading of these texts attests.

Is it not ironic, then, that an accompanying fear of the enduring, the sustaining, "the natural," and "the given" has become itself a cultural pattern—the oft-repeated pattern of incessantly moving beyond or throwing away that which was? Moreover, is it not a paradox that the kind of *change* I believe we now need is a change toward respecting "the given," and toward "letting be" the sometimes slower workings of nature, without acting upon the all-too-familiar desire to interfere and "develop" the land?

Of course, when we take the time to examine them more carefully, we see that neither Cobb's nor Braidotti's figuration should be interpreted so one-sidedly. Rather, both explicitly address one of the major issues of postmodern theory, How may we desire a specific type of change (or state of becoming)—for instance, liberation, freedom, nomadism, or creative transformation—*for* particular kinds of subjects—for instance, women—after the "death" of the modernist subject? In other words, once we have recognized that attempts to comprehend subjectivity through representative categories, such as women, men, whites, blacks, heterosexuals, homosexuals, and even human and animal, are at worst oppressive and at best problematically naive, how may we articulate and justify our desire to promote better, more liberating, and freer modes of subjectivity . . . for both ourselves and others? Since hierarchical power relations have helped to form identity categories in all their limitations and rigidity, does invoking these identity categories, even if for purportedly liberationist reasons, actually serve to reinforce the oppressiveness of power structures? And yet, if no "kind" can be designated *for whom* justice, change, liberation, and creative transformation are being advocated, then how can these ideals have any meaning? Put otherwise, if there is no enduring (for however long or short a period of time) subject or "kind," if there is no integrity of an individual event but instead only "flux," then must we not say that the ideal of transformation is merely "change for the sake of change?" For whom is change advocated if there is no value given to definiteness of location, particularity of identity, and endurance of ground? If givenness or groundedness has no other value than to supply a social identity that would be best overcome, then the ideal of relentless change has merely replaced the ideal of eternal stasis; one mono-logism has superseded another.

Because much postmodern rhetoric, especially in the forms it has taken in U.S. academia, celebrates such concepts as ambiguity, fluidity, and multiplicity at the seeming expense of notions like definiteness, stability, coherence, and "the given," it is important to assess the possible echoes of such a tone in postmodern writings. As we have seen, Braidotti's stress upon nomadism as opposed to the "paralysis of the sedentary" (NS, 30) and Cobb's emphasis upon creative transformation as opposed to "static principles" (CPA, 84) seem to embrace this dichotomous, either/or tendency. The danger, moreover, is that such a stance may help to promote an already prevalent anthropocentrism characterized by an attitude in which the only kind of change viewed as worthwhile (or even noteworthy) is *human*-caused change, such as "land development." In such a worldview there is an assumed insignificance of everything nonhuman, so that one would judge the transmutation of land devoid of human population into a parking lot or condominium complex as an indisputably valuable kind of development—quite suitable, perhaps, for those appropriating a postmodernist, nomadic lifestyle—simply because there was no apparent human use of the land before such development. Additionally, a purely anthropocentric worldview does not take seriously critical analyses of how cultural practices, such as global "free trade" capitalism, adversely influence the many nonhuman creatures dependent upon rain forests, wetlands, and other kinds of *more-than-human* (to borrow a term from David Abram[17]) "grounds." Put simply, it does not take seriously *eco-*

logical reasoning, which elucidates the interrelations within and between ecosystems, including the dependency of human life upon a healthy biosphere and the repercussions of human actions upon the natural environment, other human communities, and possible future generations.

A one-sided reading of the nomadic subject and the process of creative transformation does not heed respect for that which is given, that is, for those aspects of existence that are *more than* culturally constructed, even if we cannot "know" them outside of our linguisitco-cultural constructions. A paradigm that does not take into account these more-than-human contexts leads to a conception of humans as individuals "simply located" (Whitehead),[18] similar to Catherine Keller's description of "separative selves." This is the understanding that persons and things are exactly as we perceive them to be through one particular mode of sensory perception—sight; that they are delineated by clear-cut boundaries, and located, quite straightforwardly, in a single, three-dimensional place. This view is in contradistinction to a process-relational understanding, which comprehends people and things as *intercontextual* events or processes, continuously created by and in turn furthering the creation of their cultural, ecological, and spatiotemporal contexts. The paradigm of the simply located subject leaves the impression that the human realm is not profoundly affected by, nor has any great effect upon, the more-than-human world, and so only cultural-linguistic events are believed to have significance; only human-caused changes are deemed valuable. It is in this sense that some postmodern theories become vulnerable to the charge of cultural-linguistic solipsism; they disclose a *hyper-* rather than a *post*modernism.[19]

Of course, indifference to the nonhuman environment need not be an essential component of postmodern thought. As we examined previously, neither Braidotti's nor Cobb's figuration offers merely a one-sided emphasis upon change. To the contrary, each of these figurations embodies a critical response to the hierarchically dualistic stance of hypermodernism. Instead of extolling simplistically the virtue of "change" over "endurance," "movement" over "stasis," and "culture" over "nature," these figurations propose a more complex coalescence of innovation and reiteration, transformation, and groundedness.[20] While the "female feminist nomadic subject" calls us to account for the specificity of subjects for whom the nomadic stance is desired, "creative transformation" reminds us that the process of becoming a subject includes *both* "trans"—motility and change—*and* "formation"—definite and enduring shapes of concreteness. It also must not be forgotten that many of Cobb's subsequent writings, as is evident in the word choice for such titles as *Sustainability, Sustaining the Common Good,* and *The Earthist Challenge to Economism,* reveal a profound respect for the sustenance that is provided by "the given" and the need for practices of ecological sustainability. With these writings and his book, *Is It Too Late? A Theology of Ecology,* Cobb has "pioneered the theological critique of all that threatens the ecological ground!"[21]

Thus, rather than championing the worship of the "mono-logos" of opposi-tional dualisms, figurations such as these proposed by Braidotti and Cobb actually demonstrate that a stark separation of novelty and givenness is pos-sible only in our abstractions—and not even then, since the meaning of the one term depends in part upon the meaning of the other. Upon studying them carefully, we see that Braidotti's and Cobb's figurations illustrate the interplay of change and endurance; they offer images of the interpenetration and inter-dependence of groundedness and transformation.

It is therefore important in our appropriation and further development of their figurations that we not value change at the expense of endurance, roam-ing at the expense of rootedness, revolution at the expense of revival. There are, of course, important reasons for sometimes caricaturing the sedentary as paralyzing (Braidotti) and equating "the given" with bondage (Cobb); history has shown that it is always necessary to beware of established power regimes, be they political, religious, economic, or familial, which preach the necessity of "keeping things as they are" and stifle the unrest of liberationist impulses. Braidotti, as a feminist and gender-theorist, and Cobb, writing this book at a moment when religio-cultural pluralism was coming into people's conscious-ness, are both attuned to the need for breaking away from certain confining images, norms, and institutions. And yet, as we appropriate and develop their figurations in our *own* moment of ecological destruction and "global econo-mies," we must also recognize the danger of elevating that which is ever-mov-ing and always-changing above that which endures and provides sustenance. Today, for example, it is too easy (and too common) for multinational corpo-rations and their chief executives to "pick up and go" in pursuit of better prof-its, with little or no regard for the consequences to the ecological and human communities they've left behind. Thus, discourses tending toward disdain for the "the given" need to be critiqued in order to reveal their tacit disavowal of the intrinsic value of the biosphere's slower movements;[22] of the ongoing rep-etitions that create patterns of endurance; of the workings of our bodies and bioregions; and of all those species and events that came before and exist in many ways outside of human consciousness or control. My point is not to deny the facticity of, and necessity for, change at every level of existence, but to underscore the importance at this particular moment in history of (1) acknowl-edging and imagining the necessity of "the given"; and (2) comprehending that novelty emerges from *within* the complex intensity of inheritance, reiter-ation, relationality, and endurance.

Process may be, after all, one of the best words to signify this idea of how novelty and differentiation unfold from the reiterating patterns of speci-ficity and the concretions of interrelations. This Whiteheadian-derived under-standing of process, with its inclusion of both *concrescence* (becoming actual, "given," or a "stubborn fact of existence") and *transition* (having a dynamic, causal effect upon others, fostering the becoming of new concrescences), may

enable us to realize that neither "stasis" nor "incessant change" are very helpful for describing the fullness and complexity of existence. According to a
process view, particular relational patterns become incarnate over and again
(reiteration), thereby creating the intensity of definiteness, which in turn,
when met with contrast, spawns the desire for change. Insofar as we develop
figurations that illuminate this dynamic process of the complex coalescence
of groundedness and change, we may move beyond a modernist either/or into
a postmodern both/and.

We could say that in order to be shaped in any *specific* way there must
be enduring (and hence, reiterated) patterns of distinctive types of relation. As
Whitehead put it, "[r]estriction is the price of value" (SMW, 178). By this he
meant that *to be* at all is to be limited, and, by virtue of this very limitation, is
to have value. Were everything amorphously "one," there would be, quite
simply, no diversity, and so we would not experience differences within ourselves nor in our relationships with others. It is the act of reiteration that creates the *intensity* and *integrity* of specific kinds; the differences we recognize
come to our attention because of the endurance of these specificities, produced through the reiterative process. Furthermore, it is the encounter of different intensely experienced particularities—the meeting of diverse *kinds*—
that produces desire for transformation. Yet in order for there to exist specific
kinds, there must be endurance and reiteration—which is *not* to say sheer stasis—of intertwining patterns of relationality *through which* these distinctive
kinds have come into being. This relational matrix may be called "community," "ground," or "place," while the specific *kinds* are the distinctive and
hence limited (though not unchanging) subjects.[23]

Acknowledging that subjects in their distinctiveness emerge from and
contribute to enduring nexuses or "places" does not require reliance upon substance metaphysics. Whitehead, for example, suggested we imagine that
which we would normally categorize as a subject as, instead, a "superject"—
a designation underlining the idea that individuals emerge *from* the many
component events that create them, and in turn contribute *to* the multiple becomings of others (including their own next moment of becoming or "concrescence"). This concept of the "superject" emphasizes that the subject is
not, at core, an underlying essence onto which external relations are added,
but is instead an always-evolving process that both is born *from,* and *inter-
jects into,* the becoming of others. These interactive patterns of reiteration and
transformation constitute the vibratory grounds that germinate both new and
old genres of subjectivity.

What is needed, then, is a reimagining of "groundedenss," "givenness,"
and "place" in order to accentuate their vital, ecological resonances. "The
given" need not refer only to that which restricts, although even a certain
sense of limitation should be valued for the the intensity of particularity that
it enables. Limitations are confining, yet they are also *de*fining; they delineate

specificity, indeed difference; they are imperative to the existence of particularities, which together create diversity. Restrictions are necessary for the continual emergence of microcosms—distinctive compositions, each of which is uniquely composed from the relationships of cosmic multitudes. Hence, groundedness, "the given" and "place" refer to the prerequisite provisions for the vibratory fields that cultivate both endurance and innovation. We should therefore acknowledge and respect "ground" as our intertwining ecocultural context; as that which engenders our diverse becomings and sustains our evolutions; indeed as that which sustains stimulations rather than static substances. We should "figure" them as "grounding transformations," making possible difference and relation.

Notes

1. Cf. Catherine Keller, *From a Broken Web: Separation, Sexism and Self* (Boston: Beacon, 1986) for a description of the difference between the modernist patriarchal model of the "separative self" and the ideal of the "relational self," which emerged within strands of late-twentieth-century feminism.

2. Whitehead describes Descartes's understanding of substantive selves and material things as follows: "for Descartes, minds and bodies exist in such a way as to stand in need of nothing beyond themselves individually (God only excepted, as being the foundation of all things); . . . Those principles lead straight to the theory of a materialistic, mechanistic nature, surveyed by cogitating minds" (SMW, 144–145).

3. Charlene Spretnak uses the term *hypermodern* in *Resurgence of the Real: Body, Nature and Place in a Hypermodern World* (Reading, MA: Addison-Wesley, 1997). David Ray Griffin similarly uses the term *ultramodernism* in his introduction to the SUNY Series in Constructive Postmodern Thought.

4. Both Frederic Jameson in *Postmodernism, or, The Cultural Logic of Late Capitalism* (Durham, NC: Duke University Press, 1981) and David Harvey in *The Condition of Postmodernity* (Cambridge: Blackwell, 1989) contend that there is a connection between postmodern aesthetico-cultural modes, such as appeals to the fast-paced, ever-moving, always changing subject, and today's brand of transnational capitalism, which negatively affects people's responsibility toward, and respect for, natural environments. In Jameson's biting words, "[p]ostmodernism is what you have when the modernization process is complete and nature is gone for good" (ix).

5. Although Cobb and many other Christian theologians typically capitalize the word "christ," I follow several postmodern theologians in choosing not to do so. "Christ" is not a sir-name, but means "messiah"; "christ" when used with a proper name is descriptive, as in "Jesus, the christ," and *not* Jesus (first name) Christ (last name).

6. I use the term *ground* because of its allusion to earth and soil. Ground conjures a sense of the relative stability needed for growth and sustenance, this stability being an amalgamation, nonetheless, of a rich diversity of creatures, elements, and chemical processes. The word *ground* may serve to remind us that "the given" implies a certain

dynamism (as does decay); it is the kind of activity that creates relative stability, which in turn supplies the necessary sustenance for evolution. For a discussion on the difference between "ground" and "foundation," see Keller's introduction in this volume.

7. Although many Christians still sing hymns on Sunday celebrating the divine as an unchanging "mighty fortress," Westerners today more regularly pay homage to the market of ever-changing fashions, short-lived technological devices, nonsustainable consumption of natural "resources" (witness the ever-popular "Sport Utility Vehicles"), and gourmet foods served up in over-size styrofoam or plastic "to-go" containers. There are now several books published that look at "the market" as the new global religion, one of them being Cobb's *Earthist Challenge to Economism: A Theological Critique of the World Bank,* Religion and Politics Series (New York: St. Martin's, 1999).

8. See Carolyn Merchant's *Death of Nature: Women, Ecology and the Scientific Revolution* (San Francisco: Harper, 1989), especially chapters 7 and 8, for an interesting discussion on the depreciation of the organic view of a dynamic, animate nature corresponding with the European scientific revolution of the sixteenth and seventeenth centuries.

9. She was raised in northern Italy and Australia, and has studied and worked in various countries, becoming fluent in several languages.

10. Braidotti avers that her own claim, "I am a woman"—emerging as it does from a particular historico-cultural location—would, if spoken by someone of a different context, take on a quite different meaning.

11. Of course "kinds," such as "woman" and "Christian," can also be viewed as universals or ideals, as can all identity types. No moment of concrete-particularity can be *named* in a way that fully represents its complexity. But, for present purposes, I am making the point that some terms, especially terms of identity such as *female feminist* and *Christian,* indicate definite types of particularity more than do other, more "universal" ideals, like "transformation" or "being," which are meant to be viewed as pertaining everywhere and to everyone.

12. Surprisingly, Cobb uses the term *postmodern* in his 1975 *Christ in a Pluralistic Age* (CPA, 25–26). According to David Ray Griffin, Cobb was defining this term as early as 1964 (Griffin, *Varieties of Postmodern Theology* [Albany: State University of New York Press, 1989, 7].)

13. Such as referring to God as "King" or "Lord" in a context where "kingship" either no longer exists or refers more to dictatorship than to "just rule."

14. As per Paul Tillich's critique of idolatry in his *Dynamics of Faith* (New York: Harper, 1957).

15. While understood to be a "universal," and hence present in everyone's experience, Cobb finds it reductionistic to say that "christ" points to "the same" ultimate reality recognized in other religious traditions. Such a claim can be made or refuted only within the process of interreligious dialogue, and, from his own experience, "the power of creative transformation" is *not* the same universal that is supremely appreciated in many other religious traditions, for example, in Buddhism. (From Cobb's own experience with interreligious dialogue between Buddhists and Christians, the conclu-

sion arrived at is usually *not* "Christ is the same as Buddha.") Buddhist "emptiness," in other words, may signify a *different* ultimate reality (or a different aspect of ultimate reality), which Christians have not held as supremely important but could learn to appreciate through creative transformation.

16. Or, to put it precisely in Cobb's terminology, "logos" refers to the universal and transcendent aspect of divinity, while "christ" refers to the divine in its process of becoming incarnate, that is, becoming immanent in the world in particular ways.

17. I adopt David Abram's term, *more-than-human* (*The Spell of the Sensuous* [New York: Random, 1996]), as opposed to "nonhuman" or "other-than-human," to indicate that while everything we experience and know about is related to the human (by virtue of our vantage point as humans), reality is not merely of our human making, but includes much "more than" ourselves.

18. For Whitehead's discussion of "simple location," see SMW, 49ff.

19. See Charlene Spretnak's discussion of "hypermodernism" as "more intensified modernity" (8) in *The Resurgence of the Real: Body, Nature and Place in a Hypermodern World* (Reading, MA: Addison-Wesley). Hypermodernism is similar to Griffin's term, *ultramodernism,* which he describes in his series introduction to *Varieties of Postmodern Theology* (Albany: State University of New York Press, 1989) as the "carrying [of] modern premises to their logical conclusions" (xii).

20. Of course, as Whitehead knew well, all theorizing is abstraction. The term *concrete,* for example, abstracts from the complex actuality to which it refers. What is recommended by process thought, however, is to think as concretely as possible, that is, to remember to take account of the various and interlinking contexts from which different types of thinking arise, to comprehend that there is no "view from nowhere" nor any satisfactory "grand unifying theory," and hence to be willing to continually rethink one's abstractions in light of new material brought to one's attention.

21. Keller, in conversation. See Cobb, *Is It Too Late? A Theology of Ecology,* rev. ed. (Denton, TX: Environmental Ethics Books, 1995).

22. For instance, I cannot observe the actual movements of the opening of the fuschia flower bud on my Christmas cactus, but each time I remember to look at it again, it has slightly changed. Indeed, it is always changing, but this dynamic movement takes place more gradually than I am able to see with my eyes.

23. Though my focus in this chapter has been on modes of human subjectivity, "kinds" refers also to other species and indeed to any specific kind of being produced through the reiteration of relational patterns.

7

Processing Henry Nelson Wieman
Creative Interchange among Naturalism, Postmodernism, and Religious Valuing

CAROL WAYNE WHITE

> Resources of appreciative consciousness are not sufficient to withstand the onslaughts of change, the evil impulses of the heart, and the wearing-down of continued effort. . . . History cannot lift this fate, but it can make the glow of swift decline cumulative through a succession of generations. History can give to all things mean and noble a voice to speak from out of the past, bringing to the sensitive mind a love of earth and all things in it and the sky above.
>
> —Henry Nelson Wieman, *The Source of Human Good*

In America, the sphere of religious studies has frequently seen its own death forecast by those working within and without its disciplinary boundaries. Most recently, the challenge to traditional religious thought has been associated with the epistemological limitations and de-transcendentalizing agendas advanced by postmodern theorists. In response, many religious scholars have denied the claims of postmodernism altogether, dismissing it as the playful cant of the intellectual elite. However, it remains the case for some of us that the critical perspectives associated with postmodernism express a deeply shared sense that aspects of our conceptual, social, and political worldviews have been profoundly transformed. With an emphasis upon the importance of perspective, a rejection of universalist pretensions, and a suspicion of totalizing, closed systems, postmodern theories have influenced contemporary thinkers to forfeit the use of metatheories and transcendentalizing language and to begin focusing upon the historicity of all systematic discourses.

Embracing postmodernism has certainly forced many of us to cast a critical eye upon the intelligibility of that "Truth" that has illuminated the landscape of the West for centuries. We have become increasingly aware of the limitations and ambiguities of our various claims and the contradictions inherent in all our systems of thought. However, rigorous and sustained engagement with influential postmodern strategies (specifically deconstruction and poststructuralism) is not a subtle, seductive, dance of death for religious scholars. Rather, as I have argued elsewhere,[1] the epistemic and cultural issues emerging from postmodernism offer unprecedented opportunities for religious scholars to reconceive and reexperience the self, the other, and even our religiosity, in radically new and surprising ways. Upon surveying the morass of postmodern terrains, one may, in fact, ascertain whether, how, and to what extent possible alliances with other critical discourses can expand the imagination and help one discover fuller ways of being religious in the present era.

As one avenue to that end, in this chapter I explore possible intersections between postmodernism and process theology, which in my opinion is one of the most viable and intelligible religious discourses available to Westerners today. There are many important and diverse perspectives associated with the modern process paradigm, but in this chapter I focus upon Wieman's process theology, which developed during the early twentieth century.[2] Although Wieman's process perspective is often overshadowed by the works of such luminaries as Alfred North Whitehead[3] and Charles Hartshorne, Wieman's ideas about creativity and value offer an unique point of departure for those of us seeking some type of engagement between process theologies and postmodern theories. I specifically argue that Wieman's empirically oriented views join, even as they must be differentiated from, current postenlightenment forms of thought in presenting destabilizing elements to the ontotheological traditions of the West.[4] I further contend that Wieman's theological naturalism is devoid of the rampant rationalism often associated with process cosmologies, and that the pragmatist philosophy underlying his functional theism is suggestive of some poststructuralist epistemic assumptions.

I begin my exploration by outlining features of poststructuralist epistemologies and their impact upon religious thought. I then introduce Wieman's process framework[5] and provide a new reading of his thought within the context of poststructuralist epistemologies. Finally, in the third section, I outline a type of postmodern religious valuing informed by insights garnered from Wieman's process perspective and from my own poststructuralist assumptions. This model of postmodern religiosity emphasizes interpretations of "alterity" that exceed modernist claims.

Destabilizing the Ontotheological Game

Do we not smell anything yet of God's decomposition? God is dead. God
remains dead. And we have killed him. How shall we, the murderers of all
murderers, comfort ourselves?

—Friedrich Nietzsche, *The Gay Science*[6]

Deconstruction's impact upon religious discourse derives chiefly from its
questioning of a Western metaphysical tradition that has named and secured a
"Presence" that confers meaning and telos upon all human endeavors.
According to Jacques Derrida, all Western modes of analysis, explication, and
interpretation have reinforced a logocentric system. That system of thought
has employed fundamental terms or principles (God, Consciousness, Essence,
etc.) to designate what Derrida calls the "transcendental signified," or the
steadfast center of reality upon which rests existence as we encounter it.[7] The
ontological significance of this fixed, immutable center lies in its being
beyond the reach of free play. Its existence is substantiated by the assumption
that there is a level at which reality appears to humans directly, with an immediacy of presence.

Much of Derrida's deconstructive idiom has challenged the imperialist
tendencies of all linguistic codes and systems, especially religious ones. The
underlying assumption is that language itself is an infinitely interwoven fabric
of signifiers, with no demonstrable power of direct representation of a reality
external to it. The moment of deconstruction—the point at which the grammatical token, signifier, or vehicle of reference discloses itself as being void of
any ontological gravity—corresponds in theological thinking to a smashing of
those idols that have embodied pious assurance and doctrinal certainty. To the
extent that religionists and philosophical theologians embrace Derridean textual strategies, we face the prospect of debunking, or at least rethinking, the
myth of an originary form of presence. There is nothing (no pure, uninterpreted
presence already there) that we can try to represent in or to consciousness.

Derrida suggests instead that "the Real" is actually heterogeneous, fluc-
tuating, infinitely open and governed by chance, rather than by logic or an
immanent telos unfolding inexorably in and over time. If taken seriously, this
view of "the Real" undermines many traditional ontotheological concepts of
Truth. It generates an inexhaustible number of possible interpretations and
material for interpretations. For example, theological "Truth" can no longer
be conceptualized in terms of how adequately it reveals "the Real"; Truth is
not the representation or mirror of an eternal and universal substance
(Presence) or subject, because these do not exist. Additionally, Truth cannot
be understood in terms of correspondence to "the Real" because "the Real"
always exceeds and escapes our thinking about it.

Postmodern textual strategies unveil paradigmatic veins of traditional
Christian theology as rationalist movements aimed at controlling, labeling, and

classifying. Poststructuralist epistemologies unmask the myth (text) of classical philosophical theology as that "Truth" that would transform differences into dichotomous oppositions and reduce pluralities to a unitary centrism. Ensnared in logocentric assumptions, the influential theological (Christian) text has mandated that all theological truths necessarily become engrossed in totalistic interests. This emphasis upon firm foundations and totalizing systems has been the self-assigned task of theology (both in its classical and modern forms), which, in turn, has drawn on a tradition of rigorous explanations and extensions, ranging from Plato through René Descartes, to Immanuel Kant and Ludwig Wittgenstein. Postmodern theories challenge religious scholars who desire to hold on to the certainty of established concepts, or to keep them from sliding into nonmeaning. They suggest that, absolved of absolute knowledge, freed from the obligation to present in transparent language some alleged ultimate meaning or "unity" of reality, theological inquiry might instead situate and inscribe meanings and interpretations that become possible as human agents encounter the Other(s) and Difference(s) of various sociopolitical contexts.[8]

While not as iconoclastic as postmodernism, process thought has also resisted certain totalizing conceptions of reality that have dominated modernity. As a specific response to the clash between scientific mechanism and vitalism in the late nineteenth and early twentieth centuries, and as a challenge to the dominance of philosophical idealism, process thought helped to revolutionize theological and philosophical studies in the twentieth century. But can religionists affirm an alliance of process thought and postmodernism, while at the same time reconceiving how to think and act beyond problematic modernist claims? I believe Wieman can help us answer this question, because elements of his empirically oriented process system intersect with postmodern challenges to a tradition of modernism that has dominated our intellectual imagination for too long.

Overview of the Process Naturalism of Henry Nelson Wieman

Wieman's religious thought may best be seen as a continual endeavor to characterize what he considered to be of greatest value for humanity. In many of his published works, Wieman returns to a central query:

> What operates in human life with such character and power that it will transform man as he cannot transform himself, saving him from evil and leading him to the best that human life can ever reach, provided that he meets the required conditions? (IA, 3)

This question inevitably led Wieman to develop a mode of inquiry that he believed could apprehend, locate, and specify this transforming power within the natural realm. His empirically based process thought emerged as a result of these efforts.

Wieman's central problematic addresses a crucial issue that concerned many liberal thinkers of his time—whether one could continue to speak of the existence of God as a concrete reality.[9] The ethical movement in American theology had become so strong that many religious scholars lacked any serious interest in continuing to construct theories of the reality or ontology of God. With the rise of pragmatism and functional psychology, theological inquiry was primarily directed to what could be perceived or known, rather than to speculative or mystical ideas. The appeal to both pragmatism and functionalism was evident in the way many religious scholars (e.g., E. S. Ames and Shailer Matthews) sought to resolve the central problem of theism. Their various replies demonstrate the empirical orientation already at work within their thought. Empiricism in this context was a study of the functional aspects of phenomena. A thing or movement was known in terms of the functions it served: Find out the motives behind actions, affirmations, and words, as well as their purported purposes, and you may unmask the real nature of the event itself.[10] This new empiricism also emphasized a measure of practicality and dealing with the immediacies of existence. It was within this context that Wieman began his lifelong task of defining God as the supreme actuality of existence, identified as "creativity."

Wieman's empirical theism is concerned with the character of God as verified by the existential medium, that is, the sphere in which we live, move, and have our being. He writes, "My own purpose is a very earnest and a very serious one. It is so to formulate the idea of God that the question of God's existence becomes a dead issue, like the question of other inescapable forms of natural existence, and all our energies can be turned to living for God and seeking better knowledge about God" (ITG, 276). According to Wieman, most contemporary views of God were inadequate because they presented ideas about beliefs in God, instead of ideas deriving from experiences of God. Religious commitment, he felt, should be to the experienced reality of God and not to a mere concept: "The word 'God' should refer to what actually operates to save and not merely to some belief about what operates in this way. But in current usage the word actually refers to pictures in the mind and not to the actuality" (MUC, 12). For Wieman, the conceptions of deity espoused by influential theologians touted a rationalism that was shorn of the facticity that an empirically based theology could claim.

Wieman felt that a particular method must be followed before one could gain knowledge of God, or any knowledge at all. In his early works, he calls this method "the scientific method," "the empirical method," "the method of reason," or even "the commonsense method." This process involved, for Wieman, basic observations regarding the functional and operative meaning of creativity. In these earlier writings, the observation of certain experiences was based upon sensory data and intuition. It was not the individual, however, who was believed to produce these experiences. They were instead products of a transformative power, God, which gave particular form or character to the given context. For Wieman, God creates by giving a direction of value to a particular process of becoming. God works through the development of culture as it centers on a particular situation, in order to transform the situation into a salvific experience.[11]

However, an important shift in Wieman's thought occurred during the thirties and forties, and it is this phase of his work that concerns me most. The imagery in his writings of this time reflects his growing sensitivity to social concerns and threats to human survival. After World War II and Hiroshima, Wieman's theological writings became oriented toward a wider cultural situation. This new emphasis led him to a fuller interpretation of "God" within his philosophy of creativity. Wieman's continued interest in creativity shows forth prominently in *Normative Psychology of Religion,* written with Regina Wescott Wieman. There they provide an analysis of "supreme value" as "that connection between enjoyable activities by which they support one another, enhance one another, and, at a higher level, mean one another" (NPR, 46). Value does not lie in the events themselves but rather in the connection between these events. Value, hence, is interpreted as the combination of "what is" and "what may be," a combination of actuality and possibility.

When one gains meaning from the connections, value occurs in such a way that there is growth of value. The increase of value in the functional connection between activities should not be identified with universal programs; it means instead that only within the scope of the conditions under consideration there is growth. It sums up all that can be hoped for in terms of the best conceivable world. Growth of meaning describes the creative process (identified as God) by which the enhancement of the world takes place through the enhancement of its individual members (NPR, 48). This supreme value is superhuman, but not supernatural. The distinction is that it is not something wholly outside of human life ("supernatural"), but it does operate beyond the plans and visions of individuals ("superhuman"), bringing forth values humans cannot foresee, and often developing connections of mutual support and mutual meaning in spite of, or contrary to, the efforts of humans (NPR, 52).

In *The Source of Human Good,* his most important work, Wieman furthers his analysis of creative value within the context of human interactions and purposeful living. He appears even more intent on addressing the empirical happenings of creative value—how the act of valuing occurs concretely and dynamically within the lived experience of people—and identifying specific occurrences expressive of it. Here, Wieman speaks of God as the source of human good and asserts that human good can be increased only by the progressive accumulation of good through a sequence of generations. He further suggests that this good cannot accumulate so long as humans are preoccupied with seeking only the material "goods" of life.

A key phrase in this book is "the creative event," a highly complex concept connoting creativity as operating in human life to give it qualitative meaning. Of course, for Wieman, creativity is not merely identified with the common usages often associated with it. For example, he does not view creativity solely as innovative behavior on the part of individuals, nor as achievements produced by imaginative and artistic persons (though these would be included as instances of it). Rather, the creative event describes a process of reorganizing the many discordant parts of our lives into a more inclusive whole. The sovereign God *is* creativity, in the sense that God is the character, structure, or form that enables the events of human life to be creative. Creative ability is produced in humanity as a consequence of the prior workings of the creative event.[12] Wieman identifies the creative event not merely with the work of God, but with the *being* of God. He uses the term *being* to convey the idea that this event is a *concrete* reality embracing four unified but distinct subevents. Briefly stated, they are,

1. the emerging awareness of qualitative meaning through communication;
2. the integration of these new meanings with those previously acquired;
3. the expanding of quality in the appreciable world;
4. the widening and deepening of community. (SHG, 58–68)

The first event is the primary context from which the other three emerge. For Wieman, a stream of experience comes to us first as qualitative immediacy; only later do we become cognizant of it as knowledge relations. In other words, qualitative meaning occurs when every organism reacts so as to break the passage of existence into units or intervals called "events" and to relate these to one another. Thus, when a single organism is able to acquire the qualitative meanings developed by other organisms and to add them to its own, the human mind and its appreciable world are transformed. Events include within their structures possibilities for future development. Qualities or values are the elements of which events are made. They are the ontological reality of an event: "Every event accessible to human experience is a quality or complex of qualities; also, every event is an instance of energy" (SHG, 301).

Furthermore, a "conjunction" is a new and more complex event made up of a strand of events. When a conjunction occurs in such a way that the qualities of the event included in the conjunction fulfill their possibilities to a greater degree, there is an increase of meaning, called "qualitative meaning." According to the logic of Wieman's thought, events cannot foresee the developments possible to them, nor can the universe determine whether there will be an increase or decrease of value. There must be some determining factor responsible for integrating the values of the individual events. This one factor is God, for it is the process of progressive integration of value within the universe. Accordingly, God reveals Godself to us in events in such a way that we can understand and learn how to bring forth conditions that would allow for an increase of value. As the creative event, God is the highest value. God is part of the cosmic whole, but at the same time God is not to be simply identified with the universe. Limitations are placed upon God by the present realities at hand. In other words, God can only work with what is present. The knowledge gained through this interaction is a good example of Wieman's epistemological basis. He asserts, "The creative event as here treated includes only those events which bring a new structure whereby the human mind distinguishes and relates events in such a way that there is more richness of quality in happenings as they occur and greater range and variety of appreciated possibility" (SHG, 68). The creative event is unknowable aside from the way it functions in relation to other events.

What makes this theory so intriguing to me is the implication that human beings receive both freedom and the potentiality for creative community through creative interchange or communication. The possibility of transformation is given to humans through two sources, a primary one and a secondary one. The primary source is creativity as creative interchange; this is identified as the "transforming actuality," better known as God. The secondary source is that which human beings can learn to do, individually and collectively, when provided the right conditions for the release of creative interchange. When this secondary source is alienated from the primary source, transformation becomes merely a moral effort and not an authentic religious commitment to the primary source. It is the responsibility of humans to open ourselves to creative interchange as the *source* of good in order that we may be "saved." Here again a persistent strand in Wieman's thought appears, that is, that we cannot, as individuals, save ourselves; creative interchange is not a pseudonym for humanistic morality.

In a later chapter of *The Source of Human Good,* Wieman introduces the notion of the "perceptual event" as contributing to what is observable in the acquisition of knowledge of God. The perceptual event includes everything within and around the biological organism, which experimentation demonstrates as making a difference to conscious awareness when perceptual reaction occurs (SHG, 182). Observable experience is transformed into a God-experience when cultural imagery and sensibilities and historical conditioning converge with the experience at hand, yielding value or meaning within the present event. The present event thus becomes interpreted and validated within a larger communal context. This activity, in turn, results in a greater sense of possibilities for the future through the enhancement of others and oneself, which is another way of asserting that knowledge of God is attained. In the Wiemanian context, God alone accounts for the possibilities for new meanings and new values in human existence. Creativity is God "operating in human existence to create a wider and deeper community of shared values between individuals and peoples, while expanding the valuing consciousness of each participant individual."[13]

In his technical postscript to *The Source of Human Good,* Wieman expands upon his naturalistic metaphysics. Here, Wieman further outlines important features of the creative event. Creativity is the character, structure, or form that the event must have in order to be creative. "Creativity" is an abstraction, whereas the concrete reality is now designated as the "creative event." The creative event is changeless in respect to that structure whereby we call it "creative," even though the concrete wholeness of the event is always changing (SHG, 299). The same can be said of other events within the universe—the universe being the primary event or the basic nexus of events that contains an infinity of events. The universe is a universe only because, throughout all its changes, there is a constitutive structure whereby we call it "a universe."

Underlying Wieman's naturalism is the assumption that the mind and the universe are interdependent; they are appreciative and appreciable. Yet their interdependence is not an enduring identity. The universe that we experience transforms its nature according to the conditions of our bodies. Emphasis is upon the interaction between the psychophysical organism, its environment, and their constitutory parts.[14] That reality underlying all others, in the sense of a changeless structure of felt quality and knowable order, is creativity, because it is necessarily prior to every other form of experience. Thus, with his naturalist metaphysics, Wieman also speaks of a creative and liberating commitment to that ultimate reality. This deeper commitment is, again, to the actuality, and not merely to ideas about it (IA, 7). One must view one's ideas critically because a deeper commitment to God delivers one from bondage to one's ideas of God. This faith commitment also entails a conformity of lifestyle and behavior to the overall purpose of the creative event: the increase of human freedom, individually and collectively, is accompanied by growth of creative community (MUC, 25).

From Wieman's Religious Naturalism to a Poststructuralist Plurality of Values

> We shall have no recourse to any "transcendental grounds, orders, causes or purposes" beyond events, their qualities, and relations. . . .The richest and highest values sought and found by religion and morals are interpreted as structured events and their possibilities.
>
> —SHG, 6-7

Wieman was not a poststructuralist, but his de-transcendentalizing naturalism hints nonetheless at some of the more important epistemic changes that have emerged with the linguistically oriented analyses of poststructuralism. In this section, I assess the religious implications of Wieman's process naturalism for contemporary thinkers. I believe his philosophy of creative interchange can be interpreted in light of poststructuralism in two ways: (1) as an early de-transcendentalizing movement challenging classical and other foundationalist "modern" forms of religious thinking; and (2) as a materially based hermeneutic that challenges the linguistic authority of current postmodern theory, much of which has fostered historical abstractions or a sterile aestheticism devoid of ethical charge and material force.

Situating Wieman Within Current Poststructuralist Contexts

First, it is important to note that Wieman's process theism should not be conflated with the traditional supernatural theism of classical theology. In the opening chapters of *The Source of Human Good,* Wieman clearly rejects the transcendental, ahistorical, nonsensual affirmations celebrated within the dominant Christian theological tradition. He asserts about his own system: "Thus the active God derived from the Jewish tradition and the Forms derived from the Greek tradition are both brought down into the world of time, space, and matter and are there identified as events displaying a definite structure with possibilities" (SHG, 8). Wieman's theism is understood and described in terms of God's function. Although human need forms the basis from which this function is delineated, the stress is on the remarkable creativity that can be both discernible and elusive to reasoning individuals. And although his view of God as creativity does not totally rid itself of the residue of philosophical idealism, Wieman's pragmatism and scientific emphasis tend to avoid the subtle rationalism that characterizes much process cosmology.

A second important feature that runs throughout Wieman's writings is the notion of organic and primordial interrelatedness among all organisms. The transformation of individuals comes about through interaction with others. A healthy encounter with others helps to promote the possibility of creative community. The isolated person can never experience God, or so it seems (MUC, 73). Wieman's naturalism relies upon a compelling vision of interrelatedness, organic growth, mutual support, and meaning for all those who participate in the processes of creativity. This focus upon relationality, or active, creative interactions among fundamental events, emphasizes Wieman's uncompromising affirmation of the material base of reality; it is a point of emphasis that confounds both traditional Western metaphysical systems and the purely aesthetic (or "first wave") veins of postmodernism that have recently come under attack. For example, Wieman's method presupposes an active, concrete reality (the creative event) that participates in and helps sustain creativity within human experience. With the use of the faculties, which include rational analysis, observation, and intuition, the individual is granted opportunities to gain knowledge of this reality.

An important point here is that we come with our whole being to know and respond to that "Something" that saves us from isolation and illusions. For Wieman, the ultimate determination of truth and knowledge is the "creative event," which generates the rational principles of mind and the structure of matter in mutual determination of each other. In addition, this "progressive" creativity produces a "culture which shapes the reactions of the human body, the direction of attentive consciousness, and the technology, so that empirical findings will yield reliable knowledge inductively established within this framework of order shared in common by the mind and its appreciable world" (SHG, 201). To me, the appeal of such an arrangement is the embodied subject's complete orientation to apprehending what could be designated as creativity at work in the universe. Most notably, Wieman's conception of (ultimate) reality is materially based, where matter is conceived as a form of energy that determines the very structure of time and space, together with all else that exists or is possible. At the same time, as a natural process, the creative event is "1) the continuous creator of ideals, aspiration, and value; 2) the supreme manifestation of freedom; and 3) the source and sustainer of human freedom" (SHG, 300).

Wieman's naturalistic framework demonstrates that what was once viewed as unitary is actually constituted by a plurality; certainties are seen as ambiguities, and univocal simplicities are unmasked as complexities. His description of how growth of meaning may occur also challenges the popular notion of guaranteed intellectual "progress," which is a trap of the modernist paradigm, strongly influenced by a logic of thesis, antithesis, and synthesis. Most notably, even with his emphasis on the structure of the creative event, Wieman's naturalism foreshadows important poststructuralist insights regarding the open-endedness of our practices and struggles, and the fact that we live in worlds of paradox and uncertainty. He seems to reject modernism's triumphalism or love affair with guaranteed progress: "Perhaps the human organism does not have the nervous energy and capacity for diversified and complex feeling that is required to enter appreciatively into the riches of other races and cultures in a manner necessary to avoid destructive conflict" (SHG, 73). As such, Wieman's religious empiricism shares in the provocative "Death of History" thesis so often associated with Foucaultian-based poststructuralism. By "Death of History" I mean the rejection of Western history and theology as a seamless fabric of linear progression or as constant progress with a definitive aim or end. Grand narratives or totalistic interpretations, often cast in essentialist and monocausal terms, have accompanied this view of history and religious growth. However, totalizing theories or systems have reaped wretchedness, homelessness, and oppression, and, as such, they are no longer viable tools for understanding theological or religious values. This sentiment is found in Charles E. Winquist, who writes in *Epiphanies of Darkness,*

> The categorical imperative of Kant's moral philosophy, the realization of the absolute spirit in Hegelian idealism, or a phenomenological sci-

ence that is also a teleology are not thinkable in the same way after the insights of the great masters of suspicion, Marx, Nietzsche, and Freud. Not only did they wound the metaphysical tradition with concepts of ideology, the unconscious, and the will to power, but they also supplemented a political history of abjection where the unthinkable war to end all wars was followed by the unthinkable Holocaust and all the other powers of horror that are now commonplace in international political and economic life.[15]

To view history (theological or otherwise) as a singular process, the cultural critic is compelled to ignore discontinuities, ruptures, changes, and the vast plurality of contested values, narratives, and discourses. Questioning the themes of convergence and culmination, some of us argue (in fine Foucaultian fashion) that this idea of continuity/progress is an ideological fiction foisted upon the past to legitimate present interests and perspectives. Religionists must share with other intellectuals a "disillusionment with the ideals of progress, an awareness of the atrocities committed in this century in the name of technological and economic progress, the political and moral bankruptcy of the natural sciences which put themselves in the service of the forces of human and planetary destruction."[16]

At this juncture, it must be noted that Wieman's earlier thought was to some degree enslaved to his idealization of scientific theory. However, his later writings show his gradual relinquishment of scientific dogmatism or the ideal of having full certainty. When he asserts that every event is inexhaustible to human inquiry, or that "[w]e can never learn all that enters into an event, but we can know some aspects of its character" (SHG, 299), he anticipates some poststructuralist epistemologies that emphasize our limited knowledge and the necessity of cultivating intellectual humility. Some readers may also be eager to note that Wieman's religious thought aims to conceive of the whole, and would be confounded by a poststructuralist historiography that resists the lure of totalism. Yet to accuse him of propounding a totalizing system would suggest too facile an understanding of his various writings. It is, I contend, his religious functionalism that prevents Wieman from sliding into rationalist purity and theological totalism. As he explains, "[f]inal outcomes, as well as all original beginnings, are entirely beyond the scope of our knowing" (SHG, 92).

Granted, Wieman conceives of the creative event as changeless, unified, absolutely good, and eternal in respect to its creativity. But, as just noted, this event also displays change, plurality and temporality. As he closes *The Source of Human Good,* Wieman maintains,

We must say of this metaphysics, as we said of our interpretation of value, that it is not the only true one. There are several metaphysics, all of which are true, because a metaphysics is true if it selects some ele-

ment necessarily involved in all human existence and explains everything in terms of it. . . . The metaphysics of creativity herein developed
is chosen in preference to any other because we believe it provides a
better guide to action than any other. (301)

With these words, Wieman again demonstrates a prominent feature of his
thought that is not readily gleaned from some other process systems: that is,
that there is no single truth, but rather, at best, more or less comprehensive and
convincing versions of truth that carry with them particular social implications.

Religious Valuing as the Experience of the Other

Wieman's reply to the question, What is value? is the same answer he gives to
the question of what constitutes his new naturalism. It asserts that nothing in
reality is more accessible to the human mind than events and their qualities and
relations. He rejects those approaches to value that are "profoundly disturbed
by the transient and perishing character of value [and] are driven to locate it in
some rarified or remote aspect of experience or even in a transcendental
realm," for instance, locating value initially in the mind of God and then only
imperfectly in the minds of humans (SHG, 4). Rather, Wieman's contexualist
axiology points to the basic structures of events or things as existing in the
empirical realm. He writes, "Value is a simple relation between desiring mind
and thing desired; or it is a total complex situation, including whatever must be
taken into consideration by practical operations which determine choice so that
predictable outcomes can be known and approved" (SHG, 5).

Inspired by Wieman's process empiricism and his theory of creative
value, I now turn to my own views of what constitutes a viable model of postmodern religiosity. With reference to the deconstructive force of postmodernism, I think the import of retaining religious discourse in the present "post"
era lies neither in demonstrating its logical veracity nor in substantiating its
purported universal import. As a poststructuralist, I believe such tasks are
futile. Rather, I would prefer to argue that certain religious interpretations
depict in historical terms aspects of creativity that signify and instill value in
our lives. Religious thought provides historical and conceptual grids through
which the process of valuing is seen to be a uniquely human endeavor. It
reveals humans as constantly constructing, assessing, and reconstructing values that aim to transform the present configuration of our lives. In this context, then, I argue that religion challenges other humanistic discourses to persist in envisioning creative and responsible value systems, which may give
dignity to existence and express hope beyond the present moment.

My poststructuralist efforts are part of a wider religious paradigm inaugurated by such thinkers as Carl Raschke, Sharon Welch, Mark C. Taylor,
Graham Ward, Winquist, and Kevin Hart.[17] Despite our divergent emphases,

postmodern religionists stand united as to what is primarily suspect or troublesome in modernist assumptions. A further point on which we are agreed is that Western theological and religious systems should no longer claim full knowledge or truth. This is not to suggest that all traditional religious assertions are invalid, but rather to argue that particular configurations of them have come to us as prescriptive, exclusive, elitist, and normative. For example, poststructuralist strategies demonstrate how an obsession with foundations, certainty, and control (which has taken a unique form in modern philosophy since the sixteenth century and specifically in British empiricism) has become an integral part of Western religious and theological discourses. With other postmodern scholars, I continue to resist a metaphysics of unity or static identity inaugurated by Platonic idealism, and instead celebrate the notion of ever-changing processes, behind which there is no transcendental center of stability.

An indirect consequence of decentering the notion of the transcendental "sacred" is the recognition that death is an essential part of the life process and that humanity is not the center of the world. This has been a central theme in the readings of literary theorists employing poststructuralist interpretive methods. In his essay "What Is an Author?" Michel Foucault offers a brief and illuminating discussion on the nature of contemporary writing. According to Foucault, one major theme found in contemporary writing is the coming to terms with death. This undermines an older tradition that employed narrative as a mechanism designed to ward off death.[18] For example, in ancient Greek epics the immortality of the hero was linked with the grandeur of epic narratives. If the hero was willing to die young, this was so that his life, consecrated and magnified by death, might pass into immortality—all this was accomplished through the ingenious ploy of the narrative, which redeemed this accepted death.

Foucault notes that a similar theme of escaping death is found within Arabian narratives: one "eluded earth by telling stories into the early morning, to postpone the day of reckoning that would silence the narrator."[19] Foucault finds that, contrary to these expectations, the assumptions of modern literary criticism suggest an effacement of subjectivity and authorship: "Writing has become linked to sacrifice, even to the sacrifice of life, it is now a voluntary effacement which does not need to be represented in books, since it is brought about in the writer's very existence. The work, once thought to provide immortality, now has the right to kill, to be its author's murderer, as in the case of Flaubert, Proust, and Kafka."[20] We are brought closer to the awareness of human limitations and the necessity of living fully, especially in the face of an always-present mortality.

I further question certain unexamined suppositions regarding the theoretical subject and the nature and effects of Western rationality; this deconstructive process has found rich expression in the popular Derridean strategies employed by Taylor. Taylor provides a challenging critique to the metaphysics of presence and logocentricism inherent in such modern philosophical constructions as the self, history, text, and reality.[21] Taylor develops the consequences of Nietzsche's announcement of the death of God, where, subsequently, such concepts as self, truth, and meaning must be reevaluated if they are to remain pivotal or integral to a theological system of meaning. The value of this orientation is found in its capacity to illuminate the logical outcome of theological discourse resting upon, or anchored in, modern philosophical assumptions.

Taylor's emphasis upon the nonidentical or the nonrepresentable approaches the Nietzschean insight that philosophical "truth" is an illusion: Our first principles or concepts are no more than an order of signs, the arbitrariness of which we have forgotten. Nietzsche has written of metaphor as the very structure of or condition for the possibility of all language and concepts:

> It is only by means of forgetfulness that man can ever reach the point of fancying himself to possess a "truth" of the grade just indicated. If he will not be satisfied with truth in the form of tautology, that is to say, if he will not be content with empty husks, then he will always exchange truth for illusions. What is a word? It is the copy in sound of a nerve stimulus. But the further inference from the nerve stimulus to a cause outside of us is already the result of a false and unjustifiable application of the principle of sufficient reason. If truth alone had been the deciding factor in the genesis of language, and if the standpoint of certainty had been decisive for designations, then how could we still dare to say "the stone is hard," as if "hard" were something otherwise familiar to us, and not merely a totally subjective stimulation! We separate things according to gender, designating the tree as masculine and the plant as feminine. What arbitrary assignments! How far oversteps the canons of certainty! (Nietzsche, "On Truth and Lies in a Nonmoral Sense")[22]

More than any other contemporary philosopher, Derrida has been instrumental in bringing back this Nietzschean insight into our cultural sensibilities. Following in the steps of Nietzsche and Derrida, Taylor's theological idiom becomes a sharp reminder of the limitations demanded by language and its object of inquiry.

Derridean intertextuality contests the assumption that textual narrative, whether literary, theological, or philosophical, constitutes a single, identifiable entity or subjectivity. For example, within Taylor's poststructuralist interpretive tactics, theology as writing unfolds like a game that invariably goes beyond its own rules and transgresses its limits. There is the opening of a space into which the authorial subject and all modes of representation constantly disappear. Here the textuality of theology guards against all pretensions of authorial or determinate Truth. In this context, closure is merely an effect of a philosophical strategy, as are all systems claiming to be based on self-evident or transcendental axioms. As Mia Campioni and Elizabeth Grosz ask, "[w]hy is it necessary to unify/solidify what may be fluid, diverse, and changing, if not in order to block and control it? Diverse, changeable, strategic knowledges pose a potential threat that must be minimized—that of the incapacity of theory, of any theory to capture reality in its entirety or in its essence."[23] Poststructuralist thinking allows us to open ourselves to chance; it frees us from the compulsive need to hold onto meaning, concept, and truth, which has dominated Western philosophical discourse. Such open-ended textuality rescues the poetic or ecstatic in every discourse; it involves risk, play, and loss of univocal meaning.

Yet, while accepting the loss of certitude announced by poststructuralist epistemologies, I find it necessary that religious scholars continue to inscribe ethically charged practices that arise from the tensions and encounters of our multiple voices. Confronted with "traditional" religions' failure to change the world, I resist religion's complicity with the dominant power discourses. Thus, with Welch, I ask, Why not seek an alliance with various countercultural movements, which would produce new forms of values and theological praxis? Welch's feminist liberationist discourse, which attempts to counter the falsely universalizing, overgeneralizing tactics of modern rationalism, raises the important question of who controls the knowledge claims that circumscribe a discipline. Welch's formative work also reveals the impotence and inherent danger of modern theology (both conceptually and morally) when it is at odds with the material realities of various communities.[24]

Informed by Welch, I seek to identify the strategic practices that may reflect the interests of particular, marginalized voices and communities. (Welch recommends that those who currently engage in a deconstruction of the proclaimed purity of theorizing do so in the name of marginalized or oppressed groups.) The different interests, standpoints, and voices that Welch highlights constitute religious discourse as an internally varied, necessarily imperfect, and partial set of interpretations. Two important aspects of this religious discourse are (1) the distinction between types of values and (2) the preference for "participatory" values (e.g., antiracism, anticlassism, and antisexism), which could help us to decrease the distortions and mystifications in our dominant culture's explanations and understandings.[25]

In light of these assumptions I suggest that, in its diverse manifestations, any viable conception of postmodern religious valuing will necessarily disclose the hermeneutical dimension of human existence. Religious valuing, I mean, helps to reveal humans as primarily constituted and enhanced by our efforts to interpret, symbolize, and assess our relations with other(s)(ness). One direct implication is that we humans ought always to be expected to construct viable worlds of meaning and significance. In this suggestion I imply the Heideggerian notion of truth as "disclosive," in which a partial, open-ended, and tentative epistemology accompanies one's interpretive practices. Minimally, postmodern religious valuing suggests a particular mode of being in the world. This mode of being may be variously described as accentuating a particular pattern of discernible behaviors, or consciously choosing a distinct set of commitments as one responds to life in its varied historical, biological and cultural manifestations.

This lived reality is ontologically prior to any one particular expression in creed, ritual, or group interaction, in the Wiemanian sense of understanding how the surplusage of processes (events) are structured for creative interchange.[26] At the same time, lived experience is inseparable from these cultural expressions and cannot be filtered out or objectified. As a poststructuralist, however, I can no longer presume that the objective meaning or the totality of human experience or cultural life is ever fully encapsulated in any theory or worldview. Yet this does not mean that we must forfeit our constructions of appropriate symbols, in language and action, which express our reflective comprehensions and emotional commitments to certain forms of cultural life. Rather, this awareness of our interpretive context is what postmodern religious valuing can offer to social and academic life in the present era. Here we are led away from a modernist view that demands an "All or Nothing" epistemological framework and toward a poststructuralist one that takes into account our very complex historicity and radical relatedness, and all the possible nuances associated with these realities.

The creative event, according to Wieman, is always and absolutely good with respect to its creation of value. It must necessarily destroy values that have become too ossified in order to achieve the best possibility for new values under the prevailing conditions. This necessity brings to mind my idea that postmodern religious valuing be identified with ongoing, open-ended, hermeneutical processes that involve both interpretations and cultivation of our materiality, and that promote or increase certain value combinations over others, thus providing those involved with experiences of transformation. For Wieman, the creative event is thoroughly material yet not reducible to human cognition or control. What he identifies as the fundamental "energy" constitutive of natural events (MUC, 82-83) is akin to my suggestion that our experiences of otherness are experiences of the many worlds we inhabit, for instance, the organic or natural systems that constitute our being; the constructed and symbolic worlds of ideas and thoughts; the physical, constructed world of social institutions; the internal, psychological realms that help to configure our sense of selfhood; and the (bodily) world of other concrete organisms.

Within the present era, postmodern religious valuing must emphasize a radical historicity and an inevitable encounter with otherness. This is another way of suggesting that religious valuing accentuates crucial intersubjective experiences in which the human subject comes face-to-face with other concrete realities, grounded by the nonpresence constitutive of otherness. Granted, the category of "the other" can encompass a wide range of modalities and meanings—from the ideational, transcendental source and ground of being of traditional metaphysics, the concrete materiality of *other* selves or communities, and the nonhuman *otherness* of natural ecosystems, to the suppressed or hidden *other* of psychoanalytical theory, which challenges a dominant conception of self as an unified and transparent consciousness.

Religious valuing also implies that we are capable of reflecting on aspects of our subjectivity (which for many of us is constituted as a perceived unity); that we desire to create conceptually a sense of the whole; and, beyond this, that we seek to provide standards of virtue for the various tasks to which we apply ourselves as we relate to others. This latter component often involves constructing an assorted set of judgments connecting our knowledge of "what is" to our expectations of "what ought to be." In short, religious valuing provides an integrative understanding of human desires and perceptions, which helps to constitute us as relational, becoming, concretizing entities. Additionally, postmodern religious valuing makes explicit those precognitive, extralinguistic experiences from which arise the conviction that one is not alone. Thus, assuming that radical historicity mandates encounter with otherness, there is the further suggestion that the idea of historicity is one of the preconditions for conceiving particular notions of objectivity, transcendence, and communal moral reasoning, for it is only through an acceptance of one's material, concrete embodiment within its perceived relatedness that one might begin to envision what lies beyond one's own self-perceptions and thoughts.[27]

More than most other humanistic discourses, the religious discipline has historically demonstrated that the process of valuing (including institutionalizing some forms of value over others) is an inevitable and necessary dimension of human experience. With its emphasis upon the necessity of the process of valuing, religion continues to inspire some of us to think and hope beyond what seems immediate and available. Raising the questions of "What if?" or "Why not?" or even "Could it be?" is of paramount importance in the postmodern era. Either we attend to these questions or we cease to use our human potential to construct and interpret worlds of meaning beyond modernity.

While remaining open to the mysteries of existence, we humans must unceasingly call into question those forms of social relations, cultural formations, and ideological systems that would deny others (and sometimes ourselves) a basic dignified existence. To do so is to draw attention to what the cultural critic, Steve Connor, calls the "imperative dimension of value."[28] Connor means that we must discover the necessity or "value" of value itself, where value is defined as the irreducible orientation toward the better and revulsion from the worse. Here, there is the principle of generalized positivity or the inescapable pressure to identify with whatever is valuable over whatever is not conceived of as valuable.[29] I suggest that within the linguistic codes constructed by humans the imperative dimension of value is not only distinct from the operation of particular values, but it challenges their being reified. This imperative dimension commands that we continue evaluating in the face of every apparently stable, encompassing particular value. In short, all values must remain continually vulnerable to appraisal and to the process of being reevaluated. Acknowledging this dimension, however, does not necessitate positing or naming an absolute or intrinsic value that is wholly set apart from the process of reevaluation; to do so, or to attempt to isolate for inspection such an absolute value, draws one dangerously toward turning it into an object.

The imperative dimension of value involves extreme reflexivity, since it demands not only that we continue valuing, but also that we continue to evaluate *any* given value. The paradoxical structure of value implies, on the one hand, that there are certain values that will be upheld, institutionalized, and often reified by both individuals and communities. On the other hand, to emphasize the reflexive structure of value is to assert that every value is itself subject to the force of further evaluation. As Connor writes, "Only an institution can dissolve itself, only an identity can know plurality, only the same is vulnerable to alterity, only a kind of consciousness can embrace the unthought, only tradition can beget newness; in sum, only the commitment or imperative to value can effect any kind of transvaluation. . . . The very imperative to continue and extend the investigation of value is continually vulnerable to its own force."[30]

Postmodern religious valuing can assume a meaningful place in contemporary culture, including intellectual debates, if it continues to provide sympathetic understandings of (and critical responses to) the value-laden worlds we live in, without either necessarily clashing with other forms of human knowledge or withdrawing into a self-serving sufficiency. Yet postmodern religious valuing must be versatile enough to adapt to ever-changing cultural situations; it must grow so conceptually sophisticated and symbolically rich that we shall be able to comprehend in a more positive light the dizziness resulting from the complexities and multiplicities of life.

Of course, as various histories have shown, many religious systems fail to recognize their own contingent and institutionalized values as human constructs, conceived at one point or another as pragmatic and interventionist strategies against perceived dangers or evils. Examples of these perceived threats have ranged from the notion of an impersonal universe, through the subjective experiences of meaninglessness, to tyrannical and unjust human behaviors. Throughout the range of human experiences, religious thought has functioned, in part, to help us confront and challenge the myriad "limiting" experiences (death, suffering, anxiety, fear, pain, etc.) that partially constitute our lives.

A radically naturalized postmodern religiosity works from the guiding principle that each standpoint one takes is necessarily partial and contingent upon the way one is positioned in relation to such factors as class, race, and educational background. This recognition calls for a commonsense pragmatism that assumes that conflicts of interest and forms of social practice must continually be worked out in order to assure group survival and integrity. In this context, we may begin to accept the fact that although cohesive communities are impossible ideals and that dissent is inevitable, we can yet demand a grammar of conduct or shared vocabulary of values, and a minimal sense of belonging to our contingent communities.

Wieman's process empiricism compels contemporary critics to investigate further the notion of value within cultural theory. Throughout Western thought there has been a tendency to posit a conflict in one form or another (essentialism/historicism, universalism/particularism, intrinsic value/contingency, and use value/exchange value) between absolute and relative value. Consequently, most accounts of value theory have deplored or tried to avoid any or all inconsistencies, often choosing one polar opposite over the other. Today, a growing number of theorists seeking to go beyond the limitations of this either/or logic are positing these human constructs as requiring, confirming, and regenerating one another rather than as being discrete and antagonistic. Such gestures imply the possibility of reconceptualizing the concept of value without surrendering to the idea of a universal, absolute, and transcendent value; without yielding to mere plurality, relativity, and contingency; and without resolving the differences through a violent yet "neat" logical synthesis. In other words, the self-contradictions and unabatable paradoxes of value must be accepted and addressed creatively.

It is in and through our intimate social encounters and various communal formations that we are made cognizant of the imperative dimension of value. In more practical terms, the institutions and procedures that we employ to actualize our evaluations of values—schools, universities, local and national governments, religious institutions and traditions, and political organizations of all kinds—are always likely to become stagnant amid the desire to conserve or reproduce certain values. However, the reflexive nature of religious valuing presupposes the freedom and courage to question what has been perceived as necessary or natural in the past—here we see the importance of the hermeneutical insight of how past evaluations enter into the present. The necessary and ongoing evaluations of value itself will, it is to be hoped, undercut any tendencies to reify, or to dogmatically ontologize, our various institutionalized values.

Finally, our various forms of valuing must themselves be diversified and multiplied; we need to create and institute methods of insuring plurality through fostering differences rather than through limitation. Strategically, institutionally, politically, as well as in our dreams, desires, interpersonal relations, writing, and religious and philosophical quests, we may continue to bring about instances of valuing that are not structured by isolationist, egoistic impulses and asymmetrical power relations. This openness may lead to transformations of self and other. Such work includes, but is not exhausted by our various attempts to accept and to prehend the complex, infinite richness of the *energy* of life, to use Wieman's term, which can never be fully grasped by human cognition. Here we can expect—and should hope—to encounter the complex, infinitely rich materiality of Otherness.

Notes

1. Carol Wayne White, *Triangulating Positions: Poststructuralism, Feminism, and Religion* (Amherst, NY: Humanity Books, 2001).

2. During the 1920s, two of the most pressing issues confronting religionists and theologians were the relationship between science and religion and the problem of theism. The contemporary scene of the 1920s was marked by exciting prospects generated by the contributions of Darwin's theory of evolution and the strand of organismic philosophies emerging from the findings of modern physics. One of the prime features of a new ethos among philosophers and scientists was a shift in imagery and thought corresponding to these new scientific paradigms. Encouraged by the new physics, many of these thinkers sought to counter the prevalent notion of mechanism with expanded scientific and philosophical imagery.

3. The synthesizing capacities of Alfred North Whitehead cannot be overestimated. He ingeniously incorporated and systematized various strands of evolutionary, scientific, and philosophic thought into one worldview. Many scholars have noted that the thoroughness with which Whitehead pursued his systematic task, analyzing and drawing out explicit implications of the various fundamental notions of reality, makes his work more than a mere summation of that which preceded him. Indeed, it is a creative philosophical vision, bringing together the various aspects of organicist thinking that lay behind his systematic effort. At the same time that Whitehead's *Religion in the Making* came to the attention of some American religious thinkers, especially the faculty at the Chicago Divinity School, Henry Nelson Wieman published his *Religious Experience and Scientific Method* (New York: Macmillan, 1926).

4. In *Religious Experience and Scientific Method,* his earliest book, Wieman lays the foundation for his continued distrust of speculative metaphysics. He writes, "Metaphysics in the sense of that reasoning which abjures experience and the conclusions of scientific thought is futile" (12). For Wieman, metaphysical knowledge must be about the universe as we know it and within the bounds of human knowledge, as based upon human experience. This sentiment is consistent with his rejection of traditional, supernatural forms of revelation.

5. In 1926, shortly after the publication of Whitehead's *Religion in the Making,* the Chicago faculty invited Wieman to their institution as a guest lecturer. Wieman had already been exposed to Whitehead's writings long before the latter had addressed himself to the problems of religion and metaphysics. Wieman had read Whitehead's *An Enquiry Concerning the Principles of Natural Knowledge* (Cambridge: Cambridge University Press, [1919] 1955) and *The Concept of Nature* (Cambridge: Cambridge University Press, 1920), becoming acquainted with Whitehead's vision through these

and other works. At Chicago, there was both irritation and excitement over the reconditeness of thought presented in Whitehead's vision. Wieman's interpretation of Whitehead's canon was so successful that he was asked to join the faculty the following year. His influence there during the next twenty years shifted Chicago's focus from sociohistorical studies to philosophy of religion.

6. Friedrich Nietzsche, *The Gay Science,* Walter Kaufmann, trans. (New York: Vintage Books, Random, 1974), book 3, 181.

7. Derrida lists the following as fundamental terms or principles of philosophical thought that, in actuality, function as representative modes of presence: (1) presence of the thing to the sight as *eidos;* (2) presence as substance/essence/existence *(ousia);* (3) temporal presence as point *(stigme)* of the now or of the moment *(nun);* (4) the self-presence of the *cogito,* "consciousness," subjectivity; and (5) the copresence of the other and of the self, intersubjectivity as the intentional phenomenon of the ego. All of these terms designate what Derrida calls the "transcendental signified" (OG, 12).

8. While accepting the loss of certitude announced by postmodernism's claims, religionists are nevertheless inscribed with ethically charged practices that arise from the tensions and encounters of our multiple voices. Confronted with "traditional" theology's failure to change the world for the better, postmodern religionists must resist their own complicity with the dominant power discourses, and seek alliances with countercultural movements that would produce new forms of theological praxis. This orientation expresses my attempts as an African-American poststructuralist who understands that not all strategic and potentially "emancipating" practices emerging from critical theory will (or can) reflect the interests of all marginalized voices.

9. Apparently Darwin's *On the Origin of Species* had already been interpreted within such fields as psychology, sociology, and religion. At the Chicago Divinity School, thinkers like Shailer Matthews, Edward Scribner Ames, and Shirley Jackson Case had already begun to incorporate the emerging thought into their religious and theological projects. In fact, one may argue that the issue of science and religion had been posed for these religionists within the ethos of thought that Darwinism had created.

10. Bernard E. Meland, "Introduction: The Empirical Tradition in Theology at Chicago," in *The Future of Empirical Theology,* Meland, ed. (Chicago: University of Chicago Press, 1969), 31. See also Meland, *The Realities of Faith* (New York: Oxford University Press, 1962), 116.

11. Wieman, "The Promise of Protestantism—Whither and Whether," in *The Protestant Credo,* Vergilius Ferm, ed. (New York: Philosophical Library, 1953), 166–167, 177–178.

12. Even though Wieman confines his discussion of the creative event to its occurrence in human communication, he also views the universe as being composed of an infinitely complex structure of events, and he affirms that creative interaction occurs within and among organisms. In *The Source of Human Good* he writes the following: "The thin layer of structure characterizing events knowable to the human mind by way of linguistic specification is very thin indeed compared to that massive, infinitely complex structure of events, rich with quality, discriminated by the non-cognitive feeling-reactions of associated organisms human and nonhuman" (66).

13. Wieman, "Creativity and the Universe," *Interchange,* May, 1969–1970, 1.

14. Wieman and Walter Marshall Horton, *The Growth of Religion* (Chicago: Willett, Clark, 1938), 368.

15. Charles E. Winquist, *Epiphanies of Darkness* (Philadelphia: Fortress Press, 1986), x.

16. Seyla Benhabib, *Situating the Self* (New York: Routledge, 1992), 218–219.

17. Representative scholarship conjoining critical theory and religion include Thomas J. J. Altizer et al., *Deconstruction and Theology* (New York: Crossroad, 1982); Carl Raschke, *Theological Thinking* (Missoula, MT: Scholars Press, 1989); Edith Wyschogrod, "On Deconstructing Theology: A Symposium on Erring: A Postmodern A/theology," *Journal of the American Academy of Religion* 54(3): 523–557; Wyschogrod, Raschke, and David Crownfield, eds., *Lacan and Religious Discourse* (Albany: State University of New York Press, 1989); David Ray Griffin et al., *Varieties of Postmodern Theology* (Albany: State University of New York Press, 1989); Kevin Hart, *The Trespass of the Sign* (Cambridge: Cambridge University Press, 1989); Terrence W. Tilley, ed., *Postmodern Theologies* (Maryknoll, NY: Orbis), 1995; Mark C. Taylor, *Erring: A Postmodern A/theology* (Chicago: University of Chicago Press, 1984); Sharon Welch, *Communities of Resistance and Solidarity* (Maryknoll, NY: Orbis, 1985) and *A Feminist Ethic of Risk* (Minneapolis: Fortress Press, 1990).; Charles E. Winquist, *Epiphanies of Darkness* (Albany: State University of New York Press, 1987); and Graham Ward, ed., *The Postmodern God: A Theological Reader* (Malden, MA: Blackwell, 1997).

18. Michel Foucault, "What Is an Author?" in *The Foucault Reader,* Paul Rabinow, ed. (New York: Pantheon Books, 1984), 102. Here Foucault is concerned with the question of power and the function of the author in works of fiction. His discussion of the relationship of writing to death is part of a larger project of dissolving "the subject" as the origin and center of discourse.

19. Ibid.

20. Ibid.

21. Taylor (1984). In Taylor's deconstructive idiom, the binary oppositions, upon which theological truths have been built, ultimately collapse such that theological discourse turns back onto itself and no longer makes consistent sense. His subversive exploration of the opacity of theological language calls into question any purported separation of (or clear distinction between) "true" theology and false utterances. This conceptual opening benefits those theological traditions (or voices) that have been shunned or dismissed as deviating from orthodox interpretation; it also has suggestive potential for undermining the political/economic bases of all systematic discourses.

22. In *Philosophy and Truth: Selections from Nietzsche's Notebooks of the Early 1870's,* Daniel Breazeale, trans. and ed. (Atlantic Highlands, NJ: Humanities Press, 1979), 81–82.

23. Mia Campioni and Elizabeth Grosz, "Love's Labours Lost: Marxism and Feminism," in *Beyond Marxism: Interventions after Marx,* Judith Allen and Paul Patton, eds. (Leichardt, NSW, Australia: Intervention Publications, 1983), 127.

24. Welch (1985) and (1990). See note 17.

25. Ibid., 58–60.

26. Here I borrow imagery from Wieman's naturalism. For Wieman, nature is associated with the totality of events and their possibilities, and is the only arena for human feeling, thought, action, knowing, believing, and commitment. Nature is an ongoing process that includes multiple subprocesses, two of which are the divine and the human. Furthermore, the mind and the universe are not ultimate or self-sufficient because they are late emergents from the massive, inexhaustible fullness of the flow of felt quality, that is, nature. Thus, my appeal to ontological language should be regarded from within the context of this type of naturalist viewpoint.

27. It should come as no surprise that many religious systems have sought historically to provide integrative frameworks of the perceived whole, often in transhistorical, objective, or universal terms. The various cosmologies, metaphysics, and value systems emerging from the world religions indicate a persistent human propensity to construct worldviews that adequately express something more, beyond the commonsense knowledge and restrictions of empirical data. With Wieman, however, I argue for a religious naturalism that is appreciative of the sensual without falling prey to the reductionism of scientific materialism.

28. Steven Connor, *Theory and Cultural Value* (Cambridge, MA: Blackwell, 1992).

29. Ibid.

30. Ibid., 3.

8

A Whiteheadian Chaosmos?
Process Philosophy from
a Deleuzean Perspective

TIM CLARK

Introduction

The philosophy of Gilles Deleuze is often classified, in the anglophone world at least, under the heading "poststructuralist."[1] While there may be some justification for this categorization, it nevertheless fails to capture the theoretical scope and philosophical ambition of what is perhaps the most important of Deleuze's works: *Difference and Repetition.* It would not be completely wide of the mark to categorize this work as an exercise in speculative cosmology, a process philosophy even. At any rate, Deleuze himself invites the comparison, referring to *Process and Reality* as "one of the greatest books of modern philosophy" and linking his own use of "descriptive notions" to that deployment of "empirico-ideal notions [which] we find in Whitehead" (DR, 284). Although this essentially methodological affinity has been duly recorded and commented upon (most notably by Ilya Prigogine and Isabelle Stengers[2]), there has, as yet, been no exploration of the extent to which Deleuze's metaphysics parallels that of Alfred North Whitehead in terms of its content—the extent to which his own system of "descriptive notions" mirrors, departs from, or fractures the categoreal scheme of *Process and Reality.*

While there are, of course, no straightforward one-to-one correspondences between the components of the two systems (there is, e.g., nothing obviously resembling an "actual entity" in the Deleuzean cosmology), there are nonetheless a number of ostensible conceptual affiliations. To pick out just three: that which Deleuze theorizes as "the virtual" bears a certain similarity to Whiteheadian pure potentiality; likewise, the elements of the virtual, namely, what Deleuze calls "Ideas," play a role comparable to that attributed to eternal objects; finally, the factor in the Deleuzean system that corresponds most closely to Whitehead's notion of creativity—that ultimate principle by which the production of novelty is to be thought—goes, for Deleuze, under the name of "productive difference," or "Difference in itself."

Rather than explore these various parallels directly, my immediate concern here will be to establish the essential *difference* between the Whiteheadian and the Deleuzean systems. Perhaps the quickest way to encapsulate that difference is as follows: while *Process and Reality* represents a systematic cosmology, *Difference and Repetition* develops a speculative "chaosmology." At its most simplistic, the distinction in play here is that between a cosmos in which order is imposed upon a primordial chaos "from outside," or transcendently (as when Form is imposed upon matter by the Platonic demiurge, or harmony established a priori by the Leibnizian deity), and a chaosmos in which order is generated "from within," by a wholly immanent process of self-organization. In these very general terms, perhaps the closest approximation to a chaosmology among Whiteheadian thinkers is to be found in Donald Sherburne's vision of "a Whitehead decentered . . . a Whitehead without God . . . a neo-Whiteheadian naturalism." From this perspective, as from Deleuze's, "there is no one overarching center of value, meaning and order"; rather, "patterns of meaning and order emerge gradually, fitfully, and unevenly from [a] churning multiplicity of value centers."[3] Thus, or so it would seem, the term *chaosmology* is simply a fancy neologism for speculative naturalism—for a cosmological system that lacks a God.

This simple picture, however, is more than a little complicated by the fact that Deleuze himself—in his one and only sustained discussion of Whitehead's philosophy (TF, 76–82)—sketches out the possibility of a chaosmology within which Whitehead's *God* would have a positive, indeed an essential, role to play. My aim in the present chapter is twofold: firstly to argue, pro Sherburne and contra Deleuze's reading, that there is no place for God—even for Whitehead's God—in a "chaosmos" worthy of the name; but secondly, following Deleuze and departing from Sherburne, to outline one way in which the operation of "decentering Whitehead" might lead to somewhere other than to a naturalism. To this end, I shall focus almost exclusively upon a singular and sensitive point in the Whiteheadian system: namely, that moment at which "the barren inefficient disjunction of abstract potentialities"—the disjunctive multiplicity of eternal objects—"obtains efficient conjunction of ideal realization" within the primordial nature of God (PR, 40).

Deleuze's Reading: A Question

In the following passage from *The Fold*, Deleuze sets out what he takes to be the key difference between the Leibnizian and the Whiteheadian cosmologies:

For Leibniz . . . bifurcations and divergences of series are genuine borders between incompossible worlds, such that the monads that exist
wholly include the compossible world that moves into existence. For
Whitehead, on the contrary, bifurcations, incompossibilities, and discord
belong to the same motley world *that can no longer be included in
expressive units,* but only made or undone according to prehensive units
and variable configurations. In a same chaotic world divergent series are
endlessly tracing bifurcating paths. It is a "chaosmos" . . . [in which]
[e]ven God desists from being a Being who compares worlds and
chooses the richest one compossible. He becomes Process, a process that
at once affirms incompossibilities and passes through them. (TF, 81)

This passage concludes Deleuze's brief account of the difference between Leibnizian monads and Whiteheadian actual entities (or "prehensive
units"). As he suggests, while it is true that

the two instances . . . have no windows, . . . for Leibniz, [this] is because
the monad's being-for the world is subject to a condition of closure, all
compossible monads including a single and same world. For Whitehead, on the contrary, a condition of opening causes all prehension to be
already the prehension of another prehension. . . . Prehension is naturally open, open to the world, without having to pass through a window.
(TF, 81)

My question to Deleuze is this: Is the (undeniable) fact that Whitehead's
prehensive units are naturally open sufficient grounds for describing the
Whiteheadian universe as a "chaosmos"? Might it not still be the case that,
given Whitehead's *theology,* his universe remains "semi-open and partially
predictable"—as George Kampis has suggested, in explicit contrast to the
closed, predictable Leibnizian system on the one hand, and to the open, unpre-
dictable, unfinished-in-every-dimension system of Henri Bergson on the
other?[4] The answer to this question will depend (as Deleuze clearly recognizes) not simply upon an analysis of the nature of monadic units, but on confronting the issue at its most sensitive point, namely, with respect to the difference between the Leibnizian God, who "compares and chooses," and the
Whiteheadian God, who "affirms incompossibles and passes through them."
    In his comprehensive study of Whitehead's metaphysics, William
Christian offers an interpretation that prefigures the one adopted by Deleuze.
Like Deleuze, he recognizes that the crucial distinction lies between the Leibnizian and Whiteheadian conceptions of divinity:

Whitehead's God, like Leibniz's, envisages all possible worlds. Unlike
the God of Leibniz's system, Whitehead's God does not choose *any* of
the possible worlds. Rather he values them *all,* even though they are not

compossible. Thus . . . the function of his primordial nature is to hold the possible worlds together by his appetition for them all, so that all are relevant in one way or another, to any particular world which occurs in the course of nature. From the lack of a final and necessary order of eternal objects in the primordial nature of God it follows that there is no final order of nature.[5]

In other words, so Christian argues, the lack of a fixed, necessary, or preformed order of potentiality logically follows from the principle that God affirms (or *values,* to use Whitehead's term) all incompossibles. But if this is the case, what are we to make of those several passages in which Whitehead speaks variously of an "*inevitable* ordering of things, conceptually realized in the nature of God" (PR, 244, emphasis added), or of "*the* eternal order which is the *final* absolute wisdom" (PR, 347, emphasis added)? Indeed, Christian himself suggests that we understand the "fixed and necessary order," which appears in chapter 10 of *Science and the Modern World,* as "describing eternal objects as they exist in the primordial vision of God."[6] Should we identify here a contradiction that vitiates the Whiteheadian system as a whole, or is it the case that a more careful reading of Whitehead's theology is called for? The same question might be raised on the basis of Deleuze's own remarks: In *The Logic of Sense* he makes it quite clear that what he calls the "immanent consistency" of the chaosmos necessarily excludes the "coherence" traditionally supplied by a transcendent God (LS, 176). And yet, in his commentary on Whitehead, he seems to hold open the possibility of a chaosmos that would include a divine element. Again, if this is not a simple case of self-contradiction, does it suggest a reading of Whitehead's theology that would render it compatible with a Deleuzean chaosmology? My attempt to resolve these issues will involve a detailed examination of Christian's defense of Whitehead's non-Leibnizian God, together with an interpretation of Deleuze's highly paradoxical notion of "disjunctive synthesis."

Christian's Reading: Some Criticisms

One significant point of agreement between Deleuze and Whitehead concerns their critique of Aristotelian systems of classification within which a concrete individual is conceived as being merely a member of a certain class or an instance of a certain kind. Christian formulates Whitehead's view as follows:

> [A]n individual is something more than a member of a species. The principle of classification is inadequate to account for real individuals. A principle of synthesis is needed. This principle is "creativity" . . . "that ultimate principle by which the many, which are the universe disjunctively, become the one actual occasion, which is the universe conjunctively."[7]

Insofar as the "many" refers to the disjunctive multiplicity of eternal objects, it is not representable in terms of a logic of genera and species. The many of pure potentiality constitutes a multiplicity within which "there are no ultimate exclusions, expressive in logical terms," for the simple reason that "such exclusions are decided by the finitude of circumstance" (cf. MT, 75–76). The error of the principle of classification lies in its tendency to posit an exclusiveness of pure potentials among themselves without recognizing that such incompatibilities are established through, or decided by, the negative prehensions that are constitutive of actual entities. Similarly from a Deleuzean perspective, the error of such classification lies in its failure to recognize that the exclusiveness of incompossibles is a feature unique to the actual, a feature for which there is no precedent in pure potentiality. As Deleuze puts it in *The Logic of Sense,* "Would two events [pure potentials] be contradictory because they were incompatible? Is this not a case, though, of applying rules to events, which apply only to concepts, predicates and classes?" (LS, 170). Rather, "incompatibility is born only with [the] individuals and worlds in which events [pure potentials] are *actualised,* but not between events themselves" (LS, 177, emphasis added).

Given the Whiteheadian doctrine that the exclusiveness of incompossibles is logically dependent upon the decisions made by actual entities, the question then becomes, What effect does the "initial decision" made by God, the ultimate actual entity, have upon the logical status of pure potentiality? There can be no doubt that God makes decisions a propos of the disjunctive multiplicity of eternal objects; the difficulty is to establish in precisely what sense these divine decisions are distinguishable from the choices and calculations made by the Leibnizian deity. Whitehead's dilemma seems to be this: On the one hand, the principle of classification is to be challenged by positing the primordiality of a world of eternal objects that knows "no exclusions, expressive in logical terms"; on the other hand, positing pure potentiality as a "boundless and unstructured infinity"[8] lacking all logical order would seem to be precisely that conceptual move that renders it "inefficacious" or "irrelevant." Over and above the "special relevance" that selected eternal objects may have in relation to particular, finite actual entities, it is necessary that there be a kind of "relevance in general," a real togetherness of all eternal objects among themselves, effected by an eternal, infinite actuality: "Transcendent decision includes God's decision. He is the actual entity in virtue of which the *entire* multiplicity of eternal objects obtains its graded relevance to each stage of concrescence" (PR, 164). The question is whether this transcendent decision necessarily involves that element of limitation and exclusion characteristic of decisions in general. (Cf. PR, 164: "The limitation whereby there is a perspective relegation of eternal objects to the background is characteristic of decision.") Christian thinks not, and Deleuze appears to follow him.

Clearly, everything turns on the nature of "synthesis," that is, on the precise manner in which incompossible potentials are "held together." Deleuze distinguishes between two kinds of synthesis: the conjunctive and the disjunctive; and within the latter between two uses of disjunction: an immanent use, at once inclusive, nonrestrictive and affirmative, and a transcendent use, which is exclusive, limitative and negative (LS, 172, 176). Following Leibniz, both Deleuze and Whitehead agree that the actualization of individuals and worlds is subject to a condition of conjunctive synthesis, conceived, in Deleuze's terms, as "a method of constructing convergent series" (LS, 174) or, in Whitehead's terms, as "that principle by which the many (disjunctively) become one (conjunctively)" (PR, 21). Nor would there be any disagreement over the fact that, *once an actual world has been formed,* limitation, opposition, and negation become characteristic features of the world as actualized. But the question is whether such factors are also primary, or whether they are merely the secondary effects of an originary movement of "disjunctive synthesis," that is, a synthesis that somehow holds incompossibles together, but does so without limitation, opposition, or negation—that is, a synthesis of "total affirmation." It is in relation to this question that Deleuze's distinction between the two uses of disjunction is most pertinent: If, as Whitehead *at times* suggests, principles of limitation, exclusion, and so forth are indeed operative in creating the conditions for the production of novelty, then the disjunction involved here cannot be "properly speaking a synthesis, but only a regulative analysis at the service of conjunctive synthesis, since it separates the nonconvergent [incompossible] series from one another" (LS, 174). But if, as Deleuze insists, that factor he calls "difference in itself" creates the requisite conditions for novelty, then the disjunction involved will be a genuinely affirmative synthesis within which "divergence is no longer a principle of exclusion, and disjunction no longer a means of separation. Incompossibility is now a means of communication" (LS, 175). Furthermore, as Deleuze goes on to make explicit, any attempt to introduce a principle of limitation into pure potentiality itself will require appeal to the "form of God [as] guarantee [of] disjunction in its exclusive or limitative sense" (LS, 176). This is the truth Deleuze uncovers in Immanuel Kant's discussion of "The Ideal of Pure Reason" in the first *Critique*. In a manner that to some extent prefigures Whitehead's own recasting of traditional theology (God, not as creator, but as the first accident of creativity), Kant's God is here,

> at least provisionally, deprived of his traditional claims—to have created subjects or made a world—and now has what is but an apparently humble task, namely, to enact disjunctions, or at least to found them. . . . God is defined by the sum total of possibility, insofar as this sum constitutes an "originary" material. . . . The reality of each thing "is derived" from it: it rests in effect on the limitation of this totality. (LS, 295-296)

It is precisely *this* God, along with his humble task, which is excluded from the chaosmos theorized by Deleuze, and it is the very same deity that appears in Whitehead's "first reference to the conception of God he will later elaborate and defend."[9] The task appointed to God in chapter 11 of *Science and the Modern World* is nothing more, and nothing less, than that of instituting "an antecedent limitation among values, introducing contraries, grades, and oppositions" into the totality of possibility (the realm of eternal objects): "Thus this first limitation is a limitation of antecedent selection" (SMW, 221). Since the God who appears here is patently a reincarnation of Kant's "master of the exclusive disjunction," it follows that any attempt to interpret the system of *Process and Reality* as representing a nascent chaosmology will have to demonstrate that the theology developed in the later work positively *supersedes* and *excludes,* rather than, as Christian claims, "elaborates and defends," the theology of the earlier. Christian does, however, present a strong case for an element of elaboration by showing how, between the two works, the realm of eternal objects ceases to be a realm in any meaningful sense, since the eternal objects are no longer "related in any single fixed order."[10] His conclusions are presented as follows:

> I suggest that the primordial nature of God orders eternal objects in the sense, and only in the sense, that in God's envisagement eternal objects are together. . . . God excludes *no* possibilities and for this very reason does not *order* possibilities, in the strong sense of "order" [i.e., fixed a priori]. . . . Therefore it is truer to say that God envisages possibilities of order than that God envisages an order of possibilities.[11]

Two objections to this solution might be raised. Firstly, given that the characteristic feature of decisions in general is limitation (following Whitehead, PR, 164), Christian still has to make sense of Whitehead's reference to the "transcendent *decision* of God" a propos of pure potentiality. Secondly, there is an element of near tautology affecting the formulation of the solution, specifically in the first sentence: "order," in its "weak" (non-Leibnizian) sense, is to be defined *only* in terms of "togetherness" (on this Deleuze could perhaps agree); but the difficult question is to know how *togetherness* (synthesis) is to be defined (since it cannot be defined in terms of "order" without collapsing into bare tautology)—that is, to know precisely *how* incompossibles are held together through an analysis of the exact mechanism involved, and this Christian does not provide.

The first objection refers back to the question I just raised: Precisely how does the transcendent decision of Whitehead's God differ from the choice/selection made by Leibniz's deity? Although he does not address this question explicitly, the rudiments of an answer are implicit in the passage from Christian cited earlier: "Unlike the God of Leibniz's system, Whitehead's God does not *choose* any of the possible worlds. Rather he *values* them all, even though they are not compossible."[12] Thus, if God's transcendent decision refers *only* to this operation of evaluating incompossible worlds while refraining from selecting any one of them, then it does indeed make sense to speak here of a "decision" that is not yet a "choice." The question then arises as to whether this nonselective decision still involves any necessary element of limitation or restriction. Given that the decision is one of *value,* the answer can only be yes, as Whitehead himself clearly recognized: "Restriction is the price of the value. There cannot be value without antecedent standards of value, to discriminate the acceptance or rejection of what is before the envisaging mode of activity. Thus there is an antecedent limitation among values, introducing contraries. . . . [etc.]" (SMW, 221). Prima facie, this would seem to be the end of the line for Christian's argument in favor of a divine "total affirmation": Whitehead's God holds incompossibles together, and excludes none, simply because he values them all; but if *restriction* and *limitation* are the conditions of value, then it would appear that even here God is still required to enact, or at least to found, disjunctions that are not yet positively synthetic or wholly affirmative. The element of choice (or selection) may have been removed, but the element of *comparison* remains (standards of value implying comparisons of better and worse), and thus at least one aspect of the role Leibniz attributes to his God is still in operation.

Nonetheless, Christian can call upon some powerful evidence from the later work that would militate against this conclusion—most notably Whitehead's remark that precisely "because it arises out of no actual world [the primordial nature] has within it no components which are standards of comparison" (PR, 47). Clearly, the problem now becomes: How to square *this* claim with the earlier doctrine according to which God provides the necessary antecedent standards of value? Following Lewis Ford, there is an apparently simple solution: interpret the earlier passage in such a way that it does not (or at least not only?) refer to God, but rather (or also?) to the complex of relations an individual actual occasion has with past actual occasions and eternal objects.[13] Ford's general and surely correct thesis is that between *Science and the Modern World* and *Process and Reality* there is a shift from monism to pluralism, a devolution of creative power from a Spinozistic substantial activity to the self-creating activity of actual occasions. It would then be wholly consistent for a similar shift to have taken place with regard to the sources of value. Nonetheless, even taking this devolution into account, the precise role that God plays in the process of evaluation remains unclear. Pace Donald Sherburne's solution (viz. ditching God altogether, positing the multiplicity of actual entities as the *only* source of a plural "order, meaning and value"), one possible response might run as follows: in the primordial nature there are no general (fixed a priori) standards of value, there is only the capacity to offer "guidelines" relative to already individuated worlds. This, or something very like it, seems to be the solution implicitly adopted by Christian when he says of the primordial nature,

It is not a teleological arrangement of eternal objects into a single hierarchy. It is rather a matrix for those orderings effected by particular actual occasions in the course of nature. . . . Any particular ordering of divine appetitions in God is relative to a particular instance of becoming. . . . In the primordial nature, taken in abstraction from acts of becoming . . . eternal objects have *togetherness but not gradations of importance.*[14]

This certainly gets rid of the last remaining element of divine limitation, but at what cost? If it is true that God can find within Godself no standards of comparison, then the divine capacity to evaluate becomes wholly parasitic upon actual worlds, and Sherburne's naturalism beckons. But the most immediate problem here is that raised by our second objection to Christian's solution: specifying precisely *how* incompossibles are held together. If the requisite disjunctive synthesis cannot be explained by an appeal to the doctrine that God *values* all possible worlds, this is not so much because evaluation is logically dependent upon gradations of importance, but because (accepting Christian's explanation of the *absence* of such gradations in the primordial nature) the logic of the doctrine itself entails that God be inextricably involved in the formation of actual worlds as "circles of convergence," that is, in "the orderings effected by individuals in the course of nature." And thus, at least with regard to the process of evaluation, God is always already functioning at the service of *conjunctive* synthesis, that is, providing "guidelines" with a well-meaning regard for what is actually compossible.

The very best evidence Christian has for his interpretation—namely, that "God's . . . conceptual experience is . . . limited by no actuality that it presupposes. It is therefore infinite, *devoid of all negative prehensions*" (PR, 345, emphasis added)—remains subject to a similar qualification: all negativity may have been removed, de jure, from the primordial nature, but is this enough? If, stripped of all technical connotations, we can take the term *prehension* to mean simply "holding," then the phrase "infinite, nonnegative prehension" informs us *only* that nothing is "held negatively"—that is, that nothing is effectively excluded or "relegated to the background"—but this still does not explain precisely how everything is positively "held together." In short, removing the element of limitation/negation is a necessary but not sufficient condition for the theorization of disjunctive synthesis.

If the concept of evaluation is, at least on the argument just presented, inadequate to the problem, are there any other viable alternatives? Christian makes use of two other terms, which are themselves virtual synonyms: *entertainment* and *envisagement.* Incompossibles are held together simply because they are all entertained or envisaged within the primordial nature. One immediate (and seemingly intractable) problem arises: even Leibniz's God "*envisages* all possible worlds."[15] But the main problem here is the more general problem of vagueness or imprecision: Once again, the only definite content registered by these concepts is that the operation involved is *distinct* from that of conjunctive synthesis. As Ford puts it, "[s]ince to envisage means to confront, face, what is envisaged is that which the occasion has before it to synthesize. To envisage is not to [conjunctively] synthesize, to bring into prehensive unity, but to entertain as an ingredient for such prehension."[16] Even so, in deploying the terms *envisage* or *entertain,* nothing definite is said about the nonconjunctive mechanism involved in the primordial act of holding-to-gether-without-bringing-into-overarching-unity. Perhaps the reason why these terms remain vague, virtually empty, or at least "unpacked," is that within the system as a whole they are absolutely *primitive.* (All that Whitehead says in defense of the term *envisagement* is that it is better than certain other alternatives, for instance, "intuition" or "vision" [cf. PR, 33–34].) It is perhaps at this point that a fundamental overhaul of the system begins to look both attractive and necessary: to begin again, addressing the same problems, but with different primitives.

A Deleuzean Alternative to Deleuze's Reading

If, as I have tried to show, the Whiteheadian God is not entirely adequate to the ultimate role required of the divine, is this the cue for developing a wholly naturalist cosmology that excludes, in principle, all traces of the divine? Not quite, at least not so far as Deleuze is concerned. While for him, as for Whitehead, the Spinozist option remains overly monistic (in one way or another, Spinozism must be "pluralized"), it is nevertheless possible to discern, in provisional outline, what a "Deleuzean" deity would look like on a monotheistic model. To fulfill the ascribed role, to perform the requisite function of total affirmation, Whitehead's God would have to be profoundly schizoid, in the precise sense set out in Deleuze and Felix Guattari's *Anti-Oedipus:*

> The schizophrenic . . . does not substitute syntheses of contradictory elements for disjunctive syntheses; rather, for the exclusive and restrictive use of the disjunctive synthesis, he substitutes an affirmative use. He is and remains in disjunction: he does not abolish disjunction . . . instead he affirms it *through a continuous overflight spanning an indivisible distance.* (AO, 76)

Ripped out of its context, the phrase "continuous overflight" can be read as functionally equivalent to Whiteheadian "envisagement": incompossibles are held together, the affirmation is effected, "through a continuous overflight. . . ." The term is, no doubt, just as vague and uninformative as its Whiteheadian counterpart; nonetheless, any attempt to construct a Deleuzean theology would have to begin by substituting the disjunctive syntheses of a divine schizo for the disjunctive analyses of that primordial rational Being in whose "very nature it stands to divide Good from Evil, and to establish Reason 'within her dominions supreme,'" as Whitehead so unequivocally puts it (SMW, 223). Such a substitution forms the first principle of "the new critique of Reason" that Deleuze discerns in the work of Pierre Klossowski:

> The schizophrenic God has so little to do with the God of religion, even though they are related to the same syllogism. In *Le Baphomet* Klossowski contrasts God as master of the exclusions and restrictions of the disjunctive syllogism, with an antichrist who is the prince of modifications, determining instead the passage of a subject through all possible predicates. (AO, 77)

The same point appears in *The Logic of Sense* as follows: "[D]isjunction posed as a synthesis exchanges its theological principle for a diabolic principle," ensuring that "instead of a certain number of predicates being excluded from a thing in virtue of the identity of its concept, each 'thing' opens itself up to the infinity of predicates through which it passes, as it loses its center, that is, its identity as concept or as self" (LS, 176, 174). While these comments are clearly posed against Leibniz, the point can be restated in Whiteheadian terms simply by substituting "actual entity" for Deleuze's "thing," and then calling upon Whitehead's cosmological theory of propositions in which actual entities form the "logical subjects" and eternal objects the "predicates" (cf. PR, 186). This puts us in a position to assess Deleuze's specific claims concerning Whitehead's system, namely that it theorizes "a world of captures rather than closures," a chaosmos in which "beings [actual entities] are pushed apart, kept open through divergent series and incompossible totalities that pull them outside, instead of being closed upon the compossible and convergent world that they express from within" (TF, 81). To my knowledge, the best approximation to this view is once again to be found in Christian, insofar as what basis there is for Deleuze's interpretation would have to rest on the following principle: "To say that there is a general scheme of relatedness among eternal objects is only to say that *all relations are possible*. If some certain eternal object were actualized [for a particular actual entity], then *all* other eternal objects would be relevant in *some* way or other [to that entity]."[17] Now to say that, in principle, and a propos of the logical subjects of the system, all relations are possible and all eternal objects relevant, is *almost* to say that Whiteheadian subject-units are "pulled outside," "decentered," kept open to the infinity of predicates through which they (virtually) pass. But the telling question is this, What is Whitehead's *own* explanation of how this is possible? "His ultimate explanation is that each [actual entity] in its initial phase prehends God," as it must do, because only through the mediation of the divine nature is there an "envisagement of the *entire* multiplicity of eternal objects."[18] But if, as I have argued at length, Whitehead's all-envisaging God is incapable of performing the strange kind of synthesis required, then the God who appears in *The Fold* as "affirming incompossibles and passing through them" must be precisely Deleuze's own: the Divine Schizophrenic. And it is this God who consistently fails to appear in *Process and Reality,* other than as a negative or a kind of after-image. (Except once, in a mythic aside: Whitehead cites from John Milton, *Paradise Lost,* Book 2, and then adds, "the fact of Satan's journey through chaos helped to evolve order; for he left a permanent track, useful for the devils and the damned" [PR, 96]. In Klossowski's terms, a track left by the "prince of all modifications," first servant of the inclusive disjunction.) On this basis, then, I would suggest that—on his own terms—we must rule out Deleuze's sketch of a specifically *Whiteheadian* chaosmology and conclude that within Whitehead's system the universe remains, in principle, only semi-open and therefore partially predictable. Of course, Deleuze is correct to say that, *by contrast with the monads,* Whiteheadian subject-units are radically open. But the system as a whole remains subject to an "initial condition," which Deleuze himself consistently demands be excluded.

But what are we to make of Deleuze's own account of how the requisite synthesis of pure potentiality comes about? Is he seriously suggesting that for the "God of religion" we substitute an equally primordial (and mythical) Divine Schizophrenic, an "Antichrist," *Satan* himself? No such supremely individuated Being appears in the system of *Difference and Repetition;* in fact, any form of monotheism is ruled out in principle by the operation just referred to as "pluralizing Spinozism." Nonetheless, as I suggested earlier, Deleuze's antitheism by no means leads us straight to a naturalism, for while it certainly ensures that pure potentiality is not to be identified with God, it nonetheless maintains that "*the energy that sweeps through it is divine. . . .* Hence the sole thing that is divine is the nature of an energy of disjunctions" (AO, 13). But, to put to Deleuze the question we posed to Christian, *What precisely is this nature?* What is the precise mechanism involved in this "disjunctive" synthesis? In fact, as will become all too clear, Deleuze's response to this problem is often no less vague, obscure, at times near tautologous, than Whitehead's own. Here is how Deleuze faces up to it:

> The most important difficulty, however, remains: is it really difference which relates different to different in these intensive [purely potential] systems? . . . When we speak of communication between heterogeneous [incompossible] systems . . . does this not imply . . . an agent which brings about the communication? . . . what is this agent, this force? Thunderbolts explode between different intensities, but they are preceded by an invisible, imperceptible *dark precursor,* which deter-

mines their path in advance but in reverse, as though intagliated. . . .
(DR, 119)

I am not sure that it is possible to "explicate" this impenetrably dark notion of the "dark precursor"; suffice to say, "it" is that element that functions as the agent of communication between incompossibles, as the immanent operator of disjunctive synthesis. Almost immediately, Deleuze poses the crucial problem for himself: "The question is to know in any given case *how* the precursor fulfills this role" (DR, 119, emphasis added). A few lines later, the semblance of an answer is offered:

> Given two heterogeneous series, two series of differences [incompossible potentials], the precursor plays the part of the differenciator *[sic]* of these differences. In this manner, by virtue of its own power, it puts them into immediate relation to one another: it is the in-itself of difference or the "differently different"—in other words, difference in the second degree, the self-different which relates different to different by itself. (DR, 119)

One might, not unreasonably, want to object to this formulation, pointing out that in order to deal with the problem, Deleuze has here reverted to a tortuous syntax that could fairly be described as Hegelian dialectic "with one term missing"; in other words, that by making his primitive concept of difference do *all* the work, the inevitable result is mere vacuous repetition, empty tautology. It is indeed at this point that Deleuze, self-confessedly, attempts to think something "contrary to the laws of thought" (DR, 227) and thereby risks that lapse into vacuity for which Kant condemned all of metaphysics. But the lines that immediately follow attempt to explain why—at least within the terms of the Deleuzean chaosmos itself—this moment of attempting to "think the unthinkable" is, at the limit, ineliminable:

> Because the path it [the dark precursor] follows is invisible and becomes visible only in reverse, to the extent that it is travelled over and covered by the phenomena it induces within the system [i.e., within an actual world], it has no place other than that from which it is "missing," no identity other than that which it lacks: it is precisely the object = x. (DR 119-120)

Thus Deleuze presents his speculative, and distinctly Platonic, hypothesis: The visible, actual world is an effect of this invisible "reversion" of the potential, the infinitely rich sediment it leaves in its track. As the object = x, the (path of the) dark precursor is that virtually *unintelligible* object that corresponds to the thought of difference "in itself." Necessarily unintelligible insofar as the very conditions for the production of novelty (viz. disjunctive syntheses of incompossibles) entail that intensive (potential) differences will always already be canceled within the novel extensities and qualities in which they are actualized—(through the conjunctive syntheses of compossibles; in Whitehead's terms, through a demand for "balanced complexity," the integration of incompatibilities into realizable contrasts [cf. PR, 278]). As such, the object = x is inevitably occulted by the forms of representation (categories, concepts, and laws) under which the actual, extensive, *contrasting* "phenomena" are thinkable, and by which their behavior is explained. Thus, Deleuze concludes, "it is not surprising that, strictly speaking, difference ["in itself"] should be inexplicable. . . . For difference, to be explicated [actualized] is to be cancelled. . . ." (DR, 228).

This much at least can be said about the nature of the dark precursor: In its role as agent of synthesis it is not, like the primordial nature of God, One: "[G]iven the variety among systems, this role [must be] fulfilled by quite diverse determinations" (DR, 119). It is possible to discern in this principle not only a pluralizing of Spinozism (or perhaps a modest homage to Hume: Why not a whole team of gods?), but also an implicit answer to Plato when, in the *Sophist,* he raises the question of synthesis/analysis a propos of the Forms (or "genera"):

> Now since we have agreed that the classes or genera also commingle with one another, or do not commingle, in the same way must he not possess some science and proceed by the processes of reason [he] who is to show . . . whether there are *some elements extending through all and holding them together so that they can mingle, and again, when they separate, whether there are other universal causes of separation.*[19]

In other words, as Whitehead notes, for Plato "determinations of compatibilities and incompatibilities are the key to coherent thought" (AI, 147). If Deleuze's thought of the difference-that-relates-different-to-different is not "coherent," it is because its "objects" are precisely those elements that run through the incompossible series simultaneously effecting *both* a holding together (synthesis) *and* a holding apart (disjunction); thus it is one and the same "universal cause" in each case: "The affirmative synthetic disjunction . . . consists of the erection of a paradoxical instance, an aleatory point with *two uneven faces,* which traverses the divergent series as divergent and causes them to resonate through their distance and in their distance" (LS, 174, emphasis added). "Paradoxical instances," "aleatory points," "dark precursors": these, I would suggest, are the only divine elements in the Deleuzean chaosmos, "primitives" in both a methodological and metaphysical sense: "savage concepts" apparently resonating with "things in their wild and free [not yet actualized] state" (cf. DR, xx).

Conclusion

For Deleuze, then, the sole thing that matters is the chaosmological *function* instantiated/exemplified by his various primitives. As such, in the Deleuzean chaosmos, many factors (many features of God and of his various roles, both traditional and Whiteheadian) putatively necessary for the production of novelty are eliminated. To deal with these in turn: firstly, no supreme individual or being is required to perform the function, only "individuating acts" (multiple synthesizing agents, lacking an identity, always missing) distributed within an impersonal and preindividual field of pure potentiality. And ruled out categorically is any infinite Being "existing for its own sake" (cf. PR, 88) but entrusted with the benign function of "federating" differences between finite beings and worlds. Secondly, it is no longer the case that "multiplicity requires that any unity it may have be established for it by some outside agency";[20] it requires only a "mobile, immanent principle of auto-unification" (LS, 102) through disjunctive synthesis. Thirdly, the chaosmos need not "include a *stable actuality* whose mutual implication with the remainder of the things secures an inevitable trend towards order" (AI, 115, emphasis added); rather the "system . . . is neither stable nor unstable, but 'metastable,' endowed with a potential energy [the so-called divine 'energy of disjunctions'] wherein the differences between series are distributed" (LS, 103). Finally, no element of *consciousness* can enter into the initial conditions for the production of novelty. This is a factor that Whitehead himself explicitly, though obscurely, recognizes: toward the end of *Process and Reality* the primordial nature is described in the following terms: "free, complete, eternal, actually deficient, and *unconscious*" (PR, 345, emphasis added). And just as the primordial nature knows no *negative* prehensions, so too with the Deleuzean notion of the "virtual" as a kind of cosmic unconscious: "The phenomena of the unconscious cannot be understood in the overly simple form of opposition and conflict. . . . conflicts are the result of more subtle differential mechanisms. . . . The negative expresses only within consciousness the shadow of fundamentally unconscious questions and problems" (DR, 106).

Were such consequences to be accepted, then a process metaphysics could indeed dispense with Whitehead's God, although not with that singular function of "total affirmation" which Whitehead—the weight of ontotheological tradition bearing down upon him—valiantly attempts to grant God. However, as I have tried to show, while in Deleuze's metaphysics we find something like Whiteheadian pure potentiality reappearing in a radically decentered form, the net result is less a neo-Whiteheadian naturalism than a distinctly postmodern avatar of polytheism: a vision of multiple "little divinities" effecting random syntheses of differential elements within an immanent space of possibilities; a theory of evolution metamorphosed into Chaosmological Myth; an unqualified affirmation of the endless, goalless, production of Difference. As it was with Nietzsche, so it is with the pagan Deleuze.[21]

Notes

1. I am grateful to Isabelle Stengers and to a second, anonymous referee for their helpful and encouraging comments on an earlier draft of this chapter. Stengers rightly objects to the classification of Deleuze as a "poststructuralist" on the grounds that this heading is an American importation of no interest to the French, who were reading Deleuze since before 1968, and who recognized him as a "master," meaning deserving of a heading by himself. This is undoubtedly correct. The Anglo-American label may, however, be put to a legitimate, if rather specific, use—namely, in the context of a selective reading of Deleuze's works from the late sixties (DR and LS), and taking the logico-mathematical model of structuralism (developed by the Bourbaki school and taken up by Piaget) as the reference point, rather than the more familiar, but rather different, model derived from Saussurean linguistics. For an attempt at such a revisionist reading, see my article, "Deleuze and Structuralism," in *Deleuze and Philosophy*, Keith Ansell-Pearson, ed. (London: Routledge, 1997).

2. Cf. Ilya Prigogine and Stengers, *La nouvelle alliance* (Paris: Gallimard, 1979), esp. 387–389. See also Stengers's article, "Entre Deleuze et Whitehead," in *Gilles Deleuze: une vie philosophique,* Eric Alliez, ed. (Paris: Les empecheurs de penser en rond, 1998), 325–332.

3. Donald Sherburne, "Decentering Whitehead," *Process Studies* 15(2) (1986), 83, 92.

4. Cf. George Kampis, *Self-Modifying Systems in Biology and Cognitive Science* (Oxford: Pergamon Press, 1991), 462.

5. William Christian, *An Interpretation of Whitehead's Metaphysics* (New Haven: Yale University Press, 1959), 276.

6. Ibid., 259, 262.

7. Ibid., 251. Christian quotes Whitehead from *Process and Reality,* 21.

8. Ibid., 252.

9. Ibid., 262.

10. Ibid., 277.

11. Ibid., 276, 277–278, emphasis added.

12. Ibid., 276, emphasis added.

13. Lewis Ford, *The Emergence of Whitehead's Metaphysics 1925–1929* (Albany: State University of New York Press, 1984), 116.

14. Christian, *Interpretation of Whitehead's Metaphysics,* 274, 275, emphasis added.

15. Ibid., 276.

16. Ford, *Emergence of Whitehead's Metaphysics,* 110.

17. Christian, *Interpretation of Whitehead's Metaphysics,* 274.

18. Ibid., 269.

19. *Sophist,* 252D, 253. Cited by Whitehead (his brackets and italics), ESP, 129.

20. Granville C. Henry, *Forms of Concrescence* (London and Toronto: Associated University Presses, 1993), 120.

21. On Deleuze's understanding of evolution, see DR, chapter 5, passim; e.g., 248: "Natural selection . . . shows how differences become connected to one another and accumulate in a given direction, but also how they tend to diverge further and further in different or even opposed directions. Natural selection plays an essential role: the differenciation *[sic]* of difference"—that is, the role of a dark precursor for the actual "origin of species." On Deleuze's Nietzschean mythologizing, cf. DR, passim. As a representative passage: "The eternal return does not cause the same and the similar to return, but is . . . the consequence of a difference which is originary, pure, synthetic and in-itself (which Nietzsche called "will to power"). If difference is the in-itself, then repetition in the eternal return is the for-itself of difference" (DR, 125). Finally, for a different perspective on a similar connection, I am grateful to Stengers for drawing my attention to the quasi-Nietzschean flavor of God's insatiable "appetition for new contrasts"—a pathos especially noticeable when a difference arrives (as it does most days) between "what He cares for and my own craving for being cared for." Had I been able to pursue (among others) this intriguing observation, the paper would no doubt have had a different, less oppositional, and therefore, perhaps, more productive "feel."

9

De-Ontologizing God
Levinas, Deleuze, and Whitehead

ROLAND FABER

Ontology and the De-Ontologization of God

Ontology and theology seem to express a reciprocal relationship. As the German theologian Walter Kasper writes, "God-Talk presupposes the metaphysical question of Being and evokes it at the same time."[1] Hence, ontological God-language is a significant, although disputed, aspect of theological and philosophical discussion—one thinks of the importance of Charles Hartshorne's occupation with the ontological argument of Anselm of Canterbury. The hope for an ontological horizon of God-language still lurks on the ground of theological propositions; so we find it, for instance, behind Hans Küng's question (and book), *Does God Exist?* Under the reign of ontology, the most important question seems to be that of God's "existence."

Nevertheless, since Ludwig Feuerbach's strong reproach of projection, Friedrich Nietzsche's denial of the "existence" of God, and Immanuel Kant's deconstruction of ontological God-language in his *First Critique,* the correlation, congruence, or even reciprocity between theology and ontology can no longer be claimed naively. Criticism within and external to theology has forced theologians to think about de-ontologizing God. Language-critical, psychoanalytic, deconstructive, and ethical reasons underly this process of dissociating theology from ontology. The *language-critical reason:* "God" is the expression of general notions (like "the world"); thus, "God" is a language signifier by which the subject of speech is to be constituted as "manifestor." Subject and signifier mutually cause one another; they do not need any a priori designations or relation with "real" objects (LS, 12ff.). The *psychoanalytic reason:* "God" refers to the repressive reality of the "Super-Ego" (father and mother). Its strength of repression canalizes the "Id" and stabilizes the "Ego."

The *deconstructive reason:* "God" articulates a conceptual unity of differences, although—in reality—there is no unity. Where difference is thought *as* difference, "God" ceases to function as a unifying entity. The *ethical reason:* As long as God appears under the notion of Being, God is presupposed as a projection of our own egotistic expansion. This, and nothing else, is the notion of Being. Hence, in breaking the ties to our self-extending egos, God may appear as the totally other, or as a reality of decision, but not as a reality of existence.[2]

Given today's exorbitant problems connected with the invocation of ontological language, it should not surprise us that philosophers of the twentieth century, such as Emmanuel Levinas and Gilles Deleuze, strove to overcome the ontological language of *Sein* or "existence." Regarding the reality of God, they reconstructed notions of divinity through a new horizon, namely that of Ethics or Aesthetics. Although it may have been forgotten, we may now recall that Alfred North Whitehead's conceptualization of God avoids the language of existence and any discourse of the proofs of God's existence. In fact, quite different from Hartshorne, Whitehead was opposed to such proofs (cf. PR, 93). As Walter Jung has demonstrated, even Whitehead's step from any "cosmic order" to a God as "ordering process" does not indicate proof of God's existence, but only expresses a logical procedure, reassuring systematic consistency.[3]

The theological questions now become: Of what mode is the "reality" of God? Should God's reality be stated in ontological terms? If not, what other mode might we use? Regarding Whitehead's concept of God, I will explore these questions through developing the following complex three-part thesis: (1) The "reality" of God does not consist in an ontological reality; that is, it does not claim a judgment regarding the "existence" of God. Rather, it expresses an *aesthetic* reality. (2) However, this aesthetic reality will be more adequately expressed as the reality of *in/difference*. In reconstructing the essential moments of Whitehead's final work regarding God's reality—his article, "Immortality"—I shall suggest that God's aesthetic mode of reality could be transformed into a nondual reality, namely that of *expressive in/difference*. (3) Finally, by reconceiving Whitehead's notion of God in light of the thesis of *expressive in/difference*, we shall be inclined to understand Whitehead's move toward a conception of God as an *eschatological adventure*.

By using the term *de-ontologizing*, I claim the following transformation: from God as an ontological reality to God as an aesthetic, in/different, and eschatological reality. Thus, de-ontologization does not indicate a dismissal of ontology and the ontological question as such. Rather, since any *critical* discussion of ontological reality *qualifies* the notion of ontology positively, it leaves a wider horizon—that is, the negative possibilities—undiscussed. Although the Wolffian, Cartesian, and Kantian tradition of ontology as *modes of possibilities;* the Aristotelian, Thomistic, and Heideggerian tradition of "Being" as *that which is encountered;* and the ontic and logical tradition of the *existence-quantifier stating facts* are all covered in the writings of Levinas, Deleuze, and Whitehead, one may still doubt that all ontological traditions have been examined, much less exhausted. At the very least, we may ask whether Levinas has misread Martin Heidegger's ontological difference by identifying it with an illusionary "egology." We may also widen our view to include traditions such as the "negative ontology" of neo-Platonism, Dionysius the Areopagite, Nicolas of Cusa, the later works of F. W. J. Schelling, or the Zen position of the Kyoto-school, on the one hand, and that of the "positive-univocal ontology" of Duns Scotus, Benedict de Spinoza, Henri Bergson, and even Deleuze, on the other.[4]

Thus, the notion of de-ontologization, as expressed in the three-step thesis of *aesthetics, in/difference,* and *eschatology,* does not intend to replace ontological discussion as such. Rather, it attempts to open the horizon for these "negative" and "positive-univocal" traditions beyond the influential Aristotelian tradition, which claims "analogy" as the horizon for an adequate ontological God-language. Opposed to the analogical tradition, Deleuze writes that *negative* ontology "admits that affirmations are able to designate God as cause. . . . But God as substance or essence can be defined only negatively, according to the rules of transcendence. . . ." (EP, 53). *Positive* ontology, to the contrary, affirms "that everything expresses God. The whole order of Nature is expressive" (EP, 58). It is in the name of these traditions, be they positive or negative, that the de-ontologization of God is being performed. In the tradition of negative ontology, I take the voice of Levinas to be one of the strongest; in the positive, it is Deleuze who most forcefully evokes the expressionist tradition.

But why Whitehead? Whitehead is introduced in this context of de-ontologization for at least three reasons: Firstly, regarding Whitehead's philosophy, it may be necessary to surpass an often formal and mostly internal interpretation of Whitehead's work in order to reignite a discussion in which Whitehead appears in the context of contemporary philosophy. Secondly, it may be fruitful to introduce Whitehead into contemporary philosophical discussions because he may well generate new views of the problems under dispute. Thirdly, the interaction of Whitehead's thought with both ontological traditions—the "negative" and the "positive," represented by Levinas and Deleuze, respectively—may allow for a double-edged transformation to take place: On the one hand, we may discover in Whitehead's thought horizons for de-ontologizing God in both of these directions, the negative and the positive, with Whitehead's thought seen as uniting their paradoxical division. On the other hand, the context of de-ontologization will be presented as a catalyst for a new way of expressing Whitehead's notion of God.

On the border of language and reality, we may well be aware that we have no "certain" knowledge but only grapple with our inability to grasp.

Nevertheless, in mapping out a common plane for Levinas, Deleuze, and Whitehead, we shall find the following "drama of de-ontologization" taking place: (1) Levinas de-ontologizes God by totally dissociating God from any kind of reality that can be placed under the auspices of Being. God appears as the totally *Other of Being,* utterly transcendent to all beings. (2) Deleuze de-ontologizes God by completely dissolving God into the expressiveness of the *natura naturans.* God disappears within total immanence. (3) Whitehead, however, shall be introduced as attempting to integrate these two poles—the transcendent and the immanent—leading to the notion of God as *in/difference.*

Levinas on Alterity: De-Ontologizing God as Transcendence

In his two major books, *Totality and Infinity* and *Otherwise than Being or Beyond Essence,* Levinas develops his conception of alterity as the idea of "the other" who cannot be encountered through naive notions of subjectivity.[5] In view of this *truly* other, Levinas transforms the definition of subjectivity from that of "self-conscious being-in-oneself" to such conceptions as "to-risk-one's-existence" and "to-leave-oneself."[6] In his criticism of Heidegger's *Sein,* Levinas defines the fundamental meaning of the other as a reality that cannot be reflected by any subject nor revealed by reason.[7] The reflection of the subject would already be a "reduction of the other to the Ego" (an "alter ego"/ "like me"), a subsumption of the other under the notion of *Sein.* Thus, Levinas would argue, Heidegger's ontology fails to examine sufficiently the requirements of "the other." For Levinas, alterity stands against ontology; alterity unmasks ontology as "Egologie."[8] Only by the "horror of the other which remains the other" is philosophy "essentially philosophy of Being. . . ."[9] In contrast to Heidegger's *es gibt Sein,*[10] which assimilates "the other" under the terms *Dasein* and *Mitsein* (Being-with[11]) Levinas develops his conception of anonymous existing: *il y a.* Before all thoughts, prior to any consciousness or assimilating self, *es gibt* (there is/it gives) "the other."[12]

How, then, does the other disclose itself (give itself) for others to recognize without losing its otherness?[13] In his "phenomenology of alterity,"[14] Levinas answers by describing forms of disclosure that undermine any assimilation—such as those that occur in the concepts "existence," "Being-with," and "Being-within-the-world"[15]—and that enable recognition of "the other as the other." Disclosure of otherness occurs in extreme phenomena such as time and death, or in the dissipation of "self-ness."[16] Here, "the other" does not appear within the "egotistic spontaneity" of a subject, but through a breaking-into "the self" by "the other."[17] Indeed, "the other" constitutes "the self" by an ethical call, and this takes place *before* "the self" is able to *grasp* "the other." Here "the other" appears prior to *Sein.* Levinas calls this process *jouissance.*[18] Within *jouissance,* "the other" can never be encountered as such, but only in its "passage."[19] "The other" is encountered in/as *le visage,*[20] which we do not understand; rather, *le visage* occurs.[21] In its ingression, however, "the other" is elusive and becomes an enigma.[22] Enigma "is transcendence itself, the closeness of the other as the other. . . . The enigma is the mode of the absolute; the absolute is beyond recognition."[23]

In his extremely complex book, *Otherwise than Being or Beyond Essence,* Levinas conceives of (thereby reacting to Derrida[24]) alterity as "otherwise than being" *(autrement qu'être).* That is, not only as "another being," but as "the other of Being."[25] Thereby, Levinas breaks the sovereignty of Kant's transcendental Ego by opening it up to something preoriginal, pre-phenomenological. No "subject" is preexistent to "the other"; rather, the subject exists only as addressed (and taken up) by the other. The "I" has no privileged status of "being-oneself"; the "I" is already "deposited" *(dé-position)* and constituted by "the other." Subjectivity originally owns neither consciousness nor self-possession ("being-at-home-with-oneself"); subjectivity exists only as "leaving-itself."[26]

Four facets of Levinas's thought disclose striking similarities to Whitehead's conception of actuality: (a) "The other" appears *diachronically.* It cannot be encountered as simply present, but only as past or as future.[27] However, precisely this relationship forms the "occasion's" real internal nature (cf. PR, 41). "The other" implements this structure in three ways: as the "real potentiality" of the occasion;[28] as "initial aim"—the starting point for subjectivity beyond itself (cf. PR, 244); and in the activity named "creativity," which sustains self-becoming without being subjective itself. (b) "The other" opens itself only in a strangeness that cannot be assimilated. "Occasions" within the relative present, but also as passing, dying, having become, and being *(Gewesenes),* remain always strangers to one another; the other's presence can be only suspected.[29] In its satisfaction, a perfect occasion has "attained its individual separation from other things" (PR, 154); it signifies the "'great refusal,' . . . [as] its primary characteristic" (SMW, 158). Even Whitehead's "eternal objects" cannot be assimilated, because they appear only as ingredients of any given process. Whitehead's expression for this nonassimilation of the "eternal objects" is the incommensurability of the "primordial nature" of God. (c) The subject stands always already under the call of the other; the subject cannot voluntarily seek out the other, but finds itself already in the other's presence. "The other" manifests itself in the subject before the subject exists. Therefore, it is only when "the subject" itself is relativized that ontological thinking can be overcome. What remains after the breakdown of any totality is, for Levinas, not "the subject" of a radically pluralistic subjectivism, but "the other," which transcends all subjectivity.[30] In Whitehead's "reformed subjectivist principle" a similar perspective is found. (d) "The other" appears for both Levinas and Whitehead as trace and enigma. Nevertheless, its "face" can be touched. "The other" appears in experiencing that which has passed, which can never be possessed in the present. As past or future, "the other" evades the present.

Levinas names his de-ontologization of reality "ethics,"[31] "metaphysics,"[32] and "alterity." In this context, God's alterity does not indicate an ontologically "absolute difference," nor does it signify "another par excellence"; rather, it expresses reality differently than different *(autre qu'autrui)*, or differently in another way *(autre autrement).*[33] Levinas calls this preontological and preethical alterity of God *Illeity.*[34] The strongest formulation of such divine alterity in Whitehead is probably found in his idea that the process of God's own becoming occurs in every respect conversely to the world's becoming (cf. PR, 349).

Deleuze on Novelty: De-Ontologizing God as Immanence

Deleuze stands within the poststructuralist tradition of Michel Foucault. In Deleuze's main works, *Difference and Repetition, The Logic of Sense, The Fold,* and *What Is Philosophy?* he asks time and again *the* basic question of his philosophy, *What is an event?* (LS, 7, 66).[35]

As aesthetic reality, events do not refer beyond themselves to "exterior referents" (things, humans, history, "something that is").[36] Instead, they represent their own reality at the boundary of things and language—namely, the reality of meaning, or, better, "sense" as in "non-sense" (LS, 66ff.).

In his analysis of perception in *Difference and Repetition,* Deleuze demonstrates that what originally drives one to think appears not in "recognition" of ideas but in an "encounter" with "forces," or what he calls "intensities." They are felt only with a certain "affective tone"; they "can only be sensed" (DR, 139). Following Plato's *Republic,* Deleuze develops this distinction further in *The Logic of Sense* (1–3): On the one hand, there is that reality accessible to recognition because it is gained through the harmonious use of all of our faculties. This kind of reality corresponds to "common sense." Recognition of this reality may form ontological propositions such as "This is a finger." On the other hand, that reality that energizes thinking in the first place discloses itself only in irritating our faculties and in perplexing our thoughts. One cannot recognize this perplexing reality through abstract qualities; one can encounter it only through concrete aesthetic intensities.[37]

In *The Logic of Sense,* Deleuze establishes aesthetic reality as a "between" at the border of things and language. The aesthetic "designates" no ontological objects; it "manifests" no subject (the "I"); it "signifies" no concepts. Instead, it defines the dimension of *expression,* the level of *sense,* or the *pure event* (LS, 19–22, 28 ff., 151).[38] Therefore, the reality of sense/pure event/ expression is not directed toward facts (ontological-language), or subjects (subject-language), or truth conditions (concept-language) (LS, 12 ff.).[39]

Deleuze expresses aesthetic reality as that *dimension of the status of things* that "is" not or does not "have" any Being.[40] Aesthetic reality reveals itself as "non-existent entity," or as "extrabeing" (with Meinong), or as "?-being."[41] Further-more, it articulates a *dimension of language,* which does not indicate anything that exists, but rather that "subsists" or "insists" (LS, 34).

What is interesting is that Deleuze—in a manner very similar to White-head—situates his language of "events" within cosmology.[42] Deleuze's "events" form a cosmological space within which intensities can be trans-formed into extensities. In the language of *Difference and Repetition, The Logic of Sense,* and especially *The Fold,* Deleuze defines this space of "virtual events" as *spatium,* as formless and open *Ungrund/sans fond/"*groundlessness" (LS, 106).[43] In this groundless space, intensities are "enfolded" and can be "out-folded" to extensities or shapes in space and time. *Implicit spatium* expli-cates itself as *extensio* (TF, 20).[44] In the earlier language of *Bergsonism* and *Expressionism in Philosophy: Spinoza,* however, Deleuze defines this state of initial virtuality and the space of "pure events" in terms of Bergson's *élan vital* and Spinoza's *causa sui,* that is, as the infinite but self-differentiating sub-stance of God.[45] With respect to Bergson's *élan vital,* Deleuze writes, "Virtuality exists in such a way that it is realized in dissociating itself. . . . Differentiation is the movement of a virtuality that is actualizing itself."[46] Regarding Spinoza's "infinite substance," Deleuze recognized its absolute immanence and total expression *within* the world and *as* the world's primor-dial process of differentiation—the process of the actualization of virtuality.[47]

A high affinity appears to exist between Deleuze's and Whitehead's the-ories of occasions, which Deleuze considers in his book *The Fold.*[48] Two interesting points of similarity are the following: (a) Reference to ontological entities is subordinated to the intensity of events: Not truth, but *interest,* ex-presses the primary function of reality-referring propositions (PR, 259).[49] (b) Deleuze's "virtuality" resembles Whitehead's "creativity": Virtuality is totally immanent and thereby productive of the world. In other words, Deleuze reads Spinoza in the sense that Whitehead wishes to interpret Spin-oza's singular, infinite, and ultimate "reality"; namely, without any substan-tialization and as pure, nonentitative activity (cf. PR, 7). "Creativity" does not exist; rather, one could say, it insists.[50]

Deleuze uses his event-theory of virtuality and actualization in order to articulate *conditions of novelty* for the world. In reference to Gottfried Wil-helm Leibniz and Whitehead, Deleuze accepts as his basic cosmological inter-est the quest for a world in which *creation* is possible (TF, 81).[51] This would be a world without preformation, without preformed "order," but of sponta-neous "organization."[52] Consequently, Deleuze promotes affective reality itself as the transcendental condition of experience, concepts, and proposi-tions.[53] Perplexing forces arrange experiences, not pregiven rules or schemes. That is, novelty occurs within concrete, unforeseeable, and by no means a priori assignable categories, insofar as the forces grow together—always in another constellation. This concrete novelty, which cannot be predetermined by any rules or categories, Deleuze calls *the event* of actuality.[54] In somewhat perplexing approximation, we can recognize here Whitehead's "ontological principle": In the nexus of creative occasions, it is the abstract conditions, categories, or rules that always *follow* the event of novelty. The immanence of the field of "virtuality" creates novelty through acts of differentiation, but not by *pre*forming actuality.[55] Virtuality is a "plane of immanence"—itself a plurality, but infinitely including all of reality as "One-All," *Omnitudo* (WP, 35).

In the light of his philosophy of total immanence, Deleuze's "God" dissolves into what he may have seen as the purest statement of that immanence: the infinite, univocal, affirmative, and self-differentiating essence of God—according to Spinoza, *Deus sive natura naturans*. It would not be correct to claim that Deleuze has an atheist or even materialist bias. Deleuze offers, in fact, an extremely differentiated notion of God—as seen in his book on Spinoza–and not a "transcendent" God as is found in the analogical or negative-ontological traditions.[56] In the language of *What Is Philosophy?* "transcendence" is an illusion that arises *only* in the process "of making immanence immanent to something" (WP, 49), and thereby violating the first rule of the philosophy of immanence: that immanence is only immanent to itself as the totally expressive reality of Nature and Thought (WP, 38). The nearest we can come to such a notion of immanence in Whitehead is in his attempt to reintegrate "Creativity" and "God" in *Adventures of Ideas*. While in *Science and the Modern World* (cf. SMW, 70) and in most of his following writings, "Creativity" is Whitehead's Spinozistic account of immanence (see also, PR, 7), in *Adventures of Ideas,* Whitehead seems inclined to replace any remaining connotations of God's transcendence with a totally immanent divine creativity. As he puts it, "Immanent Creativity . . . avoids the implication of a transcendent Creator" (AI, 236).

Whitehead on "Pure Feeling": God as Aesthetic Reality

Levinas, Deleuze, and Whitehead all make use of Kant's three *Critiques* to limit ontological language. Whitehead's "philosophy of organism"—surprising as this at first may seem—has not only a constructive agenda, but also a *critical* intention: it offers a "critique of pure feeling" (cf. PR, 113). His critique has four dimensions: (a) It fulfills a *basic* intention of Whitehead's "philosophy of organism." (b) Strategically, it aims at the "philosophical position in which Kant put his *Critique of Pure Reason*" (PR, 113). (c) In its central position within his philosophical project as a whole, Whitehead's "critique of pure feeling" supersedes all three of Kant's *Critiques*. (d) It unites what was divided in Kant's *Critiques*. Like Deleuze after him, Whitehead forms a new

between Levinas's conception of total transcendence as the condition of alterity and Deleuze's conception of immanence as the condition of novelty. It is this balance that will allow us to transform the *contradiction* of transcendence and immanence, as it appears in Levinas's and Deleuze's conceptions of the de-ontologization of God, into a *creative contrast* based on Whitehead's late restatement of the notion of God, which I shall call the notion of "in/difference."

What allows us to undertake this transformation? I propose that it is Whitehead's insistence upon the difference between "Creativity" and "God" *and* their reintegration into a new contrast of "in/difference" that permit the present move. This distinction empowers us to envision as integrated in Whitehead what appears to be divided in Levinas and Deleuze, namely the transcendence of "God" (Levinas) and the immanence of "nature naturing" (Deleuze). Levinas's conception of divine alterity, one could say, corresponds to a Whiteheadian theory of occasions and God as actuality. Deleuze's "infinity of differentiation" of the manifold plane of immanence, on the other hand, corresponds to Whitehead's theory of creativity. Both models, that of Levinas and Deleuze, obviously lead to considerable one-sidedness. However, such one-sidedness can be healed by integrating them both in a Whiteheadian contrast.[78]

In order to understand this transformation into a Whiteheadian contrast, consider the following experiment: Imagine Whitehead's divine reality without the immanence of Whitehead's "creativity"; this would introduce an absolutely transcendent God, the conception of which corresponds to Levinas's concept of alterity. Next, imagine the immanence of Whitehead's "creativity" without the alterity of Whitehead's God-language; this would dissolve the divine into absolute immanence, the conception of which corresponds to Deleuze's concept of immanence. Now, imagine how immanence and transcendence might be reconceptualized through Whitehead's doctrine of "creativity" and "God."

My thesis is that it is not only possible to reconceive what is contradictory in Levinas's and Deleuze's conceptions concerning the de-ontologization of God, but, moreover, that Whitehead's later work gives us a hint at how to intersect and even unite these concepts through the mediating notion of "expressive in/difference." "Expressive in/difference" becomes the needed missing link in a Whiteheadian doctrine of "God" and "creativity." This may be explored in four stages:

First stage: This thesis may be explained further by referring to Whitehead's late differentiation of a "World of Activity" and a "World of Value" in his lecture on "Immortaltity" (Imm., 82). The two "Worlds" represent Whitehead's final restatement concerning the difference between "Creativity" and "God." According to the lecture on "Immortality," both Worlds develop within a threefold relation: "The World of Value is not the World of Active Creativity" (Imm., 90); "the World of Activity . . . is the World of Organization: It is the Creative World" (Imm., 79); the "World of Value exhibits . . . the notion of God" (Imm., 90). So what does this mean for a final contrast between Levinas and Deleuze? Firstly, in Whitehead, the distinction between the World of Creativity and that of Value is indissoluble: "Creativity" and "God" may never collapse into one reality, be it immanence or transcendence. Secondly, the World of Actuality is the universe as seen from its grounding in Immanence; that which Whitehead names "Creativity," "Immanent Creativity," or "Self-Creativity" (cf. AI, 236). Thirdly, the World of Value, on the other hand, is the universe seen from the process of valuation that ultimately grounds reality in "God."

Second stage: If the two Worlds are not to be conceived as a final distinction that freezes reality into a duality, Whitehead must allow for some kind of process that can express their unity as *unification.* And in fact, Whitehead avoids final duality by the sophisticated move whereby he performs the unification of these Worlds, namely by considering them as mere "abstractions from the Universe" (Imm., 80). We view the two Worlds as already within the horizon of "the totality of the universe" (Imm., 80). *Concrete* reality—that is, reality that is not an abstraction—happens only as *unification* of these Worlds; this is the process of their finite unification against the background of the infinite universe (Imm., 77). The *concrete intersection* of these two abstract perspectives, what Whitehead calls "evaluation" (Imm., 79), happens in the *unification* "of the coordinated value into the multiplicity of finite acts" (Imm., 82), that is, as the activity of finite actualities. Finite actualities, as they constitute concrete reality, undergo the process of unification and, hence, the intersection of Activity and Value and, ultimately, "Creativity" and "God."

Third stage: Besides *finite* unification, Whitehead knows also of a "second unification" in which Activity and Value intersect: This is the "essential unification of the Universe. . . . This is the notion of God" (Imm., 90). Accordingly, what has to be seen here is a certain turn: In a sense, God appears as the "ultimate reality" of *both* Worlds. In the World of Value, God appears as that aesthetic reality "whose existence is grounded in Value" (Imm., 90), while in the World of Creative Activity or the World of Fact, God appears as "the intangible fact at the basis of finite existence" (Imm., 90).

Fourth stage: Only when we allow for such a turn may we get a glimpse of how to extend Whitehead's terminolgy toward the direction of a *unification* of both Worlds in the reality of God. Although it may seem more consistent to remain within generally accepted terms, namely that the ultimate reality of the World of Activity is "Creativity," and that of the World of Value is "God," we may also seek the "essential unification" of the World of Fact and the World of Value within a reconstructed concept of divine reality that somehow includes both worlds, "God" and "Creativity." Although the "essential unification" (*as* "ultimate reality"/"actuality"/"virtuality") reveals itself as the *concrete* intersection of the two Worlds, this is not a *finite* unification, but an *essential* unification *from beyond* both appearances. The "essential unification" removes the abstractions of both Worlds from each other. God now appears as that reality *from beyond* the abstract division of the two Worlds, totally expressing itself *within* the two abstract Worlds, or, as Whitehead writes, "express[ing] the elucidation of one of the abstractions by reference to the other" (Imm., 79).

In terms of our investigation, Levinas's God of *Alterity* constitutes, in fact, a *de-ontological* reality on the basis of the World of Value: God is not an aspect of the World of Creativity; God exists as wholly transcendent, only as the call of "the Other" and as the nonontological "ultimate reality" of the World of aesthetic Value. Deleuze's immanent but creative infinity, on the other hand, infuses the *Order* of the World of Values totally into the World of *Organization* (cf. Imm., 79). This *de-ontologized* aesthetic reality of expressive and insistent Creativity replaces the World of Value which, for Deleuze, somehow functions only as the unnecessary preformation of creativity.[79] In this context, it is Whitehead's connection of "Creativity" *and* "God" that may create the needed space for a Whiteheadian understanding of the de-ontologized reality of God.

The paradox of Alterity and self-creative Immanence can only be resolved within that "second unification" of the two Worlds—rather than that of finite processes—that is, the *ultimate intersection* of both Worlds *beyond* their difference.[80] This is the notion of "expressive in/difference." Although God is now envisioned *beyond* the two Worlds (beyond "activity" and "actuality," "God" and "Godhead"), this ultimate reality is *not* a "third," a "different" reality; on the contrary, God now expresses the in/difference of the difference between the two Worlds and their ultimates, "God" and "Creativity." In being creative in all of the differences, even the difference between the two Worlds, God is, at the same time, to be viewed as completely *expressive within* those differences. God's reality of in/difference removes the abstraction of the two Worlds by conceptualizing God's in/different totality as the *origination of their difference* and, thereby, of *difference as such*. What follows from this is of crucial importance: God does not "exist" *beyond* the differences of the two Worlds as some kind of substantial reality, but God *insists* and *subsists* only *within* the differences of the two Worlds.[81]

Now the "affirmative" and "negative" ontological traditions intersect in the notion of the expressive in/difference of God, without stating an ontological analogy, but by including it. This notion of divine in/difference includes four aspects: Firstly, there can be more than one way in which the Worlds of Value and Activity can unite; they may unite in the "finite unification" of actualities, but they may also intersect in an "essential unification" that is God. Secondly, while the "finite intersection" is a unifying process of the abstract Worlds, the "essential intersection" is a process of their creation (analogical tradition).[82] Thirdly, since God's reality cannot be explained exhaustively *within* the differences it creates, God is de-ontologized as the *origin* of the differences, which enables ontological statements (negative-ontological tradition). Fourthly, God's "reality beyond" must not be substantialized (as if it could be stated within the differences it creates). Therefore, God's reality is in/different to/from the differences it intersects, by originating these differences (positive-ontological tradition).

Using the term *expressive in/difference,* I take up Nicolas of Cusa's conception of God as *non aliud.*[83] Cusa states that in being *non aliud* God "is nothing other than the Non-Other."[84] Therefore, divine reality is *identical* with itself as the in/difference of anything and of itself. Since God is "nothing other" than any reality, God cannot be stated *as* "another" reality. God's singularity cannot be told *within* the differences we use *to name reality* (ontologically). Hence, God cannot be *identified* as the Non-Other *like* any Other. Therefore, God is *totally expressive* of the reality to which God relates in God's being *in/different* to it; nevertheles, God as the "Non-Other" is also *not identical* to this reality.

God as Eschatological Adventure

Because of this conception of "expressive in/difference," we may go even further: The in/different God neither appears as "being" *beyond* the differences, nor as "existing" *within* them, but *ultimately* as "insisting" on the differences God expresses by creating them. Since God as *non aliud* does not hide any dark essence beyond the world, but is totally *expressive,* difference-*creating,* and turned positively *toward* the world, God's reality may be seen as an ultimate process of inexhaustibly *coming into* the differences. In other words, God is "in coming," but never "coming to be"; God subsists as "unification," but never as "unity"; God insists neither as "being" nor as "becoming," but ever as what I will call *eschatological ad-vent.* This notion indicates, firstly, that God's expressive in/difference has to be understood not as static reality, but as process, namely as a process of the origination of differences. Secondly, God now appears as *ad-vent from beyond the differences, in being totally expressive within them.* Thirdly, in God's advent, the world turns out to be an *eschatological "adventure" of the "advent"* of God.

The concept of "eschatology," implied in the reality of God as explored in this investigation, should not be confused with the doctrine of "the end," completion or perfection of the world, nor as the doctrine of the *novissima,* the so-called "last things." It indicates, rather, that God's "reality" *comes from* the eschatological future. That "eschatological future" of God does not, however, define a *futurum* into which the world develops, but expresses God's *adventus,* which comes to the world *as* its "future."[85]

That is to say: Neither "is" God, nor "was" God, nor "will" God "be"— God cannot be stated under the temporal modes of Being; God instantiates no tenses. Instead, God's reality "comes" into those time-modes; God's "coming" constitutes the tenses we use to articulate God's relation to the world (cf. Apoc. 1:4).[86] The eschatological God, now totally de-ontologized, "never really is" (cf. PR, 82), but "comes," or *ad-vents,* indicating ontological poverty, since God appears to express "nothing" rather than "being."[87] However, this poverty merely indicates the eschatological plentitude of the advent of God into all that "is," "was," or "will be." Thus, God's "coming" to (or, in certain cases, "haunting" of) all being and becoming in all modes expresses an eschatological adventure.[88]

This notion of the "eschatological adventure" of God can be demonstrated further by returning to the concepts of *alterity, novelty,* and *adventure* that have guided our investigation to create a contrast between Levinas's transcendent God of *Illeity* and Deleuze's immanent God of *natura naturans* within a Whiteheadian context.

(1) *Eschatological Novelty:* God's eschatological reality appears *beyond* "categories," "principles," and "entities." Certainly, Whitehead treats God as a concrete entity *in relation* to abstract principles[89] and categories.[90] However, when Whitehead, due to his conceptual scheme, is forced to characterize the "entity" of God, he leaves us with a series of paradoxical negations expressing that God is not like all other (actual) entities: God—the "non-derivative entity" (PR, 32);[91] God—the "primordial superject of creativity (PR, 32); God—not like other entities, but the radical reversal of their processuality (PR, 349).[92] Precisely this reversal justifies an understanding of God as the reason, the source, the organ for novelty (cf. PR, 67, 88)—as Marjorie Suchocki has shown—or as the "creativity of the future" from which the world develops: "God is forever future," says Lewis Ford, and therefore, "strictly speaking, God cannot be properly characterized as one actual entity."[93] Hence, in God's eschatological adventure, God "originates" beyond all distinctions: On the one hand, all distinctions are removed—that of "God" and "Creativity" (Ford), that of "Ultimate Reality" and "Ultimate Actuality" (John B. Cobb, Jr.), or that of "God" and "Godhead" (Joseph A. Bracken, S.J.).[94] On the other hand, God originates all differences.[95] This is God's "poetic" (PR, 346), nonontological mode of the eschatological creating of novelty.[96]

(2) *Eschatological Alterity:* In *Adventures of Ideas,* Whitehead envisions salvation as hope for a "mode of satisfaction deeper than joy and sorrow" (AI, 172). Such "eschatological satisfaction," however, demonstrates (perhaps better than any other of Whitehead's notions) the *eschatological alterity* of God: No subject experiences its own fulfillment or "satisfaction" (cf. PR, 84). "Becoming-a-subject" always indicates a process of "leaving-oneself-without-return" (cf. AI, 296).[97] The eschatological encounter with God happens beyond a remaining self, beyond its subjective (self)-"enjoyment" ("not-being of immediacy," AI, 237), and always within self-transcendence.[98] Whitehead's eschatological conception of occasions never strives for

identity, but for intensity (cf. PR, 277).[99] Only within a "satisfaction" beyond personality (although never without it), does a person become God-capable.[100] God's alterity expresses Whitehead's sense that salvation is not a process of egotistic claiming of cumulated and consumed subjectivity, but is ultimately a gaining of a self in God by losing all self-claiming subjectivity. God is not to be found in the ontological (being a subject), but in the eschatological (self-relativizing all possessive subjectivity).

(3) *Eschatological Adventure:* At the intersection of alterity and novelty, Whitehead's notion of adventure leads us back to his magnificent conclusion of *Adventures of Ideas* (AI, 295f.). Eschatology appears where "adventure" defines the transcendence beyond any status quo (cf. AI, 273–283), where "zest" signifies the "self-forgetful transcendence" of becoming (AI, 296), where "peace" is envisioned as the *eschaton* as "soteriological (re-)collection."[101] The eschatological reality of God appears as an all-embracing adventure: God as "Eros," who opens up the future from out of God's eschatological reality; God as "supreme adventurer," as the guaranty for the never-ending character of the adventure of the world; finally, God as "adventure into the universe as one," in which the world collects itself. In the concluding vision of *Adventures of Ideas,* God's reality is disguised as that of the eschatological "Harmony of harmonies," as the eschatological reality of the advent and adventurous intersection of "initial Eros" with "final beauty."

According to Kant's "third anthropological question," *What may I hope?* God now appears as a "reality" within *eschatological hope.* At this point, nevertheless, Whitehead's "de-ontologization" may lead us to discover a horizon for a *new* "ontological" discussion, in which God does not have to "exist," but does "insist" as adventurous advent originating the differences that create the world, while uniting them at the same time. Now there may grow new interest in investigating the striking connections with negative-ontological traditions, such as are found in Nicolas of Cusa, Schelling, and Levinas, or with positive-ontological traditions as found in Duns Scotus, Spinoza, and Deleuze. Within this new horizon of conceptualization, Whitehead may appear as a contemporary thinker who moved far beyond the "frozen finality" of the metaphysical system with which he is associated. In the contemporary context, Whitehead's own attempt to de-ontologize God leaves us with puzzling hints taking us far beyond any system into that which is imaginative, always proposing, always in process.[102] A new place of departure is needed for contextualizing Whitehead's thought within the contemporary philosophical context; that departure may lead us to the reconstruction of the concept of God as "poetic reality," as "expressive in/difference," and as "eschatological ad-vent(ure)."

Notes

1. Walter Kasper, *Der Gott Jesu Christi,* 3rd ed. (Mainz: Gruenewald, 1995), 27. My translation. Originally, "Die Rede von Gott setzt die metaphysische Frage nach dem Sein voraus und hält sie zugleich wach."

2. Emmanuel Levinas, *Die Spur des Anderen,* 2nd ed. (Freiburg, Germany: Alber, 1987), 189.

3. Walter Jung, "Zur Entwicklung von Whiteheads Gottesbegriff," *ZPhF* 19 (1965), 601–635, esp. 617.

4. Michael Hardt, *Gilles Deleuze: An Apprenticeship in Philosophy* (Minneapolis: University of Minnesota Press, 1993), 115. He makes this differentiation in respect to Deleuze and the univocal tradition of "Being" in Deleuze's *Bergsonism* (1988) and *Expressionism in Philosophy: Spinoza* (1990).

5. Whitehead and Levinas are arguably two of this century's most original religious thinkers. Both of them named their philosophical projects "metaphysics." Catalyzed by the surprising similarities between Levinas and Whitehead, their metaphysical agendas may be interpreted as pointed against the philosophical justification of ontology. Levinas's central concept in his de-ontologization project, namely "the other," goes back to Vincent Descombe's text, *Le Même et l'autre* (1933); cf. Colin Davis, *Levinas: An Introduction* (Notre Dame: University of Notre Dame Press, 1996), 3.

6. E. Drischler, *Die Bedeutung der Nähe Gottes. Ein Gespräch mit Karl Rahner und Emmanuel Levinas* (Würzburg, Germany: Bonner Dogmatische Studien, 22, 1996), 107. Levinas sets himself against the Western tendency toward reflective self-consciousness, because it turns "durch alle Abenteuer hindurch . . . selber wieder . . . zu sich zurück wie Odysseus, der bei allen Fahrten nur auf seine Geburtsinsel zugeht." See Levinas (1987), 212.

7. Levinas, *En découvrant l'existence avec Husserl et Heidegger* (Paris: J. Vrin, 1949). Cf. Levinas's critique of Heidegger in Davis, 7–33. Cf. Levinas (1987), 212.

8. Levinas (1987), 189; cf. I. Breuner, P. Lausch, and D. Mersch, eds., *Welten im Kopf: Profile der Gergenwartsphilosophie.* Frankreich/Italien (Hamburg: Rotbuch, 1996), 3.

9. Levinas (1987), 212. My translation.

10. For Levinas, Heidegger transforms "the other," which cannot be summarized by the notion of "Sein" without losing its otherness, into a "Neutrum, das die Gedanken und die Seienden ordnet." See Levinas (1987), 193.

11. Heidegger's "Dasein," even as "Mitsein," still remains egologically structured and solipsistically oriented, because "the other" is misinterpreted as alter ego, as "other I," as that which is like me. In this case, however, it is grasped in such a way that it is already robbed of its otherness. Cf. Levinas, *De l'existence à l'existant* (Paris: J. Vrin, 1978), 26.

12. The meaning of *il y a* is extremely difficult to decipher and has no consistency that would be conceivable without involving itself in paradoxes. Importantly, however, it signifies anonymity and impersonality. Thereby, *il y a* is comparable to

phrases like *il pleut* (it rains). Cf. the translations of Heidegger's *es gibt* in Davis, 22f. Cf. Drischler for the comparison of Heidegger's *es gibt* and Levinas's *il y a* (371).

13. Cf. Levinas (1978), 10, 26.

14. Cf. Levinas, *Le Temps et l'autre* (Montpellier, France: Fata Morgana, 1979), 14.

15. Cf. Davis, 26–30.

16. Cf. Levinas's late lectures, *La mort et le temps* (1991) in Levinas, *Gott, der Tod und die Zeit,* P. Engelmann, ed. (Vienna: Edition Passagen, 1996), 26, 43, 53, 56, 60 passim. Cf. Levinas (1979) 59, 62.

17. Cf. Levinas, *Totalité et infini* (Paris: Livre de Poche, 1961), 33.

18. Cf. Levinas (1961), 112–119.

19. Cf. Levinas (1961), 211. In reflection, otherness would be overwhelmed by the same; cf. Davis, 45.

20. *Le visage* includes both modes: "the face" and "to face"; cf. Davis, 46.

21. Cf. Levinas (1987), 221. My translation.

22. Cf. Levinas (1987), 246. My translation. Cf. Breuner, Lausch, and Mersch, 182.

23. Levinas (1987), 254–255.

24. In this later work, "the other" loses to a large extent its importance and is generally replaced by *le prochain,* "the neighbor." "The other" is thus relativized as a focal point in favor of the "subject." Over against the conversion of trusted notions, surprising meanings and new terms now appear, such as *an-archique, re-presentation,* and *dia-chronie.* Levinas even begins again to use the fundamental ontological verb *être* (being). Cf. Levinas, *Autrement qu'être ou Au-delà de l'essence* (Paris: Livre de Poche, 1974). Cf. the discussion of the complexity of Levinas's new language in Davis, 71–72.

25. In philosophical discourse, however, "the other of Being" is transformed automatically into an (ontologically) "other being" as soon as it appears as object of my discourse; cf., Levinas (1974), 74. Levinas explores this paradox within his distinction of *le Dire* (saying) and *le Dit* (the said); cf. Davis, 74–79: "The said" leads to an ontology; "saying," however, leads to "the other" within a process of "signifying"; cf. Levinas (1974), 81: *lui bailler significance.*

26. Cf. Levinas (1974), 80–83. Levinas calls this process of subjectivity *témoinage* (the state of witnessing): the witnessing of "the other" as "the other" constitutes "the subject" by "the other"; cf. Levinas (1974), 223–238.

27. Cf. Drischler, 416; cf. Levinas (1961), 64.

28. In Deleuze's analysis, "the other" is interpreted precisely as the intrusion of (foreign) possibilities into the identity of the "I" and "my world." The whole structure of perception, therefore, is grounded on those possibilities—the other as ground of perception. Cf. Deleuze in LS, 301ff. For the "facticity" of this past "otherness" cf. B. Taureck, *Emmanuel Levinas zur Einführung,* 2nd ed. (Hamburg: Junius, 1997), 91.

29. Levinas writes, "Nun macht das Nichts wie das des Todes streng genommen den Hauptteil von nichts aus. Es ist ein absolut unbestimmtes Nichts, das auf keiner-

lei Sein anspielt, und kein Chaos, das nach Form strebt: Der Tod ist Tod von jemandem, und das Gewesen-Sein von jemandem wird nicht vom Sterbenden, sondern vom Überlebenden getragen"; cf. Levnias in P. Engelmann, ed. (1996), 82.

30. Cf. A. Huegli and P. Luebcke, eds., *Philosophielexikon. Personen und Begriffe abendländischer Philosophie von der Antike bis zur Gegenwart* (Reinbek, Germany: Rowolth, 1997), 380; cf. Davis, 6.

31. *L'éthique,* in Levinas's terms, does not intend simply "ethics" but all human "Being," even politics. Nothing human can be excluded. Cf. Davis, 3.

32. Cf. Huegli and Luebcke, 380; cf. Derrida, "Violence et métaphysique: Essai sur la penseé d'Emmanuel Levinas," in *L'écriture et la différence* (orig. 1964) (Points; Paris: Seuil, 1967), 159–202.

33. God's otherness cannot be understood on the basis of the *il y a;* cf. Levinas, *De Dieu qui rient à l'idée* (Paris: Vrin, 1992), 115. Drischler notes, "Das 'es gibt' (il y a) des Seins beschreibt Levinas somit grundsätzlich anders als Heidegger. Das hängt zutiefst mit dem 'mal d'être', dem 'Übel zu sein' zusammen" (371). To some extent, Whitehead's intention to differentiate "creativity" from "God" interprets a similar problem: Because the activity of creativity is neutral, opposites—both aesthetically and ethically—are included within creativity. God, however, is only good. Cf., therefore, Whitehead's remarks in SMW, 179.

34. Cf. Levinas (1992), 113–114.

35. Cf. E. Weber, "Fragment über die Wissenschaft reiner Ereignisse," in *Gilles Deleuze—Fluchtlinien der Philosophie,* Friedrich Balke and Joseph Vogl, eds., (Munich: Fink, 1996), 198.

36. Cf. Nancy in *Deleuze: A Critical Reader,* Paul Patton, ed. (Oxford, UK: Blackwell, 1996), 110.

37. Cf. D. W. Smith, "Deleuze's Theory of Sensation. Overcoming the Kantian Duality," in ibid., 30f. Intensities energize thinking, yet they conceal themselves from our observation/perception/understanding/thinking. They do not form an ontological, but rather, an aesthetic reality.

38. "Expression," "sense," and "event"—these are not identical with any other dimension of things or language, but they identify their own reality of "aesthetics." Cf. LS, 20–22.

39. Cf. Ronald Bogue, *Deleuze and Guattari* (London: Routledge, 1996), 70.

40. Without naming Levinas, Deleuze and Guattari actually reconstruct Levinas's alterity—the alterity of the "other," which calls to itself in the mode of the "face" within its *field* of immanence—thereby identifying "the face" of "the other" as the expressive reality Deleuze was reflecting upon in *Logic of Sense* (WP, 16ff.).

41. Cf. LS: 7, 19–20, 22, 31, 35, 81, 110, 123, 180, 221; cf. Bogue, 72.

42. Cf. Bogue, 62ff. What interests us is not simply Deleuze's language of aesthetic reality or his talk of "events," for here he has his own project that aims at something partially different from Whitehead's investigations. Cf. A. Badiou, "Gilles Deleuze, *The Fold: Leibniz and the Baroque,*" in *Gilles Deleuze and the Theater of Philosophy,* Constantin V. Boundas and Dorothea Olkowski, eds. (New York: Routledge, 1994), 51–69. Deleuze's primary philosophical influences are Bergson, Nietz-

sche, Spinoza, and Leibniz. Nevertheless, when Deleuze directly addresses the question in the context of investigating Leibniz, in chapter 6 of *The Fold,* he takes account of and interprets Whitehead's understanding of actual occasions, creativity, and God; cf. TF, 76ff.

43. Cf. Bogue, 62f. This *Ungrund* signifies a nonexisting horizon of pure events or their "wherein."

44. Cf. Bogue, 63.

45. Hardt demonstrates throughout his book on Deleuze that (a) the Bergsonian and the Spinozist approach are continuous with one another and (b) Deleuze's early reading of the history of philosophy is the basis for his later language.

46. Deleuze, "La conception de la différence chez Bergson," *Les études bergsonniennes,* 4 (1956), 93. Cited by Hardt, 14.

47. Cf. Hardt, 64.

48. Cf. Bergson (2, 1996), 126ff; cf. Ch. Frémont, "Komplikation und Singularität" (1996) in Balke and Vogl, 64f.

49. For Whitehead, the value of theories consists in their "lure for feeling, thereby providing immediacy of enjoyment" (PR, 184). For Deleuze, it consists in the indication of things (truth) and the signification of concepts (conditions of truth). Finally, the function of intellectual feelings, in Whitehead, is "to heighten the emotional intensity" (PR, 273).

50. Just like the field of "sense"/"spatium"/"virtuality" in Deleuze, Whitehead recognizes the field of "creativity"/"receptacle"/"extensive continuum" within the language of intensity, explained here as "extrabeing." Deleuze's "spatium"—the metaphysical horizon of "virtual events"—calls to mind the receptacle, that nonexisting, invisible, formless, and all-receptive "wherein" of all occasions without any further reason, which Whitehead takes from Plato (AI, 187). This moment of transcendental creativity can be integrated within Whitehead's larger notion of creativity. Cf. W. Garland, "The Ultimacy of Creativity" in S. Ford and D. L. Kline, *Explorations in Whitehead's Philosophy* (New York: Fordham University Press, 1983), 227f. We could still read this language as representing an ontological account, at least within the tradition of the univocal meaning of Being (as does Hardt [113–115] for Deleuze's realm of "virtuality" and as does Joseph A. Bracken in *The Divine Matrix: Creativity as a Link between East and West* [Maryknoll, NY: Orbis Books, 1995, 52–69] for Whitehead's "creativity"/"extensive continuum"). Nevertheless, even then God could not mean anything less than this nonentitative activity. Cf. John B. Cobb Jr., *A Christian Natural Theology* (Philadelphia: Westminster Press, 1965), 209: "Creativity, for Whitehead, does not 'exist'."

51. For Leibniz, this may have been "the best possible world."

52. Cf. Hardt, 18–19, 119–121. The virtual field of forces, powers, and events, the "receptacle" of intensities and characters, hence, that force us to think but at the same time perplex our recognition, can be grasped neither by any categories of thought nor by any a priori. They are included within a transcendental field of total immanence, a field of forces that affects thinking. Cf. LS, 4ff, 52.

53. Like Whitehead, Deleuze knows that the concrete cannot be explained by the

abstract, but that philosophy is a matter of the explanation of the abstract; cf. B. Baugh, "Deleuze und der Empirismus" (1996) in Balke and Vogl, 202.

54. Baugh in Balke and Vogl says,

Denn reale Ursachen sind keine universalen und apodiktischen Regeln; . . . sie sind vielmehr genauso bestimmt und partikular wie die Wirkung, welche realen Ursachen koextensiv sind. . . . Diejenigen Kräfte, die Erfahrungen disponieren, sind weniger vorweg gegebene Regeln oder Schemata als größtenteils nicht-bewußte. . . . Kräfte ohne Form und Gesetze. . . . In diesem Fall ist die Aktualität des Empirischen-anstatt durch den Verstand gegebene Regeln oder Begriffe anzuwenden-empirisch konstituiert und durch zufällige Verkettung von Kräften, von konvergierenden oder divergierenden Serien oder Fluxationen, . . . von Differentialen an Intensitäten und Gradstufen an Veränderung, . . . die gemeinsam etwas Neues und Unvorhergesehenes ins Leben rufen. . . . Deleuze nennt das unvorhergesehene Auftreten einer neuen Aktualität "das Ereignis der Aktualität" . . . (47).

Cf. Deleuze, TF, 1ff., 52ff.

55. The constellation of Deleuze's virtuality actualizing itself within the immanent field of forces realizes the self-differentiation of the absolutely positive, infinite, and ultimate reality, in a way very similar to how Whitehead interprets the individualization of "substantial activity" in SMW (70, 107). Cf. Hardt for Deleuze's differentiation of virtuality-actuality from possibility-reality (16–17). In a certain sense, Deleuze's understanding of virtuality resembles Whitehead's interpretation of how creativity's energizing of "real potentiality" (past actuality) is different from the realization of possibilities (eternal objects).

56. Underlining the persistent "theological" background of Deleuze's philosophy of immanence on the basis of Spinoza's notion of God as a purely affirmative-ontological notion, we may not be astonished that Deleuze introduces Spinoza as *the Christ* of philosophy, that is, as the Christ of the God that is total immanence (WP, 60).

57. Cf. Davis, 53.

58. Instead of using Kant's God-language from his *Second Critique,* which recognizes "God" merely as an ethical postulate of responsibility, Levinas's "Ethics-Metaphysics" appropriates more from Kant's *Third Critique.*

59. Cf. the similarity of Whitehead to Deleuze's analysis of language in LS, 12–27.

60. For Whitehead, aesthetic reality defines the most basic account of the internal validity of actuality and thus expresses the process of valuation as its root-metaphor; cf. Michael Hauskeller, *Alfred North Whitehead zur Einführung* (Hamburg: Junius, 1994), 145–150 and Rolf Lachmann, *Ethik und Identität: der ethische Ansatz in der Prozeßphilosophie A. N. Whiteheads und seine Bedeutung für die gegenwärtige Ethik* (Freiburg i.B., Germany: Alber, 1994), 60–64, 96–98. Furthermore, for the process of valuation seeking to intensify its aesthetic value, God's intensity is the "standard of intensity" (PR, 47)—beyond any measure and grounded in God's incommensurable "primordial nature."

61. Cf. Bogue, 56ff.

62. Regarding Deleuze, cf. D. W. Smith, "Deleuze's Theory of Sensation.

Overcoming the Kantian Duality" (1996) in Patton, 29; regarding Whitehead, cf. Reiner Wiehl, "Whitehead's Kant-Kritik und Kant's Kritik am Panpsychismus" in *Natur, Subjektivität, Gott. Zur Prozeßphilosophie Alfred North Whitehead,* Helmut Holzhey, Alois Rust, and Reiner Wiehl, eds. (Frankfurt, Germany: Suhrkamp, 1990), 216.

63. Only once, when Kant in the *Critique of Judgement* speaks of the experience of the "sublime," this "reality in the encounter" announces itself. Here the disagreement of reason and imagination *confronts* us with a reality appearing within "thought," but not, however, entering into our "knowledge."

64. As Hans Poser put it once, such categories always have a hypothetical character, referring to actual processes of feeling, and representing no a priori constant structure; cf. Poser, "Kosmologie als revidierbare Metaphysik," in *Whiteheads Metaphysik der Kerativität. Internationales Whitehead-Symposium Bad Homburg,* Friedrich Rapp and Reiner Wiehl, eds. (Freiburg i.B., Germany: 1986), 105ff.

65. Cf. J. Bradley, "Transcendentalism and Speculative Realism in Whitehead," *Process Studies,* 23/3 (1994), 162–163.

66. My emphasis. Cf. Deleuze in Balke and Vogl, 29f.: As in Deleuze, Whitehead's conditions only signify the concrescing process (and nothing beyond). The "transcendental field" always marks a plane of immanence, being a projection of the sequence of events, and not, as in Kant, being an objective structure beyond this process. Cf. Deleuze, DR, 285. One could even say that Deleuze here follows Whitehead's ontological principle, according to which categories always represent abstractions from the concrete flux of occasions. At least, this becomes a main principle of his last major work, *What Is Philosophy?*

67. Cf. Balke and Vogl, "Einleitung: Fluchtlinien der Philosophie" (1996) in Balke and Vogl, 8.

68. Cf. Wiehl in Holzhey et al., 219.

69. Whitehead replaces abstract "objects" of thinking with concrete processes of prehension. In the self-constitution of aesthetic realities, the causal power of feeling has priority over the clear realization of abstract ideas.

70. Therefore, the primary place of experience/realization/thinking is the unconscious. Cf. E. Weber, "Fragment über die Wiessenschaft reiner Ereignisse" (1996) in Balke and Vogl, 202.

71. Smith in Patton, 37: "Sensations cease to be representative and become real."

72. Cf. Deleuze in DR: "Intensity is both the unsensible and that which can only be sensed" (230); cf. Smith in Patton, 37.

73. Corresponding to the removal of any plain "ontological object" of recognition, the "transcendental subject" dissolves into the flux of intensities. In the process of feeling, subjectivity appears as relation between occasions. Cf. Wiehl in Holzhey et al., 219ff.

74. Cf. Levinas (1987), 212.

75. Cf. Smith in Patton: "the power of the active 'I think.'. . ." (37).

76. Cf. Badiou in Boundas and Olkowski: "Leibniz—Deleuze's subject is directly multiple. . . ." (62).

77. Cf. P. Klossowski, "Digression vor dem Hintergrund eines apogryphen Proträts" (1996) in Balke and Vogl, 128.

78. If aesthetic reality is thought without God, then the moment of alterity disappears. If aesthetic reality is thought, however, without the immanence of creativity, then it loses its character of novelty. Aesthetic language as language of pure immanence knows of novelty; in the long run, however, one cannot indicate any reason for it. If aesthetic reality is thought without creativity, then the moment of immanence disappears. Aesthetic language as language of pure transcendence knows of immanence; however, no creative self-constitution can be thought.

79. In Deleuze's *The Fold,* on the other hand, we find an extensive passage on Whitehead in which Deleuze recognizes the special status of Whitehead's God as a "reality" that does not preform the world, but affirms and even "runs through" its incompossibilities. Furthermore, Deleuze acknowledges that Whitehead's "eternal objects" do not preform the world, and hence, do not contradict the ultimate creativity of the world's process. Cf. TF, 79–81.

80. This "second intersection"does not necessarily interrupt the principle that God should be understood as an exemplification of the common categories for all actualities, since God "represents" these categories; but God does it "from the other side," so to speak, as their organization *per creationem,* not their execution *per participationem.*

81. "Expressive in/difference" indicates a complex concept that defines a difference that is *not different of itself* and, at the same time, the *origination of difference as such.* Since this "(in)difference" cannot be grasped *from within* the differences it originates, it is *"in*different" to these (all) differences; since it is *productive* of these differences, it is *"in* the differences," that is, exposed to the differences it originates. Hence, this in/difference is *expressive;* it is no "thing" beyond the differences it originates. The term *expressive in/difference* relates to my term *nondifference,* which I use in other publications, meaning the same. It is based on Nicolas of Cusa's term *non aliud.* Nevertheless, "nondifference" does not indicate "no difference," but rather "not to be identifiable within differences (which it originates)"; similarly, "in/difference" does not indicate apathy to differences, but rather, "to be the origin of the differences that can not bear it from within." Therefore, "in/difference" is always *in differences,* that is, from beyond, but totally expressive within all differences.

82. Roland Faber, "Trinity, Analogy and Coherence," in *Trinity in Process: A Relational Theology of God,* Joseph A. Bracken and Marjorie Hewitt Suchocki, eds. (New York: Continuum, 1997), 160–162.

83. Cf. the exploration of this term, *nondifference,* in Faber, *Prozeß, Relativität und Transendenz. Zur Kritik prozeßtheologischer Theoriegestalt* (Wien, Austria: Universitaetsbibliothek, 1997), 397ff.

84. Nicolas of Cusa, *De veneratione sapientiae XIV:* "non aliud est non aliud quam non aliud."

85. Jürgen Moltmann, *Das Kommen Gottes: christliche Eschatologie* (Gütersloh: Chr. Kaiser Gütersloher Verlaghaus, 1995), 42f.

86. Cf. Moltmann, 40, but also Cobb, *Process Theology as Political Theology* (Manchester, England: Manchester University Press, 1982), 75. The eschatological

notion of God is adopted by Cobb in his discussion of the "eschatologization" of God in much political theology, such as that of Moltmann, Sölle, and Metz.

87. Thus, in his *De Deo Abscondito,* Nicolas of Cusa states that God is not precisely nothing, but neither is God anything; rather, God is all (omne)—but precisely not "the All."

88. Or as Cobb (1982) says, "No event occurs in the world without God's coming, not as a part of its past, determined world, but as the gift of freedom, the gift of transcendence, the gift of the future" (75). In this sense, God creates the events that may be seen under ontological perspective, but God never introduces Godself within the events as an ontological entity. God may be named an eschatological force and, therefore, an "ontological force" creating ontological entities, but never may God be called "ontological" with regards to Godself.

89. Principles are rules in a process that is determined by events; God "coming" from God's own novelty has no other "standard of intensity" beyond Godself (cf. PR, 47). Whitehead first grasped God as "principle of concretion" (cf. SMW, 178; cf. RM, 115). But God, understood as the "reason" of events, must be concrete in accordance with the ontological principle. Thus, God does not define an "ultimate metaphysical principle" (PR, 343); rather, God "provides, not is, the principle of concretion" (Conv. 5; cf. PR, 244). In SMW, God is still interpreted as an abstract principle: "God is not concrete, but he is the ground for concrete actuality" (178). In RM, God is interpreted as a "formative element" for the process of events—thus as a "principle." Yet, God is seen also as an "actual nontemporal entity" (88). Cf. Jung (1965): "der Tatsache explizit Rechnung getragen, daß diese Einschränkung des überhaupt Möglichen als ein Akt der Synthesis angesehen werden muß, als wertender Entwurf einer Welt. Dann erst wird auch sichtbar, was dieses zunächst nur als Prinzip bezeichnete Wesen überhaupt mit dem zu tun hat, was wir göttliche Funktionen im religiösen Sinn nennen, Z. B. Erlösung" (606). Cf. A. H. Johnson's alternative formulation of "abstract first metaphysical principles" (191) in his *Whitehead and His Philosophy* (Lanham, MD: University Press of America, 1983). In *Process and Reality* Whitehead sets up the principle that God "is not to be treated as an exception to all metaphysical principles, invoked to save their collapse," but God "is their chief exemplification" (PR, 343). This means, first of all, that God is *concrete,* and as a concrete happening, God *designates* "metaphysical principles" for the world by taking precautions for them, not by being their prisoner.

90. Regarding God's novelty (which cannot be understood by any [old] categories), God "comes" to the categories and authorizes them. Although Whitehead at times indicates "that he should have introduced God's primordial nature sooner" (Conv. 5), in PR "God" appears as a "derived notion" (cf. PR, 31–34)—derived not regarding God's reality, but as a concept. The complexity of the categories, which are necessary in order to articulate "God," demonstrate the breakdown of all categories regarding their value to grasp God's reality. A. H. Johnson notes, "the status of 'derivative' is not assigned to the entity, God, but (i) to the other actual entities and (ii) to the results of God's function as primordial, in arranging and making available the realm of eternal objects" (129). Cf. Ernest Wolf-Gazo, "Alfred North Whitehead," in Gernot Böhme (Hg.), *Klassiker der Naturphilosophie: von den Vorsokratikern bis zur Kopenhagener Schule* (Munich: Beck, 1989): "Es ist interessant, daß 'Gott' nicht in White-

head's Kategorientafel erscheint, sondern daß 'Gott' nach Whitehead in allen Kategorien kreativ tätig ist" (310).

91. God embodies no entity like an "imperial ruler" (PR, 242) nor like the "personification of moral energy" (PR, 243).

92. Cf. also the analysis of such patterns in K. Koch, "Schöpferischer Lockruf im Prozeß der Welt. Perspektiven der Gottesfrage in der amerikanischen Prozeßtheologie," *Theologische Berichte* 12 (1983), 153–156. Against absoluteness, Whitehead sets relativity. Against the conception of a "controlling power," he sets the persuasive power of God. Against the "legislator," he sets change and life; cf. Lachmann, 133. Against the status quo, Whitehead sets the "contingency" of God. Against the male conception of God, he sets the God beyond sexual duality. Charles Hartshorne in *A Natural Theology for our Time* (La Salle, IL: Open Court, 1967) pokes fun at depictions that present God as similar to other world-entities, only infinite—such as God the "world monarch"—by referring to them as God the "transcendental snob" or "transcendental tyrant" (137).

93. Cf. Lewis Ford, "The Divine Activity of the Future," *Process Studies* 11(3) (1981): "I propose we conceive God to be a future activity creating the conditions of the present" (172). Cf. Suchocki, "The Metaphysical Ground of the Whiteheadian God," *Process Studies* 5(4) (1975), 239–240.

94. Cf. Bracken, 55.

95. In Whitehead, "God" refers to that fundamental "eschatological novelty" by which everything appears marvelous: "The concept of 'God' is the way in which we understand this incredible fact—that what cannot be, yet is" (PR, 350).

96. Whitehead's designation of God as a "poet" should not be seen as a weakening of the notion of God as creator. With "poet," the Greeks named the "maker." God's power is not "smaller" than that of other "actual entities" (cf. Conv. 8). The opposite is true: God is creatively overflowing Godself as eschatological future, coming as formal novelty (eternal objects) *and* actual novelty (creativity).

97. As long as a subject becomes, it "is not yet" a subject; if it is completed, it ceases to be a subject (cf. AI, 237–238). As long as an occasion is "becoming," the occasion "is" not yet. However, should an occasion "come-to-be," the occasion would not "be" anymore (cf. AI, 237). This applies to Whitehead's dictum that "it never really is" (PR, 82). Thus, in Whitehead as well as in Levinas, the solipsism of the enjoyment of self-unity is prevented. Cf. also Levinas (1961): "Enjoyment means that absolute selfness of a subject that indicates its being-alone-with-itself without original communication" (142). Finally, Whitehead's "persons," indicating a personal nexus, are not characterized by an Odysseic consciousness of self-return. They always leave themselves for other events, although this process of permanent transformation can obtain the illusion of a "selfness" of the nexus; cf. AI, 181–183.

98. This has to be said against a misconstruction of "satisfaction," as in R. Schulte, "Eine neue Denkform im Glaubensverstäendnis?" in Leo Scheffczyk, *Rationalität* (Freiburg i.B., Germany: Alber, 1989), 324 n.10. The completed occasion is perfect—that is, completed and passed/perished. In its "perfectness" beyond all subjectivity, that is, as passed, an occasion is taken up, judged, and reconciled with God. Cf. Inada (1975), 482–483: He states the relationship between this aspect of immortality

(i.e., to remain in God as a value) and the Buddhist notion of "emptiness," *sunyata*. Although *sunyata* is called "passing," "emptiness," or "nothing," etymologically it indicates also "the state of completeness or fullness of being" (483)—in a manner beyond self-enjoyment and egotistic incurvation.

99. "Perfection within God states—quite similarly as in Levinas—'self-forgetful transcendence'." Cf. Drischler, 107. Here, Levinas turns against the Odysseic paradigm, because Odysseus—after all his adventures—finds his aim only in his coming home. Drischler goes on: "Levinas läßt ein solches Denken hinter sich und kann, mit seiner Betonung der unmittelbaren Nähe des Anderen nicht ohne absolute Trennung denken zu können, das transzendentaltheologische Modell dahingehend hinterfragen, ob es diesem wirklich gelingt, das Phänomen der Unmittelbarkeit der Nähe Gottes und zum Nächsten zur Sprache zu bringen. . . ."

100. Whitehead's notion of eschatological "peace" indicates the overcoming of any form of self-concentration. Its "aim" is situated "beyond any personal satisfaction" (AI, 288) or "selfish happiness" (AI, 289). Cf. Suchocki (1975): "[T]he actual occasion in God is felt by God in terms of the highest relationship made possible by that actualization relative to every other actuality prehended by the divine nature. . . . [God] feels the occasion in its immediacy and yet transcends the occasion by relating it beyond its own finite vision to all others in the vision of God. In God, the occasion is itself, and others, and God" (5). The conception of "eschatological alterity," the perfection "beyond joy and sorrow" recalls strongly the Buddhist conception of *anatman*. In both, "the traditional view of the self breaks down"; as the corn-seeds of which Paul speaks in 1 Cor. 15:36f., an event must disappear to live on.

101. For finite occasions the "everlasting union with their transformed selves" (PR, 347) promises an eschatological self-surrender with God: "the 'self' has been lost" (AI, 285). Cf. Suchocki, *The End of Evil: Process Eschatology in Historical Context* (Albany: State University of New York Press, 1988), 110, 118, 199–216.

102. According to Guy Emerson, this is what Whitehead thought of himself: "[Whitehead] likes Plato because he was always proposing, never finishing anything. It is always 'process,' not frozen finality." (MS Am. 1850 [14–15], from September 17, 1970, brought by Mrs. Guy Emerson.)

10

Beyond Conversation
The Risks of Peace

ISABELLE STENGERS

To intervene in an attempted "conversation" between two full-fledged products of the American tradition—"deconstructive" and "constructive" postmodernism—is a risky move for a French-speaking, European philosopher. The more so since the very word, *conversation,* is already a shifty one for me. Indeed, I am not only one of those perplexed French-speaking onlookers, wondering about the very possibility of bringing together Gilles Deleuze and Jacques Derrida, Michel Foucault and Jacques Lacan under the same label, as one party in the conversation. I am also someone passionately interested in a domain of human practices the value of which depends upon, or at least implies, eliminating the charms of conversation: the practices of experimental science.

What makes things easier, however, is that this hoped for conversation has not begun yet. We have not to accept the implied meanings of these terms, but are free to try to give them a speculative turn. Here, I feel more at ease, since I am unable to dissociate my own "speculative turn" from both Alfred North Whitehead and Deleuze—Deleuze being one of those French philosophers who for now seems to belong to "the others." The point is not, however, to start with boundary quarrels, to wonder for instance if Deleuze would not belong better to the "constructive" postmodernists. We deal with a stubborn, obstinate matter of fact. "Process people" in the United States know about Henri Bergson, but most likely not about the one French philosopher who was, already more than forty years ago, working and thinking with Bergson, and producing, as an outsider to any recognized trend, a new kind of "real togetherness," with new contrasts, new intensities and new appetites between Bergson, Benedict de Spinoza, and Friedrich Nietzsche. The fact is that most process people in the United States do not know that thirty years ago Deleuze had already written of Whitehead in the two most extraordinary pages I can think of about him, as a "speculative nomad" (DR, 284–285).

This is not a matter of chance. While process philosophy was still in the process of situating itself in its relation with process theology, Deleuze, for everybody who read him (including probably himself, but nobody can know for sure), was the atheist philosopher par excellence, tracking down any shade of transcendence in philosophy, taking the triple ideals of contemplation (Plato), reflection (Immanuel Kant), and communication (including never-ending conversation) as the very traps philosophy must escape in order to think, that is, to create, that is, to resist. Accordingly, Deleuze did relate to Whitehead, but never to the world of process philosophy *and* theology.

This leads me to one of the challenges our "conversation" may have to meet, a challenge that probably bears on the famous modern/postmodern contrast at a very emotional level. Belonging, like Deleuze, to the French philosophical tradition, the very fact of having philosophers, theologians, theists, and Christian ministers working together, as it is usually done in process thought, was indeed for me a testing challenge, a situation very hard to understand, let alone to take seriously. It must be remembered that in our part of Europe, as a result of history's perhaps starting with religious wars, we do know very well indeed about the power of the church, but not about the many paths and risks associated with a multiplicity of churches. And while we know very well about the ever-recurring danger that a transcendent reference be introduced and produce a repartition between what it selects and what it rejects, we are unfamiliar with the possibility that the worship of God, if resolutely not taken as "a rule of safety" but as "an adventure of the spirit, a flight after the unattainable" (SMW, 192), could lead away from transcendent values and toward the production of new, immanent intensities for life and thought.

In fact, the very proposition "worship" is sufficient to mobilize an easy opposition, consolidating otherwise diverging, vital, emotional values about human life, history, and the world. However, as process people, we know that oppositions are never final, that producing the possibility of enjoying new contrasts where oppositions once ruled is the adventure of both hope and reason. This, by the way, is also far from easy to accept by those of the Nietzschean-Deleuzean lineage: for them, neither reason nor hope constitutes reliable common grounds, as this lineage emphasizes the "dark" emotions of struggle, power, and madness over against anything it can identify with a consensus of "reasonable people" or with an aspiration for a general, conciliatory goodwill.

How to turn an opposition into a possible matter of contrast? Obviously, this is not only a question of goodwill. My guess is that we may do so through the experimental extension of the specific risks that singularize each position. Giving a chance for contrasts to be created where oppositions rule implies producing a middle ground but not a medium or average mitigating differences. It should be a middle ground for testing, in order that the contrast evolve not from tamed differences but from creatively redefined ones.

The middle ground, as I will propose it, addresses what I would, in first approximation, call two parties: the "French tradition" (including Foucault; with Derrida and Lacan my imagination and hope come up against their limits) and "process people," be they philosophers or theologians. It would create a double test: for the French tradition, to accept the very hypothesis of a positive reference to reason and hope; and for process people, to realize that any reassuring, direct convergence between religion and speculative thought may, indeed, condemn the opposition to remain an opposition.

What are the stakes of this double test? But first of all, why privilege the Deleuzean stance when what we call "postmodern deconstructivism" includes so many other options? I would answer with three points. The first point is that I have no choice in the matter: this is the testing ground where I was created as a philosopher. The second point is a hypothesis: maybe those who belong to the constellation of "postmodern deconstructivism" did gulp down a rather dangerous fish when annexing Deleuze under their label. I do not know if the resulting "cracks" Catherine Keller describes in her chapter in this volume will extend far enough, but they are occasions that can be turned into opportunities. The third point is that, in this case, the conversation that could be invented would not be an academic conversation only, merely producing academic machinery to roll on new tracks. Rather, emotions, values, what it is to think or resist, what it is to hope, how to inherit and tell the modern story, and which kinds of ingredients to use, are all at stake not very far from the small, ugly world of academic niceties, comparative studies, and quasi-ethical "you wouldn't dare; look, I do."

Among those academic niceties, we can include what has been called the "science wars." In this case the pleasant ideal of urbane, civilized conversation did meet its limits. In fact, the very portrayal of conversation as an ideal was viewed as an insult, and the *Sokal Hoax*[1] can be read as the angry but petty revenge of offended scientists. Those scientists understood very well that conversation as an ideal excludes them. Indeed, the adequate subjects for an interesting, open conversation between well-behaved, sophisticated people should never be "real facts." This is a true oppostion: conversation needs facts to refer to a brute, meaningless matter of fact, the interpretation of which humans should be the only masters, while experimental scientists concentrate all their passion on the extraordinary attempt to give to this "mute," brute, free-for-all "reality" the power to minimize our freedom to interpret. Since the very principle of such an attempt troubles the conversation game, deconstructing the claim that scientists can succeed is part of the game.

Taken seriously, Whitehead's statement that any "proposition proposing a fact must, in its complete analysis, propose the general character of the universe required for this fact" (PR, 11) explodes the limits of any conversation.

It implies a radical constructivism. For interpretations are not our own; they become "facts," adding universes upon universes. And if Whitehead's own proposition is to be taken as proposing the universe it requires, it is obviously pointless to try to justify it with reference to some kind of transcendent source of agreement. This last point is relevant for the struggle of the Nietzschean-Bergsonian-Deleuzean lineage against the three ideals of contemplation, reflection, and communication. Constructivist humor, happily celebrating that our speculative sentences can never define what they mean but always appeal for an imaginative leap—which produces the new contrasts—may free us from the temptation of an ironic-critical-deconstructive fascination with these ideals, as powerful traps needing ceaseless diagnosis and unmasking.

Conversely, the French Deleuzean "tradition" will always refuse any kind of settlement, conversational or otherwise, which excludes those who are already excluded, even if this exclusion *appears* to be an inclusion. As Deleuze said, to think (or create) is to think "in front of" or "for" "analphabets or dying rats or alcoholics." This does not mean addressing them, or helping them, or sharing hope or faith with them, but, rather, not insulting them with our power to justify everything. Thinking with them "in front of" us means thinking with the feeling and constraint that we are not free to speak in their name or even to side with them. In other words, philosophers belonging to this tradition will always demand that theologians think in front of the witches, pagans or what they call "fetishists"; that is, that theologians think against any possibility of justifying the destruction of pagan, idolatrous, or fetishist ways of worship. So, we must ask ourselves, What would count as a conversation "in front of" all the unknown people that our words so easily disqualify, in fact, even when those words outwardly speak of mutual appreciation, respect, and love?

The Deleuzean stance, with its built-in decision to think in front of the damned, is quite compatible with the ideal of conversation, but it may also be part of the "middle ground" I am trying to produce. This implies a double test indeed. Will it help process-people to "stammer" or "quake" when trying to produce the words for a sorely needed "relational worldview"? And will "Deleuzeans" accept a possible translation of this decision in typically Whiteheadian terms, that of a propositional (and not conversational) togetherness, the satisfaction derived from which would include experiencing the scars of its birth (PR, 226), including all its (nonacademic) absentees?

Envisaging such a possibility, I am taking a constructivist stance, since I take words to be "lures for feeling," not denouncing them because they would demarcate (we have no way to actually include fetishists, starving rats, or alcoholics), but demanding that those words be constructed with the aims of "clothing the dry bones" (PR, 85) of our demarcations with the vivid feeling of the presence of those absentees our demarcations cannot but push away. Away, not against.

Whatever their built-in demarcations, our words must be stammered out there, where "angels fear to tread," as Gregory Bateson would have said. Creating togetherness is an ideal seeking a satisfaction, and to renounce it would be to renounce the adventure of hope. To try to think together, while knowing that we are, should be, and must continue to present ourselves as unable to transcend the actual limitations of this togetherness or to escape toward some dreamed of universality, is, I would submit, the very stamp of a constructivist philosophy. Speculation thus becomes not the discovery of the hidden truth justifying reality, but a crucial ingredient in the construction of reality.

I will now attempt a more precise experimental step, the aim of which is and must be double, since it experiments with a middle ground. I will imagine "Deleuzeans" feeling that Whitehead's God cannot be dismissed as a "naive" American relic, and I will have "Whiteheadians" feeling the sort of weird interest that would arise from the Whiteheadian God if It were accepted by the "Deleuzeans." This indeed performs a double test, since for the first group it means actually disavowing any kind of socially comfortable, modernist *je sais bien mais quand même* about religious matters, while for Whiteheadians it may mean putting the already fragile alliance between philosophers, theologians, and ministers under dangerous stress. Well, it is the business of thought, as appealing to the future, to be dangerous.

I will center this experimentation not on Whitehead alone, but on Whitehead together with another great speculative philosopher and mathematician, Gottfried Wilhelm Leibniz. And on the way we can hear more precisely this most daring of Leibniz's statements: Our world is the best of all possible worlds. This indeed is one of the touchstones: No "Deleuzean" would ever accept installing any kind of transcendent reference from which the world could be judged, even as the best. But every one of them would oppose as well Whitehead's apparently weaker claim. Whitehead described Leibniz's "best of all possible worlds" as an "audacious fudge" (PR, 47), but he himself wrote about an "inevitable ordering of things, conceptually realized in the nature of God" (PR, 244). In order to address a problem, it is best taking it at its hardest: in this case, accepting as a matter of fact what would seem to provoke the objection. Let us accept, then, that there is a strong common element between the Leibnizian and Whiteheadian "Gods," as related to divine ordering, and let us experiment.

I leave outside the scope of this chapter the technical reasons why Leibniz's philosophy required the hypothesis of our world being the best possible, just emphasizing that he also stated in the strongest technical terms why nobody but God is able to define, or even approach, the function in terms of which our world can be first defined and then characterized as the best. As we know, Whitehead emphatically refused this "no way to know" solution. Metaphysics would then play the too easy trick of defining what is actual through its limitations in contrast with a reality we should look for behind the scene (SMW, 178).

Accordingly, there is no access behind nor beyond with Whitehead: even God cannot possess any definition of what would be the best world. God may be in unison of becoming with every other entity, but It is everlastingly unsatisfied with any satisfaction, Its ever-present, everlastingly repeated question being not about the best of all worlds but "what is the best for *that* impasse." This difference does not create a beyond, going beyond the self-definition an actuality constitutes for itself, only the opportunity for an actual entity to get beyond. It answers the one major contrast between God and actual occasions: while every satisfaction has for its price negative prehensions, God's experience, derived from Its primordial, infinite, conceptual nature, is devoid of negative prehensions (PR, 345). Through the transformation of Its wisdom, all realizations may well be "saved," or "transform[ed] . . . into a reality in heaven," as they are freed from obstruction or inhibition, but it is also through this transformation that each satisfaction is positively felt as an impasse, both the satisfaction and the price it was paid for being felt together.

In fact, Whitehead's final metaphysical truth that "appetitive vision and physical enjoyment have equal claim to priority in creation" (PR, 348) celebrates the most radical divorce between God and any kind of omniscience, however limited. While the initial aim of an actual entity derives from the divine challenge or lure, conjecturally answering the divine question about an objective impasse, God does not possess any advanced knowledge about what the actual entity will or even can produce with this challenge. To me it is important indeed that the initial aim does not communicate with a hypothetical model God would entertain. If God had a model, this would entail the possibility of judging the satisfaction that will be actually achieved through a comparison with this divine model. When Whitehead writes that God is the great companion, the fellow-sufferer who understands, it seems to me important to take "understanding" as devoid of any paternalistic connotation. God does not understand in the sense of understanding why the actual entity missed the best its initial aim proposed, and excusing it because of love; It understands in unison of becoming.

However, this first contrast is not sufficient because it is built as a too easy defense: claiming that Whitehead escapes the menace that would follow from any proximity with Leibniz. I will turn now toward more dangerous, because common, grounds. Indeed the Leibnizian statement that our world is the best is not a metaphysical statement only. It also plays in Leibniz's philosophy the role of a Whiteheadian proposition, a lure, explicitly and mutely appealing for an imaginative leap. What it appeals to is succeeding in being or in becoming able to affirm the justice and wisdom of God while it would be so easy and so legitimate to hate both this world and the God who is responsible for its coming into existence. This does not make a difference at the level of contents. It is not justified by any deduction from the world or human history as we observe them, and it does not allow for any explanation, any particular confidence, any prevision, any evaluation of particular matters of fact. But it makes a practical, vital difference, and furthermore it is a demanding, testing one. This test, as I will now try to show, is a proposition defining speculative philosophy as giving its chance to peace or, more precisely, as fabricating the conceptual possibility of peace in order for us to be existentially fabricated by it.

In *The Fold*, Deleuze emphasized that Leibniz's concepts provide a way to construct a subject who is not *in* the world (Heidegger and the phenomenological tradition) but *for* the world. In *What Is Philosophy?*, which we may take as a kind of philosophical testament (not will), Deleuze wrote, together with Felix Guattari,

> But, on the new plane, it is possible that the problem now concerns the one who believes in the world, and not even in the existence of the world but in its possibilities, so as once again to give birth to new modes of existence, closer to animals and rocks. It may be that believing in this world, in this life, becomes our most difficult task, or the task of a mode of existence still to be discovered on our plane of immanence today. This is the empiricist conversion (we have so many reasons not to believe in the human world; we have lost the world, worse than a fiancée or a god). The problem indeed has changed. (WP, 74–75)

The "empiricist conversion" Deleuze alludes to has obviously nothing to do with turning back toward the academic playlets that are the common references for logical empiricism and many Wittgenstein followers. But it has a lot to do with "being for the world." Believing in this world was William James's great pragmatic theme, the one that makes a difference between habits as we always already have them, and experimental habits, be they moral, aesthetic, or conceptual—habits we experiment with in order to become capable of new experiences. It was also what Leibniz asked when asking us to succeed in accepting this world as the best. For Leibniz it made the very difference between salvation and damnation.[2] And finally, the relation between the "empiricist conversion" and "peace-fabricating" propositions is at the center of Whitehead's whole enterprise, beginning with his first struggle against the bifurcation of nature, that is from the statement that "all we know of Nature is in the same boat, to sink or swim together" (CN, 148), to the very definition of the demand for adequacy, which the categoreal scheme must satisfy, that is, it should induce an experience of the real togetherness of all experiences as they are reformulated through the scheme.

The Whiteheadian demand for adequacy and coherence, Leibniz's "best of all worlds," and James's "will to believe" have nothing to do with a matter of fact, be it empirical or metaphysical. The *peace* they allude to is a fabricated peace, that is, a peace that does not preexist in any way, neither beyond, nor behind. It is a peace we should thus not conceive as both "natural" and somehow lost. What preexists is always selective, partial, specialized, and potentially conflictual.

Both Leibniz and Whitehead were mathematicians. I think this peace, the possibility of which they wanted to construct, exhibits the creativity of mathematicians who do not seek the solution *to,* but rather construct the possibility *of,* a solution to a problem. The problem comes first.

A correlative common feature is that the worst way to present both Whitehead's and Leibniz's concepts about the divine ordering of the world is to take them as expressing something that could be discussed as an opinion or even a description. If I state that "Leibniz thinks that our world is the best of all possible worlds" or that "He claims that our experience is that of monads without a window," I induce the response, "What a strange idea." If I state that for Whitehead there are eternal objects, the divine envisagement of which provides the "inevitable ordering of things" (PR, 244), I induce the hypothesis that it is only a matter of Plato's influence and that we could readily do without those objects, and probably without God as well. Again, both Leibniz and Whitehead were mathematicians. When a mathematician produces a strange hypothesis, such as that of irrational or complex numbers, it is not a matter of opinion. He or she has been constrained by the problem, and it is the problem that required, that demanded, the invention of those strange, nonintuitive numbers.

Concepts are required in the construction not of an opinion but of the possibility of a solution to a problem. Leibniz was the first to give crucial importance to the difference between prerequisite and condition. A prerequisite is always relative to a problem as it is formulated, and cannot claim to transcend this formulation. A condition, on the other hand, corresponds to a normative, purified, rational formulation of what must be conditioned; the double definition of the condition and of what this condition conditions claims to escape and transcend particularity to achieve authorized knowledge. In Whitehead's texts, "to require" or "to demand" are verbs that appear when decisive points are being made. They are the mathematician's answer to a situation. His or her job is not to impose conditions upon the knowledge situation in order for it to fit general norms of intelligibility, as Kant does in the name of the Copernican revolution. His or her job is to recognize and construct the situation as a challenge, and to make explicit what this challenge requires in order to achieve an answer.

Whitehead wrote that the categoreal scheme is a matrix (PR, 8). I think we have to understand "matrix" not in its biological sense, associated with some kind of inexhaustible source of novelty, but in its mathematical definition. In mathematics, a matrix in itself is mute. It does not describe anything or produce anything. It is a tool for transforming one vector into another vector. In speculative philosophy, it is a tool for transforming one feeling into another feeling. Correlatively, the Whiteheadian scheme is to be logically consistent, but its terms refer to nothing we can observe; all that we observe and name must be described in terms of societies. Indeed, in Whiteheadian terms, all the problems we deal with are sociological ones; they address the problems of societies.

As a consequence, the propositions and contrasts we can imagine may well be constrained by the categories of existence, but they will never directly illustrate the nine categoreal obligations that articulate the self-consistency of the scheme. They may well exhibit, through the new contrasts they produce, the imaginative leap the categories of explanation suggest, demand, and appeal to, but they will never lead back to ultimate notions like creativity, many, and one. What the scheme defines are the prerequisites for an adequate and coherent formulation of our many experiences. Only the applications of the scheme, always relative to particular circumstances, experiences and questions, and always requiring the imaginative leap to which the concepts it articulates appeal, may test its adequacy. Whatever the situation, it should exhibit, as transformed through the application of the scheme, what I would call the "possibility of peace," a possibility that should owe nothing to purification (the "brilliant feat of explaining away") and everything to a more concrete description, which together takes into account the situation as it claims to be understood and what those claims require in order to be formulated in a way that is coherent and that does not transcend relations and particularities.

Thus, not only does Whiteheadian process philosophy refer, as does any philosophy, to what Charles Sanders Peirce called a "Third," an Interpretant, but his propositions, as well as the propositions of Leibniz, vitally depend upon this element of thirdness—of a creative, peace-producing interpretation—being actually felt as such. While the seductive power of any bifurcating description, distributing what belongs to mind and what belongs to nature, relies on eliminating the Third or interpretive element, the very point of both Whitehead's and Leibniz's speculative systems is that they are constructions explicitly meant to save all that exists together. They are openly artificial constructions, which fabricate the possibility of peace. And they are lures, mutely appealing for the unending adventure that would actualize this possibility.

I have just used the term *save*. This term belongs to theology but also to the history of Western knowledge, and as such it gives me the opportunity to make more precise the kind of emotional test the "saving" stance of speculative philosophy entails, bearing on values, historical memory, and social self-definition in a tradition that has linked truth with conflict. Here I am thus no longer "defending" the concepts of either Whitehead or Leibniz; instead I am using them in order to test the French inclination for despising the very idea of "saving" anything from conflict.

Ever since Galileo, to "save" has had heavy connotations, being associated with "to save only _____." Galileo refused to accept that his description of astronomical phenomena saved "only" those phenomena. He claimed that his science had to be recognized not as saving appearances through a convenient interpretation, whatever the definition of convenient, but as making the scientist the only right interpretant, the only one to be authorized by the phenomena themselves. All other interpretants, be they philosophers or theologians, should accept and submit to this "objective authority."[3] The "dark" greatness of the science Galileo initiated is the following: There is no place for a negotiated, peaceful agreement; either you submit to the authority of science as the exclusive interpretant or it means war. Still today many scientists not only demand that we respect their faith in a scientific portrayal of the world, but also demand that we share their conviction that physical laws testify to the very rules nature would obey—on pain of being denounced as relativists or even irrationalists.

Our historical memory celebrates Galileo's greatness, the heroic way he challenged the authority of the church, his *E pur si muove* celebrating the power of the facts to confirm his polemical truth and thereby defeat those who crushed him. It is also worthwhile to recall and emphasize that Leibniz's "Irenicism" was generally derided. *Herr Leibniz glaubt nichts,* it was said even before he died, at a time when trying to construct words and sentences that would create a possibility for peace between theology, science, and philosophy was already felt as some kind of a betrayal. Division, contradiction, and even war were already, as they are now, the name of the game. Whatever the faith, a "true faith" had to give to the faithful the power to denounce and hate.

Speaking as a philosopher belonging to the Western tradition, I would state that the way Leibniz was eliminated by scientists, philosophers, and theologians all belonging to this same tradition has created my access to this tradition, that is, created my standpoint; I wish to have for my enemies those who suspect that I would lead them to betray their faith, those who would accuse me of believing in nothing. This is why it is so important to underline that the construction of a peace-producing philosophy cannot be reduced to some kind of an objective description that should be accepted once misunderstandings and illegitimate extrapolations are cleared away. Indeed, peace as fabricated, not as discovered beyond distorting illusions, is a real test, a test that concerns us as we inherit a tradition that has so terribly confused truth and power.

A peace-producing philosophy is a test because it demands that we resist the satisfaction of power, that is, of legitimately explaining away (if not eliminating). And I would claim that it is not against specialized languages that peace must be constructed. It is against the value our Western tradition attributes to conflict as the very mark of truth. In speculative or constructivist terms, to construct "against" the value of conflict does not mean to enter into conflict; it means, rather, to positively feel the "scars of birth" of any experience promoting conflict as the mark of truth, and so to dispel its dark necessity.[4]

Sigmund Freud rightly characterized this experience when he made truth a trauma, a wound against our narcissistic images; his whole idea of psychoanalysis derives from this characterization. The seduction of the idea of a truth that should hurt and disenchant, which should go beyond illusions and destroy them, is exemplified each time a scientist or somebody speaking in the name of science promotes a version of the bifurcation of nature. And this seduction may well explain the very stability of the bifurcation theme. Be it when Galileo rejoiced in making the experimental fact (dealing only with the way heavy bodies fall in a frictionless world), the possibility and power of which he had just discovered, the ground for expelling philosophers and theologians from the new territory of science. Be it when Jacques Monod deduced from molecular biology and Darwinian selection the existential loneliness of humanity in a meaningless universe. Or be it each time thinking and feeling are reduced, in the name of science, to the blind interplay of neurons: What triumphs is emphatically not scientific objectivity but a strong affective association of truth with conflict and war.

I would state that Whitehead's speculative system, or more precisely the open set of propositions that are the applications of his scheme, may be defined as an active, constructive and noncritical antidote against our fascination with the power of truth. The ongoing discussions among process people about the relevance of maintaining an explicit reference to Whitehead's technical concepts when addressing cultural, religious, political, ecological, or social problems are, for me, a mark of the practical success of process philosophy as an antidote. The conceptual matrix has no authority of its own; it claims no authority to mobilize and fight in its name; instead, it works through insinuation and transformative effects as an infectious lure for new creative contrasts. You can propose what are indeed applications of the scheme without any explicit, open intervention by the concepts it articulates. Thus, as William James would have said, Whitehead's scheme verifies itself through its practical effects, by the way its saving operation produces a more interesting world and a more demanding thinking, by the way it inspires surprising syntactic transformations and suggests possibilities for escaping dramatic either/or dilemmas, devastating injunctions to choose and polemical standpoints demanding submission. It verifies itself first and foremost through confidence in reality, as if saying, "Do not be afraid; never will reality give to anyone the power to completely deny and reduce."

Whiteheadian speculative philosophy may help us—it has helped me—not to be afraid of all those who claim they have, one way or another, "reality on their side." This includes postmodern deconstructivist claims, for those claims play again on the old traumatic truth: They first of all address and crush anyone's hope to get outside, to escape the human-only lures for meaning, which are exhibited by conversation as they propose it. However, I would insist that the fabrication of peace-making propositions cannot be identified with peace as an experience. If indeed Whitehead's philosophy may be characterized as the construction of a possibility for peace, this is because it can produce through its applications what I would call, a bit paradoxically, "peace fighters," and not because it would be a path naturally or inevitably leading to the experience of peace.

As is well known, Whitehead's *Adventures of Ideas* closes with the description of this experience. When I am teaching Whitehead, I feel the flickering of this experience. It happens, for instance, when students encounter and enjoy the possibility of acknowledging as harmonious experiences, interests, or values that they initially deemed contradictory; or the possibility of experiencing the divorce between reason and the power to judge; or again the possibility of recognizing as a contrast—which is as such part of the very construction of reality—something that they previously thought was merely an idea *about* reality. Just as Whitehead wrote that "(l)ife is lurking in the interstices of living societies" (PR, 105), I would say that the experience of peace lurks in the interstices of the many sociological applications of Whitehead's philosophy. But it is also very important not to overestimate this flickering, lurking experience, that is, not to make it the aim of the scheme, its final "application." I would claim that the *experience* of peace will never come into existence as an application of any philosophical system.

I am not producing some kind of new version of the "traumatic truth," but taking seriously and concretely into account the question of this historical tradition we call "philosophy." Other traditions, which have indeed cultivated wisdom as such—that is, have learned how to practice and stabilize an experience of peace—have produced no definition of rationality or the philosophical adventure. They do not lack it, however, and there is no point for us in paternalistically looking for their equivalent, as if it should well exist. As its very name recalls, philosophy is not wisdom. The philosopher calls herself a "friend of wisdom" (we could probably translate this as "friend of peace"), and the idea of such a "friendship relation" with "peace" is a specifically Western invention. Also, the link proposed by Whitehead between philosophy and the adventure of reason specifically designates "us" as those who belong to this tradition, since "reason," as such, is our own invention. And a fearful one, since it should well be recalled that it was first created in order to divide and disqualify.

Philosophical words and propositions are loaded with birth scars that mark the adventure of philosophy, and of rationality as defined by philosophy, as a polemical enterprise. If philosophy is indeed a set of footnotes to Plato, both Plato's text and many of its footnotes are polemical constructions addressed against those whom they would denounce as producers of illusions, starting with the Sophists, the poets, and the magicians. Paraphrasing Leibniz, I would say that the philosophical tradition is not criminal, but full of crimes.

Leibniz and Whitehead both experimented with the construction of peace-producing propositions inside the philosophical tradition, using for

their purposes the very same words that were created by this tradition to disqualify, oppose, and even destroy "others." This means that their work can be
celebrated as proposed antidotes against certain poisons this tradition has
invented or at least justified. And again, I mean first of all the power of fascination the Western tradition has, repeatedly and under many different guises,
conferred upon truth—a purifying, polemical power that makes us proud to
escape the deceptions of the world, leads us to associate progress with the
purging of past illusions, and demands that we question traditional ways of
cultivating meaning, togetherness, cooperation, and belonging, even at the
price of destroying them. Peace-producing philosophies are antidotes against
the poisons immanent in our tradition. We would build a speedway "where
angels fear to tread" if we thought their words were something other than antidotes. We would turn the antidote into a new poison if we did not associate it
with a very specific challenge: to succeed in conceiving it as resolutely and
appetitively (not traumatically) divorced from any ambition to achieve the
very dangerous self-definition we have inherited from our tradition. As antidotes, both Leibniz's and Whitehead's peace propositions produce lures for
positively resisting, just as mathematicians resist what they call "trivial solutions," any formulation that would aim at unifying humanity beyond their
diverging and conflictual definitions of cultivating the experience of wisdom.

Thus, it may happen that a philosopher experiments with the transformation of his or her philosophical concepts into words that would vectorize
an experience of peace. This was the case for Spinoza's knowledge of the
third kind, as it was for Whitehead at the end of both *Process and Reality* and
Adventures of Ideas. We may celebrate these transformations as events, but
we should keep in mind that these events, which did indeed happen for certain philosophers, are not achievements we could identify with the aim of the
experimental adventure of philosophy—designing and redesigning its language, as Whitehead defined it (PR, 11).

This is why it is important to affirm the strongest distinction between
peace as a philosophical, problematic proposition and peace as an experience.
The first is our specific responsibility, since our tradition has turned so many
words into justifications for holy wars waged in the name of traumatic truths.
As to the second, our primary task is to recognize as *our* problem that the
Western tradition, and I would stress the academic tradition therein, has not
specifically cultivated the kind of practical wisdom probably needed in order
to stabilize such an experience. We are the children of anxiety, and we should
not anxiously disclaim this fact. I would add that Whitehead's and Leibniz's
concepts of God both address this problem, since each in his own way is associated with "thinking with the hammer" or "hammer thoughts." This is a kind
of thinking which, following Nietzsche, produces its own test. What these
concepts demand is emphatically not a trauma, since it is never a question of
tearing away from what would be only illusions, but an affective transforma-

tion of the one who takes them as effective lures for feeling and produces contrasts where oppositions once ruled.

The "best of all worlds" was indeed such a "hammer thought," actualizing what Leibniz identified with damnation, but so is the proposition that I have derived from Whitehead, that is, that God enjoys no concrete predefinition of what would be "the best" for any occasion. In other words, God depends on *us* for the creation of peace-propositions and the contrasts they entail. In both cases, as Deleuze might perhaps accept it, the point is not to believe "in God," but to accept as a problematic ingredient in our experience of the world the luring proposition of "God" being "for" the world. The point is, furthermore, to accept correlatively that the more a truth is "traumatic" or the more a proposition claims to possess universality in its own right, the more it may be transformed through God's experience into an interesting contrast, but one still loaded with negative prehensions.

I come back now to the idea of a (peaceful) "conversation" between the French tradition and process people. Whatever word we might propose instead of *conversation,* resisting the hammer thought of "God being for this world" would entail that the intended coming together embrace the challenge of not accepting the facile charms of academic conversation. It would further entail not requiring a select setting of only well-behaved, disenchanted, human-only partners who tiredly turn their backs on their own disappointing stories, and not sneering at oppositional, impolite formulations, but instead actively turning them into challenging contrasts. It would entail creating the difference between "peace" as an ironic rejection of any fanatic adhesion and "peace" as actively learning to produce and feel adhesions as a plurality of contrasted affirmations "for the world." This is what is at stake in the paradoxical term—*peace fighters*—I have introduced, leading to the idea that the aim is not agreement but alliance.

I have called "cosmopolitics" the kind of experimental togetherness that makes peace a challenge and not the condition for a polite conversation. "Politics" recalls that this proposition stems from our Western tradition that linked what it abstracted as "reason" with what it invented as "politics," which has meant, since Plato, the problem of who is entitled to speak and on what grounds when the question of our common destiny is at stake. The prefix "cosmo" takes into account that the word *common* should not be restricted to our fellow humans, as politics since Plato has implied, but should entertain the problematic togetherness of the many concrete, heterogeneous, enduring shapes of value (SMW, 94) that compose actuality, thus including beings as disparate as "neutrinos" (a part of the physicist's reality) and ancestors (a part of reality for those whose traditions have taught them to communicate with the dead).

Cosmopolitics defines peace as an ecological production of actual togetherness, where "ecological" means that the aim is not toward a unity beyond differences, which would reduce those differences through a goodwill reference to abstract principles of togetherness, but toward a creation of concrete, interlocked, asymmetrical, and always partial graspings. To take the very example of what Deleuze calls a "double capture"—a concept Whitehead would have loved—the success of an ecological invention is not having the bee and the orchid bowing together in front of an abstract ideal, but having the bee and the orchid both presupposing the existence of the other in order to produce themselves.

In order to be a bit more concrete, I will conclude with a contrast organized around a group of very "impolite" people: those scientists who claim they represent reality and thus have no reason to converse with others (or even with each other) but believe instead that they should be listened to. While they would rightfully be considered as excluding themselves from any civilized conversation, they posed a major concern for Whitehead, right from the start. I will now attempt to convey how vitally I needed the Whiteheadian "do not be afraid" to envisage the possibility of becoming a "peace fighter" in this area. Such a becoming had for its condition that I would address those passionately impolite people as being able, because of their very passion, to accept the peace-proposition that I now call "cosmopolitics," in this case a proposition both celebrating the creativity of the sciences and syntactically transforming their claims into more concrete ones, thereby actively depriving them of the traditional abstract setting of the "science versus opinion" or "science versus conversation" war-game.

When Whitehead was writing *Science and the Modern World,* he was enjoying the hope that the epoch when the sciences sided with the bifurcation of nature was about to be closed. We know that he was overly optimistic in this matter: not only is the reductionist stance still dominant, but we have very good reasons *not* to believe, as he did, that scientific innovation as such might endanger it. The idea that science is at war with opinion, that its very advance means "progress" framed as, "everyone thought such and such before, but we (scientists) now know that, . . ." has proved stronger than all the revisions of what scientists may indeed claim to know. In other words, I would state that we must now accept the fact that the field of science needs a still more concrete description of the values it produces: not only its epistemological values but also its political values reproduce an opposition between a "rational," objective grasp of reality and an "irrational," subjective, culturally embedded opinion. As long as the "science against opinion" image is patiently accepted, infecting scientists and nonscientists alike, the bifurcation of nature will be produced again and again as both the condition for science and for its confirming result.

The point is not to oppose a "Whiteheadian interpretation of scientific facts" to the usual one, as if scientific facts were some kind of neutral ground to be equally shared by everybody. Nor is the point to deny the "power of scientific facts." The point, rather, is to open up the knowledge-game and to disconnect it from any kind of generalist, "view-from-nowhere" model of authority. This indeed implies first and foremost the stance of "do not be afraid"; that is, it implies that we should not believe for one minute the scientific claims that "reality" has "factually" given science the power to deny or reduce.

Scientific, experimental facts offer no neutral ground. Scientists are right when they deny that a freewheeling conversation would give their facts whatever interpretation we would like. Indeed, these facts are produced by scientists for scientists, in terms of the values they are engaged in actualizing together. Here, by the way, I feel that process people should take better advantage of the contemporary so-called social studies of science[5] in order to describe the production of scientific facts in terms of process, that is, in terms of exhibiting rather obstructive, intolerant values and maintaining and depending upon the "patience" (SMW, 119) of its larger environment. Whitehead stated that an electron belonging to a living body is probably not "the same" as an electron belonging to a dead one. If we may accept such a statement, we should not be impressed or afraid upon hearing the dramatic accusation made against the social studies of sciences, that it would reduce scientific "facts" to mere social (read "irrational") constructs. If process philosophy is not an empty designation, it should demand that we never accept the kind of sad, either/or—*either* objective, neutral, having the power to disconnect itself *or* mere construction—alternatives upon which this accusation depends. We should recognize instead that the either/or proposition is a way for scientists to obtain limitless patience from their environment, where some "impatience" should well prevail.

I come now to the very power of scientific facts. How to save this power in peace-producing terms? How not to be (conceptually) afraid of the authority scientists derive from their "facts"? How to produce the possibility of a "cosmopolitical" grasp, celebrating those facts together with what they often seem to deny? Here I think we have first to complement Whitehead's analysis in order to exhibit that experimental facts are not privileged examples of what he called "stubborn facts." For me, examples of such stubborn facts would be the death of a loved one, the crash of an airplane, or the opportunity that was missed and never will return: those facts illustrate well that nothing will undo what is stubborn, but they also ask for interpretation, and will typically induce an open process of interpretation. The very specificity of experimental facts, on the other hand, is that while they undeniably "happen," they are nevertheless anticipated, thought before, paid for in advance. Furthermore, their happening one way and not another entails an extreme contrast between, on the one hand, those human beings who passionately cared for the issue and, on the other, all the others, who may well wonder why numbers can produce such dreams or such nightmares, such joys, or such disappointments.

Another aspect of experimental facts is even more surprising: on the one hand, experimental facts happen only in a highly conscious, critical, and interpretative social environment, and the story of their coming into being requires a universe of intentional risks, of verbal statements and explicit contrasts, of passionate ambitions and controversies; on the other hand, the very success they are meant to achieve is to stop interpretation, to have ambitions bowing in front of an objective verdict, to promote reality against intentions, and to enforce the closure of until then free human controversies. The whole of human invention, imagination, intentionality, and freely engaged passion is here mobilized in order to establish that there is one interpretation only, the "objective one," owing nothing to invention, imagination, and passion. Through an experimental device, the experimental fact thus technically transforms some very select nonhuman societies in such a way that they fulfill rather strange and purely human demands: that the stories those nonhuman societies will tell about themselves both serve as an argument in human controversies and support the claim that they owe nothing to human subjective values or interpretations. This is quite an achievement indeed, a very demanding, selective one. The production of new kinds of experimental facts are true events, producing an open-ended difference between the future and the past.

However, when a scientist tells you, "that's a fact," the first thing to do is see who is talking. If the one who is talking belongs to a field in which the authority of facts is explicitly related to some kind of "objective methodology," we should remember all those factors in the environment that must have been eliminated in the name of this methodology. Many sociologically and psychologically reductionist facts are more remarkable by the negative prehensions they enact than by their innovative and relevant grasp of an aspect of reality. This is why they need as an ingredient of their "truth claim" an avowed relation with the progress of science as it is illustrated by the experimental sciences, that is, physics, chemistry, or molecular biology.

To freely engage in the enterprise, the aim of which is to have freedom of interpretation bowing down to "objectivity," is not a matter of methodology but of satisfying demanding tests. The tests experimental facts must satisfy in order to be recognized as facts, the very success of which conditions their existence as scientific facts, have one primordial goal: to demonstrate that the propositions they authorize have for their subject "a phenomenon as we are compelled to understand it." A phenomenon has been transformed into what can be called a "reliable witness," reliably testifying for one interpretation against others. Objectivity is not a general feature of science; it is an acquired feature of some select phenomenon—the feature that scientific facts acquire when they have survived the controversy that tested the possibility that the witness betray its representative, that the fact allows for distinct (competent) interpretations.

I had to add "competent," and this may seem very impolite. But I cannot leave out the reason why experimental scientists exclude themselves from civilized conversations. Indeed, controversies are doubly selective: only select facts can hope to survive them, and only select people are practically and passionately interested in the difference to be created between facts as reliable or unreliable witnesses. The "force" of experimental facts relies on the coherence of this double selection, on the coincidence between "being passionately interested" and "being recognized as competent." Indeed, where the neutrino's mass, for instance, is concerned, nobody but the specialized scientist gives a damn whether the value is zero or very very small. But when a scientist uses so-called experimental facts against "opinion," the situation is quite different: as soon as a scientific statement claims to be interesting for "ordinary people" and denies, however, the competence of those same people, its force is lost. In other words, the selectivity of experimental facts is such that experimental knowledge may well complicate the formulation of human beliefs and convictions in the ecological sense of leading to the production of new contrasts and distinctions in order to take that knowledge into account; but never can a scientific proposition as such legitimately replace "opinion."

I would claim that the way I have just reframed the problem of the power of "experimental facts" produces the possibility of a "demanding peace" as a proposition that both respects the value scientists demand we recognize in what they call "objectivity" *and* demands from scientists that they enjoy scientific achievements as selective, inventive, social events, and not as a monotonous assaulting wave of objective rationality against human opinion. Furthermore, I would claim that we need here the full scope of Whitehead's concept of "society" in order for "social" scientific events to be construed also as "cosmological" events, going beyond the bifurcation of nature; celebrating new, enduring links between human questions and nonhuman societies; acknowledging each new kind of experimental fact as the coming into existence of a new kind of hybrid society.

But the peace propositions we may, as philosophers, derive from this understanding are also demanding ones, as demanding as Whitehead's decision when he proposed that time be atomic. The atomicity of time was the speculative price to be paid in order for philosophy to define itself "for" becoming, that is, never taking scientific explanations as final, as these explanations must privilege the continuity of the functions or patterns on which they depend. This price does not mean war, but it does mean maintaining a very determinate and stubborn distance. There is and there should be a strong contrast between the kind of question we will call "cosmologically relevant" and the type of question experimental facts have the power to decide. In other words, the Whiteheadian peace proposition will accept as an event in human history the successful granting to a nonhuman society the power to tell an objective story about itself, but it will exhibit this event as a successful selection and abstractive exhibition of this society, allowing scientists to explain away becoming.

Such a proposition will not be happily greeted by many speculative physicists, nor by philosophers fascinated by physics. According to this proposition, after all, it is a nightmare to dream of a direct "summit meeting" between the speculative risks of philosophy and, for instance, the adventures of real and virtual particles, interactions, quantum void, or whatever exotic beings physics creates. No creature can be separated from its environment, and the two environments—experimental and speculative—owe their existence to diverging, noncontradictory values, "for" being and "for" becoming. Connections may exist, but no deduction from one to the other, just as between the Deleuzean bees and orchids.

If accepted, however, those connections may be vitally important. This is what I have learned working with Ilya Prigogine, who devotes his life to the inclusion of the asymmetry of time in the so-called fundamental laws of physics. His ambition and the risks he accepts are those of a physicist, and his struggle to have all the physical laws that now exhibit time symmetry to no longer testify for a perfect understanding of time, but to an insufficient, too abstract version of physical causality, is impressive. It may well lead back to Whitehead's diagnosis: for Prigogine, time-symmetrical, physical descriptions indeed exhibit the "symptoms of the epicyclic state from which astronomy was rescued in the sixteenth century" (SMW, 135).[6] However, what is most interesting to me as a philosopher is that the more rigorously the risks and results of Prigogine's endeavor satisfy the demands and constraints of physics, the more they exhibit the demanding specificity of physics: they may well allude to becoming, but they are "for being." Indeed, what Prigogine now calls the "laws of chaos" explicitly define their object not as "reality" but as a grasping together of those aspects of a chaotic, nonconformal reality that build up a "conformal pattern" or "law." Prigogine's "laws" do not exhibit "reality" as satisfying the demand of lawful regularity; instead they abstract from reality the pattern that satisfies this demand. As a consequence, "laws of physics" would be divorced from "laws of nature," and, as a further consequence, a proposition like that of Prigogine vitally needs his colleagues to accept their laws as distinct from the laws reality would obey.

A "cosmopolitical," peace-fabricating interest in human practices has nothing to do with summit meetings. The problem of the power of experimental facts is not restricted to the great problems of "theoretical physics meets philosophy." Careful attention to the negative prehensions that turn a new contrast into an opposition should extend everywhere in a fractalized manner, that is, toward each problem whatever its scale, where a formulation may "mean war." The trust and hope to which this kind of attention attests actualize the Whiteheadian "do not be afraid" as a firm belief that never will reality side with a holy war. In order to exemplify this last point, I will offer a last example, very far from physics but quite relevant to the disqualifying power of modern rationality.

Modern, so-called rational, pharmacology presents itself as proof that the only rational way to understand the living body is the experimental way, in terms of the blind, interlocked concert of molecules and their interactions. Everything that may rationally intervene in such a concert must be a molecule, it claims, and devising new molecules is the only rational, objective way to cure people. However, we also know that promising molecules must first satisfy clinical tests, mainly against "placebo effects," in order to be accepted as drugs. Furthermore, in the case of failure, the molecules return to a sad anonymity, while in the case of success, the need for the test is forgotten, while a new triumph of the success of "scientific molecules" in curing people is celebrated.

This scenario testifies for very interesting negative prehensions. It masks a crucial contrast. While the satisfaction of the clinical test is presented as verifying that the eventual cure has indeed its reason in the abstract encounter between the sick body and the molecule, those verifying cures are in fact obtained "against placebo": they do not "objectively" testify about the "encounter"; rather, they statistically testify that, one way or another, the successful molecule has contributed more specifically than a "mere placebo" in the induction of the healing process.

A peace-fabricating description of the whole situation would first rejoice in the severe tests we demand that our drugs pass, but would then emphasize that the very creation of these needed tests marks a true "social" transformation, going from an experimental environment to the complex environment of suffering-body-and-anxious-mind-with-physician. As the placebo itself testifies, the healing process cannot be abstracted from this environment. It may well be induced by nonmolecular means—means that cannot testify about themselves in the "objective" terms demanded by experimentation. Furthermore, those means cannot be explained away as a "mere placebo effect," since the abstract, measured placebo effect does not exist as such outside the purified clinical test setting. With the placebo, we meet under the guise of an irreducible residue (physicians must keep quite neutral in order for the statistics to be valid; they must even ignore whether they are distributing the molecule or the placebo) what is cultivated elsewhere. In different therapeutic practices, it is no longer a residue, as it is not only amplified and stabilized but may also be produced anew, as expressing, exhibiting, and producing different possibilities of healing, in different social environments.

Again, the development of Whitehead's concept of a society is urgently needed. Indeed, a Whiteheadian peace proposition would have to emphasize that the "social" processes that we call "disease" and "cure" do not (generally) satisfy true experimental demands (telling an objective story about themselves), which would authorize the reduction of the sick body to some molecular assembly. It would celebrate the clinical test as our way of rationally taking into account this irreducibility: we do not allow our molecular dreams to stand for reality. It would not solve the problem of how to relate our pharmacological tradition with other "traditional" ways of healing: even God does not "know" how before the event of an actual ecological togetherness. But the peace proposition may produce the appetitive envisagement of this possibility.

I have just exemplified the cosmopolitical enterprise as I inherited it from Whitehead's peace-fabricating proposition. Such an enterprise cannot converge into a conclusion, since it is an open-ended story, the end of which would coincide with the cessation of the unending list of destructive simplifications and disqualifying judgements we have produced in the name of truth as a traumatic power. This may seem a long way from the starting point of my text: the possible encounter between what I have called "process people" and the "French tradition." I started with a double test, resisting on the one side any direct convergence between religion and philosophy, while accepting on the other that we can maintain, or create, a positive reference to reason and hope while thinking "in front of" or "for" analphabets, dying rats, or alcoholics. I end with scientifically reliable witnesses, drugs, and healing processes. The point of this wide circuit is the construction, or exploration, of what I have called a "middle ground," where concepts produced through this double test could be created. If philosophy creates concepts, this very creation, Deleuze tells us, affirms or requires a plane that is nonphilosophical or prephilosophical. A plane, which primordially, should not be an academic one, should lure feelings "for" the world, and should not be defined in reference to such a "small world." Thus my conviction is that the encounter, as a risk and not as an exercise in comparative philosophy, needs some kind of physical enjoyment of the many concrete situations where the creation of new concepts is required: concepts that will affirm hope and reason "in front of" or "for" the many against whom crimes have been committed in the name of hope and reason.

Notes

1. The *Sokal Hoax* refers to the physicist Alan Sokal's submission of an article—which included much postmodern jargon and that he considered to be a "spoof"—to the journal *Social Text*. After it was published in the spring/summer, 1996 volume, Sokal revealed that it was a hoax.

2. Leibniz, *Confessio Philosophy,* French-Latin text (Paris: Vrin, 1970).

3. Isabelle Stengers, "Who Is the Author," in *Power and Invention: Situating Science, Theory out of Bounds* 10 (Minneapolis: University of Minnesota Press, 1997). See also Stengers, *L'invention des sciences modernes,* coll. "Champs" (Paris: Flammarion, 1995).

4. See Stengers, "Pour en finir avec la tolérance," *Cosmopolitiques* 7 (Paris: La Découverte/Les empêcheurs de penser en rond, 1997).

5. Two major protagonists of this field, Bruno Latour and Donna Haraway, have for their part already recognized the relevance of Whitehead.

6. See Stengers, "Breaking the Circle of Sufficient Reason," in *Power and Invention.*

Contributors

JOSEPH A. BRACKEN, S.J., is Professor of Theology and Director of the Brueggeman Center for Interreligious Dialogue at Xavier University in Cincinnati, Ohio. He is the author of six books and coeditor of a seventh, and he has written roughly sixty articles with a special focus on process theology and trinitarian theology. Recently, he has also written on issues connected with philosophical deconstructionism and the search for new forms of truth and objectivity. His latest book is *The One in the Many: A Contemporary Reconstruction of the God-World Relationship* (2001), on which his chapter in this volume is heavily based.

TIM CLARK received his Ph.D. from the University of Warwick in Coventry, England, for a thesis on the metaphysics of Gilles Deleuze and Alfred North Whitehead. He lives and works in London and has taught philosophy at Middlesex University and Richmond College.

ANNE DANIELL is a Ph.D. candidate in Theological and Religious Studies at Drew University in Madison, New Jersey. Her primary academic interests include ecological theology and the influence of deconstruction, feminist theory, and religio-cultural pluralism on theological thinking. Her dissertation subject, "theology of place," brings together incarnational and ecological theologies with theories of place, performance, and the carnivalesque.

ROLAND FABER is Professor of Systematic Theology at the University of Vienna. A research fellowship brought him to Claremont, California, and to the Center for Process Studies in 1995–1996. In 2000, he was honored with the Kardinal-Innitzer Prize in Theology. He has published widely in German and English on process philosophy and theology, poststructuralism, the doctrine of god, and eschatology. His most recent book is *Prozeßphilosophie. Su ihrer Würdigung und Kritischen Erneurung* (2000) (Process Theology: Toward Its Appreciation and Renewal). With Nicole Mantler and Eva Schmetter he coedited *Variationen über die Schöpfung der Welt* (1995).

ARRAN GARE is Senior Lecturer in the Department of Philosophy and Cultural Inquiry at Swinburne University, Australia. After gaining his Ph.D. from Murdoch University, Western Australia, he was awarded a Fulbright Post-Doctoral Fellowship to the Center for Philosophy and History of Science at Boston University. He has published widely on metaphysics, philosophy of science, philosophy of culture, politics, and environmental philosophy. His books include *Nihilism Inc.: Environmental Destruction and the Metaphysics of Sustainability* (1996); *Postmodernism and the Environmental Crisis* (1995); and *Beyond European Civilization: Marxism, Process Philosophy and the Environment* (1993). With Robert Elliot he coedited *Environmental Philosophy* (1983).

CHRISTINA K. HUTCHINS is a Ph.D. candidate in Interdisciplinary Studies at the Graduate Theological Union and teaches part-time at the Pacific School of Religion in Berkeley. She holds an M.Div. from the Harvard Divinity School and is an ordained minister in the United Church of Christ (Congregational). Her dissertation utilizes process thought and insights from feminist and queer theories to explore the contemporary ecclesial discourse on sexuality as a rupture that opens new possibilities for the philosophy of religion. Related essays appear in *Theology and Sexuality* and in *God, Process Thought, and Literature* (2001). She is also a prize-winning poet, and has published over 60 poems in many literary journals and anthologies. Her book of poetry with CD is *Collecting Light* (1999).

CATHERINE KELLER is Professor of Constructive Theology at the Theological and Graduate Schools of Drew University in Madison, New Jersey. She is the author of *From a Broken Web: Separation, Sexism, and Self* (1986); *Apocalypse Now and Then: A Feminist Guide to the End of the World* (1996); and is presently completing *The Face of the Deep: A Deconstruction of Creatio ex Nihilo and a Reconstruction of a Theology of Creation from Chaos*. John B. Cobb Jr. was her mentor at Claremont.

LUIS G. PEDRAJA, a native of Cuba and an ordained Baptist minister, received his doctorate in Philosophical Theology from the University of Virginia. He has taught at the University of Puget Sound, Perkins School of Theology of Southern Methodist University in Dallas, and is currently Academic Dean and Professor of Theology at Memphis Theological Seminary. He has written articles in philosophical theology and Hispanic theology, as well as a book, *Jesus Is My Uncle: Christology from a Hispanic Perspective* (1999).

ISABELLE STENGERS is Associate Professor of Philosophy at the Free University of Brussels and a Distinguished Member of the National Committee of Logic and the History of Philosophy of Sciences in Belgium. She is the author of numerous books and articles on the history of science, the theory of systems, and psychoanalysis. Among those published in English are *Power and*

Invention: Situating Science (1997), *A Critique of Psychoanalytic Reason* (1992, with Léon Chertok), and, with Ilya Prigogine, *Order Out of Chaos* (1984).

CAROL WAYNE WHITE is Associate Professor of Philosophy of Religion at Bucknell University in Lewisburg, Pennsylvania. She has published articles addressing the intersections of critical theory, feminist philosophy, and religion and is the author of the book, *Triangulating Positions: Poststructuralism, Feminism and Religion* (2001). Her recent research has been supported by grants from the John Templeton Foundation, the Knight Foundation, and the National Endowment for the Humanities. During the 2000–2001 academic year she was a research associate at the Five College Women's Studies Research Center and is currently completing a manuscript on the vitalistic principles of the seventeenth-century philosopher, Anne Conway.

Note on Supporting Center

This series is published under the auspices of the Center for Process Studies, a research organization affiliated with the Claremont School of Theology and Claremont Graduate University. It was founded in 1973 by John B. Cobb, Jr., Founding Director, and David Ray Griffin, Executive Director; Marjorie Suchocki is now also a Co-Director. It encourages research and reflection on the process philosophy of Alfred North Whitehead, Charles Hartshorne, and related thinkers, and on the application and testing of this viewpoint in all areas of thought and practice. The center sponsors conferences, welcomes visiting scholars to use its library, and publishes a scholarly journal, *Process Studies*, and a newsletter, *Process Perspectives*. Located at 1325 North College, Claremont, CA 91711, it welcomes new members and gratefully accepts (tax-deductible) contributions to support its work.

Index

Galileo, 244–45

Gender, 5–6, 26n.15, 115, 124–25, 136 n.2, 140n.24, 141n.28, 144n.50. *See also* Feminism, Identity, Subject and object; Subjectivity; Woman, Women

Gene fetishism, 63

Gilson, Etienne, 97

Givenness, 148–49, 158ff., 163–64n.6

Global economism, 12, 32, 63, 69n.1, 159, 161

God, 15, 22–25, 94, 101–6, 108n.8, 135, 175, 198, 210, 231nn.78–81, 232 nn.86–90, 234nn.100–1, 248; as concrete, 171, 173; and creativity, 25, 171–74, 215, 221, 227n.33; as creator, 24; and différance, 108n.8; and differences, 210; Deleuzean, 192, 196, 221; as eschatological, 224, 232 n.88, 233n.95; and good vs. evil, 201; and the future, 222–24, 233 n.93; as immanent, 215, 219, 229 n.56; justice of, 240; Kantian, 196; Leibnizian, 193–95, 197; language for, 164n.13, 233nn.91–92; limitations of, 174, 197–99, 248; as lure, 66, 240, 248; and novelty, 223; and ontology, 217, 232n.88; and order, 194, 239; as poet, 223–24, 233n.96; as process, 193, 210; and reason, 201; as salvific, 240; as schizophrenic, 200–2; as source of human good, 172, 174; as super-ego, 209; and temporality, 222–23; as transcendent, 105, 215, 219; as transformative, 172, 174, 240; trinitarian, 94, 105; and valuation, 102, 173, 194–95, 197–99, 220–21, 229n.60; Whiteheadian, 94, 193–94, 198–99, 200, 202, 210, 232nn.88–90, 240; and world, 101–2, 105. *See also* Christ, Creativity; Creative Transformation; Eschatology; Expressive In/difference; Immanence; In/difference; Logos; Other(ness); Transcendence; Ultimate(s); Whiteheadian terminology, primordial and consequent natures

Goethe, Johann Wolfgang, 33, 34

Good, the, 158. *See also* the Common Good

Griffin, David Ray, 2–5, 10–11, 15–16, 19, 23–24, 26nn.7,9, 28n.42, 72n.29, 73–74, 141n.29, 164n.12, 163n.3, 165n.19, 189n.17

Grosz, Elizabeth, 182

Ground, 12–14, 22, 27n.28, 62, 68, 148–49, 153–55, 158ff., 163–64n.6.

Growth of meaning, 172, 177

Guattari, Felix, 20–21, 39, 58, 70n.10, 200, 227n.40, 241

Gunew, Sneja, 137n.9

Hammer thought, 247–48

Haraway, Donna J., 14, 61ff., 71n.20, 151; and Whitehead, 63–66

Harding, Sandra, 62–63, 71nn.20–21

Hardt, Michael, 225n.4, 228nn.45,52

Hart, Kevin, 179, 189n.17

Hartshorne, Charles, 101, 104–6, 109 nn.24–25, 120, 209–10, 233n.92

Harvey, David, 163n.4

Hegel, G. W. F., 33, 37–39, 41, 44, 107n.4

Hegemony, 137n.10, 139n.16, 144 n.49,50, 145n.51

Heidegger, Martin, 13, 33, 37, 40–42, 44, 46, 50, 51n.19, 52n.36, 97, 99–100, 109n.21, 182, 211–12, 225 nn.10–11, 241. *See also* Presence; *see under* Metaphysics

Herder, Johann, 33

Heterogeneity, 169

Heteronormativity, 112–14, 124, 129, 136nn.1,4, 142–43n.39, 144nn.49, 50

History, 107n.3

Hobbes, Thomas, 46

Hölderin, Friedrich, 34

Holy, 133–36. *See also* God

Homosexuality, 112–13, 116, 129, 136 nn.1–2, 144n.50

hooks, bell, 63

Hope, 134–36, 223–24

Husserl, Edmund, 18